Germany and Europe in Transition

Germany and Europe in Transition

Edited by
Adam Daniel Rotfeld and Walther Stützle

OXFORD UNIVERSITY PRESS
1991

Oxford University Press, Walton Street, Oxford OX2 6DP
Oxford New York Toronto
Delhi Bombay Calcutta Madras Karachi
Petaling Jaya Singapore Hong Kong Tokyo
Nairobi Dar es Salaam Cape Town
Melbourne Auckland
and associated companies in
Berlin Ibadan

Oxford is a trade mark of Oxford University Press

Published in the United States
by Oxford University Press New York

© SIPRI 1991

British Library Cataloguing in Publication Data
Germany and Europe in transition. - (SIPRI monograph).
1. Europe. Politics
I. Rotfeld, Adam Daniel   II. Stützle, Walther   III. Series
320.94
ISBN 0–19–829146–9

Library of Congress Cataloging in Publication Data
Germany and Europe in transition / edited by Adam Daniel Rotfeld, Walther Stützle.
1. Europe—Politics and government—1989——Sources.   2. Germany (East)—Politics and
government—1989——Sources.   3. Germany (West)—Politics and government—1989——
Sources.   I. Stützle, Walther.   II. Rotfeld, Adam Daniel.
D2009.G47 1991   940.55—dc20   90–19695
ISBN 0–19–829146–9

Typeset and originated by Stockholm International Peace Research Institute
Printed and bound in Great Britain by
Biddles Ltd, Guildford and King's Lynn

Contents

Part I. A European peace order and the responsibility of the two German states

Part II. Documents on German unification and European security

Appendices

Acknowledgements

The editors would like to thank the John D. and Catherine T. MacArthur Foundation for generous financial support in organizing the SIPRI/IPW Potsdam conference. We are also grateful to Professor Max Schmidt and his staff at the Institut für Politik und Wirtschaft (Berlin) who, as hosts of the Potsdam conference, extended warm and gracious hospitality to the participants and assured the excellent organization of the discussions. The assistance of Gudrun Malina, Gottfried Kreller and Manfred Schmidt is also gratefully acknowledged. Our thanks also go to Bella Kjellgren, who assisted throughout the preparations for and proceedings of the conference. Special appreciation is paid to Billie Bielckus who spent many long hours editing, verifying and revising the manuscripts to prepare them for publication. Acknowledgement is given also to Marianne Lyons and Ricardo Vargas-Fuentes who contributed to typing the papers and documents through their endless revisions.

Adam Daniel Rotfeld and Walther Stützle
1 December 1990

Abbreviations and acronyms

APELL	Process for Responding to Technological Accidents
CDU	Christian Democratic Union
CFE	Conventional Armed Forces in Europe
CMEA	Council for Mutual Economic Assistance (Comecon)
Comecon	Council for Mutual Economic Assistance (CMEA)
COMTRADE	United Nations Trade Data Bank
CPSU	Communist Party of the Soviet Union
CSBM	Confidence- and Security- Building Measure
CSCE	Conference on Security and Co-operation in Europe
CSU	Christian Social Union
DSU	German Social Union
EBRD	European Bank for Reconstruction and Development
EC	European Community
ECE	UN Economic Commission for Europe
EFTA	European Free Trade Association
EPC	European Parliamentary Commission
EPC	European Political Co-operation
EPU	European University Center for Peace Studies
ESA	European Space Agency
EUREKA	European Scientific Co-operation project
FAO	Food and Agriculture Organization of the United Nations
FDP	Free Democratic Party
GATT	General Agreement on Tariffs and Trade
GNP	Gross national product
ICC	International Chamber of Commerce
IMF	International Monetary Fund
IMO	International Maritime Organization
IPCS	International Programme on Chemical Safety
IPW	Institut für Internationale Politik und Wirtschaft der DDR
IRPTC	UNEP International Register of Potentially Toxic Chemicals
IUCN	International Union for Conservation of Nature and Natural Resources
LDPD	Liberal Democratic Party of Germany
NATO	North Atlantic Treaty Organization
NDPD	National Democratic Party of Germany
NNA	Neutral and non-aligned
OECD	Organization for Economic Co-operation and Development
PDS	Party of Democratic Socialism
SED	Socialist Unity Party of Germany
SIPRI	Stockholm International Peace Research Institute
SME	Small and medium-sized enterprise
SPD	Social Democratic Party
UNCITRAL	United Nations Commission on International Trade Law
UNEP	United Nations Environment Programme
WEU	Western European Union
WTO	Warsaw Treaty Organization

Introduction

Adam Daniel Rotfeld and Walther Stützle

In 1989–90 the unthinkable happened: with the breakdown of political divisions in Europe the cold war came to an end. Europe entered a period of transition and of building a new security order. The fundamental political transformations in Central and Eastern Europe and the Soviet Union drastically reduced tensions and the danger of a military conflict in Europe, but the collapse of 'real socialism' did not come about as suddenly as many analysts and political writers tried to convey. The final breakdown was preceded by many symptoms of dysfunctioning, manifest for many years. In Central Europe the first massive workers' protests occurred in Berlin (17 June 1953) and were labelled in the German Democratic Republic as 'counter-revolutionary events'. The dramatic changes of 1989, initiated by the Polish round-table and the establishment of the first non-communist government in Warsaw, culminated in the opening of the Berlin Wall and the unification of Germany. In the first weeks and months all these breathtaking events were the subject of much fascination and description, for obvious reasons. They deserve, however, thorough analysis, profound reflection and evaluation.

Thinking about and planning for the future require a good understanding of the past and the present. With this in mind the Stockholm International Peace Research Institute (SIPRI) and the Institut für Internationale Politik und Wirtschaft der DDR (IPW) jointly organized an international conference on 'A European Peace Order and the Responsibility of the Two German States', held in Potsdam on 8–10 February 1990. The reason for holding the conference was simple: to help students of international affairs acquire a better understanding of German affairs and to give Germans a better understanding of international concerns. The conference was attended by the outstanding scholars of a number of European countries as well as the United States and the Soviet Union (the programme and list of conference participants are appended to this volume). Leading politicians from the two German states also participated in the Potsdam discussions. The objective of the conference was to foster a better understanding of the events in Central and Eastern Europe in general and in the GDR in particular. The discussions contributed to a sober assessment of the role of the two German states in an emerging new structure for Europe. The intention of the organizers was also to facilitate further thinking about research work required on these and other topics.

The papers addressed to the conference by Christa Luft, Deputy Prime Minister of the GDR, and Hans-Dietrich Genscher, Deputy Federal Chancellor and Minister for Foreign Affairs of the FRG, are significant political documents of the time. The first free elections were still to occur, but radical changes in the self-confidence of the GDR Government in general, and *vis-à-vis* the West German neighbour in particular, were strongly manifested without any precedent in the past. Professor Luft stated at the Potsdam conference that 'the attempt to build an independent, socialist nation in the GDR had failed'. At that moment, February 1990, she said that the GDR Government's decisions 'have to a great extent been dictated by the necessity to take immediate and urgent practicable measures that are conducive to containing the growing exodus of people undermining this country's structures in everyday life'. She was thinking of the fact that since Hungary announced the opening of its borders (10 September 1989) thousands and thousands of GDR citizens had fled to the Federal Republic of Germany via Hungary, Czechoslovakia and Poland. After the decision of the GDR Council of Ministers (9 November 1989) to open the Berlin Wall and other border crossing points to the Federal Republic of Germany the exodus continued with no sign of abatement. It was decisive. The Deputy Prime Minister of the GDR declared: 'There is no serious political force left in this country which would not come out in favour of unity in whatever form'. The next day Professor Kurt Biedenkopf (Member of Bundestag, CDU) noted: 'All political forces have determined that the two German states should be united'. The convergence of views was striking. Two essential questions remained open: when and how. The official position of the GDR Government presented at the conference by Professor Luft was unequivocal: alignment of the two German states with their present military alliances at a lower military level until the transformation of NATO and the WTO into political organizations is completed. Another option discussed at that time was the Modrow plan concerning military neutrality for the future united Germany.

The highest priority of GDR policy was not external or international security factors, but how to stabilize the situation in the GDR and how to contain and stop the population exodus. Prime Minister Hans Modrow's Government developed the political concept of the 'contractual community' (die Vertragsgemeinschaft) to organize the growing together of the two German states. In fact the beginning of the implementation of German unity through the Monetary, Economic and Social Union, based on the proposal submitted by the Government of the FRG (7 February 1990), predetermined the unification process. The signing of the Treaty between the two states, establishing this Union (Bonn, 18 May 1990), made the unification process irreversible (the Treaty became law after being approved by both parliaments on 21 June 1990; the Bundestag approved the Treaty by a vote of 445 to 60, the Volkskammer by 302 to 82). The introduction of the Deutschmark on the territory of the GDR (1 July 1990) constituted the first decisive step towards the new reality: the two German states become inseparably linked.

The external factors of the unification process were repeatedly stressed and analysed during the Potsdam conference. Four questions were discussed and considered as priority: the German borders, affiliation of the future united

German state to existing alliances, conventional arms reductions in the unification context and the emerging pan-European security structures. Federal
Foreign Minister Hans-Dietrich Genscher announced at the conference that the
two German states can make 'a joint declaration guaranteeing the borders with
all their neighbours, and they can also jointly reaffirm their renunciation of the
production and possession of nuclear, chemical and biological weapons'. The
identical relevant resolutions of the parliaments of the German states were later
approved (21 June 1990) with an aim to reaffirm definitely the recognition of
Poland's western frontiers. The Treaty signed between Poland and Germany in
Warsaw on 14 November 1990 confirmed the present and future inviolability of
the border between Germany and Poland and made a mutual commitment to
unreservedly respect their sovereignty and territorial integrity. The resolutions
expressed the desire that a united Germany and Poland will continue 'the policy
of understanding and reconciliation, shape their relations in a forward-looking
way and thus set an example of good neighbourly relations'. The hope was
expressed that German unity will make a historic contribution to the creation of
a European peace order in which borders no longer divide. In this respect, the
statement of Hans-Dietrich Genscher at the Potsdam conference was remarkable: 'When we Germans speak of unification, we have in mind two German
states, including Berlin.'

Apart from borders the main external aspects of the establishment of German
unity were connected with military alignment, with the European Community
(EC) and with the Conference on Security and Co-operation in Europe (CSCE)
process initiated in Helsinki.

It was at the Potsdam conference that Hans-Dietrich Genscher presented the
concept of how to fit the unification process to the requirements of the European Community. He particularly noted the proposal made by Prime Minister
Tadeusz Mazowiecki of Poland to establish a 'Council of European Co-
operation'. Explaining his understanding of the institutionalization of the CSCE
process, Genscher listed 10 new pan-European institutions and structures which
are required for co-operation and security reasons:

1. An institution to co-ordinate East–West economic co-operation. The European Development Bank must also be seen in this context.

2. A pan-European institution for the protection of human rights. The application of the Council of Europe's Human Rights Convention to the whole of
Europe suggests itself.

3. A centre for the creation of a European legal area aimed at legal harmonization.

4. A European environmental agency.

5. Extension of the European Scientific Co-operation Project (EUREKA) to
the whole of Europe.

6. Collaboration between the European Space Agency (ESA) and corresponding Eastern institutions.

7. A centre to develop European telecommunications.

8. A centre to develop European transport infrastructure and policy.
9. A European verification centre.
10. A European conflict management centre.

The governing Mayor of Berlin, Walter Momper, offered to establish the seats of European and CSCE institutions in Berlin, in particular the seat of the permanent CSCE secretariat.

Opening the panel discussion with the participation of the leading political personalities of the GDR, Professor Egon Bahr raised the question of whether a united Germany would be a member of NATO. The scale of views ranged from a 'united and demilitarized Germany' (Bärbel Bohley, New Forum) through 'no entry into NATO' (Walter Romberg, SPD) and 'disbanding the alliances or leaving them' (Gregor Gysi, PDS) to 'Germany in NATO with a special status for the former GDR territory' (Lothar de Maizière: 'I do not think an expansion of NATO would be right, neither would membership by [the] present-day GDR').

The decision was made some months later as the result of the Gorbachev–Kohl negotiation in Zheleznovodsk, USSR, on 16 July 1990. The fifth point of the agreement reached between the two leaders was announced by Federal Chancellor Helmut Kohl: 'While the Soviet troops remain in the former territory of the German Democratic Republic, the NATO structures will not be extended to this part of Germany. From the very beginning this will not affect the immediate application of articles 5 and 6 of the NATO Treaty. Bundeswehr troops that are not part of NATO's military organization, that is, territorial defence units, can be stationed in the territory of the present German Democratic Republic and Berlin right after the unification of Germany.'

The reader will find in this volume the full texts of many agreements and other documents on the external aspects of Germany's unification, including the decision of the GDR Volkskammer on accession 'to the area in which the Basic Law is in force' (23 August 1990). In these brief words unification according to article 23 of the FRG Basic Law was decided; it took place on 3 October 1990. The solution of the 'German question' with respect to international security problems was negotiated and achieved in the framework of the 'Two-plus-Four' talks.

The concept of such negotiation among two German states and the Four Powers was raised and discussed in public during the SIPRI/IPW Potsdam conference by Egon Bahr. A week later the six foreign ministers of the Soviet Union, the United States, France, Great Britain and the FRG and the GDR held talks in Ottawa (13–14 February 1990) and decided to search for a solution to 'external aspects of the establishment of German unity, including the issues of security of the neighbouring states'. The 'Two-plus-Four' talks conducted in Bonn (5 May 1990), in Berlin (22 June 1990) and in Paris (17 July 1990)—with the participation of the Foreign Minister of Poland, Krzysztof Skubiszewski— were concluded successfully in Moscow (12 September 1990).

The aim of this book is to give professionals—researchers and journalists as well as diplomats and politicians—documented background to the speed of evolution of the political postures of the two German states, the Four Powers and some other countries on a future security system in Europe.

* * *

The documents published in Part II illustrate how deeply the process of German unification is rooted in and interconnected with European integration and the building of a new security order in Europe. Over a few months in 1990 many decisions were taken and many statements were issued with different concepts and suggestions as to how to fit and adapt the unification of Germany to new European security structures. Some conclusions on the future of the CSCE and new pan-European institutions emerge from the concepts, proposals and documents in this volume:

1. The principles of political pluralism, the rule of law, democracy and human rights have been reinstated, reflecting the historic changes in Europe.
2. A need to institutionalize political dialogue within the CSCE framework has been accepted by all states participating in the Helsinki process.
3. An agreement was achieved at the summit meeting in Paris to establish a high level meeting on a regular basis and some new European security structures.
4. No reservations arise from the idea of adapting existing organizations to the evolving CSCE process.

These elements delineate a framework for agreement on institutionalization. More elaborate structures would not be desirable at present; if anything they would lead to bureaucratization rather than attacking new problems and tackling the challenges of developments in Europe. New institutions should be geared to the tasks that require solution.

The documents were selected to reflect German, European and global needs in security matters and to show how they were defined in the official texts. As well as basic treaties, declarations and statements, the intention was to include some not easily available documents of the time: speeches and lectures given by political leaders, proposals made by the governments of new democracies in Central and Eastern Europe, and decisions taken by/at some multilateral conferences and institutions. The main criterion of selection was that the documents be connected with the unification of Germany or European security; however, an attempt is also made to cover new trends, such as the search for sub-regional co-operation, for example, the Baltic Sea Conference and participation by the Baltic republics.

Among the almost 60 documents included, many are published for the first time in this volume: for example, the principles of the 'Two-plus-Four' talks, the Baltic Sea Declaration and corresponding guidelines, the CSCE decisions adopted after the Vienna follow-up meeting and the results of the Paris Summit Conference of the European and North American states (19–21 November 1990). All the published texts are based on official sources.

In 1990 Germany and Europe entered a new era. Much research and many studies on the 'German question' and the European security issue were rapidly overtaken by events and have become outdated. This does not apply to the documents; they remain valid as a basis of analysis and explanation of the decisive factors and driving forces. Like good wines, the older the better, many documents also become more valuable in time, not only reminding us of the facts but also irreplaceable in understanding the political aims, motivations and perceptions in the decision-making process.

This volume is part of a larger effort at the Stockholm International Peace Research Institute devoted to examining the new dimensions of European security: to research both the traditional military aspects of security and, in a broader perspective, the political, economic and structural elements of preserving stability in the New Europe.

Part I
A European peace order and the responsibility of the two German states

1. The network of FRG–GDR agreements and the future of Europe

Address by Christa Luft, Deputy Prime Minister of the German Democratic Republic

We are facing tremendous social and political changes in Europe. The feeling has grown that the East–West conflict is about to end and that our continent is entering a new stage of development. Post-war chapters of the cold war, contradictions between systems and confrontation are coming to an end. Now, there is a great chance to establish a truly European peace order for peaceful and good neighbourly co-operation among peoples and for co-operative relations among states. The German issue has been put on the agenda in a new way, namely, as a realistic task to unify the two German states in the near future. Once more, it is the key question of European politics. According to GDR Prime Minister Hans Modrow: 'The German people will take their place in the construction of a new peaceful order as a result of which both the division of Europe into hostile camps and the split of the German nation will be overcome'. This concept has brought about that inseparable linkage for which I also stand, namely, that a final solution of the German issue can be achieved only via free self-determination of the German states in co-operation with the Four Powers taking account of the interests of all European states and peoples. The most recent political developments have shown that the process of unification, which started from the bottom, has assumed a very rapid pace. This questions all predictions made so far as to the date of its completion.

Before I address the present situation and future developments, allow me a moment of retrospection. For more than 100 years the German issue has existed as a problem touching on the security of peoples and states of Europe, regarding ambitions in German politics that could interfere with their vital interests. This particularly concerned the immediate neighbours of the Germans. World War II, unleashed by German Fascism and resulting in human sacrifices and material losses on a tremendous scale, and the holocaust perpetrated on European Jewry, led to the conclusion that a reliable means of protection should be established to avert a new war emanating from German soil. The Potsdam Agreement signed here in 1945, and the regulations still in force with regard to the rights and responsibilities of the Four Powers for Germany as a whole, were to provide such securities. However, I would like to state very clearly that, apart from this security concept developed at the end of World War II, there were no stipulations that provided for the division of Germany. Quite the contrary: all commitments undertaken were aimed at exterminating the roots of Fascism and militarism and were focused on establishing a unified German state within its post-war frontiers. This unified democratic German state was not established, however. The emergence of two German states was a result of the cold war that set in soon after World War II. The fact that they were integrated in opposing military alliances, in economic alliances with totally different structures and that they drifted apart as the result of the building of different social orders, led to two different conditions. First, the existence of two independent sovereign German states had to be seen as a factor for European stability. Both states became elements of the European security architecture, an architecture that was built on confrontation, rather than co-operation, and that relied on excessive military strength. However, after the signing of the 1972 Treaty on the Basis of Relations between the Federal Republic of Germany and the German Democratic Republic, the forum of the Conference on Security and Co-operation in Europe (CSCE) was used to constitute a process of normalization between the GDR and the FRG. The political leaderships of both countries gave repeated assurance that they were fully aware of the commitments dictated by history—namely, to pursue a policy that expressed the general responsibility of Germany for peace. The term 'community of responsibility' was coined, and the commitment thus taken, to work incessantly for peace and for nothing else, was accepted by the European peoples with satisfaction. On the other hand, there were justified doubts as to whether this twin nation could be maintained in view of long-standing common national traditions in the FRG and in the GDR, and whether this division of the nation might not give rise to renewed German imponderabilities once again. Of course, these emerged in full clarity when the signs of the times in Europe were more and more in favour of co-operation and when thinking in terms of isolationism and demarcation lines turned out to be obsolete. That is to say, when the attempt to build an independent, socialist nation in the GDR had failed.

The process of transformation, originally aimed at achieving democracy and internal change in the GDR, was eclipsed, in autumn 1989, by emotional demands for unification with the FRG voiced at big demonstrations by the people. The 'German question' has re-emerged with all its aspects; no government and no political party in the GDR can overlook this fact.

Of course, reactions have been far from uniform. It is clear to me, however, that any major political decision that disregards this drive for unity, or tries to put off unification indefinitely, would not only ignore the will of the people but rather increase the danger that an unstable, uncontrollable situation will emerge in the GDR. When I say, nevertheless, that the 'German question' has arisen in its entire dimension once again, it goes without saying that I include the external dimension as well. Even a brief look towards our neighbours in the East and in the West, a look at the Four Powers and, for understandable reasons, a look towards Israel will make us realize rather quickly that the present development of the German issue has, cautiously speaking, triggered a vivid interest there.

In both German states, therefore, all politicians with a sense of responsibility must carry out an unbiased analysis of the internal conditions for a possible growing together of the two German states, taking into account those factors that result from the specific commitments taken by the Germans to peace in a European context. I fully agree with Federal Foreign Minister Hans-Dietrich Genscher when he repeatedly stressed that these factors should not be disregarded, and I also share his concern that the results of disarmament negotiations might no longer keep pace with political change in Europe. With all this in mind Prime Minister Modrow, when submitting his concept for unity, proposed a responsible national dialogue on these issues. Although I cannot make out any acute military threat to any side in Europe, I think the issue of an ongoing military confrontation, as represented by the strong concentration of troops and weapon systems in the GDR and in the FRG, is something we should not accept forever. Appropriate unilateral measures and active efforts to reach a swift and constructive agreement in Vienna would not only enable the governments in Berlin and Bonn to live up to present peace commitments, but could also make an essential contribution to shortening the process of *rapprochement* between the two German states. Clearly, without the reduction of military confrontation, without the elimination of military blocs and without a new co-operative security system in Europe all efforts to bring together the German states will rapidly face insurmountable obstacles. Any attempt to overcome these obstacles by means of nationalist solo efforts would make the 'German question' explosive once more in a way that would turn it into a destructive element for peaceful coexistence in Europe. As Soviet Foreign Minister Eduard Shevardnadze said, because the German issue is the centrepiece of European security, its solution should not be sought in one direction and pursued politically; this, and I would like to quote Mr Shevardnadze again, would not become a catalyst favouring all-European integration and consolidation, but would rather undermine the difficult construction of the 'common European home'.

I know that it is particularly difficult in any country these days to show off this insight, resulting from realistic thinking, to advantage in a highly emotional atmosphere. Nevertheless, we want and have to find a way to harmonize the eruptive German–German dynamics with the need to establish a new European peace order in which all European nations are protected against the threat of a reviving chauvinist German problem. The crumbling of the old structures, once and for all the obvious loss of confidence, the spontaneity in the behaviour of the people and the emotion expressed at and reflected by the street demonstrations in our country do not permit any talk of secure prospects even in the short term. With regard to the acting government of the GDR, decisions have to a great extent been dictated by the necessity to take immediate and urgent practicable measures that are conducive to containing the growing exodus of people, undermining this country's structures in everyday life.

In his statement on German unity on 1 February 1990, the Prime Minister of the GDR took a very bold step, which should not rush us into the abyss ahead but rather help us to jump the rift. What are the major problems to be resolved? In my opinion, it is first of all absolutely essential to attach priority attention to the problem of self-determination. The awakening that brought about the great changes in the GDR was actually started by demands for democracy and for liberating the population from internal spoonfeeding. The call for reunification, on the one hand, constituted a change in the priorities expressed at the mass demonstrations. But this call, on the other hand, could be interpreted as a continuation, a perfection of the demands for self-determination, too.

Meanwhile, there is no serious political force left in this country which would not come out in favour of unity in whatever form. The conflicts, which I believe will not be over after the 18 March election, are much more focused on the questions of time-scale, modalities and the degree of consideration of international factors. The process towards German unity will continue. Demands for the continued existence of two states are no longer a long-term prospect; the transnational process has already started. The continued existence of two opposing social systems within a confederation is hardly imaginable in view of the structural, functional and spiritual collapse—not only in the GDR—of early socialist ideas and visions shaped by outdated Stalinist ideas. At present and in the foreseeable future the right to self-determination of the German people will make itself felt in a way that aims at merging the two German states very soon. It cannot be the task of responsible German policy to put up obstacles to that process, nor to further it. However, there is a responsibility not to let the implementation of the right to self-determination drift away towards nationalist tendencies. At present this is not an easy task for the political forces in the GDR. It is quite a challenge. Without the constructive involvement of responsible political forces in the Federal Republic of Germany it will not be possible to come to grips with this question in the spirit of peace, evening out conflicts and constructing a common European home. I wonder if such warnings are sufficiently listened to, but it would really be reasonable if none of the political parties now campaigning for the general elections allowed themselves to misuse the right to self-determination in order to promote their own policy.

Another problem is that of security. I am not referring to the burning question of internal, that is, domestic security. I have in mind the growing danger, resulting from the changes in the GDR, and from disturbances to the security of Central Europe, along the dividing line between NATO and the Warsaw Treaty Organization. As during the critical phase in the early 1980s there was no dialogue in society about security policies, and differentiated concepts of enemies were maintained despite the undeniably positive contribution the GDR made to continuing the political dialogue between the systems, we suffered a loss of domestic acceptance of our basically correct security orientation. This, at present, is leading to a large degree of indifference and even rejection of a military contribution of the GDR to security in Central Europe. People do not realize the importance of the commitments made by the GDR to its allies within the WTO. Of course, the GDR has not yet fully exhausted its potential, as far as unilateral disarmament steps are concerned. But it would presumably be counter-productive if the GDR were to yield to demands for a total unilateral demilitarization in the present situation.

How can security be obtained in this critical situation—security not only for ourselves, but for others as well? I feel that an orientation to a constructive conclusion of the Vienna Negotiation on Conventional Armed Forces in Europe as early as possible could be helpful. The inception of a second round of these talks should aim at establishing a convincing structural inability to attack as well as a new co-operative security structure in Europe. This should be our goal. Those who reuse Prime Minister Hans Modrow's proposal for military neutrality on the road towards a federation of the two German states should let us know how to resolve these highly sophisticated problems of the two German states' alignment with different alliances in a way that is acceptable for all involved. I see the only alternative to be temporarily to maintain the alignment of the two German states with their present military alliances at the lowest military level possible until the transformation of NATO and the WTO into political organizations has been completed. In spite of repeated outright rejection the part of the Modrow plan concerning military neutrality has, after all, rejuvenated the discussion regarding the security consequences of our efforts towards German unity. Certainly, we have addressed a sensitive area for NATO. Discussions should continue in an unbiased manner. The present official position of NATO on that issue is not necessarily the ideal solution. The problems of safeguarding the stability of security in Central Europe surely cannot be resolved by clinging to the strict patterns of the military blocs. I think that this discussion in Potsdam will open up opportunities for reaching understanding on these questions as well.

If the GDR and the FRG now enter into far-reaching economic integration they should certainly succeed in agreeing on and taking measures towards military confidence building and the reduction of direct military confrontation while maintaining their commitment to their respective allies. When we talk about responsible German policy I cannot imagine a policy which would ignore one problem of greatest and substantive interest to all European nations, primarily to our Eastern neighbours, namely, the problem of frontiers. Those who are really prepared to draw correct conclusions from the sinister past of Germany cannot deny the Polish people the right to live within secure borders. Any questioning of the Western Polish border along the Oder and the Lusation-Neisse would cause turmoil all over Europe. Shifting of borders always means shifting of power.

The uncertainty the FRG Government still nourishes, for whatever reason, concerning the final character of the western border of Poland also brings an element of uncertainty into the forthcoming talks about a qualitatively new arrangement of the regulation between the FRG and the GDR. I am not only speaking on behalf of the GDR Government when saying that what we need is an unambiguous confirmation by the Federal Government, repeatedly made by Foreign Minister Genscher, to recognize once and for all the Polish frontiers as definite frontiers. It is no exaggeration to say that lack of clarity in this issue will have negative consequences for the continuation of the CSCE process.

Now, let me try to find an answer to the question about our road with regard to short- and long-term solutions of all-European prospects. First of all, we are interested in universal, primarily economic, stabilization of the GDR. Clearly, this would be impossible without close co-operation with the Federal Republic of Germany. At the same time we are trying not to lose sight of the all-European dimension of German–German relations at any time. Currently the GDR Government sees its primary economic and social goal as stabilizing the economy within the shortest time possible, giving it a fresh impetus for growth and becoming increasingly competitive in the international market, taking full advantage of all internal and external resources in order to preserve living standards, to maintain social security for all and thus provide quality of life for all GDR citizens within a foreseeable time by elevating it to the standards already enjoyed by other European countries. In the first place we do so in order to contain and reduce the exodus of people from the GDR. What we need is to offer a rewarding prospect to the people here. This calls for radical transformation from our old command economy to a socially and ecologically oriented market economy without delay. Of course, economic reform and stabilization measures to revitalize our own national economy must rely first of all on our own efficiency and our own performance. To this end we do have quite a sizeable potential for effective utilization and expansion, such as intellectual potentials, the highly advanced individual skills of numerous citizens, a sizeable capital stock in the GDR which can be elevated very soon to a higher level, some good market positions in Comecon countries, and the fact that the GDR is, after all, situated in the heart of Europe—which calls for determined action to make it a bridge between East and West and vice versa. At the same time we are strongly interested in what we call economic starting aid by the Federal Republic. Our economic and social backwardness, resulting from the imposed Stalinist model that has failed, is considerable. So, a considerable solidarity contribution by the Federal Republic to stabilize supply and industrial production would not only be in the interest of the GDR to enable it to catch up with Europe within a foreseeable time. It would also make improvements in the social and economic situation of our citizens felt, but at the same time it would pave the road to new markets and to an improved East–West infrastructure. So, the expansion of a contractual community and the gradual establishment of confederacy structures would thus be strongly supported.

I assume that the responsible political forces in the Federal Republic, in both government and opposition, have their own interest in stabilizing the situation in the GDR. Looking at the campaign for the general elections and state elections in the FRG, and the general elections in December 1990, I am fully aware of the fact that basic agreement may be temporarily eclipsed and concealed by campaign polemics and even sometimes denied. We will have to live with that. The present Government of the GDR will continue on its path of increasingly closer co-operation with the FRG. We do not see any meaningful alternative. A new quality we want to impart to this co-operation should, as the next step, be reflected in the substance of our bilaterally accepted contractual community, and it should also be reflected in the forthcoming confederation as another step towards a future united German state. Any hasty and premature unification of the two German states would have very detrimental consequences for both sides and for Europe at large. Such a unification *de facto* would be nothing but an incorporation of the GDR into the FRG, accompanied by a maximum abandonment of its own identity. It would mean admission of 16 million GDR citizens to the FRG. Sober considerations speak for avoiding such a development. It will be difficult enough to control planned unification because we want 10 parts to grow together. To this end the President of the FRG and Willy Brandt coined the generally accepted wording, namely, 'grow together but not proliferate together', and the GDR Prime Minister warned against 'nailing' the two German states together. It is in the interests of a contractual community to organize the growing together, to demonstrate it to the public and to prevent such unwanted proliferation, or to integrate development already under way in the mutually agreed regulations.

Therefore, even during the first-stage contracting of a community we should do much more than simply make the 1972 Treaty on Basic Relations a reality. Although the Treaty has proven satisfactory, it is far from adequate for the new situation and the needs of today. We in the contractual community must clearly point out what we have in common. The next stage in growing together should be the establishment of a confederation. This should be made crystal clear, too. When saying that the German issue has already been decided by history, I feel that this statement should not be interpreted as if that is a decision of the remote future. The Chairman of the Supreme Soviet, Mikhail Gorbachev, in his recent meeting with Hans Modrow, Prime Minister of the GDR, said that he often talked about the determining role played by history, and he expressed the feeling that history is already applying corrective actions. I agree with this. I also agree with the warning that unification of the Germans, closely associated with the destiny of Europe, cannot be solved in the streets. Everyone knows that attempts are increasingly made to stir up tension, to shake constitutional structures and to undermine the scope of the government and authorities. Such destabilization in the GDR would result in unforeseeable consequences for Europe as a whole. We are therefore trying very hard to build consensus among all forces in the GDR, to the benefit of that contractual community, with the FRG. All forthcoming stages in the growing together of the Germans must take due consideration of the properly founded national interests of the citizens in both German states and the interests of our neighbouring states and nations. Prime Minister Modrow's concept for a road to German unity might comply with these demands. It is an offer to all, and it does not specify any time-scale for any stage. So, what can happen faster, should be allowed to happen faster.

As it is regarding the next step I feel I should elaborate on a number of ideas concerning the contractual community. If our common firm intention is for a future-oriented perspective for unification, by means of a tight network of agreements and integration of institutions, we will have to establish a political consultative committee chaired by the two heads of government and equally representing the two states as the supreme body of the contractual community (die Vertragsgemeinschaft). It could be called the German council. This commission, or council, would be authorized to discuss all issues related to the contractual community, to prepare recommendations for governments and parliaments and regular assessments of developments in German–German relations, and to discuss and settle disputes. Below that level the ministries of the two German states could establish similar commissions, working on specific fields. Everything should be aimed at the establishment of an economic, monetary and social association. This association, which can only be established on the basis of a market economy, should have a clear social and ecological orientation towards the common good. We have gained very bitter experience in the past with regard to our national economic potential. Therefore, we should systematically sponsor and promote developments which are in harmony with the aims of the development and needs of the domestic and international markets. As to the new desirable qualitative forms of co-operation, we should set up appropriate institutions.

In public discussions on the *rapprochement* and unification of the two German states at present, emphasis is being placed on the question of currency. Great expectations are harboured with regard to fast economic progress. The proposals being discussed on this issue in the GDR and the FRG can be summed up in two basic variants. One provides for a gradual approach, via a monetary link in line with a process of political and economic *rapprochement* and, until most recently, this concept was greatly supported by bankers and economists. The other variant calls for an immediate introduction of the Deutschmark in the GDR. To the best of my knowledge, this concept is the one primarily supported by politicians in the FRG, and some in the GDR. On 7 February 1990, the Federal Government submitted a proposal to the public to immediately start negotiations with the GDR Government on a monetary union. This offer has created an absolutely new economic and political situation. We do not have the details as yet. Of course, we shall look at the proposal, and it is going to be one of the priorities high on the agenda in next week's talks between Federal Chancellor Kohl and Prime Minister Modrow in Bonn. In my opinion, the opportunities associated with yesterday's proposal and the economic, social and political risks involved will have to play the central role in these talks. The concept of an immediate monetary union, in my opinion, means that, aside from the political process of a contractual community and a confederation, accomplished facts are going to be established in the fields of economy and currency—facts incorporating the GDR into the Federal Republic of Germany. To prepare such political decisions, however, the political, economic and social interrelations and consequences should be discussed, and they should be explained in order to involve all political forces and movements, including the unions, in democratic decision making.

The two German states are still affiliated to different military alliances. The very existence of NATO and the WTO is generally considered to be a stabilizing factor in terms of international security as long as there is no universal security system along the lines of co-operation. Therefore, the security aspect should be given due consideration when it comes to the contractual community. At present, there are discussions that this process of the growing together of the two German states should be accompanied by an expansion of NATO to the eastern frontier of the GDR on the Oder. I regard this as a dangerous orientation. The Vienna process is aimed at reducing asymmetries, and the entire CSCE system is aimed at reducing and minimizing asymmetries. This whole system would be jeopardized. The two German states would be acting against their own interests if they embarked on a road towards destroying the CSCE process. In this highly sensitive area of security the contractual community should tell all nations in the East and in the West that the two German states are prepared to pursue common security policies without terminating their affiliations to NATO and the WTO and in full agreement with the objective trends towards international co-operation and demilitarization of interstate relations in Europe. The two German states have for some time actively supported confidence- and security-building measures. What should prevent them from establishing a joint security council which is accountable to both parliaments? It could be composed of experts from the foreign and defence ministries, the armed forces and from science and economy. Such a council could hammer out specific proposals for establishing co-operative security strategy concepts, in particular for a second CFE agreement. Both German states could give an unparalleled illustration of their responsibility for peace by undertaking joint efforts to make financial means from disarmament available for environmental conservation, for repairing environmental damages, to assist the developing countries and to form a joint disarmament fund.

To what extent such proposals and ideas could be included in the formal text for a contractual community, or whether a certain agreement on security policy should be concluded, is to be determined at the negotiating table, but I feel that a contractual community would be incomplete without clear political and security stipulations and would not comply with the mutual responsibilities for preserving stability.

To have a visually new quality, the actual human dimension of our mutual relations, that is, the co-operation of the social forces of our nation for establishing such a contractual community, should gain a particular significance. Now that the Berlin Wall has fallen and the politics of separation have been overcome, it is clear that decades of separation and stonewalling have not destroyed the sense of togetherness of the people in the two German states. Of course, the reunion of the people first and foremost is an individual decision, in which states and authorities should not intervene, but the different living standards, the currency problems and questions that make it difficult for the citizens to make full use of their potential, should cause the two governments to contrive ways and means to deal with the human dimension of the contractual community. If Prime Minister Modrow, in speaking about the qualitative aspects of newly arranging relations between the GDR and the FRG, has always linked it with the phrase 'good neighbourhood', this idea should certainly be taken literally as an expression of good neighbourly relations. Without such good neighbourly relations as a result of a joint national dialogue the sequence of steps to bring about unity could not develop. The people, the social structure and the political conditions should be duly considered when going ahead with a contractual community and beyond that towards confederation and a German Federation. The success of the first stage of a growing together—as I regard it, the contractual community—is of extreme importance.

It should provide the pillars for what must follow. That is why I thought it necessary to refer to the contractual community in my speech.

I am coming back to my starting-point. The post-war period is over. No new danger of war is in sight in Europe. Thus Europe can enter a new stage of its development. Where hostile camps become dissolved, the division of the German nation could not be maintained artificially. Connected with this development is the question about the fate of the rights of the four allied powers, which again include the question of a peace treaty. In this context avoiding a special German way means a practical approach to the solution of the 'German question', which again should be connected with the preservation of the rights of the Four Powers. These rights can only be replaced by respecting the interests of the Four Powers .

The approach of a preliminary CSCE II conference in 1990 should be saluted and not regarded passively; we should rather contemplate whether or not the two German states should come up with common ideas about concluding a peace treaty regarding the questions that remained unsolved after the war. This should not be in opposition to the Four Powers, but in close co-operation with them. If we succeed within the framework of the CSCE in winning all the European states, the USA and Canada over to a common solution to the 'German question', this certainly would be the optimum way of not turning German dynamics into an unacceptable direction for other countries. The future European peace order will only be durable if a German Federation is established in the middle of our continent, not nationalistic, but rather a functional, integral part of a united Europe. The process of forging the unity of Europe can only take place step-by-step. There will be contradictions and advice. The CSCE remains the framework. The problems that cannot be overlooked include the confrontation of the blocs, economic imbalance and entanglement with the accelerating development of global questions.

In conclusion I should like to emphasize the main guidelines again which, to my mind, are of significance to the GDR if it wants to comply in a dignified manner with its international and national obligations. First of all, it is all about the creation of stable domestic political and social conditions in the GDR in order not to allow any destabilization in Central Europe to emanate from the GDR. Second, what matters is to develop the common national features of the Germans in the GDR and the FRG and the relations we have to maintain with the FRG in such a way that all the requirements of preserving European stability must be duly considered. The obligations we have entered into with other countries and groups of countries should be adhered to. It should become clear that, through a close contractual community and a federation, the path to integration of a united Germany into a future united confederal Europe should be opened. Perhaps, by so doing, we could succeed in resolving the 'German question' in accordance with the pan-European requirements in a way that the very vision coined by Berta von Suttner in 1894 may come true: 'By the end of the 20th century there will be no human society that still faces the scourge of war as a legitimate institution.'

2. German responsibility for a peaceful order in Europe

Address by Hans-Dietrich Genscher, Minister for Foreign Affairs of the Federal Republic of Germany

In the summer of 1988 I appealed in this venerable and living city to let visions become reality. The people in the GDR, admired by the entire world, have made visions become reality and have acted peacefully and responsibly. The things achieved in Leipzig, Dresden and Berlin were conditioned by developments in Central and East European states.

Our German destiny is inextricably linked to Europe's destiny. President Havel expressed this as follows in Warsaw: 'It is hard to conceive of a united Europe with a divided Germany. Likewise difficult to conceive of is a united Germany in a divided Europe'. The firm linkage of our destiny to that of Europe imposes great responsibility on us Germans. Our geographical position, our history and our weight increase this responsibility still further. Living up to this responsibility is the European mission of the Germans.

The Germans in the GDR are in the process of defining their position on the future of Germany and Europe. The programmes of the parties who intend to contest the elections on 18 March 1990 show that they, like ourselves, seek a united Germany in a European framework, under a European roof. On 18 March the Germans in the GDR will decide in free, equal and secret elections on their future political and social system, on the GDR's relationship with the FRG and on the goal of, and path to, German unity. We in the Federal Republic determined our position earlier on as a member of the European Community and the Western Alliance, committed to the goal of German unity.

The two German states are called upon to provide not only a German, but also a European answer to the quest for national unity. The aim is to create a European framework in which the Germans can come together. The breathtaking pace of developments everywhere in Europe, but especially in the GDR, prompts many people to ask what is the foundation and framework for those developments. It is the Helsinki Final Act. The CSCE process must now come fully to bear. This requires that the signatories of the Final Act achieve a partnership for stability throughout Europe in political, economic and security terms. The basis for such a partnership for stability is also in the Helsinki Final Act and the Conference on Security and Co-operation in Europe (CSCE) process.

The CSCE process must become the Magna Carta of a stable European order, based on human rights and fundamental freedoms. The Helsinki Final Act gave the participating states a binding code of conduct for peaceful relations among them. It made the East–West conflict manageable and mitigated its consequences for the people. Today the CSCE is acquiring a new dimension: it must chart the course for overcoming the unnatural division of our continent. Following antagonism and then a *modus vivendi*, the third phase is now beginning, in which Europe will find its unity.

The renunciation of the threat or use of force continues to form the basis of peace and co-operation. The countries of Europe can and should live together without mutual fear and in peaceful competition. This was stated in the joint German–Soviet Declaration of 1989, whose significance reaches beyond German–Soviet relations.

The renunciation of force has become far more credible on our continent—between the alliances and, now that the Brezhnev doctrine is no longer applied, within the Warsaw Pact as well. This development is inextricably linked to General Secretary Gorbachev's policies, with which he has secured for the Soviet Union and its foreign policy unprecedented international recognition. His policy of greater openness at home and abroad, the restructuring of the Soviet Union and the rejection of the expansionist Soviet foreign policy of the past has led to a fundamental change in the situation in Europe, from which all nations in Europe benefit. Recent decisions by the Central Committee in Moscow steadfastly continue the policy of restructuring; they bear out my conviction that the reform process in the Soviet Union is irreversible and calls for a positive reaction by the West in every respect. This development is an important contribution to confidence building in Europe.

Confidence building leads to a spirit of coexistence in which there is no room for hegemony and threats, for distrust and hostile stereotyping. Old hostile stereotypes are fading as a result of the greater openness and democratization in the countries of Central and Eastern Europe. The democratic revolution there has thus paved the way for a new security policy.

The threat situation has changed fundamentally, although as regards military arsenals and the deployment of forces there have been no changes as yet to the extent possible, desirable and necessary. This confirms all the more our view that the huge, intrinsically dangerous accumulations of weapons, especially on German soil, are not the cause, but the consequence of tension and confrontation. As that tension and confrontation are reduced, it becomes even more essential to reduce weapons to the absolute minimum needed for defence.

The two German states must live up to their responsibility in this new situation. They must become the driving force behind a development that overcomes the division of Europe. The Germans in the West and in the East have long been in agreement on this point: 'German soil must never again be the source of war, but the source of peace.'

We thus acknowledge our special responsibility for the stabilization of peace in Europe by establishing a peaceful European order. This requires that all

CSCE participating states abandon the power politics of the past and proceed to a co-operative policy of responsibility.

The policy of the Federal Republic of Germany has, in keeping with the precepts of our Constitution, been a policy of responsibility ever since the founding of our state. To serve world peace, to be an equal partner in a united Europe, and to preserve their national and political unity—that is the mandate which the German people have been given by their Constitution. This includes the determination to firmly link the destiny of Germany to that of Europe. The Germans will not follow a separate path. Nor will they pursue a separate course of neutrality; this would give rise to new insecurity and instability in Central Europe.

The CSCE process rests on co-operation and integration into the European architecture. The architecture for the whole of Europe is emerging in the CSCE process. The CSCE must provide a framework of stability for the dynamic, dramatic and in some respects revolutionary developments in Central and Eastern Europe, including the Soviet Union. The CSCE process must become the bedrock of a partnership for stability throughout Europe. All CSCE participating states must want to maintain the momentum of development in stable conditions. The Western offer of partnership for stability, which must have a political, economic and security dimension, is a significant Western contribution to the success of the policy of reform and democratization.

In view of developments within Comecon and the Warsaw Pact, it will be necessary to pay special attention to the security interests of the Soviet Union. Nobody can clearly foretell the course of developments in Central and Eastern Europe, but there are two trends:

1. The European members of Comecon, including the Soviet Union, are increasingly focusing on the European Community (EC). This can be taken into account by a policy of ever closer co-operation and association. The European Community will be one of the components of a peaceful order in Europe reaching from the Atlantic to the Urals, the common European home. It is already an anchor of European stability.

The Soviet Union and the other European members of Comecon recognize this fact by their energetic efforts to intensify relations with the EC. Co-operation and association agreements are to be negotiated. Some of these countries view co-operation and association in the perspective of subsequent membership. For the GDR the President of the European Commission, Jacques Delors, has proposed three options, all of which take account of the GDR's special relationship with the EC since it was established. They are:

(a) A co-operation and association agreement;
(b) An application for membership, which could be negotiated before 1 January 1993, as an exception to the general rule; and
(c) Entry into the European Community via union with the FRG.

The GDR will have to decide for itself on these three options after the 18 March 1990 election. The acting government has already decided in favour of the first option in its *aide-mémoire* of 24 November 1989. These options for the GDR should be accomplished by realistic community options for all European Comecon countries, including the Soviet Union:

(a) Trade, co-operation and association agreements as well as political consultations with the European Political Co-operation (EPC);

(b) Participation in the work of international economic and financial institutions such as the General Agreement on Tariffs and Trade (GATT), the International Monetary Fund (IMF), the World Bank and the OECD. Participation in stages, including observer status, may be expedient;

(c) Membership of or observer status in the Council of Europe. Accession to the European Human Rights Convention and the extension of the jurisdiction of the European Court of Human Rights to the whole of Europe; and

(d) Membership of the new European Development Bank with all rights and obligations.

With these possibilities, co-operation in the whole of Europe can make a significant contribution to Europe-wide *rapprochement*. Pan-European transport and telecommunications structures as well as a pan-European energy grid are becoming increasingly necessary. This pan-European network of co-operation must have the CSCE process as its framework. This means that in the CSCE process too, the EC will acquire an increasingly important, stabilizing pan-European role.

2. In the Warsaw Pact, there is a growing desire in Czechoslovakia and Hungary for the withdrawal of Soviet forces, and in Poland for their reduction. The impact that this has on the structure and future of the Warsaw Pact is a matter concerning the Warsaw Pact alone. In this respect, too, we shall strictly observe the principle of non-interference.

But, particularly in view of these developments, NATO can make an essential contribution to stability by unequivocally stating that whatever happens in the Warsaw Pact there will be no expansion of NATO territory eastwards, that is to say, closer to the borders of the Soviet Union. This security guarantee is important for the Soviet Union and its conduct. It is also a contribution to the predictability of Western policy, which is essential especially at this stage.

The West must take account of the recognition that the changes in Eastern Europe and the process of German unification must not lead to a shift in the balance of power. Instead the plan for a pan-European co-operative security order must bring about more stability for the whole of Europe and more security for each country in Europe. Such a policy also takes account of the Soviet Union's legitimate security interests. We know that these are vital Soviet interests. All Western decisions must attach great importance to this aspect.

In setting out to design the future structures for Europe, especially its security structure, we must clearly define the future role of the two alliances. They are already moving away from confrontation towards co-operation. This development logically requires that they become elements of co-operative security structures throughout Europe. This means security through joint efforts and no longer security for one side at the expense of the other. Thus the aim cannot be to expand the area covered by alliances or even to seek superiority, but to link the alliances to form an instrument for co-operation conducive to security. They will become elements of the new co-operative security structures in Europe, by which they will be increasingly overarched and into which they can ultimately be absorbed. The two alliances are called upon to define their role more and more along political lines. Their significance for the disarmament process will grow.

The armed forces will also play an increasing role in confidence building and verification. The missions and doctrines of the alliances must keep abreast of political developments. If these developments proceed faster, the alliances will lose their stabilizing influence. In its threat analyses and its assessment of the balance of power, the West should not disregard the emergence of democracies in the Warsaw Pact. The process of democratization in Central and Eastern Europe means greater security for the West, which makes a resolute disarmament policy even more essential. The Soviet Union, too, has realized that the West, as an alliance of democracies, has neither the intention nor the capability to attack the East.

Gorbachev's far-reaching disarmament policy is, therefore, by no means solely determined by economic constraints, as is often assumed in the West, but by a realistic analysis of the goals and potential of the West; it reflects a new Soviet policy based on co-operation. Many studies on the role of the alliances still use an approach that is too static or even retrospective. They ignore the role of the alliances in building co-operative security structures.

Disarmament, too, must not be allowed to lag behind political developments. Without resolute steps towards disarmament there can be no united Europe and no united Germany. No one can get by this fact. The purpose of disarmament is to secure far-reaching reductions of the military elements of the East–West relationship and to cut forces to the absolute minimum necessary for defence. One of the new shared tasks of West and East is this joint task of disarmament and that of jointly meeting the economic, social, technological and ecological challenges posed by disarmament. Disarmament on the scale now required, therefore, means more than the conclusion and implementation of disarmament agreements. Rather, it opens up new areas of co-operation and of the exchange of experience.

The forces of the basing countries must also be included in the Negotiation on Conventional Armed Forces in Europe (CFE). This means including the Bundeswehr in personnel reductions. The CFE Negotiation must be followed without a break by a second round of negotiations. The same applies to the Vienna Confidence- and Security-Building Measures (CSBM) Negotiations.

It will become clear that confidence- and security-building measures have a trend-setting role to play in connection with Europe's political restructuring. Transparency, openness and the ability to correctly assess each other's potential are just as important as the reduction of forces and weapons. They are key elements of our future security structure. Following the successful completion of the CSCE seminar on military doctrines, at which the chiefs of staff met for the first time, we should consider setting up even now a committee to arrange such meetings regularly and at short intervals.

Once the implementation of a first CFE agreement begins, the way will be clear for negotiations on short-range nuclear missiles. Nuclear artillery must also be included in disarmament. If 1990 is to become the year of disarmament, two CFE agreements must be concluded by the end of the year. The same applies to the global ban on chemical weapons and the halving of the two superpowers' strategic nuclear arsenals.

The CSCE summit meeting, at which the two Vienna disarmament agreements are to be signed, will mark the beginning of a new chapter in European history. At their meeting in Dublin, the EC foreign ministers agreed on such a summit meeting. The idea of such a summit is strongly supported by the United States. The Federal Republic of Germany regards the holding of the summit in 1990 as an important contribution to stability and to overcoming the division of our continent by co-operation. I appeal to all countries to recognize its importance and to constructively prepare the summit.

This summit meeting will differ significantly from all previous CSCE meetings, especially the 1975 conference in Helsinki. At that time countries from antagonistic systems with confrontational security policies came together at the conference table, alongside the neutral and non-aligned countries. They adhered to different values and hence to completely divergent political and social orders. In retrospect, the adoption of the Final Act seems like a miracle. The faith that the Final Act's authors had in its momentum was borne out, and the faint-heartedness of its opponents refuted. The disinterest of those who voted for the Final Act but did not take it very seriously was very quickly superseded by a keen interest.

The relationship between the two German states then was as antagonistic as that between the alliances to which they belong. And yet they made an important contribution to bringing about the Helsinki conference. The treaties concluded by the FRG with the Soviet Union, Poland and Czechoslovakia, and the 1972 Treaty on the Basis of Relations between the Federal Republic of Germany and the German Democratic Republic, were essential preconditions for starting the CSCE process. Those treaties are just as significant as ever; on their basis it has been possible to usher in new developments, as the German–Soviet and German–Polish declarations of 1989 show.

In 1975, the two German states had different ideas about a common German future. This time the CSCE summit meeting will not be marked by a spirit of confrontation between the 35 countries. This applies in political, economic and security terms. It must be borne in mind that concepts have moved closer together, that the commitment to human rights and human dignity enshrined in the Helsinki Final Act is beginning to become reality everywhere.

Without wishing to anticipate the results of the GDR elections—this remains the sovereign decision of the people in the GDR—it can be assumed that at the conference table of the 1990 CSCE summit there will be two democratically elected German governments, which will be as one in their quest for unity and will already have embarked on the road to that goal through closer co-operation. Their attitude will to a decisive extent again determine whether a new chapter can be started in the history of Europe. Once more the European mission and shared responsibility of the Germans must prove their worth. They must be a driving force for strengthening and intensifying the CSCE process, East–West co-operation and disarmament.

This summit must provide an orientation for the future structure of Europe, whether it is to have a confederate structure and whether this confederate order should ultimately lead to European federalism. President Mitterrand's call for a European confederation is an important and constructive contribution.

We Germans will have to make it clear what shape Germany's future should have. The FRG cannot do so on its own and can only decide for itself, whereas the government elected on 18 March will have to speak on behalf of the GDR. Right now we can state: We Germans want to serve the peace of the world as an equal partner in a united Europe. Among our people there is a deep yearning for freedom and peace. When we Germans speak of unification, we have in mind the two German states, including Berlin.

In advance of the CSCE summit meeting, we Germans can make important stabilizing contributions: the two German states can—of course after the elections on 18 March 1990—make a joint declaration guaranteeing the borders with all their neighbours, and they can also jointly reaffirm their renunciation of the production and possession of nuclear, chemical and biological weapons. The CSCE summit can build new confidence by solemnly reaffirming the principles enshrined in the Helsinki Final Act.

The CSCE summit meeting can also contribute to the East–West partnership for stability and to the creation of a peaceful European order by intensifying the CSCE process and taking steps aimed at its institutionalization. This includes the development of pan-European institutions in the CSCE framework, such as:

1. An institution to co-ordinate East–West economic co-operation. The European Development Bank must also be seen in this context.

2. A pan-European institution for the protection of human rights. The application of the Council of Europe's Human Rights Convention to the whole of Europe suggests itself.

3. A centre for the creation of a European legal area aimed at legal harmonization.

4. A European environmental agency.

5. Extension of European Scientific Co-operation Project (EUREKA) co-operation to the whole of Europe.

6. Collaboration between the European Space Agency (ESA) and corresponding Eastern institutions.

7. A centre to develop European telecommunications.

8. A centre to develop European transport infrastructure and policy.

9. A European verification centre.

10. A European conflict management centre.

To keep the CSCE process moving, one might also set up a council of foreign ministers of the CSCE countries, which would meet at regular intervals. The proposal made by Prime Minister Tadeusz Mazowiecki of Poland for a 'Council of European Cooperation' evidently tends in a similar direction, but needs to be elucidated.

It is essential that, by deepening and reinforcing the CSCE process, all participating states are prepared to create a framework of stability and network of security for foreseeable and unforeseeable developments in Europe. This includes an assurance by all participants that they will not seek unilateral advantages at any stage and that they will strive for security through co-operation and not through confrontation. We must work vigorously for a peaceful European order from the Atlantic to the Urals, for the construction of a common European home.

The process of intra-German unification must be placed in this context. I realize that in neighbouring countries there exists a fear that the Germans will play a dominant role. This fear is unjustified in respect of Germans living in freedom and democracy. It can be dispelled still further by the resolute advancement of integration within the EC and by pan-European integration, that is, in the CSCE and disarmament process, but the pan-European process of unification requires the active and constructive participation of everyone concerned. We Germans seek this integration, but some fear that the CSCE summit might become a conference on Germany. This, too, I consider unjustified, provided that we Germans in the two states are determined to make it a conference for overcoming the division of Europe and hence a conference for German unity, too.

German unity will not be achieved without Europe, and European unity will not bypass the Germans. The Germans should not, therefore, refuse to participate in Europe, nor should the Europeans refuse to participate in Europe so as to slow down the process of intra-German *rapprochement*. The convergence of the Germans in an ordered European framework is just as important for Europe's stability as a stable framework for the revolutionary developments in Central and Eastern Europe. Within such a framework of stability the process of

German unification can take place without causing a shift in the balance of power or destabilization in Europe.

We realize that the process of German unification raises serious questions that do not concern us alone. They require thorough and responsible treatment, not just by the two German states. When, after the 18 March election, the two German governments discuss the future of the German nation and reach agreement on German unification, they will be aware of that responsibility. They will bear in mind that the GDR also has commitments, including alliance commitments; they will be aware of the interests of other European countries; they will heed the Soviet Union's security interests, which are reflected in the presence of Soviet forces in the GDR; and they will seek talks with the Four Powers.

A European-minded and -oriented FRG faces national and European responsibility in its commitment to German and European unity. The Germans in the GDR are just as good as we are. All countries in Europe can perceive that the yearning of the Germans in the GDR for German unity is growing ever stronger. That coincides with the feelings on our side. 'We are the people; Germany, a single fatherland'—this must not be ignored by anyone, by any state or government, in a Europe of self-determination and democracy. And nobody must overlook the fact that, given its economic and political problems, the GDR may become a threat to stability in Europe if it has no realistic prospect of unification. It would be a grave mistake to turn a blind eye to the true situation in the GDR. The Federal Government's offer to the GDR for economic and monetary union as well as wide-ranging co-operation is an expression not only of national solidarity, but also of responsibility for European stability. Nobody benefits if developments in the GDR move away from intra-German and European policy. The present situation is not the outcome of an irresponsible policy pursued by the FRG, but the legacy of past policies in the GDR. The rising number of resettlers is a sign of despair. Assistance is therefore needed now both for and in the GDR so as to avoid a mass exodus and destabilization. Every step that the two German states take to move closer together is a contribution to stability in Europe.

The offer of a partnership for stability to all neighbours in the East, including the Soviet Union, must encompass not only the political and disarmament dimensions, but also the economic dimension. The FRG will use its economic potential to this end. And we owe it to the peaceful revolutions for freedom not to upset the process of democratization by the old bloc-based approach, by national egoism or power politics of the past.

We Germans do not want to go it alone or to follow a separate path. We follow our path with a sense of responsibility for Europe. We do not want a German Europe, but a European Germany. We seek a dynamic development in conditions of stability. We appeal to our neighbours in East and West to open up the European perspective together with us. We want to place the process of German unification in the context of EC integration, of the CSCE process, the East–West partnership for stability, the construction of the common European home and the creation of a peaceful European order from the Atlantic to the Urals. Neutralizing Germany would not serve the cause of European stability. The Germans, who pin their hopes on Europe, must not have their European aspirations dashed. The nations of Europe should realize that we Germans want nothing but to live in peace and freedom with all our neighbours. New thinking and a sense of responsibility are demanded of everyone—first and foremost of us Germans, but not of us alone.

3. Berlin and European developments

Address by Walter Momper, Governing Mayor of Berlin

The opening of the borders, the abolition of compulsory visas and minimum exchange requirements have moved the 'German question' back to the centre of politics. The German division was the festering sore of the post-war European order. Together with the special status of Berlin, it prevented the permanent overcoming of the division of our continent. Because of the 'German question' the aim of overcoming this division and the creation of a continental, all-European federation remained latent in the background of European politics. The policy of *détente* was an attempt to approach this aim in the very long run with the continued existence of the different social systems. With the collapse of the bureaucratic–socialist systems, the time perspective has changed completely. The 'German question' is on the agenda now, but it is not a problem for the Germans alone. The German problem has determined the destiny and the lives of all nations in Europe throughout this century. The superior might of a large German Reich in the heart of the continent has twice this century been the cause of devastating wars. We understand the concern of many peoples in Europe about the restitution of the German nation-state. To take this concern seriously is the fundamental condition for solving the issues arising now. Germany without or against Europe, this cannot be. Never again do we want a Germany which is against other states.

There is also good reason for the desire of the German people for the restitution of their country's unity. No nation can be deprived forever of the right to self-determination. It is a right that other nations cannot determine. Today it becomes clear once more what power there is in the cultural cohesion of a nation. Neither the Berlin Wall nor differences in the systems have affected in any way the feeling of the Germans that they belong together. The Socialist Unity Party of Germany (SED) regime never succeeded in creating a significant separate identity in the GDR. If there ever was such an identity on the part of the people of the GDR, then it existed in those October and November days of great change. But this power is not sufficient to satisfy the wishes of the people for rapid economic, ecological and social improvements. People have run out of patience. Today the complete hollowness of the old system is evident. It was much more hollow than anyone in Europe had ever suspected.

The issue is now to take into account both the right of the Germans to self-determine their national organization and the will of other peoples for security and stability in Europe at the same time. Thus the 'German question' is embedded in the European question, in the question of the future securing of peace in Europe as such. Time is short. The dynamics of the German–German process are extraordinarily cogent. This process is not politically controlled or planned. It is determined by the mood in the GDR, the economic perspective, the supply situation and the number of resettlers. Diplomats in the European countries have no time for lengthy consultations and deliberations. They must rethink faster and act faster in order to include in this process the interests of all states.

The security order which has guaranteed peace and stability in Europe since the war was based on the failure to respect the freedom of the peoples of Eastern Europe and on the division of our continent. It is not worth shedding tears over its coming to an end. It did not represent peace but an absence of war and mutual threat and the arms spiral.

We must now together find a new system of security in Europe which is based on the free consent of free peoples and which includes the right of the German people to self-determination. Such a system can only be collective; it must include all European nations and the victorious powers of World War II.

I therefore propose that a new Conference on Security and Co-operation in Europe (CSCE) be held this very summer. This CSCE conference must not come too late. Berlin is the appropriate venue for it. This conference will work out a new CSCE agreement which will end post-war developments in Europe once and for all, and will prepare an all-European order of peace. The conference must bindingly guarantee all existing borders in Europe.

The new system of security in Europe should be a European federation. This term corresponds to President Mikhail Gorbachev's image of a common European home. This European federation must develop rapidly and simultaneously in the fields of political federation, economic federation and security partnership:

1. *Political federation* means: the step-by-step integration of other countries in the European Community (EC), first of all the territory of the GDR but also Austria, Hungary, Poland, Czechoslovakia, and so on; the strengthening of the powers of the European Parliament and the EC Commission at the expense of national parliaments and national governments; the extension of European Political Co-operation (EPC) with France and Germany at its core and with the aim of a common foreign policy, defence policy and development policy and the integration of armed forces in a European Defence Community; the opening of borders and the right of free settlement and employment; the adjustment of legal standards; at the same time, the strengthening of the rights of the regions, that is, the small units; and the recognition of all borders in Europe.

For Germany as well as for the other European powers, this model means a departure from thinking in terms of national categories. The era of nationalism is finally coming to an end in Europe. Those who discuss this topic honestly will acknowledge that it is the Germans who find it easiest to subscribe to this. These difficult debates in the European Community show that the national egotisms of individual European countries are still quite strong. We will have to address problems regionally, beyond borders. In the wider Berlin region we have made a start with working together in the Regional Committee for an area of five million people.

2. *Economic federation* means: the rapid implementation of monetary union, the extension of the single EC market to include the new member countries; the expansion of trade and particularly intensive economic co-operation with the Soviet Union; increased assistance of weakly structured member countries by means of structural aid funds; and joint environmental protection. Together with the Federal Republic, the other economically strong countries of Western Europe can help, through increased aid for the GDR, to ensure that the 'German question' is not restricted to the German nation.

3. *Security partnership* means: the complete disarmament of the ABC arsenals (nuclear, biological and chemical weapons) of the countries along the old bloc borders within two years; the reduction of the Bundeswehr to 240 000 troops; and no new Jäger 90-type aircraft. The aim of the Vienna Negotiation on Conventional Armed Forces in Europe (CFE) must be a 50 per cent reduction in the conventional field; a drastic 50 per cent reduction of medium- and long-range weapon arsenals; the beginning of joint security planning; and the redesigning of all armies into armed forces for purely self-defensive purposes. A significant step in this direction is the reduction of the armed forces of the USA and the USSR in Europe to 195 000 troops each, proposed by US President George Bush; finally the dissolution of the military blocs and a security partnership with the Soviet Union.

Nearly all political parties and groups in the GDR are entering the election campaign with the aim of creating German unity. They will have to achieve this goal quickly unless they want to be exposed to the same pressure as the present GDR Government. I expect the GDR Government to be elected after 18 March, to take office with the aim of making unity a reality quickly and thereby to make itself superfluous. This is the only way, in addition to the introduction soon of the Deutschmark as the legal currency in the GDR and the transfer to the Bundesbank of the appropriate competence in currency policy, to stop further emigration and to prevent the collapse of the GDR. This will not be a unification of states with equal rights but rather an incorporation (Anschluss) into the Federal Republic. However, the people in the GDR do not mind what it is called; their motives are not nationalistic but social and economic. The people want an improvement, at long last, in their economic situation, and they want to be assured that the political circumstances which they have just overcome will not return. They want to be assured that the SED and Stasi never come back, and they no longer feel confident that their state has the strength to reform. They see their future and the securing of democracy only in joining the Federal Republic. The old *Länder* structure will also be restored before the communal elections in May. The *Länder* parliaments could then decide in favour of an incorporation (Anschluss) into the Federal Republic of Germany, thereby determining themselves the pace of development. It would doubtless have been better and socially more acceptable not to begin with political unity but first to implement a guided process of economic adaptation and then make the political decision quietly and in agreement with all neighbours. However, there is just no time for such a timetable. The authority of the state in the GDR has already largely broken down, but without state authority the painful process of economic reforms cannot be implemented. Through the reversal of the course of events, unification will first of all bring with it a political authority in the form of an all-German Government in order then to undertake economic adaptation step-by-step. This is the only way that remains.

No destabilization of security policy, for example to the disadvantage of Poland or the Soviet Union, must be permitted to arise, between the unification of the two German states and the later creation of a new European peace order. I have therefore proposed that Four Power responsibility, as we now know it for greater Berlin, be extended to the territory of the present GDR, and that this territory and Berlin be demilitarized. That means that, as here, no German troops may be stationed in the GDR, Soviet troops could remain under the control and observation of the Four Powers in the GDR for the specified transitional period, in the same number as that of the US, British and French troops in the FRG and West Berlin. The territory of the present Federal Republic would remain in NATO as in all its other international obligations.

With regard to the alliance obligations of the GDR, the representatives of the GDR made the following declaration when they signed the Warsaw Agreement on 14 May 1955, which was stated to be an integral part of the Agreement: 'In signing this Agreement . . . the government of the GDR assumes that the reunited Germany will be free of the obligation which one part of Germany entered into in military–political treaties and agreements which were entered into before such reunification.'

This means that the GDR will be free of its alliance obligations from the moment of reunification. This does not, however, apply to the obligations arising from occupation rights as the original victors' rights and thus from the responsibility of the Four Powers for Germany as a whole.

The model I present underlines the responsibility of the Four Powers for the whole of Germany for the period of transformation. It is feasible if one thinks in categories of security partnership instead of confrontation. The clear refusal of the USA, Great Britain and France and the Federal Government to extend NATO to the western Polish border is also testimony to this way of thinking.

Today, it is actually only sections of the Christian Social Union (CSU) who still endanger unity in agreement with our neighbours by wanting to extend NATO's territory to the Oder and the Neisse and, at the same time, by not wanting to recognize this border in binding form. I am not in favour of the neutrality of all of Germany because of the lessons of history. There must not be a neutral Germany without ties in the centre of Europe, with great economic and possibly military might.

A unified Germany must be woven into the process of the union of Europe. And Berlin will be the capital again, if the Germans want this. But capital cities will see themselves as regional centres of Europe—as European metropolises. They will be the seats of European and CSCE institutions, for example, a seat of the permanent CSCE secretariat which is to be founded.

In the present phase it is important to assist in seeing that a democratically legitimized government gains authority after 18 March 1990 which will allow it to implement the transition to unity and, above all, guide it in a socially acceptable way. For this we need quick signals of concrete transitional help such as many Federal *Länder*, Berlin among them, have now approved. The greatest danger until 18 March is that the supply system in the GDR might not function adequately any longer, affected by the dissolution of the administration through lack of money or material or by strikes.

We know that there are many whose mouths water when they think how little many things cost in the GDR. After unification, the most important task will be to see to it that unity does not become the occasion for the rebirth of Manchester capitalism. Those ecological and social principles valid in the West must be guaranteed. The throwing together of two such different economic and currency systems with such different social orders can cause great social distortion, misery and proportionate speculative activities and profiteering.

Berlin will be a key region for the practical transition to unity, with all the risks, problems but also opportunities. Regional development has been organized together with the other side since December in the Regional Committee, in which representatives of the Senate, the East Berlin Magistrate, the Government of the GDR and the Federal Government are represented. Co-operation includes, in particular, the extension of the regional infrastructure, transport and communications, regional economic co-operation, regional environmental protection, the development of recreational areas close to the city and cultural, scientific and sporting exchanges, like the Olympic Games in 2004 or 2000. The Olympic peace games in Berlin will be a historic event at which the world will celebrate the overcoming of division, the end of East–West confrontation. And these games will provide a view of the real tasks of humanity, that is, the preservation of nature and the balance between North and South.

Independent of further development between the two German states, which cannot be determined precisely in terms of time, the West Berliners must at long last be granted the right to elect their representatives to the German Bundestag and the European Parliament. And the Berlin representatives must have full voting rights in the Bundestag and Bundesrat.

Berlin's status will not be affected in the short term by the sweeping changes in Europe. The rights of the victorious powers of World War II are original rights. Their practical application in the interior will, however, be reduced to the extent that the two democratic German states co-operate with one another. The function of the Western Allies as protecting powers will remain so long as the military blocs remain. The strength of the military presence will be determined by the Allies themselves. The steps in disarmament will also be translated into the reduction of the troops stationed here. The Four Powers gain political significance through the transformation of the present situation in Europe into a European confederation. With the completion of this task which will take place within the framework of the CSCE process, the victorious powers will be able to relinquish their rights in Berlin and Germany. The great powers will remain guarantee powers for the European peace order.

4. Elections in the GDR: European aspects

Panel discussion chaired by Egon Bahr, SIPRI Governing Board

Participants: Gregor Gysi, PDS; Lothar de Maizière, CDU; Walter Romberg, SPD; Gerhard Lindner, LDPD; Bärbel Bohley, New Forum; Günter Bransch, Protestant Church; Fred Dumke, NDPD

Bahr: Today's itinerary was compiled by SIPRI, together with Max Schmidt, after some preliminary talks. I am not here as a citizen of the FRG—in those shoes I would never dare allow or forbid chairmen or leading representatives of GDR parties to speak—but as a member of SIPRI's Governing Board. In our talks we agreed that I will put a number of questions to the individual participants that arise from the background of today's discussions and are partly expected by our group.

My first question is addressed to all sitting here at the table, asking you to answer it briefly. Today we have discussed the likelihood of a relatively fast unification of the two German states. We would like to know your plans concerning basic security political structures of a united Germany.

I. Will a united Germany be a member of NATO?

Will NATO be expanded; will Germany be a member of NATO; to which alliance will a future united Germany belong?

Dumke: In reply to the first aspect: in our party we hold the view that in the process of reunification NATO should not be extended to the Oder/Neisse border, and that the hitherto traditional NATO area should continue to exist. Membership is without doubt a complex question, but on the other hand it has already been answered in today's discussions to the extent that the FRG is going to retain its membership. This needs to be duly considered because, so far, a definite answer has not been given. In this context I would like to make a few remarks concerning a few aspects of the discussions here. We are of the opinion that both the Warsaw Treaty Organization and NATO will play their parts in the pan-European developments, and that the WTO has not yet lost its significance. We would like to stress this and point out that the two military alliances have potentials that could help further the European processes of unification and disarmament.

Lindner: My starting-point is identical with that Herr Genscher suggested this morning, namely, that a German unification process must be embedded in a

European scenario, and that such a scenario also calls for developing a security partnership. To this end the question of the contents of security structures must be raised more clearly than was obvious during the discussions. The focus was merely on security structures replacing bloc structures. But it is the contents that we in our party, too, are strongly interested in. Without doubt the best joint European security structures would not expand the sphere of NATO, because an expansion would most certainly lead to conflicting interests between us and the Soviet Union. Yet, this would rather hamper and not further the pan-European process of integration. The contents of such political structures should be geared to bringing about demilitarization in Europe in the spirit of a security partnership. We believe—and here I must confess again that, because worries about everyday life are at the top of the list, this question has not yet been given due consideration within my party—that questions of alliances or of membership in them will be of secondary importance within the future security structures in Europe because the military aspect will be more and more restrained within the alliances, and the political aspect will also gain ground with regard to co-operation in fields that involve both alliances.

Bahr: Let me dig a bit deeper here. The question was clearly what alliance a united Germany would belong to, given the fact that this will come about faster than your far-reaching prospects.

Lindner: The consequence of what I said is that the two German states will remain members of the two alliances they are members of today without expanding the sphere of NATO, but also to create joint security measures which are embedded in the European effort to this end.

de Maizière: To my mind the questions are relatively difficult to answer. Who would dare make accurate prognoses for tomorrow and the day after at this time. In late November and early December my party adopted the view that the future would bring a united Germany, that there would be an appropriate synchronicity of the inter-German and European processes and that they could be harmonized—we all must recognize this as a misapprehension. Hence we are facing a situation in which we can start to think about new developments without having the cut-and-dried solution at hand. I want to give a brief answer to your questions. I do not think an expansion of NATO would be right, neither would membership by present-day GDR territory. The question of the alliance of a future Germany is answered, I think. What matters is that NATO and the WTO adopt common defence structures within a CSCE framework.

Bohley: I make it a bit more personal as I am not a military expert and as I certainly belong to a small minority that will only scratch the surface in the near future. I have not made so many efforts to see my son, who objected to military service here, serve in NATO or in a Federal German army. I myself have been working with Women for Peace, and I am not prepared to accept the present military potential. We can only conceive of a united Germany as a demilitarized Germany, and those who are interested in unification today, and think it is inevitable, should start disarmament as soon as possible.

Romberg: No entry into NATO for two reasons: first, a shift in the military–political balance in Europe is not acceptable to the Soviet Union nor to the other members of the WTO; second, a solution to the security problems in the long run is no longer possible within the framework of these military alliances, but on a different level such as the CSCE and pan-European structures. I think the SPD has made it very clear in its statements that it is only possible to bring about new structures in a united Germany when taking into account the security interests of the neighbours and by establishing these new structures through contacts and constant consultations with them. Disbanding the military alliances will be a goal of the not-too-distant future. The WTO is in a crisis. Members such as Poland will no longer be interested in total involvement in situations of crisis in the Balkans and vice versa, that is, bilateral structures with the Soviet Union will more and more gain the upper hand. What the structures will be like in Central Europe remains to be seen. I think in terms of security structures overlapping military blocs. One could say a lot about them.

Bahr: I would like to put another question to the same round, namely, what is your position with regard to neutrality of a united Germany?

II. Will a united Germany be a neutral state?

Dumke: With regard to this proposal we consider it a personal proposal which corresponds to the official version: a proposal that favours dialogue mainly on the questions of the military balance of forces, disarmament as an extremely important phenomenon in the quest for resolving the issues facing Europe. We think—this is how we understood it, Herr Modrow and I have not interpreted it here—that it is essentially aimed at the military aspect of neutrality and not so much at the political one. It is also correct, and this is how we see it, that the question of neutrality cannot simply be compared with Austria of the past but needs some new considerations. I think we agree that a discussion should be held at any rate on the status in Central Europe—a development process that will spur on further considerations. The concerns I have noticed in this circle are shared by all parties involved, namely, that a united Germany, with a population of 74 million, should not be demilitarized totally while its neighbours have a substantial military presence. It is clear that this is a genuine problem, and it should be major matter of concern in this phase of the discussion to think jointly about a reasonable step towards the necessary disarmament. I want to repeat that I would, together with Herr Modrow, underline all his other concerns. This aspect is just one aspect of the whole plan. We agree with the plan as a whole. However, we regard the passage on neutrality as full of problems and consider ourselves to be participants in the discussion. We think that a lot of thinking still has to be done. Let me put it this way, at the moment we think a totality in the sense of military totality is unreal under the concrete historical conditions.

Bransch: Questions of contractual neutrality and all these things are not my cup of tea but that of the politicians. I am more interested in the ethical dimensions. If neutrality means demilitarization I cannot but agree with what Frau Bohley said. I think the churches will also share this view, at least the Protestant churches. If it means non-alignment, in an attempt to reappraise history the churches must raise the question of whether a change might one day happen which we will recognize from history, when people said: 'The strong is most powerful when he stands aloof.' That is exactly the lesson we have to learn from our German history. Neutrality can only mean to undertake developing a policy that gives our neighbours the feeling that they are dealing with a friend and not a competitor. This is easier said than done. Translating it into real policies is quite a different story, but I think a united Germany is too strong when it comes to population. Allow me to use a metaphor. Among brothers and sisters the smallest child can remain neutral when the older ones quarrel, but never the oldest brother. And from this point of view I want to repeat that a speedy withdrawal from the military alliances destabilizes trust. The incorporation of a united Germany in European contractual systems, I think, is an imperative in a successful construction of a united Germany.

Lindner: I would prefer a neutral Germany embedded in a co-operating Europe. But I think, at least at present, this is unrealistic. In the West, as I see it, neither the FRG nor the USA would support this idea and on the Eastern side, I think, it also depends on what happens to and within East European countries. That is to say that new situations would also emerge in this respect, so that this kind of neutrality, and I see it as military neutrality, would not be realistic at present.

de Maizière: I think, under the given circumstances, that what we need is not wishful thinking but what is feasible. Herr Modrow's plan is not entirely new. We know it as Rapacki's or Palme's or the like. Even their plans turned out not to be feasible, I think. I also think that the term neutrality cannot be divided into a military and political neutrality. The FRG is one of the mainstays of NATO in Western Europe or virtually *the* mainstay. A withdrawal would only be possible on the basis of consenting allies. To my mind this consensus cannot be reached at present. Another question was raised, namely, whether a neutral Germany would turn out to pose a different threat to its neighbours, that is, in the economic field. The release of forces so far engaged in the economy would possibly lead to an economic potential that could be viewed as a genuine threat to and danger for a future community. I regard the plan as nice but not realistic.

Bahr: Thank you very much. Let me only point out that I do not know of any proposal by Olof Palme concerning German neutrality . . . that is something else.

Bohley: I do not know so much about it, but I could very well imagine that a demilitarized Germany could be neutral in a demilitarized Europe. The question is much more whether we are on the verge of becoming a European military power. And I would not be afraid of our neighbours. I think it is not necessary as early as now to speculate about having no arms while all the neighbours around have them. This morning I talked to a mayor from France; he was rather worried about the next steps concerning disarmament and said: 'If there is a strong Germany next to us we have to stock up our arsenals.' I think that there are many reservations in people's minds. To me the unification of Germany always seems more dangerous for a future Europe than is generally desired. I think that we are creating many more fears than we actually want, a fact that probably would not contribute to disarmament.

Romberg: I think in German and European policies the aim has always been to establish a balance in Europe, but also on a larger scale, which the Germans are part of. I am somewhat more sceptical than Herr Biedenkopf was this afternoon. I could imagine that the potentials of both German states are not naturally absorbed in total by the European Community (EC), let alone Eastern Europe. So what is really in focus is a balance. Neutrality, I think, is a step back, because neutrality basically follows the idea of a nation. What matters now is to overcome it. Maybe there is something like a vacuum forming in the centre of Europe. The question is how we could set up Central European structures that would resolve the problem in another fashion. We shall certainly speak about them.

Bahr: May I ask you to answer my last question starting from the other end. Today we discussed that policies are meant basically to provide for a controllable process towards German unity, that is, slow and steady or fast. The whole thing must not end up in chaos. How do those gathered here, who know the GDR situation better than others, see this task or problem?

III. Whether and how to control the unification process?

Romberg: Indeed, what matters, I think, is to provide a political foundation to the development leading to unification. I can hardly tell how much time we really have. On the one hand I see growing economic problems and signs of decay also in the sphere of political structures, thinking of local government, for instance. The country is less governable every day. On the other hand I must also reflect on my impression that this rapidly growing crisis is not only caused inside the country. I do not know who has followed the Western media over the past three days. Almost every programme tries to tell us that what is left here is merely ruins, that our economy is down on its knees and that we have to push ahead with the processes underlying the monetary union. I do not want to brush the problems under the carpet. But this is a real process on the other side. I think it is evident here—and let me say it bluntly—that there are also political disputes of the FRG involved. We have the impression that this process of uni-fication is unfortunately hampered and partly undermined by the connections that are being made with the election campaign in the FRG.

Bahr: Frau Bohley, you are certainly among those who stood up for an inde-pendent GDR and, maybe, are not very happy to see unity come so quickly.

Bohley: I can only underline what Herr Romberg said. What is happening here now is not at all what I, or others in this country, set out for. We set out to change the GDR, to reform the GDR, to create democratic socialism. This idea has been superseded by that of German unity after 9 November 1989. Until then there had been no slogans demanding the reunification of Germany. People demanded freedom to travel. They have it. They demanded democrati-zation. They demanded self-development and self-determination. This would be possible. I think that the policies you have just mentioned are aimed at making this process of reunification comprehensible. So far none of them have become effective. On the contrary, we have been annexed. I consider it a spiritual annexation. At a time when people have lost orientation because of the changes. The structures were only meant to be changed; however, they turned out to be totally intolerable. This caused a certain lack of orientation. And this lack is being used for West German campaigns. And I must say that I find it scan-dalous when politicians, especially SPD, enter rooms with a victorious smile on their faces and wage their campaign over here in the GDR without considering the fact that, given the SPD will win the elections, Ibrahim Böhme will be in office and not they. I assume they will not move here, I do not know.

Bahr: Would you vote for me?

Bohley: I just mean it could be that they want to be in government here. But you are not among them. Well, I think this leads to great uncertainty and to the fact that people here do not, at least to a large degree, think about the elections of 18 March as their elections. They rather rack their brains about whom they would elect in the December elections in the FRG. I regard this as irresponsible, taking into consideration that unification is not going to happen tomorrow and how many problems all this will involve, what social problems not only for us but I think also for the Federal Republic.

Bahr: Herr de Maizière, late in November you still spoke about the opportunity of reforming socialism. You said you do not like the coldness and harshness of interhuman relationships in the FRG. Have you now, when talking to Herr Kohl, felt warmth and soft-heartedness?

de Maizière: Herr Bahr, first I thought that this evening would be free of campaign rhetoric and that is what it should continue to be. The term socialism was used to describe four facts in the past, namely: first, a form of running the economy which I regard as having failed; second, the kind and form of shaping a community that was only acceptable in part; third, it stood for a structure, for a principle of organization called democratic centralism which, because of centralization of power, rendered control of power impossible or more and more difficult; and fourth it represented a certain catalogue of values which, I think, many people in this country have accepted for many years or which has given them security. Christians also thought that they could find in it what they know corresponds to Christian life ethics. I also think that, with regard to these values, the term socialism has been discredited to such a degree, given all we learned about the reality, that we can do without this term when describing our identity, including our ethical identity. And I think we should again become more aware of the sources in the gospel.

Bahr: I did not ask out of malice. When you commented on my question my inner self agreed with you, because I personally also sense a certain superficiality and coldness in FRG society and in the way people are treated, and I have always hoped that the GDR will be capable of preserving the different values.

de Maizière: Good. I want to pick up one of Frau Bohley's thoughts. It is correct that we have a great deal of difficulties with our own identity at this time and that we have to ask ourselves in all seriousness what of all the 40 years of life we will take with us into a changed and possibly a united German republic. On another occasion I said that he who wants to think about the future has to think about the past first; at the moment we lack the time to think about the past which will enable us to think about the future. Whether we lack it for objective reasons or whether somebody is accelerating the political process I want to leave undebated. But we cannot take it for granted that the present attitudes of people in this country will be identical to those in October. When we listen to what is being shouted in Leipzig we hear: 'We want to get out', 'We stay here', 'We are the people', 'We are one people' and, finally, 'Germany—a united fatherland'; and all this within just a few weeks. It is, of course, very difficult to assess whether the roughly 100 000 gathered there are representative of what a whole people thinks, whether it is just one tendency, one opinion that is articulated this way. I also think that there are great regional differences, that in Saxony and Thuringia people have already decided that both German states are one and that we only have to create the legal basis for it and the structures. In Mecklenburg, too, there are quite a few whose thoughts are directed Westwards, while I think that in Berlin-Brandenburg and in the area around Greifswald, that is, Hither Pomerania, people have different opinions. But there is no time left to digest all this. I sometimes have the impression that time is too fast for the soul to catch up. All the more, we will have to take pains to do what we conceive of as reasonable and wise through rational thinking when emotions fail to do the job.

Bahr: Many thanks. I welcome Herr Gysi who has just arrived and I feel must be given the chance to answer the same questions before we proceed. We've had two rounds in which the representatives of this panel discussion had the chance to give short answers to short questions. These were: Let's assume a united Germany will be established sooner than the conceptions of pan-European structures anticipate. What do you think the security–political structure of a united Germany should look like? Expansion of NATO? And what alliance will a united Germany be a member of? I want to add to the second question right away, namely, your attitude towards neutrality.

Gysi: Well, assuming things happen the way you describe them I am against an expansion of NATO on principle because this would end up in a shift in the balance of power, which would be extremely dangerous to stability in Europe. In such a case I would favour either disbanding the alliances or leaving them. I think neutrality is a good idea. But I would go a step forward and I think in such a case we would need demilitarization also as an example for future European development.

Lindner: Well, Herr Bahr put the additional question of how a bit more warmth that is supposed to exist in the GDR could be preserved in the course of rapid unification. I remember what Professor Biedenkopf quoted this afternoon, and what makes me fear that a tremendous lack of warmth can be felt already, namely, the chanting 'If the Deutschmark doesn't come our way, we go where it is'. This indicates a changed way of thinking which already provokes fears of a loss of solidarity. They are growing. When it come to handling the process of unification by politics similarly to Herr Romberg I see the time factor and I do not know if there will be enough time and, therefore, I am for unification as fast as possible taking certain steps. Until this morning I would have taken monetary and economic union for the first steps. Today Herr Schorlemmer made me wonder whether an ecological union, which is even easier to bring about and even more comprehensible because it is universally known that ecological processes cannot be nationally or regionally dominated, should be given greater priority in structures of co-operation that lead to a united country. Otherwise I prefer it in the course of an economic and monetary union.

Stolpe: I simply want to introduce a few observations in this round in which I think I am not alone. First, fears are haunting this country in a rapidly accelerating development, starting from buying things out of panic up to fears about pensions. A worker told me the other day: 'If things go on like this and we are still the GDR we will have a combination of the bad points of both systems, namely, valueless money and unemployment, uncertainty, that is, dependence on the company and a lack of opportunity to create something on your own because the capital required is missing.' I think with all the analyses, starting from Western media up to what we have considered here, the silent majority, and that is logical, has not been in the focus. According to what I know people are also sceptical about the new parties and groups. I dare say that in the case of elections held in an orderly manner on 18 March, and afterwards when the two German states are united, the situation will not be essentially different from now, that is to say the exodus will start afresh. I have clear information on how many people have packed their suitcases already who say 'let's wait just a little bit longer'.

So far nobody, neither the political forces within this country nor those who kindly speak to us, has managed to bring about an emotional change, neither by means of arguments nor by announcing any kind of measures, but the trek is moving steadily in the same direction; it even speeds up. And I think that there are people today who have reached the point of saying: 'I'm not interested in free elections. I would just vote when it is for or against reunification. Everything else is irrelevant.' I'm not saying this is good, I simply have to state it. In many talks I personally had, I noted that my arguments did not change their opinions. That is why I am worried. Let me conclude by saying that if I understood Herr Schönhuber correctly he found his gap in the market. He said the occupational powers have to leave and we make it. I could imagine, though not today and not tomorrow, an escalation in which certain nationalist slogans could be supported by a majority. You may say, 'We see it the same way. What is his solution?' I have no solution and I haven't heard any solution from anybody. I can only say that time is passing too fast. In this case, if you can't stop developments, politicians necessarily take over the lead to try and curb damages.

Dumke: With regard to the picture of analysis that has been mentioned in the previous contributions I fully agree. I would rather stress one basic idea. In this very complicated situation in this country someone described it as neither slowing down nor heating up. Slowing down is out of the question when it comes to feasibility. And that is why I think that policies come first also with regard to the collapse of tremendous parts of people's visions. Herr Momper said yesterday that the choice is between social or economic aspects. And certainly when you look at things, at everyday reality, that is what it is all about. But there is more to it. I think quite a few intellectual and political questions are involved here, which make people ponder on what they have done over 40 years: Was it sensible, what was sensible, was it a waste of time? What about the FRG? How about the values? Where will I be? That is what moves people. When you see reality and talk with people you not only talk about the economy. And that is why I would basically see three levels on which efforts should be made. First, there is this country. What matters is to ensure a minimum consensus between all democratic forces in order to make sure that important political situations can be mastered. The second level is where I see quite a good potential, namely the FRG. There is an ambivalence, I would say. To my mind there is, on the one hand, a political, let me call it obtrusiveness. They come along telling us how ideas of a political nature could help us out of the crisis and how things should look in this country. On the other hand I trust in those who have made a lot of efforts since October and November of last year to find our own solutions. Many people are in distress because of what Frau Bohley called spiritual annexation, which goes beyond the idea of justice. Sometimes this creates the impression that parts of the FRG Government are already in office. I want to say that point blank. But on the other hand, and that is where the term ambivalence comes in, many of our citizens listen very carefully to what prominent FRG politicians are saying. The third level to me is Europe and the rest of the world, the weight of the two superpowers' words. It must not be underestimated. I remember statements by Mikhail Gorbachev, by George Bush, James Baker and others, in which they remind us to tackle things with a sense of perceptiveness, circumspection and common sense. I consider this to be enormously important, and that is why I think it would be very helpful for the GDR to put a lot of thought into appropriate efforts, whereby I also think that the readiness of leading FRG politicians to help should result in real, tangible and visible activities.

Bahr: Herr Gysi, you will certainly have noticed that the original question was whether to achieve a speedy unity, or slowly and steadily, can the whole process be controlled and how can it be controlled. What can be saved?

Gysi: These are quite a few different questions at once, which also require an assessment of historical and current processes, something that is very difficult to make because in this country things which took other countries that sensibly started out much earlier quite a few years, develop at a pace. I agree to the assessment that we meet with a multitude of fears in the GDR. It is my impression that many workers feel, for instance, that the democratic uprising has brought them nothing but social insecurity. They do not feel really represented in politics, nor in the social field. This nourishes their insecurity and partly helplessness, and all that results in successes for those who offer a quick solution. I think it is part and parcel of honesty not only to see and consider the international aspect but also to point out some very concrete circumstances, the mastering of which nobody has so far explained to me. In the course of quick unification—which would be an annexation rather than a unification because the GDR is in a political and economic situation which limits its basis for negotiations—I would like to know what will happen to all the leases that people entered into with trustees of houses, the owners of which live in West Berlin or the FRG and quite often on governmental order. What happens to all the landed property on which people built their bungalows or weekend cottages but which still belongs to owners in the West? Would a merger mean that factories that once were expropriated from war criminals, or other individuals or groups, be reprivatized? What will happen to the landed property of the agricultural co-operatives and the other areas under the land reform? These are just a few legal matters which seem to make at least one aspect clear to me, namely, that we need a sovereign GDR which, with a contractual community, will be able to protect its citizens by insisting on agreements and regulations to safeguard legal and social minimum standards in the course of a unification. I have repeatedly put these questions and have not yet heard from anyone in the FRG how they see their regulation. Of course, these legal matters involve more, such as the duration of labour contracts, which legislation will be valid, that of the FRG or that of the GDR, or to what extent the one or the other. Can something like that be sorted out within one week? I don't think so. That is to say, whenever things take on concrete shape, and life is concrete, it is relatively soon apparent that things cannot be resolved on the street or in just a few days. Yet, this does not change a thing when it comes to aspirations and a certain pressure that exists. This is the result of many aspects. We had a great deal of solidarity in this country owing to the ruling structures of the past. Now that these structures are crumbling and so many different fears are coming up, and a cultural identity is beginning to decline, such values very soon begin to fade. To me this is a bitter experience. I had not expected it to happen this way either. More bitter experience to me is how quickly conceptions of legality can be dismantled; he who thinks that new and better laws will help re-establish them is wrong, to my mind. In the case of an overhasty unification I fear social conflicts between the Germans, too. Because it will not work without losses for FRG citizens, and I do not know how they will react. I really do not know; maybe they will react in a very friendly manner. But it may also be that one-third of the people will not react in a friendly way at all.

We are also in a very difficult situation when it comes to leaving for the West, because today many people no longer leave because of lack of political rights and maybe not that much for social reasons. Many who leave now go because they are afraid of a speedy unity and they say that their starting position in a united Germany will be much better when they are on the side of the stronger partner, compared with the GDR citizens who will come then. They try to get integrated socially before rather than having to apply later on. There is such a variety of problems and issues that I would nominate as a Nobel laureate the person who could present a patent remedy now that would generally be accepted. I think this is impossible. But I also think, and I would like to repeat the same appeal voiced here before, that one should expect politicians in such a situation to show a particular degree of common sense, patience and level-headedness and to be prepared to say something not quite as populistic. They must also be prepared to tell a few truths, to say what is possible and what is impossible this way. And then all people have their own political, cultural and other ideas. To me this means, of course, that it matters quite a bit what kind of Germany will result from the unification process. I am not only interested in whether and how something is done but also what finally will be the outcome.

That leads us to questions that were discussed before, such as NATO and social issues, a chance for leftist and socialist forces and integration into a European process. I, for example, do not want a Germany to come into being that immediately claims territory from Poland. I do not want a Germany to come into being that suddenly feels so German and great that it means to run European affairs all by itself. A progressive and democratic Germany would be quite different. I am not sure if we can say that in the end there will be a blend of what we have on both sides or if there will be something different, where forces will dominate that play a dominant part in neither the GDR nor the FRG today. This has already been warned against. That is why I also address the worries. Other people have different worries. In the GDR everybody is worried, even though in different ways. These different worries keep clashing in a very radical fashion. A lack of political culture is gaining ground and another deficiency becomes evident that has been mentioned here before, namely, that the democratic forces, too, which recognize and see things this way or at least part of it, wage ideological battles against each other instead of agreeing on what they have in common, accepting the others, their fears and worries and the fact that they also want to shoulder responsibility in the development, thus seeking a consensus and making something of it.

Bahr: Herr Gysi, may I dig a bit deeper concerning one issue. Your party also favours unity, not so fast but in a comprehensible and controllable manner. Am I right in remembering that a couple of days ago, in an essay in *Neues Deutschland*, you wrote that it is the aim of the party to retain the community of ideas and values with the Soviet Union. How could this be imagined in a united Germany?

Gysi: What is difficult is that we say that first we consider this process of unification to be a lengthy one, and that we need a sovereign and strong GDR because otherwise it will not be able to contribute anything. That is to say that a reasonable unification process requires an independent GDR in the first place. And it cannot live in a vacuum during this time.

Of course, my party wants to maintain close relations, good contacts and common values with the CPSU, that is, stick to the ideas of *glasnost* and *perestroika* even though the circumstances differ much. And we also want to endorse these ideas in a possible united Germany. That this will not be done at governmental level but by our party alone is another story. But we may surely support ideas. At least I hope so.

Bahr: Free man in a free country.

IV. Identity of Germans from the GDR

The question of identity was raised at some point by one of the speakers. We in the West when we indulge in nostalgia, people of my generation, we buy records. And we find the music of the Beatles which evokes the 1960s. West German friends told me that when they indulge in nostalgia they simply have to go to East Germany. They find the places which they knew in their memories, which are not changed. The Germany of the 1950s. Well that Germany of the 1950s in terms of values was craving for Western values, was finding in America a kind of identity of replacement. Would a young East German still be craving for America, if not as a reality as a myth like the West Germans of the 1950s? If that is the case that would have an impact on the West German identity itself and there would be the irony of Germany having problems with NATO in terms of international structure and, in a strange way, Germany rediscovering America. In a way that would be very different from the feelings in Eastern Europe where people feel much more European than Western. Is that a valid remark or is it absurd intellectual divergence?

Romberg: I think the answer to this question depends on age. Having lived in the GDR one has gathered a lot of experience about values. Herr Gysi mentioned it. You have absorbed the values, they meant a lot. And we are undergoing a process in which we—almost week by week, at least I've noticed it for myself and I also know it from others—are changing our identity. It is as if you just left the shore of a country on a river or a sea. You do not quite know where you are headed. You are leaving a lot behind, values—I don't want to romanticize but I think lots of it is in the story. It may be nostalgia, but I think these are values out of experience, such as solidarity which, of course, evolved due to repression and a lot of circumstances in our way of life. And yet you rather want to keep them. You don't quite know how to hold on to them, if this is possible at all. I'm afraid we will lose them to a large degree. We are much more sensitive and critical concerning West German society. I do not want to expand on this. When it comes to human behaviour we have envied the West for freedom and quite a few things we haven't seen clearly yet, but we also see the tremendous individualization of people in the West, where people have to rely much more on their own resorts, have to make themselves heard, to elbow their way. In this country many things are levelled out involving inefficiency as well; productivity had a lower value. Of course, people often socialized in their factories or offices instead of working—the effects of which we can see now, not solely. But people sat together. This difference in culture and identity becomes even greater as we go East, to Poland, to Russia, and I really mean Russia. I am a little bit sceptical, Herr Gysi, as to whether we can really uphold the common values. I think we will simply enter different structures with other constraints. I can see how people in this country set their minds more and more on Western Europe, the FRG, life there and how they become less sensitive *vis-à-vis* their families and friends and the ties we used to have with friends and colleagues in the East. And I understand the Poles. All of a sudden they feel that all the Germans are going West. This creates a totally new situation for them. I can only hope that we will be able to maintain a certain potential which will enable us to function as a bridge and a mediator between cultures in this part of Germany, between Germany and Eastern Europe. This partly contradicted the structures; this contradicted education in schools. If we don't take time to reflect on our past there will be a black hole. And this untreated black hole will haunt us from the subconscious, I am rather sure. I hope that the churches, and I also belong to them, see it as an assignment that they, in place of society, will start to reflect on these past 40 years and to find out where to start.

V. Soviet security interests and the future of the WTO

Bahr: This morning Herr Genscher made some remarks about legitimate Soviet security interests. What so-called legitimate security interest of the Soviet Union would the participants in this panel see? What can be done in the foreseeable future about the WTO?

Romberg: I think the Soviet Union must be given a security–political guarantee to make sure that the balance in Europe will not be rearranged in such a way that a threat to the Soviet Union may arise. First, this means that the processes in the middle of Europe must be put on a stable basis to avoid eruptions and uncontrollable developments concerning Eastern Europe. To me this means that we must gradually set up security structures in Central Europe, that are supranational, interlinked. We do not have much time there either. I think that we must demand much more from the Four Powers of World War II and also request co-operation from the neighbours so that new supranational structures can be brought about as soon as possible. In the Vienna talks we have reached a stage at which—hopefully this year despite delaying processes—we can construct a system of verification that would at least cover Central Europe. Finally a very simple remark: what are important here are structural elements. I think thought should be given to whether the military missions of the Four Powers could gradually be turned into such a supra-national security board. They could even use the same people. This could be a useful element.

Dumke: One could possibly consider this question from two different angles. I think each state has a legitimate interest in a consensus with its neighbours so that the people can live normally and the government can organize the economy, home and foreign policies without obstacles. This general interest, I think, arises from the international relations, ties, and so on, of each state. The legitimate security interests are focused mainly on the German issue, because there lies the basic question of European security and security balance. Back in history Germany has never been only a national factor but always a European and global one. Global political constellations emerged on this territory. That is why I think there should be a considerable degree of sensitivity.

The second aspect is that these legitimate security interests are connected with the legal system established in Europe through agreements. And the Soviet Union lays emphasis on the fact that the pacts should be adhered to for its own security.

The question also referred to the Warsaw Pact. The basic tendency is to change this military–political alliance into a political alliance, not only for the sake of saving itself but also for the European process of unification. This again is a question of political culture and not simply in the sense of preserving proven elements. I think that new political thinking is heading for setting up new constellations, also with regard to the important issue of the legal system. To my surprise one point was hardly mentioned, namely, law-based government. In this context I remember something Mikhail Gorbachev said before the United Nations, in December 1988 if I remember correctly: he was interested in forming a world-wide community of law-abiding states to serve all peace-loving people. This is really important for Europe and for the 'German question' as well. I think the rule of law is an essential vehicle in the relations of both German states, as Herr Kohl has repeatedly stressed. I would see in this many a stimulus for the future. In this respect I would say the legitimate security interest could also involve the WTO, combined with the rule of law not just in the sense of national but also international law and could even be expanded.

VI. United Germany and the European Community

Merlini: According to the programme the title of this round-table discussion is 'On the eve of the elections in the GDR: European aspects'. I wonder whether it would not be the case that the issue of German participation in the EC be raised, not only that of NATO. Rapid German unification would mean that the European partners of the FRG will be faced with the fact of the enlargement of the EC to East Germany. If, on the contrary, the process is gradual and as some of the panel, and particularly Herr Gysi, underlined, a sovereign state is kept, then the process will be an application for, if it is acquired by East Germany, enlargement to a new country.

It seems to me that all these issues might be the subject of you asking the views of the panel.

Gysi: I notice that the position I and my party hold concerning this issue is somewhat too sophisticated in its dialectics, such that I never manage to put it across correctly. But this is because of the complex situation if I may emphasize it as an apology. Whether we can make it a reality is quite a different story, so I can only tell you what we are for. We favour adhering to a particular order of steps which would, at no time, go beyond the European framework. In the first place this means a contractual community. This contractual community urgently requires two sovereign states because otherwise they would not be able to negotiate about anything. Next would be the confederation already evolving during the contractual community within federal structures. A confederation means a strong *rapprochement*, a strong balance of interests. This would also require an economic, monetary, traffic and ecological union but not yet cancel the sovereignty of the two states. And this process, when organized in a reasonable and thoughtful way and within the right periods, can also lead to a furthering of the European process. And then, after a certain period, we will reach the third stage, at which we bring up the question of demilitarization and the like. The GDR could just as well join the EC as a sovereign country. This is not necessarily connected with unification. Again, what matters here is level-headedness because, apart from advantages for the EC, which I don't see at the moment but which might exist, there are also disadvantages. It would all not only be beneficial to the GDR but would also harbour disadvantages. It would require an absolute change of our social provisions and many more things. Therefore, I think, this question must be put, answered and carefully handled within a European framework. We had quite a few rash steps recently, I think. For example, I am all in favour of a comprehensive right to travel, but I also support fixing the conditions first and not creating the necessary conditions afterwards. And the different conditions in both countries show tremendous effects. I will only mention the question of subsidies. Please allow me to raise another question because the talk about a market economy always plays an important role. I do not know if my information is wrong. But, if I see it correctly, more than two-thirds of the world is based on, I may say, capitalist market structures. The question is still where some countries should be counted. Only a fraction of them are well off, so I am beginning to suspect that this fraction is living at the other countries' expense. This triggers another question, namely, whether, in the course of unification, a Germany will evolve that will live at the expense of the Third World even more than before or if this is a process which is also incorporated into endeavours made to establish a new world economic order in favour of what is called the Third World, that is, whether the GDR will be part of the unjust distribution in the world or not. This might sound like an ethical question, but it is not only an ethical question. It is also an economic question because numerous conditions for other countries also depend on it. It is very difficult to explain this to demonstrators because it is different issues that make them take to the street. But it remains a fact and you have to deal with it because in this respect it also holds that we do not live alone in this world—and, of course, we are about to become the heart of the universe and therefore we should be on guard, I think.

de Maizière: Let me refer to the question put before concerning the economic and monetary union of the EC. I think that the speedy unification of Germany could possibly slow down the processes within the framework of the EC because the FRG potential to a large degree determines the EC and this potential could now be channelled somewhere else. But I also think that when we comprehend Europe as a whole we also have to learn in the West that Europe does not end at the river Elbe and not at the Oder/Neisse line; it is much bigger, and we can only achieve a harmonization of the processes if we manage to bring about an economic situation which also covers the East European countries. With regard to the *de facto* expansion of the EC in the course of German unification I take it that the GDR, through its close ties with the FRG, has always benefited from the economic preferences of the EC, at least in part. And, if I am informed correctly, all contracts concluded by the EC have always been signed by the FRG with the reservation that in the case of a united Germany the other parts of Germany are to be integrated as well.

Lindner: Herr Merlini connected a remark with a question that had already been discussed here today. I remind you of Herr Genscher who spoke of three options the GDR has, that is, co-operation with the EC, membership in it or membership through a merger with the FRG. At this time I also want to do what is feasible immediately, I prefer the co-operation as already expressed in the *aide-mémoire* of the Government of the GDR of 24 November 1989. With regard to Herr Gysi's remark I am all in favour of not only concentrating on German–German problems, not solely European ones either but, let me use this term here, the North–South problems, too, but I am not willing to connect it with a market economy. To me this is not something that could be misinterpreted as a detrimental factor of a market orientation. I think that, looking at things the way they are, a lot more is involved than just an orientation towards the market.

Bahr: May I just add one fact to what Herr de Maizière said? If the FRG, as a member of the EC, agrees to certain regulations of the EC it does not do so with the reservation concerning German unity. Each state that joins the EC must join it without ifs and buts at the current situation of the EC and must then take over rights and duties.

I just want to mention one fact so that it will not go unsaid. One can look at Europe from the point of view of the economy, currencies and legal aspects. I think that in the past few years and decades the churches in Europe have had the strong experience of a history that has been contradictory in itself; but there have also been common features, and with regard to the future we can also witness their uniting nature. And I think that the German–German problems may constitute a certain retardation in European development and that what was aimed at in Western Europe in 1992 may have to be reshuffled. There will be the chance of discovering Eastern Europe as part of a common history and culture; we will come to create a stronger foundation which, with regard to the Third World, could bear fruit. I felt sorry when Gorbachev's book *Perestroika* was published that the whole Western world intensely discussed the first part, in which the dilemma of the Soviet economy was laid bare, and easily dismissed the second part in which first hints at a common culture were already made, including common values that can form the basis for trust. And I think Europe as a goal can only be successful if it is understood as a historical and cultural community of the peoples on this continent. Whether the churches will be able to make a humble contribution I am not capable of saying. After all, in ecumenical work experience was gained which could just as well be used.

Romberg: I would have wished that the GDR became an independent member of the EC because I think that this would also have meant a little bit more autonomy for the GDR. I think that there are a lot of members of the EC, thinking of south-west Europe, with whom there would have been a better understanding. We missed this chance and we missed it because the West European politicians did not recognize it. As a consequence a strong united Germany will emerge in Central Europe.

Bahr: I just want to remind you that we do not have to imitate the West by answering questions that could change the world in half a minute. But I would be grateful if you could shorten your answers a bit.

VII. Towards the elections

Bertram: All of you just like all of us are under the impression that demonstrations are being held every week in the GDR. As long as political forces in this country are not legitimized through free elections the demonstrations naturally have a great influence on politics. Will this change after 18 March, will the parties then represented in the People's Chamber be legitimized or will their legitimacy still be weakened because of the German–German uncertainties?

Which party will form the government after the elections? Everybody here maintains that 18 March will be the turning-point. How soon will you be able to form a government? In a vacuum of power it is not only demonstrations that matter.

Bohley: First I think we should talk about whether these free elections are truly free. I think that under the pressure society has to sustain now these elections will not be free. We all aspired to free elections but we must say that these elections are not free. They are simply manipulated and they are also pushed in a certain direction by developments within the country. In the parliamentary elections here people will vote for Western parties, by and large. One must be aware of the fact that we do not elect the SPD or SDP, as it was called until recently, but Herr Brandt and the many other speakers at election rallies. This also applies to the CDU basically, to the alliance for Germany as it is called now. Nobody is able to see what is going on. And this means that the people will again lack the conviction that this government will be legitimized— because it was not elected freely and because it could now develop according to the differences. The differences between the individual parties and groups are really very small, because all parties are basically out to meet people's needs, namely, to tell them what they want to hear, reunification, economy, dough, money, everything is supposed to be fabulous. That is what people want to hear at the moment. And this is what will be voted for. Nobody will vote for reality. Reality will go by the board. To my mind this will go on after 18 March and will end up in a sad awakening.

Bransch: I would see things a bit differently. I could not agree with saying lock, stock and barrel that all people in this country let themselves be manipulated and that they, by and large, do not understand what it is all about, and that they would not be capable of making decisions. In many talks I notice that people are still very uncertain, indeed, about whom to vote for. Most people know whom not to vote for. I say this without malice. I am just stating it. And there may also be a trace of injustice from experience. I could agree with Frau Bohley in so far as, if it is possible at all, theoretically the first elections will be the ones that will be held after a certain period of experience and calmness. When it comes to influence from abroad I can say that the liberals, as well as the conservatives, the social democratic and the socialist movements are European traditions. The fact that the new tradition of the Greens has not managed to make its mark in the political landscape may have reasons I cannot explain. I also think that in this country the European tradition, namely, to look at social issues from the point of view of these traditional lines, cannot be excluded but rather has an influence. With regard to what will happen to the demonstrations: I suppose at the moment that if there is no clear tendency towards a merger of the two parts—I avoid the word reunification on purpose—there will be demonstrations in the south of the country and increasingly so also in the north. I also guess, as things are today, that the number of those who will not vote will be surprisingly high, because of this uncertainty and taking into account that people know whom they will not vote for, and this does not only refer to one party. But they still cannot tell whom they will elect. I have, of course, an opinion as to which parties will have the greatest chances, but I do not want to state it here. It is only whether we understand the future of the two German parts as a social issue, and not a national issue, that will decide whether the demonstrations and the exodus will be stopped or will go on.

de Maizière: I have already said that we always have to ask what is desirable and what is feasible. Certainly I also wished that the elections be held on 6 May and not be brought forward to 18 March. In this case a greater differentiation and a better determination of one's own position would have been possible. However, objectively it turned out not to be feasible. I think the state of the government, also the economic situation, would not have been so stable until 6 May that we could have held elections at all. Now the question is who would have to do it? Should the UN have organized it or the like? So we have to accept 18 March. And I deem it very alarming to try and doubt the legitimacy of a then elected government as early as now because I think that the government in power then will have to do unpopular things as well, so that scratching on its sovereignty even before the elections will jeopardize it from the very outset and automatically prepare for its failure. Just thinking of the issue of the price reform, the subsidies and, in connection with it, the restructuring of the income system, the change from subsidizing products to subsidizing people, a restructuring of the pension system, that is, a whole variety of measures which may even cause more uncertainty, saying beforehand that they don't have the right to do so, would endanger the necessary steps towards matching our system with theirs and thus a unification process as I would call it. To my mind the shaping of this process will depend on such important economic issues as making results and performances comparable again. Whether the hardships resulting from this and for instance closing down factories for ecological reasons will lead to more demonstrations I don't dare say at the moment. I would support what Superintendent Bransch said, namely, if it will not become clear that everything done in politics and in the economy is geared to reach unification in the final analysis, then the demonstrations will increase from the south to the north.

Bohley: I wanted to add that I still do not understand why local elections were not held first in the GDR, because this would have really meant democratization from the grassroots level. And in the towns and villages people know very well who is credible. And this would really have contributed to becoming more certain about the new political forces, because we have to say that the parties now running in the elections are the old parties, the former allies of the SED, and the people know that they are the old parties. We shouldn't blind ourselves to this fact although they have new chairmen. And the SED, SPD, PDS ...

Bahr: We are not campaigning.

Bohley: We do not really vote. So I just want to say that this is the problem. And if it had happened at local levels it would have calmed down the country a bit. And I really regret it.

Gysi: I think ethical, political and legal terms are being mixed up here. If the elections are held properly, that is, if everyone can vote, if votes are counted correctly, if maybe the GDR citizens abroad are not shut out but are given the chance to use the postal vote and the incredible blocking mechanism will still be eliminated that was introduced on the quiet . . . Mind you, I must explain this. Unfortunately not many people have noticed it. It was stipulated that the elections in the counties are based purely on proportional representation. A certain number of candidates can be elected in the counties. Now let me take the county which is most unfavourable, having 13 seats in parliament. You simply have to calculate to find out that you need 6.5 per cent of the vote to elect one candidate. That means that all parties and groups that have less than 6 or 6.4 per cent of the votes will not send a candidate from Suhl county. Thus all these votes go by the board. Some representatives of some parties were clever enough to get it through. But some have finally found them out and now we are about to try and find and include in the election regulations a counting system that prevents votes from getting lost. Otherwise, the candidates of my party would possibly plead for a pure system of proportional representation through regional lists so that each vote would count because that would mean that it would take 0.25 per cent throughout the country to send one candidate to parliament. I only mention this to make clear what is already happening prior to the elections. This is just a minor problem. Frau Bohley really wanted to say two other things. If it refers to legitimacy in the legal sense I could not accept it. Two problems have emerged that really need to be taken seriously. One is that at times of such worries and uncertainties elections are always complicated. If, on top of this, there are even tendencies of a blood-thirsty mood, and hatred and the like are stirred up, the problems multiply. We now have the very peculiar situation that my party really benefits from the obligation to use the polling booth. This also shows the degree of renewal within my party and its followers. Apart from this it is really complicated to face elections that will not focus on the GDR. This was the dream of the New Forum, if I got it correctly, that we have the chance of making a democratic decision on the political situation in this very GDR. All of a sudden, and I am not reproaching anybody for it, simply stating the fact, it is not this that matters but much more how to become a different country. So very few political options are focused on the issue of what is to be done in the GDR, what to preserve, how to renew what and what to change, but the options are centred on how best to stop being the GDR. This really makes these elections complicated. If you consider what she described, namely, that politicians particularly from one other country take part in the campaign in a massive way, and I do not mean material support, that does not interest me at all, but appear as speakers in the campaign, thus giving the impression that they themselves would be elected, we will be faced with another problem. Whereby I always said forbidding it is of no use and I am also against it. But I would appeal to West German politicians: let the GDR parties present themselves to their electorate to make people know for whom they are voting. I have no objections to realistic prognostication—of course you can prognosticate consequences—but I am a little against discrediting results in advance. Some people say that should the result be like this there will be a disaster. Should there be another outcome something else horrible will happen. So there are people who do not say well, we'll accept any kind of outcome. No they express loud threats. They say, OK, there can be many results which are acceptable, but if a result would be like this it would be a disaster. I suppose this is another kind of manipulation that should not be permissible. It is not part of political culture. Concerning the businesslike questions, cultural and ethical questions: these are questions for any government, no matter what its composition will be. We all have to deal with those problems, but I sincerely hope that the need for democratic consensus will be put into practice or will be observed in parliament. It should be possible after the elections to co-operate within a wider range in parliament. Of course, the rules of the game in campaigning are to fight each other. But I suppose we have to learn, we have to have more practice in political culture. My last remark: one must learn democracy first, and that is why one also has to learn a certain kind of political culture. Learning democracy also means learning to put up with results one personally does not like or that do not correspond to one's own aspirations. In this respect I have some qualms. I believe we have not learned it yet.

Lindner: Initially we promised not to campaign here. However, I feel obliged to remark on two aspects concerning the elections because I did not know that the PDS is strongest in the Suhl county which is generally accepted to accommodate a shrewish hill people in small quantity, but is one of the smallest counties; proportional representations will also turn out in other regions. What we have deliberately refused to include in the draft law on the elections, which is still in its second reading and not yet passed, is a mixed election system, because we believed that in these first free elections in 40 years the election system should be as transparent as possible and the multitude of parties and associations unfortunately blurs this transparency again. In this respect I agree with Frau Bohley. What matters is to practice a little bit more fairness in the campaign. The second remark I wanted to make refers to the local elections. I repeatedly participated in the central round-table talks and I know, if my memory does not betray me, that when we talked about the local elections and also about the parliamentary elections, particularly the new parties and groups in the GDR preferred a later date in order to consolidate their organizations. In contrast to our conviction, I speak about my party, we submitted to this because we said that it would be fair to give them the chance to consolidate, but nevertheless the political developments in the GDR require bringing forward the elections in order to have legitimized representations as soon as possible. This is best done through parliamentary elections which have been brought forward to 18 March. We as a party insisted on the local elections being held on 6 May,

the initial date, which is also very close to the day the elections were held last
year. I think that this is a correct decision.

Gysi: I only want to make one remark concerning this. I must take the part of
the New Forum here. It is not true. I was present in the round-table talks. The
New Forum always demanded local elections first, this is a fact. And my
remark concerning the blocking mechanism did not refer to my party. I am not
afraid of the 6.5 per cent either. But I referred to the new and smaller parties
which would all stay small.

Romberg: I would have wished that the contributions were more future-
oriented. We have the situation on 18 March that we will have to form a government which will be able to act. The question is how this can be achieved,
how it can be composed. I personally would plead for a big coalition. Presumably the SPD will be very strong. I do not want to mention the individual
aspects. We also need to be encouraged from the outside to organize independent work by this government. What matters is to argue with the FRG, and I
really mean it, because our interests must be endorsed in this process. I also
invite representatives of other European countries to think about how to stabilize this process, which will not be easy. We have to reckon with social tension.
We hope that the days of the Weimar Republic will not repeat themselves. But
this does not depend on us alone. I think that the whole of Europe has to shoulder some responsibility, also *vis-à-vis* the FRG on the part of the other European countries. We hope and wish that we will bring about intensive talks with
all Europeans in this process and that we can co-operate.

de Maizière: I only wanted to give you my view about the accusations concerning the law on the elections. They are objectively wrong. The list will not
be compiled countywise, but there will be regional lists that will be split among
the constituencies and the votes will be counted on a national basis and only
then will the proportions be fixed and the mandates distributed. The reproach is
incorrect, objectively speaking, and I think that one should obtain ample information before making such accusations.

Dumke: I just wanted to make a critical remark about the fact that we now
finally entered the phase of making prognoses about the outcome of the elections which may not make a lot of sense, because it will turn out one way or the
other. What I want to say is that with all the problems involved in these elections we should think ahead. And one more point needs to be mentioned here
because worries were mentioned about manipulating the elections by foreign
political forces during the campaign. In the round-table talks a majority spoke
out in favour of no foreign speakers during the campaign. There are some difficulties, as we can see, when trying to put it into practice. A second aspect, from
the point of view of my party, Frau Bohley said, and I agree with her in this

respect, is that some voters view the old parties as having remained the old parties. Objectively this is not the case. For my party I would say that there have been essential and basic changes both in the political image and in the programme and aims of the party. The last remark I want to make refers to the demonstrations. This issue has been dealt with from various points of view in a very up-to-date way. I think that grassroots democracy has produced a totally new conception of demonstrations. Herr Genscher recently said that he considers the revolutions in Eastern Europe, including the GDR, to be of great momentum for preparing the basis for a new security policy. And I think with certainty the impetuses given here by grassroots democracy, especially also through the processes in the GDR, will cause the one or the other modification to the classical concept of democracy.

Bahr: I now call on the participants, hoping that the answers will be somewhat shorter.

Morgan: I would like to ask the representatives of the parties, if a coalition government will have to be formed, with which other parties would you be able to form a coalition without difficulties and with which parties would this be possible but with difficulties and, if with difficulties, what difficulties are there?

Childs: Herr Lindner spoke of fairness. Where are the other opposition parties tonight? A second question. Will the media be fair, will all the parties have the opportunity, have equal chances to present themselves in the media? At the moment this is a problem for the genuine opposition, indeed. And a last question to Herr Dumke. In the beginning, in 1948, his party was a party of reformed former Nazi Party members. What does this party represent today?

Livingston: The first question goes to Dr de Maizière: How does the centre alliance see itself? I have heard from acquaintances in the GDR that the alliance calls itself a bourgeois bloc. What are the differences between CDU, Democratic Awakening and the DSU? Do they feel as a bourgeois bloc?

The second question is for Dr Romberg. Let us assume the SPD would turn out to be the strongest party in the 18 March elections and you, Dr Romberg, might be Prime Minister. To what degree would your economic policy differ from an economic policy pursued by the alliance, would they become the strongest force, or that of the PDS with Dr Gysi as Prime Minister with regard to the pace of the unification, with regard to privatization, with regard to breaking up the combines and all these things? Would the SPD support and pursue an economic policy that is different from those of Dr de Maizière or Dr Gysi?

The last question is for Frau Bohley: What will the GDR introduce into this combination if what Herr Gysi called Neues Deutschland (New Germany)—I would rather call it a Federal Germany—came about? Thanks to you, Frau Bohley, I think we received Professor Jens Reich of New Forum a couple of days ago. I cannot quote exactly what he said, but by and large it was that we in the GDR are not used to the bargaining of the West; we cannot buy and sell in that political bazaar (these were certainly not his words but his opinion). And my fear is, as Professor Reich said, that we sell ourselves too cheaply to the FRG. We have something we can introduce even if it is just our cheap labour and our connections with the Eastern economies.

My question to you, Frau Bohley, is: first, whether you share his opinion and second, what will become of the GDR, maybe not economically speaking—it can also refer to the cultural, or ethical or solidarity fields? What will it be that the GDR will introduce into the new German state?

Dumke: Our party was mentioned when it was founded in 1948. The National Democratic Party of Germany was founded on the basis of existing legislation as an anti-Fascist and democratic party whose objective was to organize medium-size entrepreneurs for the development of a new society, as we then said, for establishing a new Germany, which had drawn lessons from history, namely, that no more war should emanate from German soil and no more Fascism should come into existence. At that time the approach was that the main political lines will be decided on by the working people, by those who were main producers of the social wealth. That was the fact. Perhaps an uncommon term was introduced here.

In revolutionary processes it always shows that in times of total changes, just like in 1945, the people try to bring about a totally new way of thinking. Two world wars had destroyed the country and Fascism provided much substance to think about. In this respect my party has always stood for the right of those who had erred in the past, but personally were not guilty of any crimes, to be given the moral, political and social chance to change. This is what the party did and, still today, we hold on to this anti-Fascist tradition. This was the point which particularly struck me because a misinterpretation might otherwise have been possible. Another aspect in similar frankness: it is a mistake to assume that the majority of members of our party were those who have simply changed sides. About 80 per cent of the membership had not belonged to any Nazi organization.

Lindner: With regard to the possible coalitions: no coalition with right-wing or left-wing extremist parties and second, as the Liberal Democrats are not willing to undergo another socialist experiment we are not ready to form a coalition with the PDS. That much I can say about the question of the coalition at this time. Concerning the question about the media: the People's Chamber adopted a resolution on the media because we do not have a Media Act yet; there is a media supervision board. I am not fully informed at the moment whether it is already fully staffed and ready to work. This board is to guarantee that there will be equal chances for everybody, that old parties and new groups will be equally represented. The electronic media have already promised to produce programmes and clips. At the moment I see slight disadvantages for the LDPD. The same applies to the NDPD and the CDU. That is because the interest of the media is concentrated on the new groups and movements, and to some extent the old structures still make their influence felt. Great tasks lie ahead of the media supervising board in safeguarding the promises made.

de Maizière: First question concerning a coalition: you know that we formed an electoral alliance a few days ago. We agreed that we could only jointly allow another party to join this alliance so that I cannot tell you anything without discussing it with the other parties of the alliance beforehand. But I want to mention one criterion, that is, that we would support such parties that stand for law-based government, the unity of Germany and a socially sure market economy. When it comes to fairness I would agree with what Herr Lindner has just said, to avoid repetition. How does the alliance see itself? To the question of whether we see ourselves as a bourgeois bloc, I could simply reply yes. We think that we should form a liberal, bourgeois and also conservative counterweight. Our target group will be businessmen and other self-employed people. We want to form a basis for people establishing medium- and small-size industries. And we also do not want to forget the traditionally strong group of artists and cultural workers.

Bohley: What will the GDR give the whole of Germany? I think, first and foremost it is 40 years of history: this is, 40 years of experience with a dictatorship, 40 years of oppression and nevertheless being able to laugh, to see the Stasi in front of your door and laugh about it. This is experience not many West Germans have had, but you cannot underestimate it because there is something good in it as well, and we also learned. It was also an experience for the people in the GDR when they toppled this dictatorship, when they said 'We are the people', that they were strong, and when they really managed to crack the strongest security machine in the world. It does not exist any more. People have managed to show a party which had claimed leadership for 40 years where it belongs, namely, next to other parties. This is experience which I think is submerged at the moment. If people could manage to get it back into their heads, they would be very self-assured. This experience will certainly surface again, and then I think something will have to be changed in the FRG as well. With this experience in mind you can change something. Maybe some people in the FRG should ponder what it would mean if such a power entered their country. That is what I wish.

Romberg: First question: coalition with whom? The SPD has not made any statements about this. I personally hope that it will not totally commit itself. I can only answer as a private person. It depends on the situation. If we manage among the parties then represented in the People's Chamber to arrive at a consensus, namely, that it is our joint mission to represent the interests of the people in the GDR during the process of unification, in this case I could think of a very broad-based alliance, not only the CDU but even more parties. This is something that concerns all of us and where we have to find a consensus to defend our own interests. It may also be, and there is a lot to it, that immediately after the government is in office the West German election campaign will be continued over here. That means that decisions made here cannot be separated from what will develop in the FRG. I would consider this a disastrous development. I am afraid it is not only not impossible but very much possible. In this case I could say even less about a coalition. It would be clear that if a government is formed with SPD participation we will endeavour to form a government with a position contrary to that of the bourgeois centre should the voters enable us to do so.

Next question: the media. I don't think there are equal chances for all. A few days ago we discussed the media bill in the People's Chamber. This also includes the question of equal supply of paper for newspapers. At the moment we have the situation that the established parties have an absolute priority. Certainly something has changed in some papers. But in no way can we speak of an equal representation of the new parties and groups.

Third question: where does the SPD differ from the other parties? Naturally there are a few different aspects. I would say in social policies our goals surely differ from those of the CDU. It is important to us that the trade unions play an important role, that social policies are spelled with capital letters, it is important to us to create such an educational policy that we do not carelessly throw away things that have proved to be good over the 40 years, that is, equal chances, a certain form of egalitarian approach, I think, should be preserved. It is important to us, and I hope we will adhere to it, that we feel committed to uphold the legacy of the European anti-Fascists. We will not be able to form a coalition with the PDS, because of its history. I hope that personal contacts with people who are members of this party will be maintained so that we jointly digest the history that we also have partly in common. The name PDS is a challenge for us and I think we have to face it.

Gysi: The question of a coalition is not imminent for my party because all the others have answered it already. I do not have to think about it. Things can look different after some time. Then we will be relatively open, including everything that makes policies really social and represents the interests of the people in the sense of independence, of individuality. I would like to make an additional remark concerning fairness. You have probably noticed that we are disadvantaged, but we will also do everything possible to get our time on TV. This, of course, was totally different in the past but usually in the course of events things turn upside down. It is a bit awkward because it concerns me in person, but I found it remarkable and funny that when I met Gorbachev in Moscow it was top news in the FRG; in the GDR newsreel it was the last news before the weather forecast for fear they could be reproached for giving preference to this party. So the worries are becoming more diverse. With regard to news-papers . . . We have one paper, *Neues Deutschland;* all the other papers in the counties have declared their independence, and they are in fact independent and, partly, very harsh in their polemics against us, that is, this monopoly position was broken as well. You know our decision about party property, so I need not repeat it here. I want to add something to what Frau Bohley said about values. I feel sorry about the following: when the uprising began, in October, it was marked by a great self-assurance. And this self-assurance has been totally destroyed in the meantime. There are various reasons, factors and influences which one could probably not enumerate in full. This is really a great problem. Of course, this is also the case because we have looked at past history in a very undifferentiated manner, and I also include myself and others. If you tell some-body that he has been lied to and deceived for many years you are telling him at the same time he has really been daft and a coward for 40 years because he had not done anything against it. This can kill self-assurance. And we cannot justify an undifferentiated approach leaving out of consideration the time, circum-stances, historical conditions of the year 1945, of the year 1949, of the 1950s, also the atmosphere of the 1950s. I think this people has achieved a lot in these 40 years and also created a cultural identity for itself. It has also created certain ethical values, and when a process of transformation started in the USSR in 1985 it did not put up with a leadership in this country that tried to prevent it but has finally chased them away, and it has tried to create its own circum-stances. And at some point the situation tipped over, other tendencies took over and the self-assurance vanished. Even though I may stress different aspects, I agree with Frau Bohley in saying that we will also introduce a strong psycho-logical and human strength apart from many other experiences in the cultural, social and economic fields which will also entail difficulties for the FRG, which harbour chances but also dangers. One must be aware of this. And that is why I hope the process will remain controllable, that it will go on in a level-headed fashion, and that it will not produce what is to be prevented but make clear that not only the GDR has to undergo reforms and changes but also the FRG, to my mind. If this is done, and nobody is speaking about it at the moment, I hope that this topic will be talked about. I also hope the people will raise this question.

Dubois: I wanted to ask a brief question concerning neutrality. Let us assume a majority of the Germans would favour neutrality but the majority of Germany's neighbours are against German neutrality. What policy would you suggest and how would you react?

Ferraris: I am very confused. On the one hand all of you want freedom, democracy, wealth, a market economy, the lot. But you do not want to pay the price, namely, a loss of warmth, a loss of solidarity. Politics is not in the realm of common sense but in the realm of demagogy, maybe. To me as an Italian, a son of Machiavelli, it seems that you are, let me say, a bit too idealistic. And politics is not only marked by ideals and convictions but is a tough business as well. On the other hand I am very impressed by what Herr Romberg said, namely, that if I had come from the moon and heard this debate I would have the impression we are not living in 1990 but in the Germany of 1928, a debate that centres on election laws and procedures after a successful revolution. And I do not want to disappoint Frau Bohley, whom I admire much, but to think that a peaceful revolution will leave much behind is an illusion. I may be cynical, but I must say that bloody revolutions will leave memories in people's minds. Peaceful revolutions will be forgotten soon. There are also examples in Europe such as the Portuguese revolution. My last remark is also a question. Whoever will be forming the government will have to make difficult decisions, unpopular decisions—not only the currency reform but also how to stop the exodus of people, how to arrange measures for the economy, and so on. I have heard very little about what you think about it. I want to quote Herr Romberg again. We as non-Germans are also worried about the stability of the GDR. You all say you want to be united with the FRG but not at once. But in this transitional period, I think, we need stability in this country. How do you intend to achieve this stability. We would like to know which concrete measures you will undertake to stabilize the country. If I hear that, as early as now, the legitimacy of the new government is doubted, for goodness sake, the most important thing after a revolution is to have elections and to have a more or less elected parliament, not the perfect MP, all of you excluded, but I mean in general. And I think that this is most important. But we want to be reassured and I am not very reassured by what I heard about the stability in the GDR. Herr Gysi has insinuated many concrete facts. I would also have wished that the others told their opinion about them.

Gysi: I only want to make a remark concerning the last point. If you've come here to be reassured, your journey was in vain, indeed. You cannot get reassurance here.

VIII. What after the elections?

Romberg: I will be brief as well. Herr Gysi has said that he is not in a position that would oblige him to think about coalitions. This way it is, in fact, easier to mention aspirations in a situation for which you do not have to shoulder the responsibility. Maybe you understood how dynamic the situation we live in is, where conditions change week by week and day by day. In such a situation I would consider it absolutely absurd if a politician made clear statements concerning everything. They will have to be made at the time of an event or shortly before. I think we have to accept this because in the time prior to the elections a lot can happen, and it would be absolutely counterproductive for a politician to get nailed down now and to be torn to pieces for it in the election campaign. I did not speak about the election laws. That was somebody else. I thought that we really think ahead, although I do not want to play the problems down. Politics as a realm of demagogy is a very dangerous statement. I think of Willy Brandt, not only because he is from the same party as I am. I think that there are people who through their personalities give a certain credit in certain situations. The credit can last long or not so long. But they give their credit for people to trust in a political strategy for a while. We shall see whether there will be people on 18 March who have this credit; whether this credit will still last until a few days after the formation of the government and also make trust possible in times of tension I do not know. But I consider it a very important point.

Bohley: We are not a party but a civic movement. We started out as a civic movement and we want to remain the same. Our main objective really is to emancipate people and to make them aware of problems. And the more the problems become obvious the clearer it becomes that there is a necessity to solve the problems as there is no strong union in the GDR, but very soon we will have a lot of unemployed. People are afraid of losing their housing. They form civic committees and try to find out whether the houses they live in belong to people in the West or if it is possible to buy these houses. Everywhere, in the social field, in the educational sector and in many other fields, people become active and try to preserve something and possibly change the course of events their way. And I think that this country needs nothing but emancipated citizens. We have started out of distrust regarding the parties and policies. We wanted to make our own policy, and now we try to influence this policy from the grassroots level. I think we have got our objectives and we do not dodge problems. We are more in favour of social security than of a social market economy. This is our main issue at the moment.

IX. On neutrality

de Maizière: I want to pick up Madame Dubois' question, on neutrality. If a majority of the people wanted neutrality and the neighbours did not, the decision would be made in favour of neutrality. I think a certain calculability is part of politics. This also includes the inviolability of contracts. Both countries are members of alliances which they entered in agreement with their partners. And to my mind they could only leave on the basis of a consensus reached with their allies again. It is impossible that one of them simply withdraws. Concerning the programmes let me pick up what Dr Romberg said. The identity of most of the parties and groups was at the beginning that they knew that they did not want to continue by any means. And it was not that clear if the development was irreversible, so that all efforts were first directed at making this process irreversible. What matters now is to name the goals of the individual parties and where are the differences. Because it is the differences that give the voters a clear orientation in the elections. Asking what the objectives of my party are, let me tell you that I think the most important of them is to change from an energy-

and material-intensive economy to an intelligence-intensive light industry and that we have to take care that an economy will evolve which will give strong support to small- and medium-size businesses, thus ensuring an organic structure of the economy. Second, we will make efforts to improve the health and social policies. We also have to make important decisions on the right to education and on the situation in the field of education. As a main line I only want to mention that we have to abandon a government-dominated educational system and goals of education the government imposed and have to give parents the chance to decide what education their children should receive.

Lindner: Concerning the first and exaggerated question I want to remind you of the quotation with which Herr Genscher began this morning, namely: not a German Europe but a European Germany is what we need. To me this means that a decision about neutrality must be a European decision. When it comes to election programmes and stability, how can it be ensured? Since there would not be enough time to present the whole election programme here, I would like to concentrate on the question of stability and only mention two aspects which I think are important: namely, first law-based government as an inevitable prerequisite for everything that follows and second, speeding up those measures designed to bring about a market economy which can have social provisions, because, in contrast to Frau Bohley, I think that only a functioning market economy can provide the resources for a true social security.

X. On competence and political and moral integrity

Stolpe: I think there are a few psychological problems for which it is very hard to find solutions. One of them is that many who would be able to do so, or who present themselves here in the field of politics, are viewed positively regarding moral integrity but their skills on the job are doubted, or vice versa. That is to say there may be people who are doing excellent jobs but whose moral and political competence is doubted because of their past. And quite often good will is faced with lack of experience and on the other hand there may be experience but, well time is over, to put it this way. A classic example for this is a talk show last week, where Helmut Schmidt was also present, and there were lots of questions to Herr Modrow about how to elect him without electing his party. I say this to illustrate the discrepancy between political and moral integrity and competence on the job. I think that there is one common base that should not be neglected, not even in the election campaign, and that is non-violent relations. I think it is also our obligation to be non-violent in what we say. Something that is normal in the West, because they all have a thick skin and know that you have to be noisy to be heard at all, can be fatal in this country because we come from a background where you quite often had to be soft-spoken to be heard or listened to at all, so words can be much more harmful and fatal in this country than in countries with a longer parliamentarian background. This non-violence needs to be preserved. In addition there is a certain responsibility to our neighbours, to learn in only a few weeks what other countries have had decades of time for. And in this respect I would offer support to anyone feeling politically responsible. Because it is hardly possible to present recipes for highly sophisticated economic problems after having only dealt with them for three, or six, or eight or ten weeks. It would be of great help if the European neighbours took these facts into consideration. We were a country that was easily influenced by the media. We quite often tried to make it clear to journalists what they were doing to us. Well journalists have a profession, they deal with news and it must be sold well. Quite often we did not reach an understanding. And here are the expectations we have concerning Western politicians, namely, that they give us the opportunity to clear things up with one another and among ourselves so that we will be good partners for all the others around us. I can only ask for that.

Bohley: I wanted to say something about competence and integrity. I do not think it has to be all that contradictory. Well I am not an economist and cannot speak on behalf of the whole New Forum. We also have competent people there. On the other hand there are questions that really have not been discussed in society, such as whether it is easier and cheaper to import another system or whether it is easier and cheaper to change an existing system. These questions are not asked any more. The decision reads market economy for a planned economy. Why not a planned economy. As a layman I cannot imagine any modern market that is not planned. And that is why I say that all people concerned should take part in the discussions. And that is what we want so that we do not again sit and wait for 40 years until we wake up and say look what they did to us.

XI. Concluding remarks

Bahr: I think we have seen a part of the reality in the GDR tonight. And if I may say this, hardly anyone around me was a politician half a year or three months ago and almost all of them have become professionals now. That must also be taken into account when applying standards to them that are normal in our country, although we cannot say that we have resolved all issues delightfully and without problems. We also have some answers still to give. Sometimes I was quite tempted to say the one or other thing but I successfully suppressed it. And there is one question of Mr Childs' open: why other parties have not been invited. Dr Walther Stützle has to answer this, I am unable to do so.

Stützle: Mr Chairman, the dynamics of the political developments in the GDR on the one hand and the short time Max Schmidt and I had to prepare this conference also lead to the fact that we invited parties that do not exist any longer and invited people who are no longer members of certain parties. But the fact that we have gathered here tonight and the house is really packed is an expression of great admiration for those who presented the GDR to us tonight. And on behalf of the organizers I would like to thank you very much for coming.

5. German unity and security in Europe

Max Schmidt, Director, Institute of International Politics and Economics

East–West relations in Europe are in a major upheaval, initiated primarily by substantive domestic changes in the East European countries. Four decades of antagonism, predominant in East–West relations, have for all practical purposes largely disappeared. The hitherto East–West inter-system conflict has been settled in favour of the Western world and is no longer effective as such; in other words, the cold war is over. Conditions have thus emerged, and are visibly growing, for overcoming the division of Europe into two hostile blocs and for getting it replaced by a situation of co-operative inter-state relations across Europe, a condition definitely shaped by the principle of common security.

On these developments is superimposed the fact that the 'German question' has been put vehemently on the agenda in a way hardly expected even a few months ago. Unification of the GDR, the Federal Republic and the whole of Berlin has been elevated to the level of a realistic possibility and necessity because of domestic developments in the GDR: this is due first of all to the irreparable collapse of the rule of the former Socialist Unity Party of Germany (SED) leaders and their power apparatus and the concomitant failure of the associated society model. The prospect of a new techno-scientific, political and, last but not least, military centre of gravity in Europe has thus taken palpable shape: a possible united Germany in a few years from now. Would the danger of a German quest for hegemony over this continent, after two abortive attempts—disastrous for Europe and the world at large (and for the Germans too)—crop up again? Questions along those lines have already been raised in East and West. They are likely to outline the major security problem relating to the restoration of a united German state and to general change in Europe at present. The answer will determine decisively whether desirable trends in Europe will be consolidated for good or jeopardized again.

Restoration of a united Germany is intermingled with quite a few weighty security aspects. These relate primarily to the consequences that the German unification process might have for the future relationship between the Germans, on the one hand, and their European neighbours, on the other, with Poland's western border being one of the issues. Consequences for the security balance in Europe as a whole and, finally, for vital interests of the Germans themselves, both in the GDR and the FRG, may be just as important. There are anxieties in East and West that a united Germany might be strong enough to dominate Europe, economically and politically, or even, once again, to endanger European peace.

The following question is being asked in this context: Can all the associated problems be interconnected such that in the process of German unification a substantial gain in security can be achieved for Europe, just as for the Germans themselves? Or: Can solutions be found to satisfy the basic interests of all neighbours, and can German unification be designed to add a strong momentum to the European disarmament process? An important promise has been pronounced by Lothar de Maizière, Chairman of the GDR Christian Democratic Union (CDU): 'The process of German unification must in no way be allowed to cause concern among Germany's neighbours.'

Such an approach in terms of political practice is not only necessary; it is also practicable, but not on the basis of the two security models now predominant in the debates between East and West, as well as within each of the two sides, that is, neutrality or NATO membership. These models have a severe shortcoming in common. They actually by-pass the interests and visions of several states without whose consent and active involvement implementation is unthinkable.

With the status of neutrality, a future Germany would be dismissed 'without compensation' from those international links with East and West which have so far prevented any single-handed German action in foreign and security policies.

There are grave reasons, on the other hand, against exclusive NATO membership by a united Germany. This would necessitate a decoupling in security policy terms from the USSR, Poland and Czechoslovakia, countries which suffered much at the hands of Germans in World War II. Neither these nor other countries to which the FRG is linked today in terms of security policy can be expected to be enthusiastic about such decoupling.

This problem cannot really be settled comprehensively and satisfactorily for all parties concerned unless a course is taken towards establishing an independent, institutionalized security dimension for the CSCE or, in a nutshell, an all-European security union. This should be an organization to include and eventually absorb the WTO and NATO (as well as the neutral and non-aligned countries) in the form of co-operative, inter-bloc and, finally, bloc-merging structures.

However, such a development would require basic consensus of all the states involved, at least on the following major issues:

1. The nature, substance and security goals of the CSCE process should be redefined on a co-operative basis, in keeping with the requirements of our time, free from those inhibitory elements which result from inter-system antagonism and placed a burden on the first phase of the CSCE, such that even *détente* was repeatedly degenerated on either side to an instrument of struggle against the other.

2. Commitment to stepwise institutionalization and an all-out binding nature for security arrangements within the CSCE would be indispensable to give all parties involved confidence in the reliability of the process. This, in turn, would pave the way for ceding certain sovereignty rights to such a security union in a

more advanced phase of its development since, without transfer of some of those rights, real European integration would not be achievable.

3. Merger or combination of alliance-related with inter-alliance security structures must be part of the original design for a desirable association of CSCE countries. This should involve the prospect of absorption of the WTO and NATO by an all-European umbrella organization, once such an organization is accomplished.

Such institutionalization of the security dimension of the CSCE process should be initiated in the foreseeable future, but it will not be possible to complete its creation overnight. More jumps in the German–German embrace, on the other hand, will occur before long and without advance notice. These two processes might well be harmonized to the extent necessary to avoid their different aspects, velocities and time horizons leading to contradictions counterproductive for Europe and for the Germans themselves. For example, the security aspect of German unity should be viewed from an all-European perspective and, with every single step towards unity, due consideration should be given to basic elements of this perspective. An answer, therefore, should be given to this top-priority question: How can the security component of German unity, in the process of its making, be designed to the effect that continued coalescence of Europe is not only not inhibited or blocked but encouraged and stimulated?

I strongly feel that the international security structures now existing in Europe should be retained until new, generally accepted structures are established and have become effective. As to the master concept for security in the forthcoming phase of German unification, it is in agreement with Zbigniew Brzezinski's proposition of 'a German confederation in concomitance with special security arrangements', supplemented with the idea of having such arrangements linked to really radical disarmament steps on German soil. The following scenario might be imaginable:

1. Drastic reduction of conventional forces and armaments in Europe, especially in Central Europe, would be an urgent prerequisite for acceptable intermediate steps towards harmonization of security with German unification, in order to remove the military burden from the foundation of the future military status of a united Germany. A first CFE agreement would just be the first step and should be followed by another agreement, with much wider reductions at the CSCE summit planned for late 1990. The two German states should take a lead in disarmament, both in implementation of the Vienna agreements and as an advance contribution to them.

2. The GDR and the FRG (as well as West Berlin), beyond the forthcoming economic, monetary and social union, are likely to set up one common political roof for a certain transitional period under which either partner will retain a certain amount of independence in foreign and security policies. The GDR would continue to exist as a subject of international law in its own right throughout such an intermediate or transitional phase.

3. Under such conditions, the GDR might continue to be a *political* member of the WTO. Its system of valid treaties with the USSR, Poland, Czechoslovakia and other states might be smoothly transferred to the GDR–FRG security union, it might be substituted by something else or transformed to multilateral CSCE arrangements. This, in practice, would come to temporary retention of the two alliances on German soil. I feel it would be absolutely thinkable as a transitional solution. At least, we cannot see any substantial security problem in opposition to such a settlement.

4. As to the armed forces of the GDR, I am very much in favour of total demilitarization. The National People's Army should be disarmed and disbanded in a socially, economically and ecologically tolerable process in the course of the 1990s. In terms of security policy, this army has been stripped of most of its purpose, a fact additionally compounded by German–German developments. There is no longer a military adversary that ought to be deterred, and this highly vulnerable patch of land in between the Elbe and the Oder has long ceased to be in a defendable position.

Demilitarization through disarmament of the GDR National People's Army is a position shared by many GDR peace researchers, politicians and military as well as by movements, such as the 'Appeal of 89'. This will be a process that will no doubt take some time and will not make the army vanish overnight.

There are different views on the subject, some assuming the continued existence of the GDR Army in reduced strength or as a territorial army (separate from the Bundeswehr and not integrated in NATO). Such views and the demilitarization idea do not necessarily rule each other out. They can be compatible, provided the definite objective and time horizon are borne in mind.

5. The FRG might continue to be a member of a changing NATO. Emphasis should be laid, in this context, on change of purpose and doctrine (e.g., renunciation of so-far valid strategies, such as forward-based defence, flexible response and nuclear first-strike). As the European disarmament process is going on and as an advance contribution to it, armed forces in any case should be strongly reduced (in the context of a second-stage CFE Negotiation—CFE-1A) to, say, 200 000 men, in the first place. This, too, has already become a subject of discussion and would, necessarily, take a number of years. In the longer run, sights might be raised to assigning the Bundeswehr to an all-European security union (together with military formations of other CSCE countries in East and West). This might be a practicable way 'to internationalize Germany's military role' as suggested by ex-CIA Director Richard Helms.

6. This would be a good way for the alliances to play a new, stabilizing role in the process of German–German unification.

Also, with a view to a definite overcoming of NATO–WTO confrontation, to stepwise interlinkage of the two alliances and to their transformation to a new pan-European system, possibilities should be studied for according to the GDR and FRG some sort of a political guest status in the other alliance (associated with the right to attend each other's periodic Foreign Minister meetings).

7. It should be one of the foremost responsibilities of a GDR–FRG security union to eliminate once and for all any doubt about a future Germany's attitude to Poland's western border. This should be done in a way binding in international law. A settlement of this kind should be just as unambiguous as the 6 July 1950 Zgorzelec Agreement between the GDR and Poland.

8. Full political and reduced military presence in Germany will be ensured during this transitional phase of the 'big four' of World War II—at the level of 195 000 men each for the time being, as agreed by the USSR and the USA. The total number might be reduced, later on, to 70 000 allied troops for all (25 000 each for the USSR and the USA plus 10 000 each for the United Kingdom and France). These troops should symbolize continued responsibility for and commitment to developments in the centre of Europe. To maintain Soviet troops in the GDR, at least during the initial phase of German unification, has already been positively taken into consideration on the Western side.

9. Embarkation on such or a similar road, accomplishable, perhaps, via the Two-plus-Four talks and, possibly, verified by a CSCE summit this year, would also eliminate any need for continued deployment of nuclear weapons on German soil. They might all be withdrawn at a relatively early date, along with general dismantling of military potentials in Germany, so that German soil would be free of ABC weapons.

A situation thus achieved in the centre of Europe might be maintained until an all-European security union were completed in which more thinking might be done on wider arrangements, including definite replacement of all post-war settlements for Germany. The process of FRG–GDR unification, in the meantime, would not be inhibited. With constructive political intentions by all potentially involved parties, it would rather be placed within a security framework, such that no one would need to be afraid of that process.

6. The research agenda ahead: lessons for institutes

Address by Karl E. Birnbaum, Director of Programme, European Centre for Peace Studies, Austria

A few points that came up in the discussion should be considered in the work of our institutes. One thing is a truism but I think it is worth emphasizing, namely, that Germany looms prominently on the agenda of both politics and research. Research on German problems seems to be quickly outdated these days since all studies on German problems imply attempts to shoot at a fast-moving target. This leads me to the conclusion that there is no substitute for presentations, exchanges and discussions like the ones we have had the privilege of listening to and participating in at this very conference. So what I want to suggest is some form of semi-institutionalization of this kind of discussion, perhaps on the model of the Conference on Security and Co-operation in Europe (CSCE) procedure where decisions are made on the time and place of the next meeting. This may be enough in order to keep up the momentum. We need to look at Germany closely and quite frequently in order to understand what is going on.

The other conclusion is more long-term and relates to the items on the research agenda. In addition to Germany—to the extent we can do research that will not be immediately outdated—the CSCE process should come high on our agenda as a framework rather than a model, as Christoph Bertram rightly suggested, for an emerging new order in Europe. It is in that framework that governmental negotiations will be conducted about changes in the present security structures in Europe. In this context we should also be studying the stages and elements of that new emerging order. With the fall of the Berlin Wall and the opening of borders between the German states a central goal of Western and FRG policy in the CSCE has in fact been achieved. Controversies about minimum exchange-rates, which agitated negotiators only a few months ago, seem to belong to a totally different historical period. The CSCE has thus lost much of its importance as an instrument for opening up Eastern societies, which for a long time was one of the main perceptions of the West, and of the West Germans in particular. But instead, governments in the East and in the West have lately begun to emphasize the role and importance of the CSCE as a potential stabilizing mechanism for both societal and political transformation in Central and Eastern Europe. The Helsinki Final Act undoubtedly contains many relevant provisions for this kind of stabilization. But at the same time, as Adam Daniel Rotfeld has rightly pointed out, the general philosophy of the CSCE is to look beyond the pacts and existing power structures. Hence the conceptual challenge facing researchers would seem to be to find criteria for the combination of stability and change that will be required. This research must tackle the problems of the means and limits of future efforts to control the pace and direction of processes of transformation. Politicians are using the term stability very loosely; they seldom have the time or inclination to indulge in a conceptual analysis. So this must become or remain a task for researchers.

Another aspect of the CSCE process that is relevant for the future political and research agenda relates to its security dimension. Overcoming the division of Germany without serious destabilizing developments presupposes parallel efforts to overcome the European division. But these efforts in turn are predicated on the dismantling of military confrontation including its nuclear element; Catherine Kelleher reminded us of that fact. Now, the CSCE is the only inter-governmental negotiating framework whose agenda encompasses the two aspects of impending change, namely, its military and its societal dimension. This suggests—to me at least—that the security component of the CSCE, which has so far been underdeveloped but is of growing importance in any case, should be further developed, and that its two main elements—the CSBM and CFE negotiations—will eventually have to be merged. One of the reasons for this relates to the role of the neutral and non-aligned states. Once we move into a stage in intra-European politics when we are really talking about steps towards a security system other than the one dominated by the two blocs, these states would seem to have a legitimate and useful role to play. Hence, for no other reason, the security element in the CSCE will have to be upgraded.

My last point refers to the functions of research institutes in the evolution of a process leading to a European peace order that would really deserve that name. I should like to refer to the fact that a number of institutes represented here are already involved in this kind of exercise. The Italian institute has a very ambitious project on the future architecture of Europe. The Polish institute, in co-operation with other institutes, is involved in a similar endeavour concentrating on the military aspects of a future European peace order. The organization which is being started with my help, the European University Center for Peace Studies (EPU) in Schlainingen, Austria, will be doing something on models and processes for a future European peace order. The fundamental, common challenge would seem to me to be to analyse the interrelationship between the three main dynamics at work in Europe: German unification, European unification and the future security arrangements for the Old Continent. The challenge would seem to be in particular to come to grips with interaction between the different places and different frameworks for these dynamic developments. This should be a common task for our institutes. Perhaps the Germany-watch meetings, which I suggested at the very beginning, could be combined with an exercise which in the first instance would aim at comparing notes on our respective views with regard to roads and steps towards a new European peace order.

7. The future of Europe and of Germany: conference summary

Adam Daniel Rotfeld

The responsibility of the two German states for a European peace order on the one hand and the responsibility of Europeans and Americans for a peaceful process of German unification on the other were the main topics discussed at the SIPRI/IPW Potsdam conference. The key question addressed was: What kind of security structure is needed for this new Europe and a united Germany?

In this context some specific questions were raised on the challenge of unification in the process of European economic and political integration, on relations between the two German states and the changes in Central Europe, and on the future role of the alliances in Europe.

I. Change and reform in the GDR and European integration

Professor Kurt Biedenkopf, a member of the Bundestag (CDU), the director of the Institute for Economic and Social Policy in Bonn and a guest professor at Leipzig University, raised some questions about intra-German relations and European economic integration. He characterized the current process as a revolutionary one. With the dike of European division broken, 'The water that had flown through this dike has to be channelled into a new river as quickly as possible', said Professor Biedenkopf.

In German–German relations this process is characterized and influenced by two special conditions which distinguish it from comparable processes in Poland, Hungary, Czechoslovakia and, increasingly, also in the Soviet Union:

1. All citizens of the GDR are potential citizens of the FRG—they can achieve this simply by going West. That means that theirs is not an autonomous economy in the usual sense of the word.

2. All political forces have determined that the two German states should be united.

Unification is therefore essential. The integration of the two German economies must be seen under two headings. First, European Community (EC) compatibility, that is, the change of the national economy in the GDR to an extent that enables complete and unrestricted participation in the division of labour within the EC and second, the integration of the two German economies, which is to precede the projected European integration. What will be created between the two German states in the coming months and years is what ought essentially to happen in the EC.

Irrespective of the question of national unity this process must integrate the economy, the labour market, the social systems, the transport systems and other infrastructure institutions or facilities such as communications. General conditions for freedom must be created. This also applies to European integration and to the standardization of the legal systems.

The development under article 23 of the Basic Law (Constitution) of the FRG to come to grips with its automatic dimension was considered as inconceivable; 'in this complex process we are at the mercy of an accidental automatic enforcement of a clause in the constitution that was meant for totally different situations'.

The pressure for unity is guided by the desire for equal living standards. This is also a major goal of the EC—although not automatically associated with the creation of equal living standards with a united Germany. This goal would reduce the prospect of European unity.

One of the decisive questions in connection with the integration of the two German national economies in the EC is whether a united Germany would turn out to be a new European superpower, a giant in the new Europe. Professor Biedenkopf asked: 'If the Germans had not learned enough, could they go ahead with such intentions in the first place?' In the classical analysis of power in Europe, the size of a country and its population figure prominently. The territory of a future Germany would only constitute two-thirds of the area of former Germany. Up to the end of World War I, Germany was the biggest country in Europe after Russia in territorial terms. A united Germany would be the fifth largest country in Europe, after Russia, France, Spain and Sweden, and would be a little larger than Finland, Norway and Poland. In 1900 the German population totalled 60 million—not essentially smaller than the Russian population of 90 million and far larger than the British or French populations. In future the 74 million Germans and 5 million foreigners that currently live in the two German states can be compared with 55 million French, 55 million British or roughly 200 million people in the Soviet Union. The population equation is totally different and, what is more significant, the population in the two German states is on the decline—in about 30 years it will be about the same as the population of France or Britain, where no parallel demographic decline is in evidence.

As regards economic potential, on the basis of the Deutschmark the gross national product (GNP) of the GDR should be devalued by 50 per cent because of the difference in productivity; the GNP of the two German states will rise from 2.3 billion to 2.6 billion DM—probably half that of Japan and just as big as that of France and the Benelux countries.

Biedenkopf's conclusion was that: 'The combination of the two German states resulting in an economic superpower position is something highly unlikely'. The potential of the GDR roughly corresponds to the industrial potential of the German province of Hessen in the FRG. In the most favourable case, if the GDR attained the same degree of productivity as Nordrhein-Westphalia the FRG would effectively be increased by the size of that region. Professor Biedenkopf stated that a united Germany would fit into the European structure much better than the German Reich did at the beginning of the century.

A united Germany would be composed of seven large conurbations: Berlin; the industrial area in Saxony, Prussian Saxony and Thuringia; Hamburg and Schleswig-Holstein; the Ruhr area; the Rhein area from Dusseldorf to Bonn; the Rhein-Main area; and Stuttgart and Munich. These areas will retain their relative positions and no cultural, social or financial set up in a united Germany would essentially change the structural features. At the same time the competition between these locations will continue. Society in the provinces in the FRG can already be said to be developing along different lines. There are marked differences in regional views on lifestyles, social structures, family structures, and so on, which are also reflected in the industrial potential of the regions. The same would apply to a united Germany.

Strong regionalization and decentralization in a highly complex industrial German society will be a model for developments in other European countries, rather than the other way round. The potential efficiency of the structures that have developed—not intentionally but because of historical conditions—will soon turn out to be attractive to other European countries, and it will be less attractive for Germany to repeat or revive the centralization as still found in Britain and France. The economic dimension of the integration is characterized by an FRG–GDR population ratio of 4 : 1, and a GNP ratio, on the basis of the Deutschmark adjusted for productivity, of 10 : 1. These differences, of course, will affect the integration ahead no matter how the issue of national law is dealt with in this process.

The economic risk of integration, within the framework of a monetary union, is no larger than the growth of the GNP assuming adequate economic growth. The growth in GNP totalled 85 billion Deutschmarks in 1989. It is impossible to spend such sums during the course of an integration process. The essential part of infrastructure financing in the reconstruction must, of course, come from private and public capital.

A transitional period of adaptation to structural unemployment is possible until new jobs are created to finance current spending by current subsidies. These are neither sacrifices nor aid but rather investment or assistance by the FRG to pay for war burdens that resulted from the Stalinist order of the past few decades in the GDR.

Finally, the entry of the GDR to the EC is comparable to the effort that would have been involved in absorbing half of Spain in 1986. The increase in the EC population would be 5 per cent and the growth in GNP 2 per cent. Given an adequate distribution of the burden—most of which would of course have to be shouldered by the FRG—the EC would not even notice the integration of the GDR.

In Professor Biedenkopf's view the problem under debate should not concern Europe. The outstanding siting conditions of GDR industry make it a sensible and future-oriented investment. The GDR not only has large amounts of land, with only half the population density of the FRG, but is also uniquely located between East and West, in a good position to tackle the future tasks of Europe, namely, the construction and renewal of Eastern national economies.

Once we have a system of overlapping security instead of an antagonistic security order—said Professor Biedenkopf in conclusion—we will have established human rights in the Western tradition. These rights can only be part of a pan-European orientation.

II. Alliances and co-operative security

'Co-operative forms, common security—these notions are good friends of mine', said Egon Bahr discussing an introduction by Hans-Dietrich Genscher, Federal Minister of Foreign Affairs. 'I also have in mind co-operative forms, developments in which the two alliances eventually may be absorbed by pan-European structures.' Egon Bahr also shared the view that a first CFE agreement must immediately be followed by a second, and that pan-European structures must also be established for the benefit of a united German republic. Clearly the German military forces will have to be included in this process. In this context, he raised two questions:

1. Is it not high time to think of a six-power conference—i.e., the two German states and the four powers, namely Two-plus-Four—to discuss the road, the prospects and all the highly sophisticated international legal and security issues and to have them settled such that the two German governments are fully aware of the framework within which they are moving forward together with the Four Powers?

2. You have outlined here as a trend an overall prospect with regard to pan-European structures within the framework of which a united Germany would find its place such that we, as an equal member, are able to work, but also such that at the same time none of our neighbours need be afraid or concerned. Most of us are in agreement with this; what matters is whether it would be all too beautiful if it really happened that way. The Republic of Germany will emerge most probably before the establishment of pan-European structures. How do you visualize that? Both questions were addressed to Foreign Minister Genscher.

In response, Hans-Dietrich Genscher pointed out the significance of the alliances: NATO is a community of values, the second function of which has been to engender the military presence of the United States in Europe. There is consensus in Europe, and the Malta summit meeting made it quite clear that this consensus also exists between the two superpowers. The United States will continue to play an important role in the security of Europe. The Soviet Union is present in Europe with and without alliances. Its European region is part and parcel of Europe, and the WTO has the function of enabling Soviet presence in Central Europe. This means that US participation in the political, economic and security–political shaping of Europe will be significant.

'I consider it necessary', stated Genscher, 'that responsible discussions on the future of Germany should be held with the government to be elected in the GDR on 18 March. Responsible discussions with the *four* can only take place once the *two* have a concept. I spoke about discussions in plural—that was not a terminological inaccuracy; it was deliberate because I did not want to stipulate whether they should meet or whether we should have individual talks. Let us see how things emerge. The Germans should state after the 18 March elections whether they can agree on a joint concept with the help of which they would be able to talk to the other states.'

Anne-Marie Le Gloannec raised the question of priorities within the European communities, asking: 'How can you have the European monetary and political union at the same time?' She asked Hans-Dietrich Genscher: 'Could you outline your vision and define the dialectics existing between the consolidation of democracy in Eastern Europe and the strengthening of the political union within the EC? How can these two things be reconciled?'

Genscher replied: 'Let me start off with the most important problem of European Parliamentary Commission (EPC) consultation. Consultations with various groups of states are already under way. The significance of the European Community for pan-European development cannot be overrated provided it preserves its own dynamics'. He also expressed the view that the formation of a German economic and monetary union 'may have an influence on our position within the European monetary system'. The development in the GDR should take place in such a way that sooner or later this economic and monetary union would become indispensable 'unless we are prepared to put up with stability risks in Central Europe . . . Our European partners should realize that they have a great chance. This is also an important contribution to the Europeanization of the Germans', said Genscher, adding 'It is a unique chance, and unless they do so it will be done by others. So if France does not do so, and Italy and Britain and others, I know people who are interested from further away who are already occupying themselves with very intensive market analyses. I can only advise you not to see this chance slip by'.

III. A need for stabilization

The representative of the Protestant Church in the GDR raised the problem of the massive flows of Germans from East to West. He said that the overwhelming majority violate their duties in the GDR, and are even favoured in the FRG. Two thousand emigrating each day creates a great concern. 'This is a time bomb ticking away and it will certainly not come to an end on 18 March', said Manfred Stolpe, 'we will have to deal with it for quite some time to come. We are approaching a disaster. I make use of this opportunity to voice the concern that really bothers us. When we say human rights they also have to be used in a civilized way.'

Responding to this question Hans-Dietrich Genscher said: 'They are not 2000 but 3000, which makes the problem even more dramatic. I spoke about the fact that help is needed in the GDR, below the level of the alliances. Medical assistance for the GDR is particularly urgent . . . On 20 July 1989 I had a heart infarct. If this had happened in the city of Halle I would not be able to chair this conference. I would require help, if I was able to sit here at all—this cannot be considered right and proper . . . The stabilization of the community in the GDR is an elementary requirement, not only for social justice; the security of old-age pensioners will become an increasing problem unless we will also set a sign. We can do an awful lot.'

IV. The future of the alliances as bilateral treaties

Professor László Valki from Hungary commented on the future of the alliances. Addressing the question to Hans-Dietrich Genscher, he said: 'You were saying that there will be a future for the Western alliance and you did not mention the future of the Eastern alliance. My weather forecast would be that the future of the Eastern alliance is very gloomy. Both alliances have lost their functions since the threats disappeared from the scene. Hungary or Czechoslovakia, for instance, do not feel any threat any more from any part of the world, including the Eastern side'.

'The Eastern alliance', continued Professor Valki, 'will probably be replaced by bilateral treaties between individual East European countries and the Soviet Union, or rather the old bilateral agreements on friendship, co-operation and mutual assistance will stay alive because they can reassure the security interests of the Soviet Union. None of the East European countries would join any alliance directed against the Soviet Union (saying this I am using the well-known Finnish formula: the Finnish–Soviet Treaty of 1948 stated that there will be no treaty signed on a coalition directed against any of the parties).' Professor Valki asked: 'How would you look at this process, dissolving alliances, remaining bilateral relationships, bilateral treaties?'

In response, Hans-Dietrich Genscher said that 'through the CSCE process we have been able to achieve co-operative pan-European developments and bilateral developments. I would consider it a step back if we withdrew again to bilateral agreements. . . . They should be retained, just to mention two important declarations, the German–Polish and German–Soviet treaties.'

The opportunities of the co-operative process within the Conference on Security and Co-operation in Europe (CSCE) framework should not be underestimated; the alliances should be considered to be undergoing a change in their function. Hans-Dietrich Genscher said: 'I do not yet know of a recipe for how disarmament could be handled, each with everyone or each against everyone'.

The two alliances acquire additional functions; they will be affected by the pan-European structure. Their stabilizing effect should not be underestimated.

V. A Soviet view on the future of the alliances

The Soviet participant, Vladimir Razmerov, commented that it is the end of the post-war period of international relations. Events in Central and Eastern Europe in 1990 have demonstrated the inevitability of revolutionary transformations. The new era opening up to the peoples of Europe and the world will be one of revolution and peace rather than war and revolution. In this new stage of history there is no place for military blocs—these have been instruments of policy conducted by military means. Consequently, politicizing blocs on the one hand enables their continued survival and, on the other, is a transitional phase to their complete elimination. Transforming a military alliance into a political one has another aspect: the establishment of new relations with old allies that have radically altered their internal structures. These relations must be based on genuine equality and mutual advantage. The establishment of such relations is not an easy task. Perhaps the very process of politicization of blocs will open up some new opportunities for the Soviet Union and its partners. The optimal course for Europeans and the nations of the world would be to put an end to blocs at once. But, regretfully, that is not possible for a number of reasons.

A most important influence on the future of blocs is the political conduct of the superpowers. The Soviet Union has done its bit to improve its political image in the West and also the international atmosphere. 'We have renounced an unproductive and sometimes foolhardy foreign policy', said the Soviet participant. New thinking calls for a realistic perception of what is taking place, and political reality today calls for recognition that there are significantly influential forces in both West and East that are interested in the continuation of functioning blocs. While an important aspect of this in the West remains stereotypes in mass consciousness, plus the interests of weapon manufacturers, in the East, particularly the Soviet Union, the main difficulties facing the disarmament process are found in the economy, or more accurately, its completely abnormal condition. If the withdrawal of two divisions from Mongolia created complications and even dislocations in the Soviet economy, what kind of problems would the withdrawal of an entire army group from the GDR present?

'The liquidation of blocs,' continued Dr Razmerov, 'is a question of time, but apparently this time period will not be very short.'

The discussion about the future of blocs recalls another military–political debate, once conducted with great heat and intensity, between conflicting views in Soviet military circles about the role of the cavalry in the imminent war. Many who took part in that debate paid with their lives for their ideas. Today we know that the cavalry played no role in World War II.

VI. Unification from the perspective of neighbours

A Polish view

Professor Wojciech Lamentowicz presented specific reactions by Poland and some other countries in the region to the German unification process. Public opinion polls in Poland have shown that some 62 per cent of the adult population do not fear the unification process in Germany, and that some 35 per cent do feel somewhat threatened by this process for many different reasons. This is a tremendous shift in Polish public opinion. Only two years ago, the structure of perceptions was just the opposite. A tiny minority of 20–25 per cent was in favour, not threatened, and a majority of more than 60 per cent felt threatened by the process of unification. What happened to Polish society that such a shift was possible at all? In Professor Lamentowicz's view efforts were being made inside Poland to go beyond Yalta. Although it was primarily a German achievement, the Poles actually did a lot to help destroy the wall between the two German states.

Another reason is the tremendous sympathy to all democratic movements from below in the GDR, a prevailing mood in Poland. 'Whatever we achieved', continued Lamentowicz, 'though not properly secured, is still some sort of achievement. We did it by pressure from below and by something perceived by many Europeans at the beginning of the 1980s after our August peaceful revolution as a bit anarchic, disordered, threatening, irrational, romantic or whatever you like. This sort of description prevailed; after a very few years in a completely different context very similar processes took place in our neighbouring countries with democratic outcomes and possibly successful institution-building of the re-emerging democracy.'

The third reason presented by the Polish speaker is that many hopes are pinned on the German unification process in Poland as well. Some of the older generation are a bit afraid of this process and of risking the dominance of German technology, German capital, German culture and German presence in general. On the other hand there are people, mainly of the younger generation, who are afraid that German unification may lead to an economy and political scene so involved in intra-German problems as to frustrate the hopes of Hungary, Poland, Czechoslovakia and other countries of the region. These opposing views both contradict and supplement each other.

About Soviet troops in Poland, Professor Lamentowicz said that there are two diverging Polish positions; these are not contradictory. The position taken by Lech Walesa is supported by the majority of the nation and the government is considered to have an interest in the security aspects of the democratization process. In the unification process, the withdrawal of Soviet troops from eastern parts of Germany and from Poland are somewhat linked. It is very unlikely that Soviet troops being withdrawn from the GDR would be stationed for good or for any length of time in Poland.

From the Polish point of view, it would be fortuitous if withdrawal of troops from the GDR were achieved in more or less the same time as a withdrawal of Soviet troops from Polish soil. This, of course, does not depend on Polish wishes; it is rather beyond our influence.

In a search for a new kind of security, Professor Lamentowicz discussed three sorts of treaty that might solve European problems:

1. A European treaty providing for security and perhaps some sort of political pan-European co-operation bringing us a little closer to the idea of a confederation (which is, of course, not very precise);
2. A kind of peace treaty, although not signed by all 35 participants of the Helsinki process since they were not all involved in World War II;
3. A treaty providing for unification in terms of economy, culture and many pragmatic problems (as mentioned by Hans-Dietrich Genscher).

The real trouble is that the 'German question' has its own dynamics and intra-German dynamics are the quickest in Europe: quicker than West European integration, quicker than pan-European integration and perhaps quicker than East European disintegration (as a matter of fact, there are three integration processes in Europe and one very important disintegration process in the East).

The two German states, once they are ready with a joint posture on their own unity, may and should get in touch even with non-neighbouring countries. Professor Lamentowicz suggested that the best procedure would be to deal with the Four Powers and perhaps with neighbours of Germany. He said: 'I would suggest trying to get in touch with any country which may feel interested, which may feel as involved as all 35 Helsinki states'.

Concluding his remarks Professor Lamentowicz said that a federation is going to be the future shape of a German state in Europe. This is an entirely German domestic policy problem.

A French view

Commenting on the remarks made by the Polish participant, Professor Dominique Moisï of France said that in the past the Poles and the French had a common interest—to keep Germany down. It is symbolic of the change which we have witnessed in Europe that we are able to discuss the evolution of the European scene in a serene, open manner.

The problem is both emotional and subjective, and at the same time rests on very objective considerations. What we are living through is a combination of German frustration and French suspicion. The nature of the German frustration is that the Germans did not share French emotions as the French would have liked. France's celebration of the crumbling of the Wall has been ambivalent. Emotions were real but they were mitigated with apprehension and second thoughts. It was a victory for freedom but also for Germany, and the French sometimes had difficulties distinguishing these two aspects. It could therefore be seen as a risk for the stability of Europe and even more so for the status of France. To paint the picture of an inward-looking country, frustrated deep down and dominated by fear, is not only an exaggeration but a misrepresentation. Public opinion in France at large was much more positive than that of the political, economic or intellectual elites. From that point of view the polls were unambiguous. Eighty-two per cent of Frenchmen considered that the crumbling of the wall was the most important event of 1989, and more than 60 per cent were in support of the unification of Germany. Elite groups were much more ambivalent.

The French know what they are but they are not sure of what they can achieve. In French eyes Germans may be too sure of what they can achieve but do not necessarily know who they are. Professor Moisï said that these feelings have been disguised in the French debate under three categories of concern:

1. Concern for the stability of the world order: before President Gorbachev's latest declaration accepting the idea of German unity, people were happy to emphasize the fact that the Soviet Union would never accept it, and therefore it was going to be dangerous.

2. The calendar of the diplomats was emphasized over that of the people by those who were showing concern for the stability of European unification at the level of the 12 EC countries. So you moved down. It was not only that the world order was going to be destabilized but also that the 12 would not make it according to their own calendar.

3. Germany is already too strong. With 80 million people it will dominate Europe and, in particular, the French economy. Both French economic and diplomatic status will see a downward process of revisionism.

Concluding his analysis of French feelings about Germany, Professor Moisï expressed a note of warning. Some gesture could have been made, he said. President François Mitterrand was not very far from the Brandenburg gate when it was opened and it would have been a beautiful gesture if he and Chancellor Helmut Kohl had been together. They had been together in Verdun, celebrating the end of the past. They could have been together at the Brandenburg Gate celebrating the beginning of the future. It would have been nice if, on the eve of his declaration with his famous 10 points, Chancellor Kohl had said a few words to the French President. Professor Moisï concluded that, while disappointment is present on the German side and worry is present on the French side, basically the countries stand together. At the highest level the situation is under control; there is a feeling on both sides that Europe is their common destiny and that there is no alternative.

Speaking about the international consequences of the process of unification, Professor Moisï said that 'clearly the difficulty stems from the fact that the calendar of the people has dictated its law to the calendar of diplomats'. The crumbling of the Wall and the implosion of authority in the GDR is imposing a calendar which no one was prepared for. Unity is now seen as the condition for stability inside Germany. While it will not ensure freedom and democracy for all Germans, it is a way to stabilize the situation domestically at the heart of Europe. But this concept of stability in the domestic political sense runs against the concept of stability in the international sense. Can a stable Europe accommodate a united Germany in the immediate future if Germany is to be united this year, as Hans-Dietrich Genscher had said that morning? What do we want in the coming years? Moisï referred to Lord Ismay's famous goals for NATO in the early 1950s: to keep the USA in, the Soviet Union out and the Germans down. These three goals need a process of adaptation.

VII. Some concluding remarks[1]

The discussion at the SIPRI/IPW conference in Potsdam reaffirmed that the search for new structures and mechanisms adequate to the unprecedented situation in Europe is now the main subject not only of the debate but also of a decision-making process.

Some broad political concepts have been advanced by Mikhail Gorbachev, François Mitterrand, Willy Brandt and other statesmen. The idea of building a 'common European home' was specified in the preparatory process for the summit meeting of leaders of the 35 CSCE states of Europe and North America (CSCE II), and the President of France has put forward an idea for a European confederation which corresponds to a 'common European home'. In Germany the idea of remaking Europe has been subordinated to the debate on prospects for a united Germany.

The imminent prospect of politico-economic unity for Germany has had the effect of adjourning an intensification of West European integration within the framework of existing communities (the EC and the EPC). Unification of Germany also poses a challenge to such Central European states as Poland, Czechoslovakia and Hungary, quite irrespective of public reactions to the initiated unification process. The Atlantic Alliance is also on the agenda. It was not easy for the Soviet Union to accept membership of a united Germany in NATO, a position voiced repeatedly by Mikhail Gorbachev and Eduard Shevardnadze. European members of NATO have suddenly found themselves facing the possibility of the Atlantic Alliance being dominated by a united Germany. Attention has been drawn to the possibility of the two German states leaving their respective alliances and becoming neutral as a price for unification which would threaten neither Germany's neighbours nor European stability. A more practical and functional solution seemed to be sharp reductions in German forces, membership of the enlarged Germany in NATO, and the preservation and establishment of new relations and ties between NATO and the former WTO members.

---

[1] This part of the SIPRI/IPW conference summary is to some extent brought up-to-date and refers to documents on German unification and European security published in part II.

In Central and East European countries an increasingly popular scenario for the future is: to bring the Atlantic Alliance closer to Europe as a whole and enable the stability of Western Europe to affect positively the still fluid situation in Central and Eastern Europe and to have a bearing on the potential dangers there, as Foreign Secretary Krzysztof Skubiszewski suggested to the London session of the North Atlantic Assembly (November 1990). Such radical systemic changes would make it possible for these states to join West European communities within the next 10–15 years, with consequences in economic as well as political life.

The partisans of positive action aimed at re-making the existing structures, which represent a product of the bipolar division, proceed from the following two assumptions:

1. The democratic and liberal changes sweeping the states of Central and South-Eastern Europe should be rewarded with appropriate institutional guarantees in pan-European structures and mechanisms; and

2. An alternative to the previous bipolar system based on subordination must not be atomization and chaos but a peaceful order predicated upon the rule of law and mutually agreed principles or rules of conduct.

The CSCE process, and the set of decisions and recommendations adopted within its framework, offers itself as a natural starting-point and a platform for the elaboration of a new multilateral pan-European solution.

It seems that the prevailing view among the new political leaders in Central Europe is twofold:

1. To modify and join existing Western institutions, such as NATO, the European Community, the Council of Europe, the Western European Union, and so on; and

2. To construct the new pan-European security structures based on CSCE principles, procedures and institutions.

The specific proposal to create a Council of European Co-operation—in the framework of the CSCE process—was presented by Polish Prime Minister Tadeusz Mazowiecki on 18 January 1990. This concept was then developed in his speech at the Parliamentary Assembly of the Council of Europe (30 January 1990) and in the Memorandum of the Polish Government submitted to all CSCE states (10 March 1990). A convergent concept has been presented by the new Government of Czechoslovakia (6 April 1990). The documents of these two governments enabled a common proposal on the institutionalization of the CSCE process to the Summit Preparatory Meeting (10 July 1990). The creation of a modest international secretariat to assist the Council and operate as a centre of documentation and information was also suggested. Similar proposals were submitted in different forms by the governments of the FRG, Denmark, Sweden, Finland and the Soviet Union.

The London Declaration on a transformed North Atlantic Alliance issued by the heads of state and government participating in the meeting of the North Atlantic Council in London on 5–6 July 1990 stated that NATO was beginning a major transformation. The NATO summit meeting proposed that WTO members conclude a joint declaration stating that the two alliances 'are no longer adversaries' and reaffirming non-use of force commitments. President Gorbachev accepted the invitation addressed to him and representatives of the Central and East European countries to come to Brussels and present their views to the North Atlantic Council. NATO leaders proposed the establishment of regular diplomatic liaison between the WTO states and NATO. They expressed readiness to continue the Negotiation on Conventional Armed Forces in Europe (CFE) in Vienna once a first treaty is signed. Apart from the CFE agreement the CSCE summit meeting—which was held 19–21 November 1990 in Paris—sets new standards for the establishment and preservation of free societies in Europe (the rule of law, free elections and market economies). This summit meeting of 34 nations decided how the CSCE could be institutionalized: regular meetings at head of state or ministerial level, follow-up meetings (like those in Madrid or Vienna), a small secretariat, a mechanism to monitor elections, a CSCE centre for the prevention of conflict and the conciliation of disputes, and possibly a European Parliamentary Assembly. The London Declaration reads: 'The sites of these new institutions should reflect the fact that the newly democratic countries of Central and Eastern Europe form part of the political structures of the new Europe'. It was agreed that the seat of the CSCE Secretariat will be in Prague and the Office for Free Elections in Warsaw. It was also decided that a Conflict Prevention Centre be established in Vienna.

The profound systemic changes in Central Europe are not accompanied by adequate transformations of institutions and organizational structures for a system of security and co-operation in the region. Not only have the WTO and CMEA shed their character of ideological and political communities, but in fact both structures are in ruins ('hollow shells'). The WTO has to some extent retained its significance as an instrument to harmonize a common position during the Vienna CFE Negotiation. The CMEA does not play any role of consequence even in regard to matters for whose regulation it was created, that is, co-ordination and economic co-operation. What is left is an unwieldy bureaucratic structure which ought to be eliminated, with the possible utilization of some of its elements in an effort to set up an organization of another sort. It is doubtful whether the WTO, reduced to performing functions of a classical geopolitical alliance, will survive. It could be transformed into a multilateral co-ordinatory instrument to control and reduce armaments. It can certainly no longer play the role of an instrument whereby pressures could be brought to bear on the allies consistent with the will and interests of the dominant power in the alliance.

The security interests of Central European states in the period of transition require:

1. *Rapprochement*—on new lines—in relations with all the neighbouring countries;

2. A new type of relations with the EC and other West European institutions;

3. The promotion of new structures of security, with their point of departure in the direction of and their common denominator represented by existing CSCE procedures and decisions. These can play a major role if they get a new dimension: they will take on the character of new security structures, and will be durable and legally binding.

The transformation of NATO alongside the London Declaration into substantially new co-operative security arrangements in the framework of the CSCE cannot be excluded.

Acceleration of change requires the elaboration of an imaginative and comprehensive concept for a new European security system. The documents in Part II of this book illustrate the significant evolution on both sides of the former line of division. In post-war European history there has never been as favourable a climate in which to replace the bipolar system, identified with stability based on subordination in the framework of two opposing blocs, with a new one based on interdependence, partnership and respect for common values by all states party to such a system. This chance and opportunity must not be missed.

Part II
Documents on German unification and European security

I. US documents

Four proposals to overcome Europe's division

Speech by President George Bush, Mainz, FRG, 31 May 1989

Excerpts

(. . .)

The Cold War began with the division of Europe. It can only end when Europe is whole. Today, it is this very concept of a divided Europe that is under siege. And that's why our hopes run especially high, because the division of Europe is under siege not by armies, but by the spread of ideas that began here, right here. It was a son of Mainz, Johannes Gutenberg, who liberated the mind of man through the power of the printed word.

And that same liberating power is unleashed today in a hundred new forms. The Voice of America, Deutsche Welle, allow us to enlighten millions deep within Eastern Europe and throughout the world. Television satellites allow us to bear witness from the shipyards of Gdansk to Tiananmen Square. But the momentum for freedom does not just come from the printed word or the transistor or the television screen. It comes from a single powerful idea—democracy.

This one idea is sweeping across Eurasia. This one idea is why the Communist world, from Budapest to Beijing, is in ferment. Of course, for the leaders of the East it's not just freedom for freedom's sake. But whatever their motivation, they are unleashing a force they will find difficult to channel or control—the hunger for liberty of oppressed peoples who have tasted freedom.

Nowhere is this more apparent than in Eastern Europe, the birthplace of the Cold War. In Poland, at the end of World War II, the Soviet army prevented the free elections promised by Stalin at Yalta. And today, Poles are taking the first steps towards real elections, so long promised—so long deferred. And in Hungary, at last we see a chance for multi-party competition at the ballot box.

As president, I will continue to do all I can to help open the closed societies of the East. We seek self-determination for all of Ger-many and all of Eastern Europe. And we will not relax, and we must not waver. Again, the world has waited long enough.

But democracy's journey east is not easy. Intellectuals like the great Czech playwright, Vaclav Havel, still work under the shadow of coercion. And repression still menaces too many peoples of Eastern Europe. Barriers and barbed wire still fence in nations. So when I visit Poland and Hungary this summer, I will deliver this message: There cannot be a common European home until all within it are free to move from room to room.

And I'll take another message: The path of freedom leads to a larger home—a home where West meets East, a democratic home— the commonwealth of free nations.

And I said that positive steps by the Soviets would be met by steps of our own. And this is why I announced on May 12 a readiness to consider granting to the Soviets a temporary waiver of the Jackson–Vanik trade restriction, if they liberalize emigration. And this is also why I announced on Monday (May 29) that the United States is prepared to drop the 'no exceptions' standard that has guided our approach to controlling the export of technology to the Soviet Union—lifting a sanction enacted in response to their invasion of Afghanistan.

And in this same spirit, I set forth four proposals to heal Europe's tragic division, to help Europe become whole and free.

First, I propose we strengthen and broaden the Helsinki process to promote free elections and political pluralism in Eastern Europe. As the forces of freedom and democracy rise in the East, so should our expectations.

And weaving together the slender threads of freedom in the East will require much from the Western democracies. In particular, the great political parties of the West must assume an historic responsibility—to lend counsel and support to those brave men and women who are trying to form the first truly representative political parties in the East, to advance freedom and democracy, to part the Iron Curtain.

In fact, it's already begun to part. The frontier of barbed wire and minefields between Hungary and Austria is being removed, foot by foot, mile by mile. Just as the barriers are coming down in Hungary, so must they fall throughout all of Eastern Europe. Let Berlin be next. Let Berlin be next!

Nowhere is the division between East and West seen more clearly than in Berlin. And there this brutal wall cuts neighbor from neighbor, brother from brother. And that wall stands as a monument to the failure of communism. It must come down.

Now, *glasnost* may be a Russian word, but openness is a Western concept. West Berlin has always enjoyed the openness of a free city. And our proposal would make all Berlin a center of commerce between East and West—a place of cooperation, not a point of confrontation. And we rededicate ourselves to the 1987 allied initiative to strengthen freedom and security in that divided city. This, then is my second proposal—bring *glasnost* to East Berlin.

My generation remembers a Europe ravaged by war. And of course, Europe has long since rebuilt its proud cities and restored its majestic cathedrals. But what a tragedy it would be if your continent was again spoiled, this time by a more subtle and insidious danger—the chancellor referred to it—that of poisoned rivers and acid rain.

America has faced an environmental tragedy in Alaska. Countries from France to Finland suffered after Chernobyl. West Germany is struggling to save the Black Forest today. And throughout, we have all learned a terrible lesson—environmental destruction respects no borders.

So my third proposal is to work together on these environmental problems, with the United States and Western Europe extending a hand to the East. Since much remains to be done in both East and West, we ask Eastern Europe to join us in this common struggle. We can offer technical training assistance in drafting laws and regulations, and new technologies for tackling these awesome problems. And I invite the environmentalists and engineers of the East to visit the West, to share knowledge so that we can succeed in this great cause.

My fourth proposal, actually, a set of proposals, concerns a less militarized Europe, the most heavily armed continent in the world. Nowhere is this more important than in the two Germanys. And that's why our quest to safely reduce armaments has a special significance for the German people.

To those who are impatient with our measured pace in arms reduction, I respectfully suggest that history teaches us a lesson—that unity and strength are the catalyst and prerequisite to arms control. We've always believed that a strong Western defense is the best road to peace. And 40 years of experience have proven us right.

But we've done more than just keep the peace. By standing together, we have convinced the Soviets that their arms buildup has been costly and pointless. Let us not give them incentives to return to the policies of the past. Let us give them every reason to abandon the arms race for the sake of the human race.

In this era of both negotiation and armed camps, America understands that West Germany bears a special burden. Of course, in this nuclear age, every nation is on the front line. But not all free nations are called to endure the tension of regular military activity, or the constant presence of foreign military forces. We are sensitive to these special conditions that this needed presence imposes.

To significantly ease the burden of armed camps in Europe, we must be aggressive in our pursuit of solid, verifiable agreements between NATO and the Warsaw Pact.

On Monday (May 29), with my NATO colleagues in Brussels, I shared my great hope for the future of conventional arms negotiations in Europe. I shared with them a proposal for achieving significant reductions in the near future.

And as you know, the Warsaw Pact has now accepted major elements of our Western approach to the new conventional arms negotiations in Vienna. The Eastern bloc acknowledges that a substantial imbalance exists between the conventional forces of the two alliances. And they've moved closer to NATO's position by accepting most elements of our initial conventional arms proposal. These encouraging steps have produced the opportunity for creative and decisive action, and we shall not let that opportunity pass.

Our proposal has several key initiatives.

I propose that we 'lock in' the Eastern agreement to Western-proposed ceilings on tanks and armored troop carriers. We should also seek an agreement on a common numerical ceiling for artillery in the range between NATO's and that of the Warsaw Pact, provided these definitional problems can be solved. And the weapons we remove must be destroyed.

We should expand our current offer to include all land-based combat aircraft and helicopters, by proposing that both sides reduce in these categories to a level 15 percent below the current NATO totals. Given the Warsaw Pact's advantage in numbers, the Pact would have to make far deeper reductions than NATO to establish parity at those lower levels. Again, the weapons we remove must be destroyed.

I propose a 20 percent cut in combat manpower in U.S.-stationed forces, and a resulting ceiling on U.S. and Soviet ground air forces stationed outside of national territory in the Atlantic-to-the-Urals zone, at approximately 275,000 each. This reduction to parity, a fair and balanced level of strength, would compel the Soviets to reduce their 600,000-strong Red Army in Eastern Europe by 325,000. And these withdrawn forces must be demobilized.

And finally, I call on President Gorbachev to accelerate the timetable for reaching these agreements. There is no reason why the five-to-six-year timetable, as suggested by Moscow is necessary. I propose a much more ambitious schedule. And we should aim to reach an agreement within six months to a year, and accomplish reductions by 1992, or 1993 at the latest.

In addition to my conventional arms proposals, I believe that we ought to strive to improve the openness with which we and the Soviets conduct our military activities. And therefore, I want to reiterate my support for greater transparency. I renew my proposal that the Soviet Union and its allies open their skies to reciprocal, unarmed aerial surveillance flights, conducted on short notice, to watch military activities. Satellites are a very important way to verify arms control agreements. But they do not provide constant coverage of the Soviet Union. An Open Skies policy would move both sides closer to a total continuity of coverage, while symbolizing greater openness between East and West.

These are my proposals to achieve a less militarized Europe. A short time ago they would have been too revolutionary to consider. And yet today, we may well be on the verge of a more ambitious agreement in Europe than anyone considered possible.

But we are also challenged by developments outside of NATO's traditional areas of concern. Every Western nation still faces the global proliferation of lethal technologies, including ballistic missiles and chemical weapons. We must collectively control the spread of these growing threats. So we should begin as soon as possible with a worldwide ban on chemical weapons.

Growing political freedom in the East, a Berlin without barriers, a cleaner environment, a less militarized Europe—each is a noble goal, and taken together they are the foundation of our larger vision—a Europe that is free and at peace with itself. And let the Soviets know that our goal is not to undermine their legitimate security interests. Our goal is to convince them, step by step, that their definition of security is obsolete, that their deepest fears are unfounded.

When Western Europe takes its giant step in 1992, it will institutionalize what's been true for years—borders open to people, commerce and ideas. No shadow of suspicion, no sinister fear is cast between you. The very prospect of war within the West is unthinkable to our citizens. But such a peaceful integration of nations into a world community does not mean that any nation must relinquish its culture, much less its sovereignty.

This process of integration, a subtle weaving of shared interests, which is so nearly complete in Western Europe, has now finally begun in the East. We want to help the nations of Eastern Europe realize what we, the nations of Western Europe, learned long ago. The foundation of lasting security comes not from tanks, troops, or barbed wire. It is built on shared values and agreements that link free peoples.

The nations of Eastern Europe are rediscovering the glories of their national heritage. So let the colors and hues of national culture return to these grey societies of the East. Let Europe forego a peace of tension for a peace of trust, one in which the peoples of the East and West can rejoice; a continent that is diverse, yet whole.

Forty years of Cold War have tested Western resolve and the strength of our values. NATO's first mission is now nearly complete. But if we are to fulfill our vision—our European vision—the challenges of the next 40 years will ask no less of us. Together, we shall answer the call. The world has waited long enough.

A new Europe, a new Atlanticism: architecture for a new era

Address by James A. Baker, III, US Secretary of State, to the Berlin Press Club, Berlin, 12 December 1989

Excerpts

(...)

Free men, and free governments, are the building blocks of a Europe whole and free. But hopes for a Europe whole and free are tinged with concern by some that a Europe undivided may not necessarily be a Europe peaceful and prosperous. Many of the guide-posts that brought us securely through four sometimes tense and threatening decades are now coming down. Some of the divisive issues that once brought conflict to Europe are reemerging.

As Europe changes, the instruments for Western cooperation have got to adapt. Working together, it is up to us to design and gradually to put into place what I refer to as a new architecture for this new era.

This new architecture must have a place for old foundations and structures that remain very valuable—like NATO—while recognizing that they can also serve new collective purposes. The new architecture must continue the construction of institutions—like the European Community—that can help draw together the West while also serving as an open door to the East. And the new architecture must build up frameworks—like the CSCE process—that can overcome the division of Europe and that, at the same time, can bridge the Atlantic Ocean.

This new structure must also accomplish two special purposes.

First, as a part of overcoming the division of Europe, there must be an opportunity to overcome through peace and freedom the division of Berlin and of Germany. The United States and NATO have stood for unification for forty years, and we will not waiver from that goal.

Second, the architecture should reflect that America's security—politically, militarily and economically—remains linked to Europe's security. The United States and Canada share Europe's neighborhood.

(...)

American military presence in Europe

State of the Union Address by President George Bush, Washington, DC, 31 January 1990

Excerpts

(...)

I agree with our European allies that an American military presence in Europe is essential—and that it should not be tied solely to the Soviet military presence in Eastern Europe.

But troop levels can still be lower. So tonight, I am announcing a major new step—for a further reduction in US and Soviet man-power in Central and Eastern Europe to 195,000 on each side.

This number reflects the advice of our senior military advisors. It is designed to protect American and European interests—and sustain NATO's defense strategy. A swift conclusion to our arms control talks—conventional, chemical and strategic—must now be our goal. That time has come.

(...)

Soviet Foreign Minister Eduard Shevardnadze and US Secretary of State James Baker met in Moscow on 7–9 February. They discussed President Bush's 31 January proposal on manpower, presented by NATO in Vienna on 8 February, and NATO's aircraft proposal presented on the same day. Differences on personnel were narrowed. They agreed to continue these discussions in the context of the Vienna Negotiation on Conventional Armed Forces in Europe (CFE) and at the 'Open Skies' Conference in Ottawa.

German unification and Europe

Statement by President George Bush, Washington, DC, 14 February 1990

Excerpts

(...)

I want to congratulate Secretary Baker for his superb job at Ottawa, and also for following through on his meetings in Moscow on the agenda that President Gorbachev and I agreed on there—set out at Malta. And I'm delighted that the 23 members of the Vienna negotiations on conventional forces in Europe accepted the NATO initiative, which I proposed in my State of the Union Address on January 31, to resolve the issue of manpower.

The United States and the Soviet Union each will station no more than 195, 000 troops in the Central Zone in Europe. And this will be the overall ceiling for Soviet troops stationed on foreign territory in Europe. The United States will be permitted to station the additional 30,000 troops in Europe outside the Central Zone.

Now, this is an important breakthrough which removes a major obstacle to the early conclusion of a CFE treaty. And it also establishes the principle that U.S. forces in Europe are not to be treated as equivalent to Soviet forces in Eastern Europe.*

The other major breakthrough was on German unification. And I called Chancellor Kohl yesterday to discuss the final details of the agreement that Secretary Baker reached at Ottawa.

We and our German allies are in full accord. Things moved quite fast there. And the agreement we've reached calls for the foreign ministers of the two German states to meet with the foreign ministers of the four powers—the United States, France, the United Kingdom and the Soviet Union—to discuss the external aspects of the establishment of German unity. This brings us a step closer to realizing the long-standing goal of German unity. And as I said in Mainz last May, it's a goal we and our allies have shared with the German people for more than 40 years.**

These steps, along with the inspiring march of democracy in Eastern Europe, bring within sight the objective that I have stressed throughout the first year of my presidency — a Europe that is whole and free.

(...)

---

* The foreign ministers and senior representatives of the governments of the 23 NATO and WTO states participating in the CFE Negotiation gathered on the fringes of the Open Skies Conference in Ottawa on 13 February 1990 to review progress in the CFE talks. They welcomed an agreement reached in Ottawa between the United States and the Soviet Union on the reduction of their stationed forces in Europe.

** For the statement made during the Open Skies Conference in Ottawa on 14 February 1990 on the agreement to initiate 'Two-plus-Four' talks see section XIX—Documents on unification.

A Europe that is whole and free

Address by President George Bush, Oklahoma State University, 4 May 1990

Excerpts

(...)

Because of our political commitment to peace in Europe, there hasn't been a war on that continent in 45 years. This 'long peace' should be viewed through the long lens of history: Europe has now experienced the longest uninterrupted period of international peace in the recorded history of that continent. The alliance is now ready to build on that historic achievement and define its objectives for the next century. So the alliance must join together to craft a new Western strategy for new and changing times.

Having consulted intensively with Prime Minister Thatcher in Bermuda, President Mitterrand in Florida, Chancellor Kohl at Camp David, and by telephone or cable with NATO Secretary General Wörner and all of my other allied colleagues, I am calling for an early summit meeting of all NATO leaders. Margaret Thatcher, one of freedom's greatest champions of the last decade, told me that while NATO has been fantastically successful, we should be ready now to face new challenges. The time is right for the alliance to act.

The fundamental purpose of this summit should be to launch a wide-ranging NATO Strategy Review for the transformed Europe of the 1990s. To my NATO colleagues, I suggest that our summit direct this review by addressing four critical points:

One, the political role NATO can play in the new Europe.

Two, the conventional forces the alliance will need in the time ahead, and NATO's goals for conventional arms control.

Three, the role of nuclear weapons based in Europe—and Western objectives in new nuclear arms control negotiations between the United States and the Soviet Union.

Four, strengthening the Conference on Security and Cooperation in Europe—the CSCE—to reinforce NATO and help protect democratic values, in a Europe whole and free.

The first task the NATO summit should consider is the future political mission of the alliance. As military threats fade, the political dimension of NATO's work—always there but seldom noticed—becomes more prominent. So at the NATO summit we should look for ways to help our German friends sustain freedom and achieve unity—something which we and our allies have supported for over 40 years. And we should reaffirm the importance of keeping a united Germany a full member of NATO.

The alliance needs to find ways to work more closely with a vigorous European Community that is rightly asserting its own distinct views. And in Eastern Europe, governments once our adversaries are now our partners in building a new continent. So we must also talk about how to encourage further peaceful democratic change in Eastern Europe and in the Soviet Union.

But even as NATO gives more emphasis to its political mission, its guarantee of European security must remain firm. Our enemy today is uncertainty, and instability. So the alliance will need to maintain a sound, collective military structure with forces in the field, backed by larger forces that can be called upon in a crisis.

Which brings me to the second task for the NATO summit—a review of how the alliance should plan its conventional defenses. While we need to recognize that it will take some time before the Soviet military presence is gone from Eastern Europe—and before the major reductions contemplated by both sides can be implemented—we need to develop our strategy for that world now.

Obviously, Soviet actions will be critical. Yet even after all the planned reductions in its forces are complete, even if our current arms control proposals are agreed to and implemented, the Soviet military will still field forces dwarfing those of any other single European State—armed with thousands of nuclear weapons. Militarily significant US forces must remain on the other side of the Atlantic for as long as our allies want and need them. These forces demonstrate, as no words can, the enduring political compact that binds America's fate with Europe's democracies.

If the Soviet withdrawal continues and our arms control efforts are successful, we must plan for a different kind of military presence focused less on the danger of an immediate outbreak of war. We must promote long-term stability and prevent crises from escalating by

relying on reduced forces that show our capability—and readiness—to respond to whatever may arise.

The Conventional Forces in Europe Treaty, we have proposed, would be the most ambitious conventional arms control agreement ever concluded.

We must finish the work on this treaty soon, and plan to sign it at a CSCE summit this fall. But at the NATO summit we need to look further ahead, preparing for follow-on negotiations after the conclusion of a CFE treaty. The NATO summit should develop the alliance's objectives for these talks.

Third, the NATO summit should also assess the future of US nuclear forces in Europe. As democracy blooms in Eastern Europe, as Soviet troops return home and tanks are dismantled, there is less need for nuclear systems of the shortest range. The NATO summit should accelerate ongoing work within the alliance to determine the minimum number and types of weapons that will be needed to deter war—credibly and effectively.

In light of these new political conditions and the limited range and flexibility of short-range nuclear missile forces based in Europe, I've reviewed our plan to produce and deploy newer, more modern, short-range nuclear missiles to replace the Lance system now in Europe. We've almost finished the research and development work for these new missiles. But I've decided, after consulting with our allies, to terminate the Follow-On To Lance program. I have also decided to cancel any further modernization of U.S. nuclear artillery shells deployed in Europe.

There are still short-range U.S.—and many more Soviet—nuclear missile systems deployed in Europe. We're prepared to negotiate the reduction of these forces as well, in a new set of arms control talks.

At the NATO summit, I will urge my colleagues to agree on the broad objectives for these future U.S.–Soviet negotiations and begin preparations within the alliance for these talks. I would also like to suggest that these new U.S.–Soviet arms control talks begin shortly after a CFE treaty on conventional forces has been signed.

In taking these steps, the United States is not going to allow Europe to become 'safe for conventional war'. There are few lessons so clear in history as this: only the combination of conventional forces and nuclear forces have ensured peace in Europe.

But every aspect of America's engagement in Europe—military, political, and economic—must be complementary, and one place where they all come together is in the Conference on Security and Cooperation in Europe—an organization of 35 states of Europe and North America. The CSCE is already a beacon for human rights and individual freedoms. Now, it must take on a broader role.

So the fourth task for a NATO summit is to reach common allied objectives for the future of the CSCE. It can help the victorious forces of democracy in Eastern Europe secure their revolutions, and—as they join the commonwealth of free nations—be assured a voice in the new Europe.

The CSCE should offer new guidelines for building free societies—including setting standards for truly free elections, adopting measures to strengthen the rule of law, and pointing the way in the needed but painful transition from centralized, command economies to free markets.

The CSCE can also provide a forum for political dialogue in a more united Europe. I agree with those who have called for regular consultations among senior representatives of the CSCE countries. We should consider whether new CSCE mechanisms can help mediate and settle disputes in Europe. I believe my allied colleagues and I should agree to take up these new ideas at a CSCE summit later this year, in conjunction with the signing of a CFE treaty.

(...)

US assurances given for Soviet concerns (at US–Soviet summit meeting in Washington, DC)

Statement by Secretary of State James Baker at the North Atlantic Council meeting, Turnberry, Scotland, 7 June 1990

Excerpts

(...)

The president reiterated our approach to unification and the Two-Plus-Four process. He said the peaceful unification of a democratic Germany was the realization of a long-held Western goal, and that it could be accomplished in a way that made all of Europe stronger and more secure. He stressed that Four Power rights should be terminated at the same time as unification—with no discriminatory constraints on German sovereignty and no singularization of a united, democratic Germany. President Bush also assured President Gorbachev that no one wanted to isolate the Soviets. But the Soviets' own policies on Germany could well have this effect if the Soviets were to take negative stands on the external aspects of unification. In this event, their approach would put them in conflict with most European governments, East and West. The very logic of new thinking would be contradicted. It would be a lost opportunity for the Soviet Union to develop constructive relations with a united Germany and the other democracies of Eastern, Central, and Western Europe.

We laid out nine assurances that we and others have offered and which we believe respond to many Soviet concerns. *First*, we are committed to follow-on CFE negotiations for all of Europe, which would also cover forces in the central region of Europe. *Second*, we have agreed to advance SNF negotiations to begin once the CFE treaty is signed. *Third*, Germany will reaffirm its commitments neither to produce nor to possess nuclear, biological, and chemical weapons. *Fourth*, NATO is conducting a comprehensive strategic review of both conventional and nuclear force requirements and strategy to fit the changed circumstances.

Fifth, NATO forces will not be extended to the former territory of the GDR for a transition period. *Sixth*, the Germans have agreed to a transition period for Soviet forces leaving the GDR. *Seventh*, Germany will make firm commitments on its borders, making clear that the territory of a unified Germany will comprise only the FRG, GDR, and Berlin. *Eighth*, the CSCE process will be strengthened. *Ninth*, Germany has made it clear that it will seek to resolve economic issues in a way that can support perestroika.

While Gorbachev was reassured by these points, German membership in NATO—and the Soviet position in Europe after unification—remained his major concern. President Bush stressed that a unified, democratic Germany would pose no threat to Soviet security and that Germany's membership in NATO was a factor for stability and security in Europe. He reiterated his support for Germany's full membership in NATO, including participation in its integrated military structures. He said that Germany must enjoy the right, as stipulated in the Helsinki Final Act, to choose freely its own alliance and security arrangements. Gorbachev seemed to accept this point.

We can and should be prepared to meet reasonable Soviet concerns. But we cannot acquiesce in an effort to block a full return to Germany sovereignty or to use ostensible security concerns over Germany as a surrogate for weakening the alliance.

(...)

The USA welcomes Soviet acceptance of Germany in NATO

Statement by President George Bush, Washington, DC, 16 July 1990

I welcome President Gorbachev's statement, at his press conference with Chancellor Kohl, accepting a united Germany's right to choose to remain a member of NATO. This comment demonstrates statesmanship and strengthens efforts to build enduring relationships based on cooperation. It can be seen as a response, perhaps in part, to the outcome of the NATO Summit in London, where the alliance displayed its readiness to adapt to the new realities in Europe and reach out to former adversaries in the East.

Five months ago, in February, Chancellor Kohl and I agreed that a united Germany should remain a full member of the North Atlantic Alliance, including its military structures. East German Prime Minister de Maizière joins us in supporting continued German membership in NATO. The Helsinki Final Act guarantees Germany's right to make this choice, and we think this solution is in the best interests of all the countries of Europe, including the Soviet Union.*

---

* Soviet acceptance was expressed during the Gorbachev–Kohl press conference in Zheleznovodsk (16 July 1990). The agreement reached between the Soviet Union and the FRG can be found in section XIX—Documents on unification

II. Soviet documents

Interview given by President Mikhail Gorbachev to *Pravda*, following talks with Hans Modrow and Helmut Kohl, Moscow, February 1990

Pravda: Our newspaper is continuing to receive letters from our readers asking for explanations regarding the German unification issue. Diverse opinions have been expressed in this respect in the West and in the Soviet Union, including those on the results of your meeting with Chancellor Helmut Kohl. Would you comment on this?

Gorbachev: The issue is very important indeed, being among the overriding ones in modern international politics. I would single out two aspects here.

The first is the Germans' right to unity. We have never denied them this right. And I would like to remind you that even right after the war, which brought our people both legitimate pride in the victory and immeasurable grief, together with a natural hatred toward those who had brought about this suffering, the Soviet Union was opposed to the partitioning of Germany. The idea was not ours, and we are not responsible for the path events took later, during the cold war.

Let me add to this that even after the emergence of the two German states, the Soviet Government, together with the German Democratic Republic, continued to uphold the principle of German unity. In 1950, the USSR supported the GDR's proposal for restoring single German statehood.

On March 10, 1952, the Soviet Government put forward a plan for the unification of Germany into a single democratic and neutral state. The West rejected that proposal, too. At a foreign ministers' conference in Berlin in 1954 we suggested again the creation of a united demilitarized Germany. And once more we were given the cold shoulder.

A year later, on January 15, 1955, the Soviet Government proposed the creation of a united Germany with a freely elected government, with which a peace treaty would be signed. That proposal was also left unanswered.

In 1957–1958, a proposal for the establishment of a German confederation, put forward by the GDR and actively backed by the Soviet Union, wasn't even considered. Another Soviet proposal followed in 1959 at a conference of the foreign ministers of the four Powers. It was for a peace treaty with a single, united Germany which, though not a part of any military–political alliance, would have a certain military potential. The result was the same as before.

Even when concluding the Moscow Treaty, the USSR did not rule out ending Germany's division some time in the future. One illustration here is that our Government accepted the 'Letter on German Unity', which had been submitted by Brandt and Scheel at the signing of the Treaty.

These are the facts as they stand.

As you see, the issue is nothing new to us. We proceed from the premise—and I have had many an occasion to say this both in public and in my contacts with German politicians—that history decided there would be two German states, and it will also decide which form of statehood the German nation will finally adopt. And history has suddenly accelerated its pace. In these conditions we have affirmed once again that the Germans themselves should decide on the course, the forms and time-frame of their unification. This was also discussed in meetings with Hans Modrow and shortly afterwards with Helmut Kohl. But this is just one aspect of the matter, and our meetings covered more than that.

Pravda: What in particular?

Gorbachev: First of all, the fact that the unification of Germany concerns not only the Germans. With all respect for their national right to take this step, the prevailing situation makes it impossible to imagine that the Germans will come to terms and then let all others merely endorse the decisions made by them. There are some fundamental matters which the international community is entitled to know about and which must leave no room for ambiguity.

It should likewise be made clear right from the start that neither the process of rapprochement between the FRG and the GDR nor a united Germany should represent a threat to or harm the national interests of their neighbors or anybody else for that matter. And, of course, any encroachment upon the borders of other states should be ruled out.

In addition to the inviolability of the post-war borders, which is most important, the war also had other consequences. Nobody has rescinded the responsibility of the four Powers; only they themselves can take this step. There is still no peace treaty with Germany. It is this treaty that can finally determine Germany's status in Europe in terms of international law.

Security has been maintained for a long time by the existence of two military–political alliances—the Warsaw Treaty Organization and NATO. Prerequisites for forming a fundamentally new security system in Europe are only just emerging now. Therefore, these alliances retain their role, although this role is being radically modified as the armed confrontation decreases, the military component of security diminishes and political aspects of the two blocs' activities increasingly come to the fore.

Consequently, the reunification of Germany should take account of these realities, namely, the inadmissibility of disrupting the military–strategic balance of these two international organizations. There should be complete clarity on this issue.

And the last thing. It follows from what has been said above that the process of German unification is inseparably linked and must be synchronized with the main direction of the all-European process, i.e. the formation of a fundamentally new structure of European security which will replace the one based on military–political blocs.

Pravda: Foreign ministers agreed in Ottawa on a mechanism for discussing the German issue with the participation of the Soviet Union, the United States, Britain, France, the FRG and the GDR. How is the role of this mechanism conceived?

Gorbachev: Indeed, the question is one of a definite format, for discussing the German issue by the six afore-said states. Incidentally, the idea of such a procedure was born in Moscow and Western capitals simultaneously and independently of each other. We spoke about this with Hans Modrow and then with Helmut Kohl. Any references to 'priorities' seem hardly appropriate here.

The legal basis of this mechanism is linked with the results of the war and the four Powers' responsibility for Germany's future role in the world. At the same time, it takes account of the great changes that have taken place since then in Europe and the world, and in the two German states themselves, and therefore includes them in the formula of this mechanism, conventionally designated as 'two plus four'.

The task is to discuss in a comprehensive and step-by-step manner all the external aspects of German reunification to prepare its inclusion in the all-European process and to consider the fundamentals of the future peace treaty with Germany.

The effectiveness of such consultations, and the authority they command, depend on the degree of trust and openness between all the parties involved. Naturally, sovereign states can engage in any contacts, including on the German issue, on a bilateral or any other basis. But we resolutely reject an approach where three or four parties initially arrange things and then inform the other participants of their decision. This is unacceptable.

Pravda: Isn't there an element of discrimination against other countries that also took part in the war?

Gorbachev: A legitimate question. It is exactly for this reason that, without belittling the historical right of the four Powers, we link the 'two plus four' mechanism with the all-European process and treat with understanding the special interest of other countries left out of this formula, thus recognizing their legitimate right to protect their national interests. I refer primarily to Poland: the inviolability of its post-war borders, like the borders of other states, must be guaranteed. Only an international legal act can provide such a guarantee.

Pravda: What do you think about the certain anxiety being felt among Soviet people and also other European peoples with regard to the prospect of the emergence of a united German state in the heartland of Europe?

Gorbachev: This concern is understandable both historically and psychologically, although there is no denying that the German people learned lessons from Hitler's rule and World War II. New generations have grown up in both German states. Their view of Germany's role in the world is different from the one that prevailed over the past hundred years or so, and particularly during the Nazi period.

It is certainly important that the whole world has been told on more than one occasion, and not only by the public of West Germany and the German Democratic Republic, but also by officials of the two countries, that war will never again emanate from German soil. Helmut Kohl has an even more binding interpretation of this: Only peace should come from German soil. He said this during the conversation we had.

Be that as it may, no one has any right to ignore the negative aspect of Germany's past. In particular, we cannot fail to consider people's memory of war, its horrors and losses. Therefore, it is also very important that the Germans, in deciding the question of unification, should be conscious of their responsibility and of the fact that not only the interests but also the feelings of other peoples must be respected.

This applies particularly to our country, to the Soviet people. They have an inalienable right to expect, and must do everything in their power to ensure, that our country will not sustain any kind of moral, political or economic damage from German unification and that the long-nurtured 'design' of history will in the long run be realized. History made us neighbors. It has linked our people by ties and profound mutual interests, and has made our destinies cross, sometimes in tragic circumstances. In this new age, history gives us a chance to start trusting each other and cooperate fruitfully.

Pravda: How do you view the agreement made in Ottawa to reduce Soviet and US troops in Central Europe to 195, 000?

Gorbachev: I regard it as an important and positive step. This proposal, made by US President George Bush, has been realized in the improved atmosphere of the international situation and of Soviet–US relations, which were given a new strong impetus as a result of the Malta meeting. George Bush's proposal is in line with the Vienna talks on the reduction of armed forces and conventional armaments in Europe.

Therefore, having thoroughly studied it, we responded favorably, and we even came out with a more radical option: the limit of 195, 000 men to apply not only to Central Europe, but to all of Europe outside the Soviet

Union. But at the same time we said that the President's option also suited us.

As you are aware, we have proposed that all troops be recalled within their national boundaries by 1995–1996, and that all foreign military bases be eliminated by the year 2000. Negotiations about the withdrawal of our troops from Hungary and Czechoslovakia are being conducted with their Governments.

In short, the agreements about the reduction of the US and Soviet military presence in Central Europe is fully in keeping with the positive trends of international development and it is promoting peace.

Pravda: To implement the agreement, the Soviet Union will have to make greater cuts of its troops than the United States. Besides that, the United States will keep in Europe, outside the central part, some 30, 000 more men. Will this not affect the balance of forces and our security?

Gorbachev: No, it will not. But this question requires a more detailed answer.

No doubt, we are calculating the balance of military potentials. But the traditional notions of ensuring security mostly through building up military force have been relegated to the past. The new character of interstate dialogue and the stability of the negotiating process have given political factors much greater weight in this area, too. The forces involved in European and international politics are so powerful that real military danger has decreased considerably, and a fundamentally new system of international security is taking shape.

I believe that the Soviet–US arrangement makes it much easier to work out an agreement in Vienna which can be signed at a European meeting at the end of the year.

As to the military aspect of the matter, which we have thoroughly analyzed, and taking into account the military–political situation today, the reduction of armed forces outside the boundaries of our country will not weaken our defenses. They are sufficient to ensure our security.

English translation from the Soviet magazine *Vestnik: Soviet Diplomacy Today* (Soviet Ministry for Foreign Affairs), April 1990, pp. 41–42.

On Germany

Statement by the Soviet Foreign Ministry Collegium,
Moscow, 24 February 1990

A session of the USSR Foreign Ministry collegium took place today. It examined a broad circle of questions linked to the development of the situation in Europe.

The USSR Foreign Ministry collegium considered it necessary to make the following statement on the results of the discussion of the 'German question':

'Recently in the discussion that has been taking place concerning the complicated set of questions linked to the possible unification of the two German states, the question of what the military and political status of a united Germany should be has come to the forefront.

Interest in this aspect of the problem is understandable since fundamental questions of security on the European Continent are indeed involved here. Less understandable are those prescriptions some countries in the West are bringing forward. They lead to the inclusion of a united Germany in NATO. Moreover this is presented in such a way that such a variant corresponds to the interests of the Soviet Union since, they say, a possible future united Germany cannot be left to its own devices without establishing some kind of external control over it.

It is not acceptable to the Soviet side that someone is trying to determine on its behalf what the essence of Soviet security is and what the best way to guarantee it is. The Soviet Union in this respect has its own conceptions. In no way do variants envisioning the membership of a united Germany in NATO fit into these conceptions. It is clear to everyone, including those who are not very knowledgeable in military issues, that their implementation would in contemporary conditions lead to an unacceptable disruption of the military strategic balance between the Warsaw Pact and NATO. M. S. Gorbachev indicated this circumstance quite definitely in his answers to the questions of a PRAVDA correspondent on 21 February, where our principled approach to German affairs as a whole is laid out.

A determining factor from our point of view is that, in the process of building German unity, a point of discussion should be that Germany should cease, for once and for all, to be a place from where there could be a threat of war. This is precisely required by the Potsdam agreements, the UN Charter, and the security interests of European, and not only European, people.

Another issue of a fundamental order also arises. It is well known that an accord was recently reached in Ottawa to the effect that the FRG and GDR foreign ministers would soon discuss the external aspects of building German unity with the foreign ministers of France, Great Britain, the Soviet Union, and the United States, including issues of the security of neighboring states. A machinery was thereby defined within whose framework solutions should also be found to a question of such indisputable priority as that of the military-political status of a united Germany. In consideration of this it would be, at the least, unproductive to run ahead, and especially, to attempt to impose upon the other side, even before the meeting of ministers, any models that disregard the interests of its security. We must even now dispose ourselves to practical work and a search for solutions that would ensure genuine security and stability in Europe. The Soviet Union is in favor of embarking upon this within the framework of the machinery of "the six" which has been set up without delay, particularly on the level of experts.'

Too fast and too slow

Interview given by President Mikhail Gorbachev, following talks with Prime Minister Hans Modrow,
Moscow, 6 March 1990

Question: What is the Soviet attitude to the idea of a reunited Germany joining NATO in any form?

Answer: We cannot agree to that. It is out of the question. In our opinion, the reunification of the two German states is a natural process, and, as I have said many times before, history itself will decide what is to be done about the reality it has created for us. Today history has quickened its pace, so to speak. And, I think, it is clear that the interests of the Germans should be taken into account, and we agree with this. But the Germans and all who are concerned with this process should also consider the natural interests of the neighbors of the two German states, and of all

Europeans. Considering that the German issue is a major one in world politics, the interests of the entire world community should also be taken into account. This is a question that must not be oversimplified. It is inadmissible to act hastily, 'in a rush', when we are dealing with crucial problems affecting such fundamental things as the interests of nations, of the Germans themselves, of Europeans, and of the entire world for that matter. Such a method is not suitable when we are considering a matter that is of world importance. A phased solution is required, and the GDR people, too, I think, have an interest in such an approach. They want to know their future, what their fate and the fate of all generations that live and work in the republic will be. It is also in the interests of the Germans in the FRG. They want to know what unification will mean for them, too. It seems that the industrialists and businessmen are thinking it over. This is a big problem, indeed. Therefore, from the domestic and foreign policy point of view, and from the point of view of the real state of affairs in the two German states, I believe that stage-by-stage unification and a carefully weighed approach are wise. This process could be merged with the general process of European unification which, incidentally, we should perhaps speed up. If these two processes proceeded at a similar pace, it would remove any concern which might be felt otherwise. And the people are beginning to show some concern regarding this matter. In particular, there is a lot of talk now about the postwar frontiers.

Chancellor Helmut Kohl has made some corrections in his stance on this issue in recent days. I welcome this, because manoeuvring and vagueness in such fundamental matters do not make for a serious policy. People should be made clear on all these issues. That is the first question. The second one is: Where will a united Germany be? I think that if the European and Vienna processes go on, if we have Helsinki-2, and if NATO and the Warsaw Pact transform themselves from military into political organizations, there will be no need to bargain over the issue of where a reunited Germany should be. A spokesman of the leadership of a Western country asked me recently: 'Why on earth are you concerned over this matter, Mr. Gorbachev? The Germans are different now'. Yes, the Germans in the East and West alike want peace and have done a lot to that end. All this is true. This

being the case, I suggested to him that they enter the Warsaw Treaty, if this made no difference at all. His reaction was immediate: 'No, why should they?', and that made things quite clear indeed. So let us weigh every solution, calculate, that is, do things with responsibility.

Today, as before, if you remember, I stressed that the current changes in the world and in Europe will bring us a new Europe and new relations among people, states, and nations. So we must not miss this chance. But at the same time this calls for great responsibility. We should not destroy what we have created through so much effort. Because everything going on now is a result of joint efforts expended over decades. There have been not only positive but also negative results, and we have learned lessons from that. And now that a historic chance has presented itself, we should act with great responsibility. So this is my extensive answer to your brief question. This is important to all of us. We shall take an active and constructive part in the current processes, but we shall not allow any undermining of the positive tendencies that have emerged in Europe and are gaining strength, including the renewal of relations among the European nations. This is the starting point for us.

Q: You said that current processes in Germany were very complicated and called for a responsible approach on the part of all. Is there, in your opinion, enough responsibility in Germany today, before the elections?

A: There are some things, you know, that are delicate, and there must be no interference in internal affairs. Our position is firm: not to interfere in the internal affairs of other states. This does not mean, however, that we are indifferent to everything. On the contrary: we are in favor of some processes and regard other processes negatively. But in the long run the people themselves will decide. So, watching the election campaign from Moscow, I see that someone is in a hurry, that someone wants to impose his views and assessments on others. I also see attempts to bring pressure to bear on the Germans in the GDR in order to serve certain party interests, to suit certain political calculations. Your question provoked this answer. I hope people in the FRG and the GDR will not regard it as interference on my part in the election campaign. But I know that many FRG visitors are arriving in the GDR and meddling in its affairs, as if the GDR had already lost its sovereignty and were no longer an independent state recognized by the world community. All this is going on there. But let the Germans themselves decide what is right or wrong for them. I believe the people themselves should think carefully before deciding who they should give their preference to, because it is especially important at this stage that there should be people in parliament, in the government, in all bodies of power, capable of acting with responsibility, in cooperation with all the governments and nations concerned.

Q: How do you visualize future relations between the Soviet Union and a reunited Germany? Will they be of a different kind from those which existed with the FRG and the GDR?

A: I think our relations will change, of course. I have just expressed my opinion on this matter to members of Hans Modrow's Government. I think these relations have good prospects. But, again, this depends on how we cooperate now. One approach could help strengthen and expand cooperation, while another could create suspicion and have negative effects.

I think our bilateral relations would benefit if responsibility was displayed on both sides. Our contacts with the GDR were, and are, the widest and on the largest scale among the socialist countries. And our relations with the FRG are the widest among the West European countries. This in itself is very important. We hope that once unification is under way—and it will concern every sphere of activity, including the economic—these interests will not suffer, either with respect to a united Germany, or to the Germans themselves, or to us.

Speaking about relations between Germany and Russia, they have a long record, as you know. There were periods when lessons had to be learnt. We cannot forget what happened when the fascists came to power in Germany and what that led to for our two peoples—for the Soviet people and for the Germans. We made appropriate conclusions, took the road of peace, began restructuring relations on a new basis and started to cooperate for our mutual benefit and in the interest of peace—all this is a very important achievement for our peoples and states. This should be preserved. We, for our part, will do all we can to this end. Since there

are mutual interests, reciprocity is required. The prospects ahead are good, I think. I see that the Germans in the FRG, businessmen in particular, display a great interest in pooling intellectual and research efforts and the technological resources of our two countries. This could serve our peoples and Europe well. In this sense, I am an optimist.

English translation taken from the Soviet magazine *Vestnik: Soviet Diplomacy Today* (Soviet Ministry for Foreign Affairs), April 1990, pp. 31–32.

Europe: a generation's mission*
Article by Eduard Shevardnadze, *Izvestia*, 30 May 1990

The changes that have taken place in Europe are today posing politicians a question: What next?

For decades people used to talk about the dangers of confrontation between the two military-political alliances, the high price of the cold war for Europeans, the need to end the division of the continent, German unity, the progress of the Helsinki process, and the strengthening of security and cooperation.

Now all this appears in a different light, in different dimensions, and opens up formerly inconceivable prospects, but it also creates new problems.

That is why, amid the torrent of euphoric statements, assessments, and commentaries, doubts can be heard—as to whether we will find ourselves back on the old road leading to the rebirth of rivalry among nation states and a repetition of the mistakes that more than once led Europe to tragedy.

I do not think this will happen, provided that we do not forget the past and that we remember our obligation and duty to think and work to prevent hitches in our common progress and to make full use of the opportunities that history has given us.

I am confident that it will not happen, provided that politicians have sufficient ability to analyze the situation realistically and critically and to grasp the pressing need to reinterpret many familiar ideas on the foundations of European security and cooperation.

There must be no delay here, especially in light of the processes associated with the building of German unity.

The alternative, as M. S. Gorbachev stressed in his interview for TIME Magazine, has already become clear: It is the institutionalization of all-European development and the creation of totally new structures on an all-European basis, with, of course, the active participation of the United States and Canada.

I would be naive to suppose that in the new circumstances, the old political and organizational instruments will suffice. It will certainly be necessary to create a structure that will oppose the forces that are working to break up the still fragile European community [obshchnost].

Fortunately we already have some elements of this structure. There is the Final Act of the Conference on Security and Cooperation in Europe and the associated accords, rules, procedures, and standards.

The Helsinki package of principles and agreements is a living, active political organism with enormous potential for evolutionary development.

Its main strength lies in the principles of consensus—not simply proclaimed consensus, but actual functioning consensus. During difficult periods the European countries have succeeded in finding mutually acceptable options in virtually all spheres of interstate relations.

Consensus is the only foundation on which it is possible to build collective—as we say, or cooperative, in the terminology of some of our partners—all-European security structures. Given this approach, nothing can be imposed and no one's interests will be flouted or disregarded.

The principle of common consent is not easy to adhere to—really new thinking is needed here, but then the outcome is a lasting, reliable decision that is strictly observed by all parties.

In the new conditions of the assertion of high standards of democracy, to conduct international affairs in any other way is impossible and will not work.

Why are all-European security structures needed? Because the bloc system was designed for a scenario of direct, face-to-face confrontation between the sides' armed forces—and confrontation at an ever higher qualitative level of means of mutual destruction.

Behind the talk about the blocs' defensive nature there has always been another reality—the orientation of their armed forces toward the conduct of offensive military operations.

The blocs sprang up as a consequence of the cold war. They cannot remain the same when the cold war has become a thing of the past. The Warsaw Pact was the first to react to this—both through large-scale unilateral reductions in troops and armaments in the member countries and through the transition to a defensive doctrine as a whole, as a bloc, and the building of its armed forces on the basis of the principles of nonoffensive defense and reasonable sufficiency.

This process is developing in the West too. Thus the communique of the NATO Military Planning Committee adopted on 23 May this year says:

'We have decided to undertake a review of NATO military strategy and bring our defensive tasks into line with the new, developing situation in future. We will have to adjust our concepts and operational doctrines'.

The North Atlantic alliance has abandoned the goal of an annual three-percent increase in military spending and adopted measures to reduce the level of combat readiness of certain of its permanent forces. NATO has dropped the program for modernization of American tactical nuclear missiles in Europe and expressed readiness to enter into talks on the limitation and reduction of this type of weapon.

We will, of course, watch carefully how these intentions are realized in NATO's practical activity. But another objective necessity also arises: to take a fresh look to see whether the foundations exist today for establishing relations of partnership between the blocs. They cannot go on indefinitely confronting and standing up to each other!

In the new situation, the question of security guarantees for those European states that do not or will not belong to military blocs arises in a new way. Only new all-European security structures can give them such guarantees.

The real situation in Europe dictates the need to go over to the resolution of all aspects of the problem of security, disarmament, and confidence-building within the framework of forums of all 35 CSCE states.

A most important component of European security is the talks of the 23 and the 35 in Vienna. These talks cannot be conducted actively and productively without due attention being paid to them at political levels.

That is why political institutions of the all-European process should be created.

In our opinion, these should be:

– The Council (Assembly) of Greater Europe—a forum of the top leaders of all the CSCE member states. This would examine cardinal questions of European policy and formulate fundamental political principles and concrete decisions on a consensus basis.

Sessions of the Council (Assembly) would be held at least once every two years.

– The Committee (Council) of Foreign Ministers. It would prepare questions for examination at meetings of the top leaders and monitor the fulfilment of their decisions. The ministers would be responsible for leadership of other organs that might be created.

Obviously, between meetings of the top leaders and conferences of ministers, problems and situations could arise that would require examination at political levels.

Here it would help to set up 'triumvirates' ['troyki'] (the former, current, and future chairmen) of the leaders and ministers, endowed with mandates of some kind for holding urgent consultations.

For day-to-day needs, it would be worth coming to an agreement on the operation of a consultative machinery consisting of envoys of the 35 countries in the capital where the CSCE's permanent secretariat will be, with the minimum necessary number of experts and technical staffers.

In our view, it is important to create a center for ensuring stability in the military–political sphere throughout Europe as the first module of the future new security structures. It could comprise two organs: The first would tackle questions concerning the collection and dissemination of data on states' military activity and would help enhance its transparency. Its functions would also extend to questions of coordinating inspections, clarifying unclear or disputed situations, and preparing appropriate reports and recommendations for the foreign ministers' committee.

The second organ would concentrate on the task of solving crisis situations. It could dispatch good offices missions, mediate between sides, and assist in easing frictions and tension.

Of course, the activity of this center should fit in with the already existing Stockholm accords on confidence building and security measures and with other control and verification [kontrolnyye i verifikatsionnyye] procedures agreed at the Vienna talks.

We advocate the siting in Berlin of the center for prevention and solution of conflicts. This would be of considerable symbolic importance.

In our opinion, the question of establishing such a center could be agreed during preparations for the all-European summit meeting, with the meeting itself announcing the establishment of this organ.

It is well known that all participants in the future summit meeting have already agreed that it would discuss questions of the future Helsinki process in breadth.

It is obvious that the leaders of CSCE states will speak out firmly in support of the principles of democracy, free elections, political pluralism, and the multiparty system and will emphasize association and other aspects of the humanitarian and legal spheres.

We assume that the summit meeting at year's end will form a special group to prepare recommendations for coordinating the activity of already existing organizations dealing with the economy, the ecology, communications, and exchange of information and people.

Evidently, this will also require the creation of some new institutions; but the main point will be to make utmost use of the potential of the Council of Europe, the EC, the UN European Economic Commission, CMEA and its organs, the European Bank for Reconstruction and Development, the OECD, the European Free Trade Association, the Nordic Council, and other European organizations and associations in the West and the East alike.

It is understandable that we will attach special importance to synchronizing and interlinking the institutionalization of the Helsinki process and the building of German unity.

The fundamental questions associated with the external aspects of German unity will be examined, as already agreed, within the framework of the 'Two-Plus-Four' mechanism which has already been created especially for this purpose. It is already functioning and, as everyone agrees, it is not functioning badly. The results of its work and the accords which have been reached will be submitted to the meeting of top leaders from all European states.

Of course, 'the Six' still have to solve some very difficult questions, such as Germany's future military–political status.

The Soviet leadership's views on this problem were recently outlined yet again by M. S. Gorbachev at the joint news conference by the presidents of the USSR and France in Moscow.

An option must be sought here which would be acceptable to all and would take into account the interests of Germany, the Soviet Union, and others.

I would like to say the following in this context: We do not think that this question ought to be approached exclusively from today's positions, the positions of current realities. The situation here will not remain static. Therefore, the final settlement formula ought to be geared more toward the future than toward the present, let alone the past.

The determining factors when we decide on our position will be: first, the dynamics of changes in NATO's concepts and strategic doctrines and the degree of this bloc's transformation into a political–military rather than a military–political alliance.

Second, the pace and depth of the all-European process of disarmament and, naturally, the Bundeswehr's military parameters.

Third, the speed and scale of the creation of all-European structures and institutions, primarily in the security sphere.

We would like to think that we will soon be able to obtain a clearer picture of what could be expected along these three avenues.

If the process of building German unity were to be organically and properly incorporated in the multifaceted European security context, a solution to what now appear to be its burdensome aspects could be found without detriment to anyone.

Only one aspect of the need to create all-European structures and institutions touches upon the problem of German unity.

An incalculably more significant goal of this large-scale enterprise concerns the future stability and predictability of the European situation and solves the task of preventing a new split and fragmentation of Europe.

All states are certainly interested in this, because peace, tranquility, and mutually advantageous cooperation in a Europe marching along the path of integration and creation of single spaces—in security, the legal sphere, humanitarian cooperation, and economic and ecological collaboration—will ultimately depend on it.

I would like to say that the submission of the question of institutionalizing the all-

European process and creating new security structures within its framework is widely supported.

A nucleus of practical proposals and conceptual approaches is already taking shape. It is gratifying that our proposals in this regard follow along the tracks of other countries' ideas, that there are many similar and close elements.

We welcomed with interest President F. Mitterrand's idea of a European confederation, U.S. President Bush's idea of an integral democratic Europe, Foreign Minister H.-D. Genscher's idea of a new peace order in Europe, Foreign Minister M. Eyskens' idea of a European confederative community, Prime Minister T. Mazowiecki's idea of a European Cooperation Council, Foreign Minister J. Dienstbier's idea of a European Security Commission, and others. Despite all their nuances and differences, they are imbued with concern for Europe's peaceful future.

They are all in active political circulation.

We exchanged opinions on questions of all-European building with U.S. Secretary of State J. Baker; with Foreign Ministers H.-D. Genscher of the FRG, R. Dumas of France, D. Hurd of Britain, and De Michelis of Italy; and with other colleagues.

Their response is positive and promising. We consulted at the working level with representatives of a number of other West and East European states and encountered understanding by them.

It must be said that other states' politicians have also expressed quite a few original ideas about ways to further develop and improve the Helsinki process. They contain valuable rational elements and promising notions.

It has been agreed that experts from all 35 CSCE states will begin consultations on all these questions in the first half of July.

Our delegation will actively and constructively work to find consensus.

I would like to end on the following idea: The United Nations Organization emerged after the end of World War II. The task of modern diplomacy is to draw a line beneath the cold war by laying firm foundations for the future all-European home.

---

* Eduard Shevardnadze further developed this concept in his article 'Towards a greater Europe—the WTO and NATO in a renewing Europe', *NATO's Sixteen Nations,* June 1990, pp. 18–22.

III. British documents

Great Britain and German unification*

Speech by Prime Minister Margaret Thatcher at the Königswinter Conference, Cambridge, 29 March 1990

Excerpts

(...)

German unification

Mr Chairman, this year's conference is being held at the moment when the German people's aspiration for unity is soon to be realised.

None of us can fail to recognise how much that means to the German people themselves—any possible doubts have been dispelled by the outcome of the East German elections. As that unity draws near, I would like for a moment to recall the very considerable part that Britain has played in it.

From very early on after the war, we concluded that a prosperous democratic Germany was essential. We promptly put in hand the process of reconstruction in the British zone: and in the first year alone, over one million tons of food was delivered from Britain, even though we ourselves were still living with food rationing. During the Berlin blockade, the Royal Air Force flew over 60,000 sorties into Berlin delivering essential supplies. Later, in 1954, it was Britain's proposal to hold the London Conference which paved the way for the Paris Agreements and the Federal Republic's entry into NATO and the WEU.

We also then entered into our commitment to keep a specific and substantial number of British forces in Germany, a commitment which we have honoured over the years, despite the heavy cost across the exchanges. The British Army of the Rhine and Royal Air Force Germany remain in the Federal Republic, the visible evidence of our commitment to Germany's defence and the defence of Western Europe as a whole.

It was NATO's staunchness in defence through the difficult years that brought about the great changes in the Soviet Union. It led them to the realisation that the West would *not* be intimidated and that a policy of confrontation would gain them nothing. And it was this, combined with Mr Gorbachev's vision and courage, which led in turn to the opening of the Berlin Wall and the opportunity for Germany to achieve its unity. I recite those facts, Mr Chairman, because I think it important to underline that Britain, at least as much as other countries, has been instrumental in creating the conditions in which German unity could be achieved in freedom.

I am not, of course, suggesting that our relations with our German friends throughout those 40 years have been a one-way process. The Federal Republic has been the staunchest of allies in NATO, and we shall always be grateful for the strong support we received from successive German governments for our membership of the European Community.

But just as the conditions for German unification were created by the efforts and resolve of many different countries, so the *consequences* of that unification also affect us all. We are all entitled to express our view on the implications for NATO, for the European Community, for Four Power rights and responsibilities and for Germany's neighbours and their borders. Now we *have* established a clear framework, which we did not have before, within which those consequences will be examined and worked out.

We have the Two-Plus-Four Group: we have discussions in NATO and the prospect of a Foreign Ministers' Meeting: we have the Meeting of European Community Heads of Government on 28 April: and we have the firm commitment that Poland will be involved in discussions about its borders, which will be guaranteed by a legally-binding treaty.

All that is a great step forward and I am very grateful to Chancellor Kohl for his cooperation.

Mr Chairman, we cannot put aside history, it would be absurd to try to do so.

We must try to learn the lessons of past peace settlements.

The Americans must not go home.

Nor must Britain retreat from the Continent.

The security interests of all those concerned must be taken into account.

No-one must feel threatened, humiliated or resentful.

Above all, we must ensure that a Germany
– *rooted* in NATO and the European Community,
– *content* within its borders,
– and *democratic* in its government, strengthens the security and the stability of Europe as a whole.

The future of NATO

Your Conference with its theme 'Germany and Europe—undivided' will deal with all these issues. I shall pick out only two of them for the remainder of my remarks this evening. The first concerns Germany and NATO. Experience has taught us very clearly that we need the collective security which NATO provides, together with the presence of American forces in Europe alongside our own, to safeguard stability and security at a time of uncertainty and change.

If there had been something of that sort in the 1930s, we would never have had the Second World War. NATO has given us 40 years of peace and security, and I believe we shall need it just as much in the future—irrespective of what happens to the Warsaw Pact.

That does not mean that we expect *everything* to go on just as before. If the conventional force reduction talks in Vienna succeed, then there will be a significant reduction in the threat currently facing NATO and we shall be able to reduce conventional forces accordingly.

If in time the Soviet Union withdrew its military presence completely from Eastern Europe, 'then we could probably afford to reduce our ready forces even further. But these reductions must be carried out in a co-ordinated and disciplined way in NATO, not in some wild scramble.

As far as the United Kingdom is concerned, we may need to adapt our commitment under the Brussels Treaty, so that we can make *some* reductions in the level of British forces in Germany—although I believe the needs of collective defence will require us, like the United States and France, to continue to keep sizeable forces there.

We may also need to adjust NATO's strategy in some respects. We shall not be afraid to consider these options and discuss them

openly, always preserving the basic structure of NATO.

I can foresee, too, that NATO may be able to reduce further the total number of its short-range nuclear weapons in Europe—and we have already made substantial reductions in recent years. The comprehensive concept which we agreed at last year's NATO summit set out the conditions on which these reductions could be made. But we shall need to retain adequate nuclear forces, both here in the United Kingdom and based forward in the continent of Europe as at present.

There are therefore three essentials for our continued security:
– that a united Germany should remain part of NATO;
– that American and other stationed forces should remain in Germany, although we hope in reduced numbers;
– and that NATO should continue to have nuclear weapons based in Germany.

There will of course have to be special arrangements for the territory of the GDR, and these must take account of the Soviet Union's natural security concerns. That will mean accepting that Soviet forces will remain there for a transitional period.

But there must be no doubt that Germany will be a part of NATO: this offers the best security for Europe as a whole. Your strong and categoric assurances on that essential point, Chancellor Kohl, have been a tremendous encouragement.

Building on the CSCE

Alongside NATO—but *not* as an alternative to it—we need to find a way to reinforce democracy and human rights throughout Europe, while at the same time involving the Soviet Union and the Eastern European countries fully in the debate on Europe's future security.

We have already a framework in the Helsinki Agreements: and they of course have the particular advantage of bringing in fully the United States and Canada.

But we must try to give them greater substance and permanence. And the time to do that is surely the forthcoming CSCE summit, which we shall hold later this year.

I am going to set out tonight some proposals which could make that summit a major step towards the creation of a great alliance for democracy, which would stretch from the Atlantic to the Urals and beyond.

First, the summit should strengthen democracy by agreeing a new provision setting out the conditions to be fulfilled for elections to be considered as truly free. Britain and the United States put forward an outline proposal, including a suggestion for independent observers, at the Paris meeting last June. We want to see a commitment to free elections become one of the new CSCE principles.

Second, we should do the same for the rule of law and human rights. The CSCE countries should set out the essential principles for a sound legal system, and should all commit themselves to respect and uphold the rule of law according to these principles.

Third, we should extend political consultation through the CSCE, as a way of involving the widest possible number of countries in discussions about Europe's future. There should be meetings at the level of foreign ministers twice a year: there might also be a procedure for convening extraordinary meetings in times of tension or crisis.

Fourth, we should consider giving the CSCE a conciliation role in disputes rather on the lines that the GATT has in the trade field. The CSCE could offer its good offices in any dispute between two or more of its members, for instance on matters concerning minority rights.

Fifth, the summit should add to the Helsinki principles the right to private property, the freedom to produce, buy and sell without undue government interference. These rights are fundamental to a free and prosperous society. Their importance is now acknowledged throughout Eastern Europe and private property has just been made legal in the Soviet Union. The CSCE should reflect and encourage this.

Sixth, the summit should solemnly reaffirm the original Helsinki commitments on European *frontiers*: that frontiers are inviolable, and can only be changed by peaceful means and by agreement, in accordance with international law.

Finally, the summit should not only sign the CFE agreement which we hope will be ready by then, but look ahead to the next steps in arms control in Europe.

If we can agree on these new principles and procedures, the Helsinki Accords will be strengthened for the future—and let us remember how well they have served Europe

over the *past* fifteen years. Without them, we in the West would not have had a locus to insist on observance of basic human rights in the Communist countries: and those groups of courageous people who formed Helsinki monitoring groups to insist on respect for their rights would never have been able to play a role in Eastern Europe's peaceful democratic revolution.

Let me stress that I do *not* believe that the CSCE can in any way take on a defence role. That must remain the task of NATO and WEU. What it *can* and *should* do is strengthen democracy, the rule of law and human rights. If we can get to a stage when they are practised and observed throughout Europe, that in itself will be an enormous contribution to Europe's security.

We shall be putting forward the proposals which I have made tonight more formally over the next few weeks.

Conclusion

Mr Chairman, I know you will all be eager as I am to hear what Chancellor Kohl has to say. May I just wish you well in your work at this Conference, held against the background of the most exciting changes since the war. I will conclude with some words of the poet Schiller, which describe what we all feel about the great events taking place in East Germany, and in Eastern Europe and the Soviet Union as a whole:

Das Alte stürzt, es ändert sich die Zeit und neues Leben blüht aus den Ruinen.

The old falls, time changes and new life blossoms out of the ruins.

---

* For the corresponding speech delivered by Helmut Kohl, Chancellor of the FRG, at the Königswinter Conference (Cambridge, 28 March 1990), see section V—FRG documents.

Vision of Britain in shaping the new global community

Speech by Prime Minister Margaret Thatcher,
Aspen, Colorado, 5 August 1990

Excerpts

(. . .)

We fight *hard* for what we believe in:

– a Europe based on willing cooperation between independent sovereign states;

– a Europe which is an expression of economic freedom, without which economic freedom could not endure;

– a Europe which rejects central control and its associated bureaucracy;

– a Europe which does not resort to protectionism but remains open to the outside world;

– and—of supreme importance—a Europe which always seeks the closest possible partnership with the United States.

(. . .)

Mr Chairman, what are the fundamental tenets of true democracy? For me they are:

– *first,* a sense of personal responsibility. People need to realise that they are not just pawns on a chessboard, to be moved around at the whim of politicians. They can influence their destiny by their own efforts.

– *second,* democracy means limitation of the powers of government and giving people the greatest possible freedom. In the end the strength of a society depends not on the big battalions, but on the foot-soldiers: on the willingness of ordinary men and women, who don't seek fame or glory or high office, to play an active part in their community, not as conscripts but as volunteers.

– *third,* democracy and freedom are about more than the ballot and universal suffrage. At the beginning of this tumultuous century, Britain rightly believed herself a free country. Yet we went into the First World War with only a 30 per cent franchise.

A strong rule of law is the essential underpinning of democracy. The steady growth of the common law over centuries; the process by which statute law is passed by an elected Parliament or Congress; the independence of the judiciary; these are as much the pillars of democracy as its parliamentary institutions.

And the *fourth* essential, Mr Chairman, is an economy based on market principles and a right to private property. Wealth is not created by regulation and instruction, but by ordinary enterprising people.

It's hard for those who have only experienced life in totalitarian societies to think in these terms, because it's outside anything they've ever known. That is why one sometimes wonders whether some of the countries trying to introduce economic reform have yet understood what a market economy is really about.

So the challenge of spreading democracy and the rule of law is an awesome one. But we must not be pessimistic. One can point to countries—Spain, Portugal, Chile, Nicaragua—where the transition from authoritarian rule to democracy has succeeded. And to those who suggest that some countries are too large for democracy, there is the remarkable example of India with its 700 million people, where democracy is well established.

Mr Chairman, it will take the united efforts of the West to shape a new global community, based on democracy, the rule of law and market principles. We need a plan of campaign. And I suggest these should be its main elements.

A European Magna Carta:

At the East–West summit of 35 nations to be held in the autumn I propose that *we should agree on a European Magna Carta* to entrench for *every* European citizen, including those of the Soviet Union, the basic rights which we in the West take for granted. We must enshrine for every individual:

Freedom of speech, of worship, of access to the law, of the market place.

Freedom to participate in genuinely democratic elections, to own property, to maintain nationhood, and freedom from fear of an overmighty state.

Europe's institutions:

Next we must bring the new democracies of Eastern Europe into closer association with the institutions of Western Europe.

I propose that the Community should declare unequivocally that it is ready to accept all the countries of Eastern Europe as members if they want to join, and when democracy has taken root and their economies are capable of sustaining membership. We can't say in one breath that they are part of Europe, and in the next our European Community club is so exclusive that we won't admit them.

It will be some time before they are ready for membership: so we are offering them intermediate steps such as Association Agreements. But the option of eventual membership should be clearly, openly and generously on the table. The European Community has reconciled antagonisms *within* Western Europe:

it should not be held to overcome divisions *between* East and West in Europe.

This does not mean that the further development of the existing community has to be put on ice. Far from it. The completion of the single market by 1992 will be an enormous change, one of the biggest since the community began in 1957. It should herald a fair and open Europe—and one which should be immensely attractive to the newly free peoples of Eastern Europe. The same is true of closer co-operation in foreign policy.

But if instead we set off down the path of giving more and more powers to highly centralised institutions, which are not democratically accountable, then we should be making it *harder* for the Eastern Europeans to join.

They have not thrown off central command and control in their own countries only to find them reincarnated in the European Community. With their new freedom their feelings of patriotism and national identity are flooding out again. Their newly restored parliaments are full of vitality. We must find a structure for the Community which accommodates their diversity and preserves their tradition, their institutions, their nationhood.

And we need to do this without introducing the concept of first and second class membership of the community, which would be divisive and defeat much of the purpose of bringing their countries into Europe.

The framework of economic freedom:

Mr Chairman, all the messages we are getting indicate that the Soviet Union and Eastern Europe desperately want to have the policies of economic freedom, but don't know how to acquire them.

Many of us are providing practical assistance through knowhow funds and joint ventures. But such is the scale of the problem that we shall need to devise new and more imaginative ways to help.

For example, we might identify a whole sector of the Soviet economy, such as transport and distribution or food processing or oil exploration or the banking system, and offer to help run it on market principles, to demonstrate what can be achieved.

After all the Soviet Union has natural wealth. It's not resources it lacks, but the capacity to turn them to advantage. One day the Soviet Union will be a highly prosperous country—and so will China— and it's not too

soon to be thinking how to bring them into the world economy.

But the most difficult step is for governments which have been accustomed to running a regimented economy to think in a different way.

If we can begin to associate them with the international institutions which have done so much to help ensure our *own* prosperity, in particular the GATT and the IMF, that could make it easier for them.

We might also bring the Soviet Union gradually into closer association with the economic summit. Britain will be hosting next year's meeting in London. If my colleagues agree, I would not be averse to taking a *first* step along that road on that occasion.

Defence in a just cause:

There is a further crucial point. None of this could be contemplated unless we in the West had been resolute to maintain a secure defence. The fact that our peoples were willing to bear the burdens, sustain the expense and brave the dangers of defence for over 40 years is a proof of how much they value liberty and justice.

We failed to do this after the First World War. Instead armies were disbanded, weapons laid aside, and American forces went home. The result was once again World War—war in Europe and war in the Pacific—and a whole generation paid a terrible price.

After the Second World War we were wiser. We threatened no one, but kept up our defences. We halted the great expansion of Communism. Today nations and people are free who would otherwise be in bondage were it not for our perseverance—and above all that of the United States.

But now, in the moment of success, it's wise to be cautious. History has seen too many false springs.

The Soviet Union remains a formidable military power. Even the Russian Republic on its own would be the largest country in the world, stretching from the Baltic to the Pacific across 11 time zones.

Moreover, with the spread of ballistic missiles and chemical weapons, it is all too likely we shall face ugly situations in other parts of the world.

We shall continue to need NATO. And that means we shall continue to need American forces in Europe—in your *own* interests as well as ours.

Do you remember some lines from T. S. Elliot's Chorus from the Rock?

'It is hard for those who live
near a police station
to believe in the triumph of
violence

Do you think that the faith has
conquered the world
and that lions no longer need
keepers?

Do you need to be told that
whatever *has* been, can
still be?

Mr Chairman, as we look to the future, there are other issues which call for a much higher level of international cooperation, more intensive than anything we have achieved so far: the spread of drugs, terrorism, intimidation, disease, a decaying environment. No country is immune from them.

Our ability to come together to stop or limit damage to the *world's environment* will be the greatest test of how far we can act as a world community.

Science is still feeling its way and some uncertainties remain. But we know that very high population growth is putting enormous pressure on the earth's resources. Primitive methods of agriculture are extending deserts and destroying tropical forests. As they disappear, nature's capacity to correct its own imbalances is seriously affected.

We know, too, that our industries and way of life have done severe damage to the ozone layer. And we know that, within the lifetime of our grandchildren, the surface temperature of the earth will be higher than at any time for 150, 000 years; the rate of change of temperature will be higher than in the last 10, 000 years; and the sea level will rise six times faster than has been seen in the last century.

The cost of doing nothing, of a policy of wait and see, will be much higher than those of taking preventative action *now* to stop the damage getting worse. And they will be counted not only in dollars, but in human misery as well. Spending on the environment is like spending on defence: if you don't do it in time, it may be too late.

Most of us have been brought up to give praise and thanks for the miracles of creation. But we cannot give thanks with our words, if

our deeds undermine the beauty of the world to which we are born.

The same lessons apply to the evil of *drugs*. We must use all means to warn young people of the blandishments which will be used to entice them into drug addiction. We must ram home that to succumb would utterly ruin their lives and devastate their families. The contemptible and callous men who prey upon the young for their own material gain must be hunted ruthlessly until they are brought to justice.

This problem is not limited to a handful of countries. There are now 40 million addicts world-wide and the number continues to rise.

We have to grapple with every aspect of the problem: the demand, the production, the money-laundering, the international networks.

Hard as we have tried, we are still far from success. There's only one way to attack the problem, wherever it occurs, and that is by bringing together all the resources and knowledge of each country to slay this dragon.

That goes for *terrorism* and intimidation too.

The terrorists fight with the weapons of war. We respond with the rule of law. The dice are loaded against the law-abiding and the innocent.

Terrorism will only be beaten when all civilised governments resolve that they will never harbour and give safe haven to terrorists.

Anything less than a proven total dedication to hunting down the terrorists within, should make those countries the outcasts of the world.

Mr Chairman, intensified international cooperation is needed just as much on more familiar problems. A world which formed itself into inward-looking blocs of nations would be taking a sad step backwards.

Yet I see a real danger of that: a European bloc based on the European Community's proposed economic and monetary union, a western-hemisphere bloc based on a US–Canada–Latin America free trade area; and a Pacific bloc with Japan and some of the East and North-East Asia Countries.

Such an arrangement would encourage protectionism and stifle trade at the very time we need to be driving forward to a positive outcome from the Uruguay round of world trade negotiations. That means we shall *all* need to make concessions, particularly on agriculture, where we are all far from perfect.

To slide back into protectionism would be damaging for all of us, and the developing countries most of all.

Of course *they* need help, particularly the poorest. They all seek investment. But there is going to be unprecedented demand, and therefore competition, for the world's savings over the next decade.

When you look at the problems of developing countries, you frequently find it is the politics which have led the economics astray.

These problems don't always stem from lack of resources or natural wealth or some other similar handicap. Quite often they are the result of bad government, corruption, the breakdown of law and order, or cynical promises which could never be kept.

The developing countries certainly need sustained help. But they also need democracy, good government and sensible economic policies which attract foreign investment. That will go to the countries which offer the best prospect of stability, which welcome enterprise, and give a fair rate of return, with the right to repatriate a reasonable proportion of the profits. Investments won't come into a country unless it can also get out.

All these problems underline the need for an effective global institution where we can agree on certain basic standards, resolve disputes and keep the peace. We *thought* we had created that at San Francisco in 1946 when we founded the United Nations. Sadly it has not quite worked out that way.

Iraq's invasion of Kuwait defies every principle for which the UN stands. If we let it succeed no small country can ever feel safe again. The law of the jungle takes over.

The UN must assert its authority and apply a total economic embargo unless Iraq withdraws without delay. The United States and Europe both support this but to be fully effective it will need the support of *all* UN members. They must stand up and be counted because a vital principle is at stake: an aggressor must never be allowed to get his way.

As East–West confrontation diminishes, as problems which have long dominated the UN's agenda such as apartheid in South Africa are being resolved, we have an opportunity to rediscover the determination that attended the founding of the United Nations. And the best time is now, with our present very able and widely respected Secretary-General.

It was never realistic to think of the United Nations as a world government. But we can make it a place where truth is told and objective standards prevail. The Five Permanent Members of the Security Council have acquired authority in recent times by working together. Not enough, but a basis on which to build.

Some would say all this is a triumph of hope over experience. But let us not be hypnotised by the past, otherwise we shall always shrug our shoulders and walk away. Shakespeare reminded us:

'Our doubts are traitors
And make us lose the good we
   oft might win,
By fearing to attempt'.

Mr Chairman I thank you most warmly for giving me this occasion to explain how I believe we can shape the future as we move into the third millennium. If we are to do better than our best, Europe and the United States must continue to make common sense, attracting others as we go, but remaining faithful to the principles which have brought us so far. Winston Churchill expressed so well the positive approach we shall need in his description of the Journey of Life:

'Let us be contented with
what has happened to us
and thankful for all we have been spared.
Let us treasure our joys but
not bewail our sorrows.

'The glory of the light cannot
exist without its shadows.
Life is a whole, and good and
ill must be accepted together'.

We must work together for more joy and less sorrow; to ensure more light and less shadow. If we achieve that, we shall have done well.

IV. French documents

European Political Union

Statement by Roland Dumas, Minister of Foreign Affairs of France, during the joint press conference with Hans-Dietrich Genscher, Minister of Foreign Affairs of the FRG, Dublin, 21 April 1990

Excerpts

(...)

Indeed, during the informal meeting held today, we presented to our colleagues, the Ministers of Foreign Affairs of the Twelve, the Franco-German proposal, signed by Chancellor Kohl and the President of the French Republic, M. François Mitterrand, with a view to organizing European political union.

The way had been opened by our colleague, the Belgian Minister of Foreign Affairs, Mr. Eyskens, who had in the same manner informed the Community Ministers of Foreign Affairs of some thoughts on this political union.

But the Franco-German proposal wants to go further. It suggests that at the next European Council meeting, to be held in Dublin next week, important decisions be taken to steer the European construction definitively towards political union.

Indeed it seemed to both the Federal Republic of Germany and France that the moment was particularly appropriate for taking the Community forward in this direction. That is the purpose of the proposal sent by the two Heads of State and Government which Mr. Genscher and I have commented today.

To pass very quickly to the main point and also let Mr. Genscher speak, I shall say that this proposal basically consists of three major parts: first of all one relating to the very substance of what we want to see achieved. We consider that today, to take account of Community patrimony, the preparation of economic and monetary union and all the events occurring in Europe, it is time to move on to political union, that is to take a leap forward.

Of course, to achieve this result we are making proposals and these will be considered by our partners in the course of the preparatory work. These proposals concern the strengthening of the parliament's prerogatives, the Council of Ministers' decision-making and the drawing-up of common security and external policies.

The second part of our proposal relates to the timetable: we think the Community must keep to the 1993 deadline (1 January) and that this date might also be that for the materialization of political union. If we adopt that cut-off date, it becomes evident that the whole of 1992 would have to be devoted to ratifying a new treaty, and therefore 1991 to construction, to getting this treaty down on paper.

(...)

A new Europe and Germany

Speech by President François Mitterrand at the Spring Session of the North Atlantic Treaty Association Assembly, Paris, 1 May 1990

Excerpts

(...)

I don't need to explain the new situation in which Europe finds itself. You know what it is and most of you are experiencing it first hand. We are seeing the central and eastern European countries once more exercising their full sovereignty and evolving, admittedly at different speeds, towards democracy; all are seeking to become reintegrated in our continent's life at every level, on the economic plane most certainly and on many others. Germany has begun the process that will lead her to unification, a major event and a natural one if you consider the logic of history and reality of a people. Let us, as I have already, wish her good luck.

An order is disappearing in Europe. It must give way to a new balance. There is to be greater military stability thanks particularly to the disarmament measures currently being negotiated in Vienna with a view to reducing the asymmetries so as to achieve a balance of power at the lowest possible level.

The European Economic Community has decided to make itself stronger through economic and monetary union while beginning to think seriously about—and to get to grips with a timetable for—defining a political union.

A great deal remains to be done, but we're going the right way, towards the peace and security that the countries of Europe want so much to enjoy. We still have to establish the bases of a contractual agreement by signing, if possible this year, the agreement on reducing conventional forces. Ahead of us too is the CSCE meeting planned for the end of this year, perhaps in Paris or any other capital that is chosen. We shall be able to discuss together, all the European countries, plus our friends from the United States of America and Canada, everything to do with cooperation and security in Europe.

It's there that the Alliance must play its role and we have the greatest need of the advice of the parliamentarians who are devoting themselves to this task.

People are naturally speaking about developments within the Alliance. That is a reasonable prospect given that the situation has changed and there are no grounds for loosening the terms of our agreements. There is talk of a new European balance. It will be necessary.

At a recent meeting with President Bush in his country, we spoke about this. I myself proposed—and I wasn't alone in this—the idea of holding a meeting of the Alliance as soon as possible—you know that some dates have been put forward—in a country which has already been sounded out on this matter.

It will plainly be impossible this time, for example in June or July, to complete these talks, but that meeting will enable us to pave the way for the next stage for the end of this year.

You are aware of France's special situation within the Alliance's integrated command. This position will be maintained, with France staying loyal to her allies and retaining the very many links which presuppose cooperation between us.

As regards the situation in NATO and its vocation—you are aware of Mr. Baker's position which was only the first of a whole series of other proposals emanating from different countries—we very clearly understand the need to give a fresh orientation to the approach that is going to be developed on

new ground in a different Europe. What is meant by a political role? The term is a necessary, but also a vague one. Let us say that it is normal for all those participating in Europe's security, and particularly the North Americans, to have their say on this new balance and for them to be involved in the decision-making.

People are talking about Germany's new situation. We agree that unified Germany, the whole of the new Germany, is naturally destined to belong to the Atlantic Alliance. There's no going back on that otherwise we would end up with preposterous arrangements. Simply, sensible measures must be taken. That does not mean it will be necessary to move the military capabilities further East. No posture capable of arousing the Soviet Union's fear or suspicion must be adopted. Simply, as we have always said, there must be balance, symmetry, a joint, concomitant and comparable démarche and, once we have those, we shall see what changes are going to take place within the Warsaw Pact, what the balance of forces will be and in what terms we shall be able to envisage security in future years. We are making sure, as we ask the others opposite us to do, that we don't undertake any unnecessary action that might be imprudent.

(...)

On NATO, the CSCE and Germany

Statement by President François Mitterrand, following the North Atlantic Treaty Organization summit meeting, London, 6 July 1990

In the text of the Final Declaration there are some fairly new and interesting statements, several are thanks to us, for example the assertion of a European identity in the security domain. This is still only a phrase, but it constitutes progress as the text says, 'The move within the European Community towards political union, including the development of a European identity in the domain of security, will also contribute to Atlantic solidarity and to the establishment of a just and lasting order of peace throughout the whole of Europe'. So we find in the same sentence, in the same context, the European identity in the security domain, Atlantic solidarity and CSCE Europe.

There is mention of the creation of new partnerships with all the European countries. That is a potent idea in this text which revalidates the CSCE's existence, structures it, organizes it more, extends it. This idea is stated clearly: we invite all other CSCE member States to join us in a commitment to non-aggression, to the establishment of regular liaison between the East European countries and NATO.

There are too all the passages on a new approach to defence, on strategy, which include a rather new element, as I believe this is the first time it is said that a commitment concerning the manpower levels of a united Germany will be given at the time of signature of the CFE Treaty, that is that the Germans are for the first time accepting the idea of a limitation applying specifically to unified Germany.

A concept was inserted on France's initiative, that of new conventional arms control negotiations within the CSCE framework in the next few years.

Articles 14 to 20 are to do with defining strategy: on all these articles when it came to the delegations' explanations of vote which were completed fairly swiftly, very few delegations commented. I spoke for longer than anyone else in order to emphasize that France had not seen strategy in the same way as the Alliance in the past any more than she did today: not the previous strategies of flexible defence, forward battle or the current weapon of last resort . . . I recalled that we agree to none of that, that the purpose of deterrence was to prevent war, even to make it impossible and not to win it. So any idea which gave the impression of degrees in the use of nuclear weapons, that there could be a long process of conventional war that would end up in the last resort in a nuclear war, seemed to us totally contrary to reality. We don't think a war can be regulated like manuscript by a slow progression, that is using ever more sophisticated weaponry. We think that's a purely abstract idea. And as we want there to be no war, if everyone knows that everything is triggered from the very outset, there won't be any.

So I explained my point of view and argued against the concept of nuclear forces being weapons of last resort. As we do not belong to NATO's integrated command, I asked my partners to draw the relevant conclusions on every article bearing on NATO's strategy or military structure. Everything contained in this text commits them, not us; which does not mean that France is against everything said in this text, but that she is not committing herself on the integrated command's strategy and structures. That is why you will find the expression 'countries concerned', which is in fact in constant diplomatic use, but there are countries which are in this case not concerned: ours. The French position is well known: France, who possesses nuclear weapons does not intend to be dependent upon a foreign decision.

There are some interesting passages on the structuring of everything that will come out of the CSCE conference. Articles 21 and 22 stress the CSCE's more prominent role involving the subsequent setting-up of a whole series of institutions, regular meetings. At the end of the text there is even the prospect of 'a parliamentary body—the Assembly of Europe—to be based on the existing parliamentary assembly of the Council of Europe in Strasbourg, and including representatives of all CSCE member States', that is all the CSCE member countries, those of Europe plus the United States and Canada.

In my explanation of vote I made it clear that I approved the proposal to transform this alliance, giving it from now on a greater political and perhaps reduced military content, although this is less certain, and considered that this opening-up was reflected by excellent proposals even though in themselves these did not solve the basic strategic problem. From my point of view, the statement on the European identity in the security domain is crucial.

The abandonment of the German position on special treatment for Germany as regards the limitation of her arms is an important point for consideration.

The CSCE's general development involving relations that are no longer bloc-to-bloc but inter-European, the invitation to Mr. Gorbachev, the bodies that will be established, the CSCE meeting in which the representatives of the various States of Europe's two former parts will meet as they please, all seem to me very positive. I am not going back over the reservations of a strategic nature that I have just pointed out.

V. FRG documents

A 10-point plan for overcoming the division of Europe and Germany

Speech by FRG Chancellor Helmut Kohl in the German Bundestag, Bonn, 28 November 1989

Excerpts

(. . .)

We all know that we cannot plan the way to German unity simply in theory or with our appointment calendars. Abstract models may be all right for polemical purposes but they help us no further. Today, however, we are in a position to prepare in advance the stages which lead to this goal. These I would like to elucidate with the following 10-point plan:

1. Immediate measures are called for as a result of events of recent weeks, particularly the flow of resettlers and the huge increase in the number of travellers. The Federal Government will provide immediate aid where it is needed. We will assist in the humanitarian sector and provide medical aid if it is wanted and considered helpful.

We are also aware that the welcome money given once a year to every visitor from the GDR is no answer to the question of travel funds. The GDR must itself provide travellers with the necessary foreign exchange. We are, however, prepared to contribute to a currency fund for a transitional period, provided that persons entering the GDR no longer have to exchange a minimum amount of currency, that entry into the GDR is made considerably easier, and that the GDR itself contributes substantially to the fund.

Our aim is to facilitate traffic as much as possible in both directions.

2. The Federal Government will continue its cooperation with the GDR in all areas where it is of direct benefit to the people on both sides, especially in the economic, scientific, technological and cultural fields. It is particularly important to intensify cooperation in the field of environmental protection. Here we will be able to take decisions on new projects shortly, irrespective of other developments.

We also want to extensively increase telephone links with the GDR and help expand the GDR's telephone network. The Federal Minister of Posts and Telecommunications has begun talks on this subject.

Negotiations continue on the extension of the Hanover–Berlin railway line. This is not enough, however, and we need to take a thorough look at transport and rail systems in the GDR and the Federal Republic in the light of the new situation. Forty years of separation also mean that traffic routes have in some cases developed quite differently. This applies not only to border crossing-points but to the traditional East–West lines of communication in central Europe. There seems to be no reason why the classical Moscow–Warsaw–Berlin–Paris route, which always included Cologne and was of great importance at all times, should not be brought into consideration in the age of high-speed trains and just as Europe's transport network is to be extended accordingly.

3. I have offered comprehensive aid and cooperation should the GDR bindingly undertake to carry out a fundamental change in the political and economic system and put the necessary measures irreversibly into effect. By 'irreversible' we mean that the GDR leadership must reach agreement with opposition groups on constitutional amendments and a new electoral law.

We support the demand for free, equal and secret elections in the GDR, in which, of course, independent, that is to say, non-socialist, parties would also participate. The SED's monopoly on power must be removed. The introduction of a democratic system means, above all, the abolition of laws on political crimes and the immediate release of all political prisoners.

Economic aid can only be effective if the economic system is radically reformed. This is obvious from the situation in all Comecon states and is not a question of our preaching to them. The centrally-planned economy must be dismantled.

We do not want to stabilize conditions that have become indefensible. Economic improvement can only occur if the GDR opens its doors to Western investment, if conditions of free enterprise are created, and if private initiative becomes possible. I don't understand those who accuse us of tutelage in this respect. There are daily examples of this in Hungary and Poland which can surely be followed by the GDR, likewise a member of Comecon.

Our sincere hope is that the necessary legislation will be introduced quickly, because we would not be very happy if private capital were to be invested in Poland—and with developments progressing so well—even more so in Hungary, which I would also welcome, but not in the middle of Germany. We want as many companies as possible to invest as much as possible.

I wish to emphasize once again that these are not preconditions but simply the foundations needed for effective assistance. Nor can there be any doubt that the people in the GDR want this. They want economic freedom which will enable them at long last to reap the fruit of their labour and enjoy more prosperity.

When I consider how this matter of the GDR's future economic system is being discussed by the SED itself—it will all be heard publicly at its special convention in a few days' time—I cannot for the life of me see how anyone saying this can be accused of meddling in the GDR's internal affairs. I find that rather absurd.

4. Prime Minister Modrow spoke in his government policy statement of a 'contractual community'. We are prepared to adopt this idea. The proximity of our two states in Germany and the special nature of their relationship demand an increasingly close network of agreements in all sectors and at all levels.

This cooperation will also require more common institutions. The existing commissions could be given new tasks and new ones created, especially for industry, transport, environmental protection, science and technology, health and cultural affairs. It goes without saying that Berlin will be fully incorporated in these cooperative efforts. This has always been our policy.

5. We are also prepared to take a further decisive step, namely, to develop confederative structures between the two states in Germany with a view to creating a federation. But this presupposes the election of a democratic government in the GDR.

We can envisage the following institutions being created after early, free elections:

– an intergovernmental committee for continuous consultation and political coordination,

– joint technical committees, and

– many others in the light of new developments.

Previous policy towards the GDR had to be limited mainly to small steps by which we sought above all to alleviate the consequences of division and to keep alive and strengthen the people's awareness of the unity of the nation. If, in the future, a democratically legitimized, that is, a freely elected government, becomes our partner, that will open up completely new perspectives.

Gradually, new forms of institutional cooperation can be created and further developed. Such coalescence is inherent in the continuity of German history. State organization in Germany has nearly always taken the form of a confederation or federation. We can fall back on this past experience. Nobody knows at the present time what a reunited Germany will look like. I am, however, sure that unity will come, if it is wanted by the German people.

6. The development of intra-German relations remains embedded in the pan-European process, that is to say in the framework of East–West relations. The future architecture of Germany must fit into the future architecture of Europe as a whole. Here the West has shown itself to be the pacemaker with its concept of a lasting and equitable peaceful order in Europe.

In our joint declaration of June this year, which I have already quoted, General Secretary Gorbachov and I spoke of the structural elements of a 'common European home'. They are, for example:

– Unqualified respect for the integrity and security of each state. Each state has the right freely to choose its own political and social system.

– Unqualified respect for the principles and rules of international law, especially respect for the people's right of self-determination.

– The realization of human rights.

– Respect for and maintenance of the traditional cultures of the nations of Europe.

With all of these points, as Mr Gorbachov and I laid down, we aim to follow Europe's long traditions and help overcome the division of Europe.

7. The attraction and aura of the European Community are and remain a constant feature of pan-European development. We want to and must strengthen them further still.

The European Community must now approach the reformist countries of central, Eastern and south-eastern Europe with openness and flexibility. This was also endorsed by the heads of state and government of the EC member states at their recent meeting in Paris.

This of course includes the GDR. The Federal Government therefore approves the early conclusion of a trade and cooperation agreement with the GDR. This would give it wider access to the Common Market, also in the perspective of 1992.

We can envisage specific forms of association which would lead the reformist countries of central and south-eastern Europe to the European Community, thus helping to level the economic and social gradients of our continent. This is one of the crucial issues if tomorrow's Europe is to be a united Europe.

We have always regarded the process leading to the recovery of German unity to be a European concern as well. It must, therefore, also be seen in the context of European integration. To put it simply, the EC must not end at the Elbe but must remain open to the East.

Only in this way can the EC be the foundation for a truly comprehensive European Union—after all, we have always regarded the Twelve as only a part, not as the whole, of the Continent. Only in this way can it maintain, assert and develop the common European identity. That identity is not only based on the cultural diversity of Europe but also, and especially, on the fundamental values of freedom, democracy, human rights and self-determination.

If the countries of central and south-eastern Europe meet the requirements we would also welcome their membership of the Council of Europe, and especially of the Convention for the Protection of Human Rights and Fundamental Freedoms.

8. The CSCE process is a central element of the pan-European architecture and must be vigorously promoted in the following forums:
– the Human Rights Conferences in Copenhagen, in 1990, and in Moscow, in 1991,
– the Conference on Economic Cooperation in Bonn, in 1990,

– the symposium on the cultural heritage in Cracow, in 1991, and
– last but not least the next follow-up meeting in Helsinki.

There we should also think about new institutional forms of pan-European cooperation. We can well imagine a common institution for the coordination of East–West economic cooperation, as well as the creation of a pan-European environmental council.

9. Overcoming the division of Europe and Germany presupposes far-reaching and rapid steps in the field of disarmament and arms control. Disarmament and arms control must keep pace with political developments and thus be accelerated where necessary.

This is particularly true of the Vienna Negotiations on the Reduction of Conventional Forces in Europe, and for the Agreement on Confidence-Building Measures and the global Ban on Chemical Weapons, which we hope will materialize in 1990. It also requires that the nuclear potential of the superpowers be reduced to the strategically necessary minimum. The forthcoming meeting between President Bush and General Secretary Gorbachov offers a good opportunity to add new impetus to the current negotiations.

We are doing our best—also in bilateral discussions with the Warsaw Pact countries, including the GDR—to support this process.

10. With this comprehensive policy we are working for a state of peace in Europe in which the German nation can recover its unity in free self-determination. Reunification—that is regaining national unity—remains the political goal of the Federal government. We are grateful that once again we have received support in this matter from our allies in the Declaration issued after the NATO Summit Meeting in Brussels in May.

We are conscious of the fact that many difficult problems will confront us on the road to German unity, problems for which no one has a definitive solution today. Above all, this includes the difficult and crucial question of overlapping security structures in Europe.

The linking of the German question to pan-European developments and East–West relations, as explained in these ten points, will allow a natural development which takes account of the interests of all concerned and paves the way for peaceful development in freedom, which is our objective.

Only together and in an atmosphere of mutual trust will we be able to peacefully overcome the division of Europe, which is also the division of Germany. This calls for prudence, understanding and sound judgement on all sides so that the current promising developments may continue steadily and peacefully. This process cannot be hampered by reforms, rather by their rejection. It is not freedom that creates instability but its suppression. Every successful step towards reform means more stability and more freedom and security for the whole of Europe.

In a few weeks' time we enter the final decade of this century, a century which has seen so much misery, bloodshed and suffering. There are today many promising signs that the 90s will bring more peace and freedom in Europe and in Germany. Much depends, and everyone senses this, on the German contribution. We should all face this challenge of history.

Bundestag Resolution on the Polish Border

Bonn, 8 March 1990

With reference to its declaration of 8 November 1989 the German Bundestag proposes that, as soon as possible after the elections in the GDR, the two freely-elected German parliaments and governments issue an identical declaration essentially stating the following:

The Polish people are assured that their right to live in secure borders will not be questioned by us Germans through territorial claims either now or in future.

The purpose of this declaration is, in accordance with the principles of the CSCE Final Act, to reaffirm in the light of German unity the inviolability of the borders with Poland as the indispensable basis of peaceful relations in Europe.

In this spirit, the border question should be settled in a treaty between an all-German Government and the Polish Government that seals the reconciliation of the two nations.

Poland's waiver of reparations from Germany dated from 23 August 1953 and the joint declaration made by Prime Minister Tadeusz Mazowiecki and Chancellor Helmut Kohl on 14 November 1989 remain valid for a united Germany.

Corresponding identical resolutions were approved by the two German parliaments—the Bundestag

and the Volkskammer. The text adopted by the Bundestag on 21 June 1990 was conveyed the next day by the Foreign Minister, Hans-Dietrich Genscher, to the Polish Foreign Minister, Krzysztof Skubiszewski. Texts of the letter and the Bundestag resolution are published in *Mitteilung für die Presse des Auswärtigen Amtes*, no. 1134/90, Bonn, 22 June 1990. On 14 November 1990 in Warsaw the FRG and Poland concluded the Treaty on the reaffirmation of their existing frontiers, signed by Ministers Genscher and Skubiszewski.

As German Europeans and European Germans

Speech by FRG Chancellor Helmut Kohl at the Königswinter Conference, Cambridge, 28 March 1990

Excerpts

(...)

II

We are currently experiencing a radical change in Europe's post-war history. The dismantling of the East–West confrontation and the democratic awakening in the countries of Central, Eastern and South-Eastern Europe offer the first realistic opportunity since the Second World War to end the division of Europe, and with it the division of Germany, by peaceful means. That division has always been a source of instability and insecurity. Its termination therefore benefits the whole of Europe.

The threat to the Western democracies did not only come from an ideology inimical to human dignity. More than once the confrontation—especially in Germany—assumed proportions which made it a grave danger to peace.

It was above all the people who suffered under the division of their country and under the bondage imposed upon them. And it was they, the peoples of Central, Eastern and South-Eastern Europe, who gave the decisive impetus for the breakthrough to democracy and freedom. They enforced a change in the status quo to which many of us in the West, too, had grown accustomed.

As a German, I am proud that my countrymen in the GDR, through their peaceful revolution, have helped write a chapter of

German and European history marked by freedom.

III

We have reason to be grateful to all who have helped make this historic change possible. Thanks are due in the first place to our friends and allies in the West, especially the Americans, the British and the French. They have stood by our side in times of danger, when the blockade, the wall, and the barbed wire threatened to keep our country permanently divided.

In the Bonn Convention they agreed to cooperate 'to achieve, by peaceful means, their common aim of a reunified Germany enjoying a liberal-democratic constitution, like that of the Federal Republic, and integrated within the European Community'.

But we also thank President Mikhail Gorbachev who, in conjunction with his domestic reforms, has turned Soviet foreign policy in a new direction. 'New thinking' is now also changing Soviet policy towards Germany and permits of a constructive, future-oriented solution to the German question. It is therefore in our mutual interest that President Gorbachev's domestic reform policy should prove successful.

But the recent developments in the GDR would not have been possible without the example of extensive reforms in Hungary and Poland either. This in itself indicates how tightly our national fate is bound up with that of our neighbours.

IV

The 18 of March 1990 brought the first free elections in the GDR. They resulted in overwhelming victory for those who advocate freedom, democracy and social market economy.

Our friends and partners know our unequivocal response to the question as to Germany's position in a future Europe. Forty years of the Federal Republic of Germany— that is to say, 40 years of democracy and the rule of law—allow no doubt as to where we stand: on the side of freedom, on the side of our friends. And the free elections in the GDR, too, can only be regarded as a manifestation of democratic maturity.

The unification of the two German states is taking place on the basis of the right of self-determination. But it also affects the interests of our neighbours. We have from the very beginning made sure that the process of unification takes place within a stable European framework. We intend it to stay that way and will not present anyone with a fait accompli.

The words chanted by the people in the GDR 'we are *one* nation!' made it clear from the start what the great majority of my fellow-countrymen want: unity in freedom.

In the first two months of this year alone the number of resettlers increased dramatically. To date over 150, 000 have come to the Federal Republic—many more than the entire population of Cambridge, for instance. They include mostly young people, doctors, engineers and many other skilled persons who are urgently required to rebuild the GDR's economy. But this exodus is not only threatening the GDR's recovery; it poses problems for the Federal Republic, too.

Since the elections on 18 March the number of settlers has dropped. The prospect of reunification is inducing people in the GDR to stay there. We must refrain from anything that would weaken their hope.

My Government has proposed that the Deutschmark also be made the GDR's currency and that a 'social market economy' be introduced there. It has thus given an answer to the question asked by people of what will come next. At the same time the coalescence of the two German states must be harmonized with the external aspects of this process. These external aspects concern:

– the rights and responsibilities of the Four Powers with regard to Berlin and Germany as a whole,

– border questions,

– the existing and future security structures and

– the integration of the present-day territory of the GDR into the European Community.

Talks in accordance with the '2 plus 4' formula agreed at Ottawa were started by experts in mid-March. I would very much like to see these talks making progress. My aim is that they be completed before the CSCE summit this year.

In addition, we make sure that our partners in NATO and the European Community are kept informed of developments and are consulted on important questions concerning them. Together we shall have to pay special attention to ensuring that Europe's security is guaranteed in future, too. This is a vital, long-term question for which a spirit of partnership is particularly necessary. I know that Britain holds a sober and firm position in this matter, and I greatly appreciate such reliability.

In assessing the security interests of a future Germany and all its neighbours, indeed of Europe as a whole, we set out from the following parameters:

First: the future united Germany must not be neutralized or demilitarized. A Germany integrated in Western security policy is an essential element of European stability.

Second: the future united Germany must therefore remain embedded in the Western alliance. Secession from NATO must not be the price for German unity. Such a policy is not acceptable to me.

Third: the transatlantic security link between Europe and North America continues to be of vital importance for us Germans and for Europe as a whole. Our aim must therefore be to further deepen cooperation between the European Community and the United States in the field of foreign policy.

Fourth: for the sake of our national interests we must not encumber progress towards German unity with border issues. In 1985 I declared in the Bundestag: 'In the areas beyond Poland's Western border Polish families live today for whom those regions have become their home in the course of two generations. We shall respect this and not call it into question'.

I strongly advocate that the two freely elected German parliaments and governments issue as soon as possible an identical declaration reaffirming the inviolability of the borders with Poland as the indispensable basis of peaceful relations in Europe. This declaration should unequivocally express the idea that *immediately after* unification of the two German states the all-German government and parliament will definitively settle the border question along these lines in an internationally binding treaty with the Republic of Poland.

Such a settlement can only be made by an all-German sovereign state. An identical declaration by the two governments and two parliaments is politically the strongest undertaking that can be expressed by the Germans *before* reunification. An overwhelming majority in the two German parliaments are in favour of such an undertaking, and thus there can be no doubt either about the position of a future all-German parliament and government.

The overwhelming majority of my fellow-countrymen seek definitive reconciliation with the Polish people. Lasting peace throughout Europe presupposes such reconciliation—just as the unification of Western Europe was only possible once the French and Germans had become friends after 1945.

I myself have time and again—for example in my policy statement on 1 September 1989—recalled the untold suffering inflicted on the Polish people by Germans. It would no doubt be beneficial for the relationship between our two peoples if Poland were to refer with equally clear and noble words as President Vaclav Havel did for Czechoslovakia to the injustice committed by Poles against innocent Germans. We Germans are not entitled to such words, and even less must we try to balance accounts in one way or another. But I am certain that such a gesture would point the way to a future in which the relationship between the Polish and German peoples is marked by a spirit of good-neighbourliness in a common Europe.

V

On 28 April the heads of state or government of the European Community will meet in Dublin. Questions concerning the integration of the GDR into the European Community will be at the forefront of the summit.

I strongly welcome the fact that the EC Commission, the European Parliament and the EC Council of Ministers began at an early stage to make intensive preparations for the process of German unification and its implications for the Community. I intend to ensure that my Government consults consistently and closely with these three Community organs on all essential issues.

A united Germany will also be a reliable member of the European Community. The larger German market will, moreover, afford additional opportunities for all our European partners. I am certain that in five years the disastrous effects of 'Socialism in practice' will be overcome. Thuringia, Saxony and the other Länder of what is now the GDR will flourish and achieve new prosperity.

VI

Just as we resolutely strive for German unity, we seek early realization of a European

Union. Strengthening the rights of the European Parliament and expanding European Political Cooperation are important stages along the path to that goal. Those who want a united Germany to be firmly integrated into European structures must logically support further progress in European unification.

We seek speedy progress with a view to the completion of the single market by the end of 1992. We would like this year's intergovernmental conference to make constructive, intensive and swift efforts so that economic and monetary union can be completed.

At the special EC summit in Dublin at the end of April I shall again propose, as I did in Strasbourg, that a further intergovernmental conference be convened this year with a view to making faster progress towards political union.

We want to follow the path of German and European unification together with our British friends. For us Germans, close relations with Britain marked by mutual trust have for decades been a cornerstone of our foreign policy.

In his famous speech at Zurich in September 1946, Winston Churchill indicated with his vision of a 'United States of Europe' a path on which we have since then jointly made considerable progress.

Europe has now again reached a turning point in its history. But there is less cause than ever for faintheartedness. As the past year in particular demonstrated, time is working in favour of, and not against, the cause of freedom. This awareness should encourage us.

As Karl Popper explained at the end of his splendid work entitled *The Open Society and its Enemies*, progress towards freedom is not the outcome of anonymous historical processes. It rests exclusively 'with our watchfulness, with our efforts, with the clarity of our conception of our aims, and with the realism of their choice'. We Germans want to contribute—as German Europeans and European Germans—to a future marked by freedom. The 1990s must become Europe's decade.

Declaration on the German contribution to the reduction in conventional armed forces in Europe

Statement by Hans-Dietrich Genscher, Minister for Foreign Affairs of the Federal Republic of Germany, Vienna, 30 August 1990*

The government of the Federal Republic of Germany, acting in agreement with the government of the GDR, makes the following binding declaration today before the plenary of the Vienna Negotiations on Conventional Armed Forces in Europe:

The government of the Federal Republic of Germany undertakes to reduce the personnel strength of the armed forces of the united Germany to 370, 000 troops (ground, air and naval forces) within 3 to 4 years. The reduction will commence on the entry into force of the first CFE treaty.

Within the scope of this overall ceiling no more than 345, 000 troops will belong to the ground and air forces which, pursuant to the agreed mandate, are exclusively the subject of negotiations on conventional armed forces in Europe.

The Federal government regards its commitment to reduce ground and air forces as a significant German contribution to the reduction of conventional forces in Europe. It assumes that in follow-on negotiations the other participants in the negotiations, too, will render their contribution to enhancing security and stability in Europe, including measures to limit personnel strengths.

---

* An identical statement was made at the same meeting by the Prime Minister and Minister for Foreign Affairs of the GDR. Translation from *Pressemitteilung* of 1 September 1990, published by the Embassy of the Federal Republic of Germany, Stockholm.

VI. GDR documents

Statement by the Prime Minister of the
GDR, Lothar de Maizière, on the occasion
of the signing of the State Treaty,*
Bonn, 18 May 1990

This is an important day for us; it marks the
beginning of the realization of Germany's
unity. Monetary, Economic and Social Union
makes the unification process irreversible.
What we are doing here today constitutes a
decisive step towards our goal of achieving
German unity in freedom with a peaceful
European order. The State Treaty is a treaty
between the two Governments in Germany.
Its content shows that both Governments are
determined not to tailor the unification
process from above. The coalescence of the
divided Germany begins rather with the
people and their living conditions. In our discussions and negotiations over the past few
weeks we are guided by the interests of the
people in the two German states. The spirit in
which this treaty was formulated is consonant
with the aspirations and desires of the people
in the GDR for freedom, prosperity and social
justice. This was not a case of foreign states
negotiating, but compatriots and friends who
refuse to be estranged any longer.

Both sides have been working on this
Treaty full speed night and day since the
policy statement was delivered a month ago. I
wish to thank the hundreds of people who
were involved in this task. The Treaty is a
great accomplishment. I should like to thank
in particular the chairmen of the two delegations, Herr Tietmeyer and Dr Krause, and all
their staff.

This Treaty is a compromise. Yet it is not
the result of haggling, but a good and balanced piece of work. It is a sound blueprint for
the introduction of an ecologically-oriented
social market economy.

At this juncture I should like to turn first of
all to the citizens of the GDR:

The introduction of the Deutsche Mark, of
dynamic pensions and unemployment insur-
ance, and the aid for the GDR's national
budget, are a generous political gesture on the
part of the Federal Republic of Germany. No
one should forget what the Ostmark would

really be worth today on a free market. And
no one should be under any illusion as to the
seriousness of the crisis in the GDR's economy. We could not and cannot carry on as
before.

Not every rosy dream which some people
have associated with the Treaty could be fulfilled. But no one will be worse off than
before. On the contrary: what country has
ever been afforded as good a starting position
as we have with this Treaty?

We in the GDR must now make the best of
it. Adopting a realistic view of the situation,
we must set to work with a new pioneering
spirit, with commitment, faith and confidence
in our own strength. In doing so, we will
never lose sight of social justice. Our social
commitment will hardly be surpassed by
anyone.

To the citizens of the Federal Republic of
Germany I should like to say the following:

My Government is responsible first and
foremost for the Germans in the GDR and for
their interests. This is in line with the mandate
given us by the electorate in our newly-won
democracy.

At the same time, however, we and the
Federal Government are jointly responsible
for an undivided future. Our aim in the GDR,
too, is to ensure the stability of the Deutsche
Mark and to safeguard an overall economic
balance in the Federal Republic and in the
GDR, in other words in the new joint economic area. I promise that we will do everything
in our power to ensure that the funds from the
Federal Republic of Germany are invested
wisely.

We consider your aid to be help for self-
help. In the long term, we should receive no
free gifts. We wish to safeguard our future
through our own efforts.

In view of the scope of the proposed
monetary, economic and social union, it is
quite natural that discussions should take
place in both German states. I find it astonish-
ing, however, that in some places there is
more concern than hope. Too many of us feel
discouraged by the host of problems which
we undoubtedly face.

Perhaps we Germans should not focus
excessively on ourselves in this regard either,

but rather look to Europe. I am confident that no German will be poorer as a result of the unification process, but that we will all be better off. And this will not be at the expense of Europe, but in the interest of pan-European development in peace, freedom, prosperity and social justice.

German unity should thus emerge not from envious confrontation, but from fruitful cooperation. We and you, Westerners and Easterners—these and similar words should soon disappear from our vocabulary.

The Government of the GDR will now present this Treaty to the freely-elected Volkskammer. I underline our firm intention to adhere to the timetable with Monetary, Economic and Social Union coming into effect by 2 July 1990.

The outcome of the negotiations on the State Treaty is courageous, unique and promising.

Courageous because this Treaty, which directly affects the existence and future of all Germans in the GDR, was negotiated in only four weeks, following forty years of socialist planned economy.

Unique because never before has a command economy been transformed into a social market economy on a fixed date.

And promising. We will succeed because both sides are bound and even condemned to succeed.

We face a truly great and unique opportunity. As a rule, history does not repeat chances like these. We wish resolutely to use the opportunity for freedom, peace and social justice for the sake of Europe in order to create a better world for our children.

---

* Treaty between the Federal Republic of Germany and the German Democratic Republic establishing a Monetary, Economic and Social Union, published in *German Tribune Supplement* (Documents of German Unity), Bonn, 1990.

The decision of the Volkskammer (GDR Parliament), Berlin, 23 August 1990*

The Volkskammer declares accession to the area in which the Basic Law is in force according to article 23 until 3 October 1990. It assumes that by this date the deliberations on the treaty of unification will have been

concluded, the two-plus-four negotiations will have reached a stage at which the foreign policy requirements and security prerequisites of unification are regulated, and the formation of the Länder will have been prepared such that elections for the parliaments of the Länder can be held on 14 October.

---

* The decision was based on a draft prepared jointly by parliamentary factions of the following parties: the Christian Democratic Union (CDU), the German Social Union (DSU), the Social Democratic Party (SPD) and the Free Democratic Party (FDP). The decision was accepted by 294 votes for, 62 against and 7 abstentions.

Statement by the Prime Minister of the GDR, Lothar de Maizière, at the Concluding Session of the Two-plus-Four Conference,*
Moscow, 12 September 1990

1. The Government of the GDR has deemed it appropriate, and has always hoped, that the foreign and security policy requirements of German unity would be worked out by common consent before the accession of the German Democratic Republic to the Federal Republic of Germany. With the adoption of the Treaty on the Settlement with Respect to Germany this goal has been attained. It is very gratifying for us to know that the efforts to produce an outcome acceptable to all sides have been successful.

The treaty on the final settlement with respect to Germany is, unquestionably, an historic document. It ranks among the outstanding European treaties of the post-war period. This accord marks the end of the post-war era. It is the foundation stone for an era of peace, freedom and cooperation. At the same time, it prepares the way for the German people to regain its unity in free self-determination.

2. I would like to thank all those involved very warmly. They have shown great understanding for the fact that the process of German unification has gathered extra momentum in recent months because of the political and economic realities, and the popular desire for unity.

The legitimate interests of all negotiating partners have been taken into consideration in a process of give and take that was by no means easy. Mutual trust and a willingness to meet one another halfway have provided signposts and set new standards during this negotiating process. What has been accomplished here should continue to serve as a pattern as Europe continues to grow together.

It is good to know that under the new political conditions obtaining on this continent even the most complicated and sensitive issues can be resolved. This encourages us to believe in a new quality of goodneighbourly relations in Europe. The crux of the matter has been that all were governed by a desire to make use of the opportunities for the establishment of an all-European structure of freedom, peace and cooperation.

3. The fact that the Two-plus-Four talks are being brought to a successful conclusion here in Moscow is of symbolic importance. It was Mikhail Gorbachev's courageous policy of perestroika and new thinking that opened the way to peaceful change in Central and Eastern Europe. This is renewed evidence that any pattern of security and stability in Europe needs to include the Soviet Union. The vision of a common European home is nearing fulfillment. The awareness of a European identity is overcoming the old divisions, and the greater Europe extending from the Atlantic to the Urals is taking shape again.

4. For our European neighbours it is a matter of prime significance that the united Germany, too, recognizes her post-war frontiers definitively and without reservations and raises no territorial claims whatever vis-a-vis her neighbours. The statements issued by the Volkskammer and the Bundestag to this effect, the 'Principles for the Settlement of the Frontier Question'** and the provisions for corresponding amendments of the Basic Law contained in the inter-German Unification Treaty provide reliable safeguards here. The definitive recognition of the frontiers is a requirement of meaningful cooperation in Europe that is imbued with the spirit of reconciliation.

Trust can and must take the place of mistrust, and candour must replace suspicion and scepticism. The Polish Foreign Minister, Krzystof Skubiszewski, last week described the territorial order that has now emerged in Europe as a basis for reconciliation and for a new departure. This accords with our own notions of future developments in Europe.

5. In connection with the unification of Germany, it has been necessary to resolve complicated matters of security policy. The consensus reached has taken into account the interests of all involved. This also goes for the special military status of the territory of the present GDR. It will be possible to thin out military forces in the centre of Europe considerably as a united Germany forgoes the possession of ABC weapons and its total armed forces are limited to 370, 000 troops, in line with the announcement made in Vienna. To this one should add the agreed withdrawal of Soviet troops from the present GDR territory within the next four years. The German territorial army units in the territory in the present GDR will not have a nuclear capability, nor will they have an offensive one in terms of size, structure and armaments. It has been possible to master the difficult task of balancing out different interests because all those involved were prepared to stop thinking along the lines of military blocs. This reflected a desire to adapt the security structures in Europe to the new situation. Confrontation and a maximum concentration of military resources are giving way to cooperation and disarmament. In the East–West relationship we can now move on from the preservation of peace to the building of peace. The new developments in the East–West relationship and in Europe can be partly put down to widespread distrust of outdated military doctrines and to an awareness that ever-mounting military expenditures and a relentless escalation of the arms race would, in the final analysis, serve neither security nor human interests. Far-reaching disarmament measures today hold out the hope that the resources thus becoming available can be used for economic, social and ecological purposes. It should be our aim, by scaling down the armed forces, to continue building mutual trust as we find more and more common ground.

The current crisis in the Gulf region indicates how fragile peace in the world can be. But it also demonstrates how strong the international community is when it comes to jointly standing up to an aggressor. For the first time in such a conflict, the great powers are not facing each other as antagonists. This success is due to trust built up over a period of years.

6. The results of the Two-plus-Four talks provide a good basis for taking, at the forth-

coming CSCE summit, the decisions needed to end the era of the Cold War and of oppression once and for all. The Iron Curtain has come down. It is being replaced by new bridges, by goodneighbourliness and constructive cooperation.

The document to be signed today will restore full sovereignty to a united Germany. A major prerequisite has been the confident belief that no more war would emanate from German soil. The united Germany-to-be will preserve the memory of history and view its lessons as a permanent obligation.

One sign among several is that the two German states, in a letter from their Foreign Ministers to the Four Powers,*** have affirmed that the graves and memorials of war victims will be protected. Political parties and associations directed against the constitutional order of the united Germany or against the notion of international understanding are inadmissible. And the results of the land reform carried out between 1945 and 1949 will be expressly recognised.

7. Our government has made a special point of ensuring that in a united Germany protection of good faith will apply, as a matter of principle, to international treaties concluded by the GDR. This finds its binding expression in the letter from the two German Foreign Ministers and in the Unification Treaty between the two German states. The same goes for contractual obligations towards member countries of the Council for Mutual Economic Assistance. They will continue to enjoy protection of good faith in a united German state.

8. Finally, I should like to tell you how happy I am that the whole German people, in concert with its neighbours and the other peoples of Europe, is in joining together in a united sovereign Germany. From the experience of the last 40 years people in the GDR know only too well that an absurd policy of self-isolation can only lead to a country being shut out and excluded from the mainstream of international development. We have never seen German unification as a go-it-alone operation, but always as a contribution to overcoming the division of Europe. Therefore, I support the proposal that the participants of the Foreign Ministers' Meeting of the CSCE states in New York should be officially informed about the results of the Two-plus-Four talks.

Formerly cut by the East–West divide, the united Germany is assuming a bridge-building role in Europe. The great old continent can now address itself to new tasks together with the North American democracies. It can turn its attention to the solution of the most pressing issues facing mankind, which are to preserve peace in freedom, to narrow the gap between North and South, and to maintain the natural foundations of human existence.

---

* The text of the Treaty on the Final Settlement with Respect to Germany can be found in section XIX—Documents on unification.

** For the Principles for the Settlement of the Frontier Question mentioned by Lothar de Maizière see section XIX—Documents on unification.

*** For the text of the joint letter of the FRG and GDR foreign ministers to the foreign ministers of the Four Powers see section XIX—Documents on unification.

VII. Polish documents

Belonging to Europe

Speech by Tadeusz Mazowiecki, Prime Minister of Poland, to the Council of Europe,
Strasbourg, 30 January 1990

Excerpts

(. . .)

Europe is living through an exceptional period. Part of our continent torn up from its roots almost half a century ago is now aspiring to return. Back to Europe! This expression is gaining currency these days in the countries of Central and Eastern Europe. Politicians and economists are speaking of a return. The same applies to members of the cultural world, although it was easier for them to feel they still belonged to Europe: Europe was felt to be their spiritual home, a community of values and traditions. Perhaps the expression 'back to Europe' is too feeble to describe the process we are experiencing. One should speak rather of a European renaissance, the rebirth of the Europe which virtually ceased to exist after Yalta.

(. . .)

The Polish people are acutely aware of belonging to Europe and the European heritage. They are as conscious of this as are the other European peoples situated at the cultural crossroads adjacent to the superpowers, experiencing alternating phases of political existence and non-existence and hence feeling the need to strengthen their identity. In all these situations, Europe has always remained a beacon, an object of affection which the Poles felt ready to defend. The idea of being the 'ramparts of Christendom' and, by the same token, of Europe itself has remained alive in Poland throughout three centuries. Europe is therefore present in the Polish conscience as a value which it is worth living for and sometimes, indeed, dying for. But at the same time, Poland has borne a grudge against Europe and this sense of reproach has remained engraved to the present day in our collective consciousness. We continue to regard Europe as an ideal, the home of liberty and the rule of law, and we continue to relate closely to it, but we also continue to feel reproachful because of Yalta, because of the division of Europe and for having been left on the other side of the Iron Curtain.

Today, however, now that the return to Europe, the renaissance of Europe as a single entity is becoming more and more of a reality, we are wondering more and more frequently what we have to offer, what our contribution can be today to the European treasure house. I believe that we do have a lot to offer. Our contribution to Europe is both our strength and our weakness.

We are like someone recovering from a serious illness. For years we have undergone the tremendous pressure of totalitarianism but we have stood firm. However, we are still convalescing. Our economy is still in a critical condition which we are trying to alleviate; the democratic institutions of our state are only just being resuscitated and rebuilt. But we have acquired experience which we shall not forget and which we shall pass on to others.

If we have managed to survive as an entity, we owe this partly to our deep attachment to certain institutions and certain values regarded as the norm in Europe. We owe it to religion and the Church, our attachment to democracy and pluralism, human rights and civil liberties and to the ideal of solidarity. Even when we were unable to give these values their full potential or put them into practice in our public life, we still held them in esteem, we clung to them and struggled for them and therefore we know them and know their value. We know the price of being European, the price of the European heritage which Westerners today have inherited without even having to pay the rights of succession. We can remind them of this price. We therefore offer Europe our faith in Europe.

Today, we are lodging an application for membership of the Council of Europe. We desire to 'achieve a greater unity between its members for the purpose of safeguarding and realising the ideals and principles which are their common heritage and facilitating their economic and social progress'. We wish to share in promoting human rights and fundamental freedoms. The Council of Europe, which has performed wonders in the defence of rights and freedoms and which is a rich fountainhead of European ideas and initiatives, seems the right place for Poland, which has itself achieved a great deal in the defence of these same rights and freedoms.

Ladies and gentlemen, the gash across Europe symbolised until recently by the Berlin Wall can now begin to heal. This can be a fascinating process, although undoubtedly a very complex and lengthy one. And yet today, as opposed to yesterday, the principal political requirements exist, or are taking shape, which will make this process possible.

Our country is confronted with the enormous task of reconstituting the rights and the institutions which characterise modern democracies and rebuilding a market economy, after an interruption of several decades. Added to this, there is the need to overcome enormous economic problems. We not only have to recreate rights and institutions but, in cases where they were non-existent, we have to start from scratch. Otherwise our two European worlds will never manage to live in harmony.

Poland has already set to work. The government which I have been leading for barely five months has drafted and had enacted numerous laws which provide a legal framework for the independence of the judiciary, for freedom of the press and freedom to organise, for freedom to found political parties, and for local self-government which, with the forthcoming municipal elections, will soon become effective. We are preparing a new Constitution of the Polish Republic which will become a democratic State subject to the rule of law.

(...)

Just as the Berlin Wall not so long ago was both the symbol of the divided Europe and a physical barrier splitting Germany into two separate states, so its collapse, while offering an opportunity to unite Europe, at the same time raises the problem of German unification. No people can be denied the right to live within the same state. But the division of Germany resulted from a major disaster caused by the Nazi state which destroyed tens of millions of human lives. It is therefore not at all surprising today if, at a time when the prospect is emerging of a reunited German state, the memory of this disaster arouses

anxieties which cannot be alleviated even by obviously weighty counterarguments such as the fact that today the situation is different and the Germans themselves are different. We acknowledge these arguments. But we must understand these anxieties and overcome them by settling the German question with the agreement of all the interested parties and in a manner which, from the outset, will offer a credible sense of security to all those who require it and which above all will guarantee the inviolability of the Western frontier of Poland.

The upheavals in Central Europe and the Soviet Union are creating unparalleled opportunities but also carry risks. In some countries the supporters of the old regime are no longer in a position to determine the course of events but can still impede it. In others, although they are on the defensive, they have not given up hope, and have not lost the capability, of regaining their former position. If severe symptoms of destabilisation, together with economic chaos, were to persist, these people's chances would increase. They will diminish if the peoples in our region, who at the moment are proving active, can carry through the crucial transformations resolutely but as calmly as possible, and above all if they can resist the temptation to try to achieve everything at once. That approach is often counterproductive.

Another danger is that of Balkanisation of part of the European continent, or of the various countries, because of acute tensions between the peoples or states, tensions whose origins lie in the present as well as the past. If partisan or national interests were to surface and the notion of regional or European interests were to be lost sight of, it would be a major obstacle to establishing healthy cooperation and mutual understanding in this continent of ours which is in the throes of change.

But the events unfolding in Central and Eastern Europe, although they carry risks, are first and foremost an unbelievable and historic challenge. And although obviously the challenges are mainly for us, the people of Central Europe, they are also a historic challenge and a task for the whole of Europe. The scope is vast. There is room for Western Europeans who see what we are trying to do and believe in our aims. With them—with you—it will be easier to narrow the distance between us. The wall which divided free

Europe from enslaved Europe is down. Now we have to fill the gulf between poor Europe and affluent Europe. If Europe is to be a 'common home' whose door is open to all, such great disparities cannot be allowed to continue. A huge job of work awaits us all.

We now need new guidelines to point our endeavours down a common European road, to no-one's exclusion and everyone's advantage. It is not easy to chart such a course, for it takes thought and collaboration. But as, in your part of the continent, post-1992 Europe is even now taking shape, why not start thinking in terms of a Europe of the year 2000? To be realistic, what kind of Europe might that be if we unite our efforts?

It will certainly not be a European area with free movement of goods, capital and people but it might be a Europe where borders and tariffs would be much less of an obstacle, a Europe wholly open to the young. For the fate of our continent depends on what kind of young people we bring up.

It might be a Europe in which contact between the creative and the scientific communities, fostering permeability of national cultures and thereby bringing them closer together, will be richer than it is today.

It will not be a Europe with a common currency but it might be a Europe in which economies will be complementary and where differences in living standards will be smaller and international economic exchange richer.

It might also be a Europe with a healthy climate, pure water and unpolluted soil, an environmentally clean Europe.

But above all it will have to be a Europe which has made distinct progress towards disarmament, a Europe which will make an impact on the rest of the world as a factor for peace and international co-existence.

By applying our minds, we could find many other spheres of social life which we could arrange better in this last decade of the 20th century. We need but apply ourselves to the task.

In this continent of ours there are institutions in which a labour of this kind has long-term prospects, because it has already been going on quite a while. One of these institutions is the Council of Europe, one of whose aims is to achieve greater unity among its members for the purpose of safeguarding and realising the ideals and principles which are their common heritage and facilitating their economic and social progress.

Now that events are speeding up in Europe, it is beginning to be possible for us—states, groups and organisations—to reflect about these matters together, and we can glimpse the possibility of and need for pan-European structures to take change of these tasks.

I think the time has come to realise the 'common home' and the European confederation which eminent statesmen have recently proposed. It is time to establish institutions genuinely encompassing the whole of Europe.

That is why I would draw attention to the suggestion I recently put forward in our parliament, for a Council for European Co-operation embracing all signatories of the Final Act of the Conference on Security and Co-operation in Europe. The council would have two functions: firstly to make preparations for summit meetings of the CSCE states and secondly to examine pan-European problems arising in between regular meetings of CSCE states. We think this would lend needed impetus to the CSCE process and at the same time facilitate future initiatives concerning our continent and aiming to secure its unity.

I am addressing you in Strasbourg, the capital of Europe. A city which, like our country, has often been caught up in the turmoil of history. A city which has several times changed hands and has wondered about its identity. But also a city which, though the capital of a region which has been fought over since time immemorial, a place that has suffered the ravages of revolution, is now an oasis of peace and prosperity. This city is a symbol of hope for us who live in the heart of Europe, where echoes of age-old quarrels are still audible. Today the whole of Europe is faced with the historic challenge of restoring its unity. Will we be equal to it? That depends on us and on you. Over a year ago, Pope John Paul II, addressing the Parliamentary Assembly, said:

'The member countries of your Council are aware that they are not the whole of Europe: in expressing the fervent wish for intensification of co-operation, already sketched out, with other nations, particularly in Central and Eastern Europe, I feel that I share the desire of millions of men and women who know that they are linked by a common history and who hope for a destiny of unity and solidarity on the scale of this whole continent.'

When he said this, probably no-one suspected the climate would become auspicious and that his hopes would begin to be realisable.

Among Strasbourg's many symbols, on the cathedral façade, are statues of the wise virgins and the foolish virgins. Let us be wise virgins. Let us be capable of recognising a historic juncture and rising to its challenge—cautiously, boldly and clear-sightedly.

Polish proposal on the outline of the Council of European Cooperation in the framework of the CSCE process, Warsaw, 10 March 1990*

1. The Council of European Cooperation would constitute a permanent political organ of the CSCE and perform consultative and coordinative functions related to all areas of the CSCE, taking into account their full balancing in the course of implementation of appropriate provisions. The activity of the Council would ensure continuity of the CSCE process.

2. The tasks of the Council of European Cooperation would include:
– reviewing and assessment of current all-European problems in respect of political, military, economic, humanitarian and environment issues; the Council would in particular work in favour of resolving common problems concerning military aspects of security in Europe (including the functioning of confidence- and security-building measures) and preventing potential threats, conflicts and disputes and would accept and consider new proposals relating to expansion of cooperation and contacts in all fields;
– coordination of activities of institutions and organs established in the CSCE process;
– promotion of contacts and ever wider engagement of the CSCE system into cooperation and contacts with regional and subregional organizations, especially with the European Communities, the Council of Europe, the Nordic Council, the United Nations Educational, Scientific and Cultural Organization, the United Nations Environment Programme, the United Nations Economic Commission for Europe and the Council for Mutual Economic Assistance;
– preparation of the conferences of the CSCE states at the highest and/or foreign ministers level;
– implementation of other tasks resulting from decisions taken at the meetings in the framework of the CSCE system.

3. The structure of the Council:
– Participating in its work would be ambassadorial rank permanent representatives of the states participating in the CSCE. In perspective, regular sessions of the Council with participation of foreign ministers would be considered.

The work of the Council would be assisted by an international secretariat of several persons. The secretariat would operate a centre of documentation and information.

The Council would have its permanent seat, with the possibility of rotation of session venues.

Plenary sessions of the Council would be held periodically with a possibility of calling extraordinary sessions, e. g. on urgent matters constituting the subject of particular interest of participating states. The Council would replace the meetings of representatives of CSCE states convened periodically.

In the work of the Council organizational procedures and working methods agreed in the final recommendations of the consultations preceding the Helsinki Conference on Security and Cooperation in Europe would be applied *mutatis mutandis*.

The Council could, on the basis of consensus, adopt joint documents in the form of communiques and recommendations.

In creating the Council of European Cooperation the existing experience and infrastructures could be used to avoid excessive extra costs.

The proposal to create the Council of European Cooperation could be considered during the course of preparatory work leading to the 1990 summit meeting of 35 states participating in the CSCE which, in its turn, might decide on the matter.

Presenting the foregoing position of the government of the Republic of Poland, the Embassy requests that information on this proposal be transmitted to the government of Sweden.

Simultaneously the Embassy wishes to inform that the government of the Republic of Poland is open to dialogue on the subject of creation of the Council of European Cooperation on all convenient levels and planes, including the Bonn Conference on Economic Cooperation in Europe to open on 19 March, 1990. The government of Poland would appreciate any remarks and comments which might help develop and perfect the foregoing proposal.

---

* An initial concept of the Council of European Cooperation was presented by the Polish Prime Minister, Tadeusz Mazowiecki in his speech at the Sejm on 18 January 1990 and developed at the Parliamentary Assembly of the Council of Europe on 30 January 1990. The published proposal was contained in the note addressed by the Polish Embassy in Stockholm to the Swedish Government.

Problems of peace and security in Europe

Address by Krzysztof Skubiszewski, Minister of Foreign Affairs of the Republic of Poland, at an Extraordinary Session of the Assembly of the Western European Union, Luxembourg, 22 March 1990

Excerpts

(...)

I have referred to the changes in Central and Eastern Europe. They have set Europe in a dynamic motion. They have demonstrated the influence that freedom and democracy exercise on inter-State relations.

Politically, the modifications that have been brought about have opened up a possibility for rearranging the European system in accordance with the aspirations of all the nations of the continent. Born ten years ago in Poland, the idea of 'Solidarity' fostered this process and added to it two essential values: first, the moral dimension, and second, the emphasis on moderation in reforms without detracting from their fundamental nature. Our approach is that of change in stability.

As a result, the traditional dichotomy of East–West relations, not to speak of division, has lost its validity.

Old structures usually outlive the circumstances that have led to their creation. The traditional security mechanisms and structures which have been inherited from the past are clearly not adequate to the challenges we face

today. They are not relevant to our aspirations and to the new situation that arose in the heart of Europe. Yet the old structures are still in existence. We all want to move away from Yalta and are afraid to come back to Sarajevo. Nonetheless, the legitimate fear of instability should not prevent us from working out a concept of pan-European relations. Our effort must be accompanied by the necessity to preserve a stable framework for transition. That way of thinking is part of the Polish foreign policy.

We do not reject the lessons of the past from which we draw several conclusions. But we must concentrate on the present and especially on the future. In building up the new system of security we must first base ourselves on the rule of international law. In particular, I would refer to the following principles governing the relations of States:

– prohibition of the threat or use of military force;
– prohibition of intervention;
– settlement of disputes by peaceful means alone;
– equality before law and in the protection afforded by law;
– self-determination of peoples, including the right of a people to establish an independent State;
– respect for and observance of human rights and fundamental freedoms for all;
– integrity of State territory and inviolability of frontiers.

The latter principle is particularly important in the present transition in Europe. The unification of the two German States can take place only within their existing frontiers and it must be linked to the corroboration, in treaty form, of the German–Polish frontier. Such a treaty, which should have the status and effect of a peace settlement with Germany, will have as its purpose the elimination of any questioning of the Oder-Neisse frontier or any discussion on its revision at the start of unified Germany and thereafter. In the moment of German unification, which is part of the process of unifying our continent, European relations and especially Central European relations at a vital geostrategic point cannot and should not be burdened with a frontier issue of that dimension. The final settlement, arrived at now, lies in the interest of the whole of Europe and is an imperative of European statesmanship.

From the Polish perspective, the new security system should reflect the concept of a single Europe and the values of democracy, pluralism and humanism. We want to close the chapter of the rule of force, political dictate and 'limited sovereignty', we wish to overcome the syndrome of zones of influence and to banish the concept of security as a 'zero-end' game.

The new system cannot, of course, limit itself to a mere negation of what was, until recently, wrong in Central-Eastern Europe. It should give everybody such sense of security and stability as to render every alliance-like security arrangement no longer necessary.

The new system of European security will be based on the elimination of the domination by a State or States over another State or States. The prohibition of the use of force is an obvious element of the scheme. But we know all too well that respect for State sovereignty and equality does not automatically remove conflicts. The future system should contain crisis-management and conflict-prevention mechanisms.

The function of alliances, and especially multilateral alliances, in Europe is another problem. Their role is changing. The Warsaw alliance, of which Poland is a member, has lost its ideological colour. It is no longer an instrumentality of political satellitism. It remains an agreement on collective self-defence in accordance with Article 51 of the United Nations Charter. In the process of building up European unity it will lose much of its significance. It will be dissolved the moment an all-European system of security becomes a reality.

We believe that the North Atlantic Treaty Organization and the Western European Union fulfil a stabilizing function.

The alliances continue to exist but their nature is changing. Since their creation they have been regarded as mutually opposed. From our perspective we want them to lose that nature. We wish that they acquire a non-confrontational and co-operative character.

By remaining in the Warsaw alliance, Poland does not pursue any ideological or political objectives that could make her differ from the ideas represented by the members of the NATO and the Western European Union. We do not regard our membership in the Warsaw Treaty as an obstacle to developing relations with the West. Sovereignty is the governing principle of our military doctrine

and its practical implementation. That doctrine is not directed against any Western alliance, but against any aggressor whoever he might be. In her history Poland knew aggressors who came from different geographical directions. Our membership in the Warsaw alliance does not imply any involvement in the global big-power rivalry.

The multilateral alliances should become more transparent. They will thus emphasize that they have no hostile intentions with regard to each other.

Disarmament is the key element of the new security order in Europe. To be effective it has to be politically and conceptually in line with the vision of a united Europe.

We focus our attention on the Vienna conference and on the elaboration of a treaty on conventional forces. While we already know what the main elements of the treaty are, we still have to ask the question whether the treaty can meet everyone's expectations. That is a legitimate issue to raise as the treaty's concept was designed long before the present developments in Europe. My answer is that the ongoing changes should not delay the conclusion of the treaty. The heart of the matter is deep and stabilizing cuts and that requires no modification. Later on, there should be a follow-up and a second stage of negotiations. In any case, we press for the early conclusion of the treaty.

The treaty will not solve all the problems and, therefore, one should make it flexible enough to include additional arrangements. In particular, such arrangements may become necessary as a result of the unification of Germany.

We should start thinking about the agenda for Vienna II. It should bring deeper cuts, especially in all the sensitive areas of Europe. Reductions of new weapons and equipment should be considered. There is need for the restructuring of armed forces and putting them into a clearly defensive posture, and one should further limit the offensive capabilities by placing constraints on logistics and deployment of forces. Vienna II should solve the problem of the destabilizing nature of new technologies and the qualitative arms race. It should create guarantees against rapid reconversion of the industrial potential to military purposes and mobilization of resources for offensive purposes. It should further develop the sufficiency rule and deal with the problem of forces stationed on foreign territory. The next phase should be based on a negotiated settlement in which all States will act as fully sovereign and independent participants.

The first agreement reached in Vienna will provide, I hope, an impetus for other disarmament efforts which would strengthen its security-building effect. I am referring, first of all, to the problem of tactical nuclear weapons.

European security is also linked to the presence of the two superpowers. The Soviet role stems from its geopolitical position in Europe. The United States' involvement has proved to be of a stabilizing nature and that role may increase with the unification of Germany.

Eurasia and, consequently, Europe has always constituted the central priority of the American–Soviet contest. The American–Soviet relations seem now to evolve from contest to co-operation. This may have, we hope and wish, its effect on Europe in the sense of gradually decreasing the intensity of the collision of the superpower interests on our continent. That, in fact, should be one of the main goals of establishing a new system of security in Europe: we all should make an effort to turn the presence of the two superpowers in Europe into a factor that supports and fosters European security, while at the same time Europe should lose in importance as an area of superpower rivalry. President Mitterrand's idea of a European Confederation has many facets, one of them being related, I think, to this aspect. And the reduction of superpower contest in Europe and the transition to superpower co-operation is of primary importance for finding a solution to the most difficult problem of German unification, which is the political and military status of the unified German State. That State must be fully integrated into what now is called the new architecture of Europe. A segment of that architecture is the Council of European Co-operation proposed by Poland.

Europe is now facing important decisions which will shape its image for a long time to come. If democracy is to be the cornerstone of the European relations, the preparation of decisions must be based on democratic rules. Each State must have a say in the discussion of matters of common interest and of those concerning its particular interests. Poland attaches a great importance to the CSCE summit to be held this year.

VIII. Czecho-Slovak documents

Speech by Jiri Dienstbier, Foreign Minister of the Czech and Slovak Republic, at the Warsaw Treaty Organization Meeting, Prague, 17 March 1990

Again Europe is talking about Germany. A strong economic formation, probably with a common currency, will soon emerge through the unification of the two German states as early as this year. The political and economic structure of this economic formation is already within reach. We fully support the right of the German people to self-determination in conformity with the moral principles of our foreign policy.

We often hear expressions of anxiety over the possible political influence of the future German state and the revival of traditional German expansionism.

Attempts to exercise pressure on this big nation may lead to the strengthening of extremist political trends and groupings, to the renewal of the so-called 'Versailles complex'. We believe it to be in our interest, as well as in the interest of the future of Europe as a whole, for the Germans themselves to choose the means of their unification as long as these are democratic.

It would therefore be pointless to argue over which article of the West German Constitution the Warsaw Treaty countries should give preference in the actual process of unification. This is the affair of the citizens of both German states, their Parliaments and Governments. In the same way we shall, in principle, have no objections as to the form in which the GDR will be integrated into the West German economic mechanism, and more particularly, in the European Communities. Czechoslovakia itself endeavours to establish the closest links with these groupings. We have no doubt that the very existence of the European Communities and of other European institutions constitute a guarantee of the democratic character of future Germany.

Czechoslovak interests have not been affected by German unification efforts for the time being. We do not assume that they will be. If an issue directly related to Czechoslovakia were to come up at the negotiations we would wish to be present. This is not an expression of distrust towards the negotiating parties, but never again shall we tolerate negotiations affecting us without our participation.

Too much time has elapsed since the end of the Second World War to organize a peace conference attended by the 51 members of the Anti-Hitler coalition. Nevertheless we should look for a way to conclude the chapter of this war with all its adverse consequences once and for all. The cold war and the division of Europe were among these negative consequences. This could be done, in our view, by a summit meeting of the Helsinki states to be held before 1992, if possible next year. We are of the view that an agreement on this could be achieved at this year's summit conference at which the heads of states will sign an agreement on conventional weapons.

The prospect of German unification also creates a new situation at the Vienna talks on conventional disarmament and confidence-building measures. It may be assumed that German unification will take place at the time of the implementation of the first agreement on conventional forces. It will therefore be necessary to look for some new solutions which will take the unification process into account, enable the necessary corrections in the adopted agreements and ensure a general balance, including balance in the most sensitive region—Central Europe. The process of German unification should be a further incentive for the Vienna talks on conventional disarmament to move without unnecessary delays from the first agreement to its second stage, e.g. further substantial reduction of military confrontation. We think it a good sign that there is general consensus in this respect as I have been able to confirm in my conversation with Western partners and at NATO Headquarters.

Developments in Germany have revived the issue of security in Europe. This issue has been raised time and again by European nations with every change on the European political scene.

Under the influence of the past the whole range of security problems in Europe sometimes escapes us. Some catastrophic alternatives of German development keep emerging in our considerations. But there are other sources of conflict in the contemporary world. Nationalist turmoil in various parts of Europe, the threat of environmental disaster, explosive economic imbalance, an eventual conflict instigated from the Third World, etc. This is why we believe that the issue of European security should be viewed in a broader context.

Our proposal is to set up a Commission for European security as the executive body of a European agreement on collective security concluded in the spirit of and in conformity with the UN Charter. Such a European Commission on Security could operate in parallel with the Economic Commission for Europe. It is my conviction that as opposed to all past and largely proclamatory attempts to conclude an Agreement on Collective Security in Europe, we now have a real chance to make this idea a reality.

The Agreement on Collective European Security should certainly stem from the Helsinki accord and would be the logical culmination of the Helsinki process. It would include the commitment of peaceful settlement of disputes in the whole region from San Francisco to Vladivostok, a clear definition of the aggressor, the commitment to mutual assistance, including military assistance, and the decision to set up an executive and consultative body—the European Commission for Security.

The Commission for Security in Europe should have two chambers; a political chamber and a subordinated military chamber. Both would meet at the level of the respective ministers. A secretariat would be responsible for day-to-day agenda. Issues of appointment of specialists, definition of competence, systems of control, equipment, etc., would be processed by a commission of experts. The staff of this body would be limited, with powers proportional to their mission.

NATO and the Warsaw Pact would go on existing for some time but their significance would gradually diminish. Both alliances would naturally cease to exist after the setting up of common structures. The gradual integration of central and East European countries into all European integration processes, the revival of traditional institutions, such as the Economic Commission for Europe, the establishment of the Security Commission for Europe and the application of the results of the Helsinki process could lend a universal

character to European unification. We offer Prague as headquarters for the European Commission for Security. This suggestion is submitted as a first outline for future discussions that would specify its structures.

We believe that the establishment of a European system of collective security equipped with an effective mechanism would be a first step to the Europe we want to live in.

The second step, if we succeed in this first endeavour, would be the foundation of an Organization of European States based on consensus. At this phase we could make the most of and expand proven institutions of West European integration, such as the Council of Europe, the European Parliament, etc.

Memorandum of the Czecho-Slovak Government on the European Security Commission, Prague, 6 April 1990

Political developments in the world and, particularly, in Europe are unfolding with such speed that the existing institutions are no longer in step with them. After years of confrontation Europe finds itself at the start of a new stage. This gives rise to new possibilities but also to certain risks.

The security structure of the continent stemming from the post-war realities is still based on the principle of a balance of forces between the two blocs. Its foundations, however, are not solid because they rest on artificial dividing lines. The division of Europe in two parts, as well as the division of Germany in two States has outlived itself.

The sources of potential European conflicts are more heterogeneous than has until now been envisaged by the bipolar confrontational system. From this follows the necessity of conceiving European security more broadly and of including in it, in addition to political and military, also economic, environmental and humanitarian aspects as well as the possibility of other threats. Such security, however, cannot be safeguarded by the existing confrontational security system, but only by a new European-wide structure of peace, stability and confidence. The profound political changes in Central and Eastern Europe add to the urgency of the need for such a modern structure.

The Warsaw Treaty and NATO operate today in different conditions than those in which they came into being. These organizations which until now have divided Europe should shift the focus of their activity primarily to the field of disarmament. We assume that further development will enhance their political role and will gradually tone down their military role. This process, at the same time, will not have to proceed symmetrically, since, in many aspects of their activities, the two groupings are not identical.

We believe that the best suitable basis on which to build a unified all-European security system is provided by the CSCE process. The new situation in Europe demands of this process to be heading with greater momentum in the direction of a second generation of Helsinki understandings. These should create the prerequisites for the gradual establishment of a common system of European security. The attainment of this goal calls for institutionalizing our joint efforts within CSCE and creating effective mechanisms of a new type.

A longer-term outlook of building a modern security system calls for making full use of the experience of the existing institutions of multilateral cooperation, such as the Council of Europe and others, which should gradually become European-wide.

Seeking new possible approaches, we proceed from the positive lessons learned so far in the CSCE process, as well as from the need to respond to the development in Germany and to the profound changes in Central and Eastern Europe.

In keeping with the purposes and principles of the United Nations Charter and of the Conference on Security and Cooperation in Europe, Czechoslovakia proposes, in the first stage, the establishment of a European Security Commission comprised of the participating States of the Helsinki process. Its justification is seen by us in the fact that it would provide an until now missing permanent all-European platform for the consideration of questions relating to security on the continent, and for seeking their solution. This European Security Commission would operate side by side with the existing two groupings and independently of them.

The formation of an effective system of European security would in the second stage be facilitated by the establishment, on a treaty basis, of an Organization of European States, including the United States and Canada.

The third stage would culminate in a confederated Europe of free and independent States.

The European Security Commission would operate on the basis of consensus. It would initially fulfil consultative, co-ordinating and certain verification functions and, later on, such functions as would be agreed by the participating States. This would include, in particular, the following tasks:

– Considering international political correlations of European security and proposing the adoption of appropriate measures;

– Forestalling threats to European peace and security, the rise of exacerbated situations, disputes, military incidents and conflicts and recommending as well as offering means of their settlement / good offices, mediation, fact finding, conciliation, etc. /;

– Dealing with questions of threat to, and violations of, security that are due to economic, ecological and humanitarian causes and assume large proportions and have international implications;

– Creating a scope for direct contacts and negotiations of the two groupings and their members, attended, if need be, also by the European neutral and non-aligned countries;

– Commenting on the conduct of negotiations by the European disarmament and security forums and proposing their further orientation;

– Considering the possibilities of expanding the agenda of the existing disarmament forums and the establishment of new ones;

– Considering reports by verification and consultation centres on compliance with European arms control and security agreements;

– Informing each other on doctrinal, structural, organizational and budgetary changes relating to the armed forces of the participating States and on the introduction of new weapon systems by them;

– Informing the United Nations as well as regional organizations on the results achieved in the sphere of European disarmament and security.

The Commission would meet at the level of Ministers of Foreign Affairs and their Permanent Representatives. Regular sessions at the level of Ministers would be held at least once a year. Extraordinary sessions could be convened at the request of participating States.

Sessions of Permanent Representatives would be held once a month or more frequently if so requested by a participating State.

Subordinated to the Commission would be a Military Committee composed of military representatives of the CSCE participating States. It would be meeting at least once a year and would deal with questions specified by the Commission. For the purpose of the implementation of its tasks the Commission may establish auxiliary bodies. The necessary technical services for the Commission would be secured by a not very sizable, operative, permanent Secretariat.

Czechoslovakia offers Prague as the permanent seat of the Commission. At the request of the participating States the Commission could also meet elsewhere.

The forthcoming Summit of the 35 participating countries, which will consider important questions of the further development of security and cooperation in Europe, could adopt a decision on creating organizational prerequisites for the establishment of the European Security Commission as a nucleus of a new security structure on the continent.

Czechoslovakia, for historical, political-strategic and other reasons, has an eminent interest in the creation of such a structure. While drafting our proposal, we took into account the suggestions which have so far been submitted by the other CSCE participating countries and which came close to our concept of European security. This proposal is open to discussion.

The dynamic development on the continent creates conditions for various approaches to the shaping of all-European structures and their appropriate mechanisms. However, the goal should be to create a new, sufficiently flexible and future-oriented model of European security.

Such development should be in the interest of not only Europe but of the whole world.

IX. Hungarian–Soviet document

Agreement concerning the withdrawal of Soviet troops temporarily stationed on the territory of the Hungarian Republic, Moscow, 11 March 1990

The government of the Hungarian Republic and the government of the Union of the Soviet Socialist Republics (henceforth referred to as the parties),

guided by the endeavour to develop friendly and good neighbourly ties between the Hungarian Republic and the Union of the Soviet Socialist Republics,

consistently observing the basic principles of international law as endorsed in the United Nations' fundamental document and in the Final Act of the Conference on Security and Co-operation in Europe, including the observance of sovereignty and of non-interference in internal affairs,

regarding the issue of the withdrawal of Soviet troops temporarily stationed in Hungary as an organic part of the common endeavour aimed at the strengthening of European and international trust and security, agreed the following:

Article 1

The withdrawal of the Soviet troops temporarily stationed on the territory of the Hungarian Republic, will take place during the period of 1990 and 1991. The withdrawal of the Soviet troops from the territory of the Hungarian Republic will commence on 12th March 1990 and be concluded on 30th March 1991.

The entire personnel of the Soviet troops will be withdrawn, including civilians who are Soviet citizens, as well as arms, military technology and material equipment.

The schedule of the withdrawal of Soviet troops from the territory of the Hungarian Republic is contained in the supplement to this agreement, and comprises an indivisible part of that.

Article 2

The government of the Hungarian Republic will co-operate in the withdrawal of Soviet troops from the territory of Hungary, by securing the necessary conditions for the implementation thereof.

Article 3

The transportation of the Soviet troops, and the leaving behind and destruction of various materials and waste, will be implemented in keeping with the interests of the civilian population and with the observance of the laws of the protection of the environment.

Article 4

There will be a limit to the movement—including flights—connected with the military training and activities of the Soviet troops stationed on the territory of the Hungarian Republic.

Article 5

The parties will appoint authorised agents to secure the implementation of the provisions of this agreement, to oversee the withdrawal of the Soviet troops from the territory of the Hungarian Republic, and for the recording, valuation, handing over or the selling, by agreed methods, of the objects, equipment or other material implements.

Article 6

Until the permanent withdrawal of the troops from the territory of the Hungarian Republic, the legal status of the Soviet troops, and the property laws and other issues pertaining to the temporary stationing of the Soviet troops in Hungary, will be decided by the agreement made on 27th May 1957 between the government of the Hungarian People's Republic and the government of the Union of Soviet Socialist Republics regarding the legal situation of the Soviet troops temporarily stationed in the Hungarian People's Republic, as well as by the regulations of other Hungarian–Soviet agreements currently in force.

Article 7

Those property, financial and other economic queries, arising from the withdrawal of Soviet troops, which are not settled by contracts already in force, will be brought under regulation by separate agreements. The parties shall make arrangements as soon as possible, aimed at the solution of the above queries until the complete withdrawal of the Soviet troops.

Article 8

Any disputed questions in connection with the understanding and implementation of this agreement, and with the execution of the withdrawal of Soviet troops according to schedule, will be settled by the parties within 30 days of their submission to the Hungarian–Soviet mixed committee, formed by the government of the Hungarian Republic and the government of the Union of Soviet Socialist Republics on the basis of Article 17 of the agreement made on 27th May 1957 regarding the legal position of the Soviet troops temporarily stationed on the territory of the Hungarian People's Republic.

Should the mixed committee prove unable to reach a decision in a question submitted to it, the dispute will have to be resolved by diplomatic means.

Article 9

The regulations of this agreement do not touch such obligations in force between the parties which originate from bi- or multi-lateral agreements, including those arising from the friendly co-operation and mutual assistance pact made in Warsaw on May 14th 1955.

Article 10

This agreement comes into force on the day of its being signed. Two original copies of it were prepared on Moscow on March 10th, 1990, in Hungarian and Russian; both texts are equally authentic.

Note: A similar agreement on the withdrawal of Soviet troops from Czecho-Slovakia was signed earlier during the official visit of Czecho-Slovak President Vaclav Havel to the Soviet Union. The agreement was signed by the two respective foreign ministers, Eduard Shevardnadze and Jiri Dienstbier, in Moscow on 26 February 1990.

X. Finnish document

Speech by Mauno Koivisto, President of the Republic of Finland, at the Parliamentary Assembly of the Council of Europe, Strasbourg, 9 May 1990

Excerpts

(. . .)

Europe is changing. This change is so swift and fundamental that hardly anyone could have predicted such a chain of events only a year ago. All those who regard themselves as experts on international politics feel incompetent.

Yet, even this is not unprecedented. It is possible to predict or at least extrapolate stable development, whilst upheavals are always impossible to foresee.

As a statesman once said: 'Not a single principle in the management of our foreign affairs, accepted by all statesmen for guidance up to six months ago, any longer exists. There is not a diplomatic tradition which has not been swept away'. Those words were spoken by the British Prime Minister, Benjamin Disraeli, nearly 120 years ago, when the German Empire had just been born and the politics of Europe were reshuffled.

Change liberates, but it also brings uncertainty and tension.

We are living in a time when old wrongs are being put right and accusation of new ones are laying the groundwork for future tensions.

When traditional confrontations recede, new ones or—indeed old-latent ones—may arise. There are signs of that in today's Europe.

Yet, I am confident that the positive elements will prevail in the future. I believe that Europe is maturing to a security that will endure.

Europe is fulfilling the commitment made in Helsinki in 1975. The Final Act laid the groundwork for today's changes in the political, military, economic and social relations of our continent.

No single factor has contributed to the recent rapid developments more than the change in the Soviet Union and in its international politics.

But it is the new spirit of understanding between East and West that has made it possible for us to leave the Cold War.

A year ago, this Assembly had the opportunity to hear President Gorbachev's views on the reconstruction of Europe on a basis of common values and a balance of interests. Politics based on blocs and the traditional balance of forces must be left behind, was his message.

It is in the nature of this process that it will never be completed. A Europe that is one and peaceful, co-operating and progressing to its full potential, can only emerge through consistent work and mutual learning.

Setbacks will lie ahead as well, but they can be overcome if we have a proper sense of priorities.

We have to strengthen common structures in Europe. To continue the process, we must rely on the principles and experiences that made our gains to date possible. But to meet the challenges ahead, we shall have to develop our methods of co-operation further.

Even during the unnatural division of Europe, the authors of the Helsinki principles respected European diversity. They safeguarded national identity and self-determination then and for the future.

As we upheld the ideals of human rights, we also freed the creative power of individual aspiration. We gave individuals the crucial position they can and must have in the spiritual and material well-being of Europe.

Last month, at the CSCE economic conference in Bonn, the participating states recognized the relationship between political pluralism and a market economy.

The orderly conduct of political change in Eastern and Central Europe is encouraging.

Multiparty democracy, the rule of law and human dignity foster economic development and facilitate reform. Those things, in turn, create a foundation for just social progress and stable peaceful relations in Europe as a whole.

Political pluralism and the marketplace have become the focus of a heavy burden of expectations.

With advancing democracy and improved co-operation, the whole of Europe will be better equipped to meet the challenges of economic restructuring that lie ahead.

As the Bonn document declares, Europe is undergoing a profound and rapid change. In Western Europe, the challenge is economic integration. In Central and Eastern Europe, the goal is, first and foremost, economic recovery.

Europe cannot expect to reap the reward for overcoming political and ideological division if the gap of economic inequality remains or even becomes wider.

The Bonn conference showed that European countries see their chance to, and recognise their responsibility for, expanding economic co-operation in an effective and yet balanced way. Markets can only perform in an economic environment of openness and reciprocity.

The transition to a market economy will be facilitated through the gradual creation of a common economic area in the whole of Europe. Co-ordinated support for sustainable economic reform will be a vital component in the coming together of European economies.

Co-operation in the development and introduction of environmentally sound technology would be a prime example of what a new Europe that is united in its purpose could achieve. Only through co-operation can the damage be remedied and the environment preserved for future generations.

The arms race has become an economic burden on Europe. The new political opportunity and hard economic necessities speak for a profound reassessment of investment in the military factor and of its role in our security relations.

The historic results in sight in disarmament negotiations will give us a chance to break the endless cycle of arms expansion and modernisation.

Europe is on the threshold of freeing itself from the overarming that has kept it captive for so many years and decades.

Individually, European countries are drawing their conclusions from the strain that armament puts on their national economies. This is especially true in countries whose economies have been under such excessive strain that they must now make a clear choice between armament and economic reform and recovery.

Just as vital is the fact that the military reality is being changed through disarmament. An emerging new strategic landscape will lessen and diminish the danger of military instability and conflict.

The negotiators in Vienna will have a chance to be true to their mandate and abolish the threat of surprise attack and large-scale offensive in the area where military confrontation was the symbol and basis for such fears in a divided Europe.

But what really makes us believe that deep cuts in armaments will give us more security is that they will be associated with effective verification, confidence-building measures and openness. The CSCE military negotiations in Vienna have an important task in this respect.

The more openness is an integral component of military matters, the more credible armament measures and new security arrangements will be.

Judgements need no longer be made on the basis of mistrust or uncertainty. States can also reassure their neighbours and other countries of the peacefulness and sincerity of their policies and intentions.

Europe will then enjoy co-operative security.

Within the military alliances, a search for future roles and new functions seems to be taking place. Such functions may be found in the field of arms control and verification. We welcome this.

We are living in a period of transition that may last for a long time.

Historic steps are in sight, although not completed yet.

Growing stability—even if it is the general trend—is not necessarily comprehensive or uninterrupted.

As East–West confrontation recedes, the major military powers continue to bear the greatest responsibility for security relations in Europe.

Regional sources of instability and conflict may assume greater significance for the whole of Europe. Relations between neighbouring states are likely to affect the maintenance of security and stability more than in the past.

Joint security arrangements function if neighbours and rivals are responsive and willing to solve their problems. A common security institution cannot solve our problems for us.

We greet with great satisfaction efforts towards regional co-operation in Central and Eastern Europe, with the aim of going beyond old barriers and former practices and grasping both the opportunities and responsibilities that exist for co-operation and resolving conflicts.

One of Finland's main policy principles is that of maintaining good relations with our neighbours and contributing to security and stability in Northern Europe and the Baltic region. That is a vital environment for our national security.

We are following with great concern and sympathy the efforts of the Baltic peoples to find their way to independence, to which also the Soviet constitution entitles them.

Our own experience tells us that with a great-power neighbour one has to reach negotiated solutions that will stand the test of time.

I speak as a representative of a country for which the greater powers projected the same fate as the Baltic nations. But we went another road. This road led first through great difficulties and sacrifices but later to a stable relationship with our neighbouring great power. The Soviet Union has become a good neighbour.

History cannot be undone, but the new chances that today's Europe offers for all countries and peoples should be fully utilized.

The foundation of security is evolving together with, and as a result of, European political and economic change. In this way, learning from experience, a new and stable security order can take shape.

When we speak today of a new European security system, it needs to be seen in the light of a comprehensive development.

As Europe changes, more and more security functions will be entrusted to joint arrangements, procedures and institutions. In the long run, such a common system may become vital for national as well as international security.

The CSCE has a central role in the management of the ongoing change. There is a growing consensus that it will also provide the essential framework for future common security arrangements and co-operative regimes.

Finland has long spoken for strengthening the CSCE follow-up in a measured way.

We concur with the idea of holding periodic meetings of the foreign ministers of the CSCE participating States. This is one of the issues to be considered at the summit meeting of the CSCE countries planned for later this year.

As a neutral country, Finland has been active in the CSCE process from the beginning. We are proud that the process carries the name of our capital, where the first summit took place.

As the CSCE process enters a new phase, we look forward to further opportunities and responsibilities.

The capability of the CSCE to respond to new and growing tasks should be strengthened. Finland is ready to offer her contribution and her services to this process.

As the host country, we look forward to the Helsinki follow-up meeting in 1992 with a sense of great responsibility. We expect the meeting to find new tasks for the CSCE process and to make decisions on such new principles, institutions and working methods as will be deemed necessary by the participating states.

Helsinki 1992 will give Europe new guidelines to continue the journey begun at Helsinki 1975.

XI. Swedish document

Building a more secure Europe in the 1990s

Keynote address by Sten Andersson, Minister for Foreign Affairs of Sweden, at the 1990 International Conference of the Institute for East–West Security Studies, Stockholm, 7 June 1990

I would first of all like to welcome you to Stockholm. It is a great pleasure for me to have this opportunity to welcome the distinguished participants in this conference to our city.

The Institute for East–West Security Studies has played a pioneering role in bringing people closer together—people from East and West, from the United States, Europe as well as from other countries. At the Institute's annual conferences and at various other meetings under its auspices, representatives of different aspects of society from many countries made highly constructive contributions to the ongoing discussion on how to create together, a more secure and peaceful world.

This ninth Annual Conference is entitled 'The Challenges and Opportunities for Building a More Secure Europe in the 1990s', a subject which has long been on our agenda. But this topic has now become topical in a way we would scarcely have believed possible only six months ago.

For the third time in this century, the political structures of Europe are being radically rebuilt. On the two previous occasions, this took place after devastating world wars. This time it is the result of a peaceful revolution. The reform policies in the Soviet Union, the changes in Central and Eastern Europe, the fall of the Berlin Wall—these events have all combined to pull down the artificial barriers which have been dividing Europe for more than 40 years.

This provides a different and much better basis for creating 'a new European architecture' than in 1918 and 1945. This new European architecture is to replace the Cold War division of Europe dominated by two blocs confronting each other.

A completely new political and security situation has been created in Europe. Central and Eastern European countries are now undergoing rapid democratization. They have initiated a transition, in many respects painful but necessary, from centrally planned economies to market economies. At the same time, however, we have been reminded of a number of national and minority conflicts.

Mikhail Gorbachev's reform policies—glasnost and perestroika—have liberated the Soviet Union from Stalinism. This has been the most important single factor in creating opportunities for forming a new Europe of peace and democracy. But the economic transformation has brought with it enormous strains, and the outcome of the reform process is still uncertain.

Even the future extent of the union is uncertain. Lithuania and the two other Baltic republics, Estonia and Latvia, have made it clear that their just and legitimate demand for national self-determination means total independence.

The clock cannot be set back. The unification of the two German states is irrevocable. For the German people this implies the end of an intolerable situation which has lasted more than 40 years. 'What belongs together, grows together'—as Willy Brandt once expressed it. The existence of two German states has been the foremost expression of the division of Europe. Their unification confirms that the old order has ceased to exist.

In Western Europe, integration is well under way. The twelve EC countries have declared their intention to form an economic and monetary union and also a political union when the internal market is realized. Negotiations between the twelve EC countries and the six EFTA countries will soon be starting to create a European Economic Space.

When Olof Palme launched the concept of common security in the early 1980s to replace the concept of nuclear deterrence, he defined it as 'security in a different and more stable form, which takes into account the legitimate security needs of every nation'.

This present development in Europe is extremely positive and promising, but it also presents many challenges to all of us who are endeavouring to build a more secure Europe than that of nuclear deterrence.

A new European order must accommodate the Soviet Union's legitimate security needs while facilitating and promoting continued reform in the Soviet Union—including the realization through negotiations of the Baltic republics' demands for independence.

At the same time, we must bear in mind that no matter what the outcome of the reform process, the Soviet Union will remain the strongest military power in Europe and one of the two leading nuclear powers. Therefore the legitimate security interests of other countries in relation to the Soviet Union must also be accommodated in a new European security order.

It is generally agreed today that a new European security order must embrace all European countries as well as the United States and Canada.

It is also agreed that military security and economic and cultural cooperation—and also human contacts and respect for human rights—are intimately linked together. This is clearly expressed in the CSCE Final Act.

A new European security order embracing all the CSCE states must develop gradually. At the same time, it is crucial that political détente in Europe should also produce rapid results in the field of disarmament.

All sides appear to agree that the unification of the two German states must not imply that Western defence positions are moved further to the East. Instead, the withdrawal of Soviet units from Central and Eastern Europe must encourage more far-reaching agreements on conventional disarmament and confidence- and security-building measures.

Future European disarmament negotiations must include all types of weapons. It is high time that all tactical nuclear weapons are removed from Europe.

Naval armaments must also be the subject of negotiations. The aim must be to achieve military stability at the lowest possible level—not just in Central Europe but in Europe as a whole.

The Conference on Security and Cooperation in Europe is the natural forum for the emergence of a new European security order. The CSCE offers a framework for negotiations on disarmament as well as on confidence- and security-building measures. In the future, these negotiations should involve the participation of all the CSCE states.

Mechanisms can also be created within the CSCE framework for solving conflicts and dealing with crises. This is highly important, particularly in view of the remaining risk of conflicts within, and perhaps also between, European states as a result of the flaring up of nationality and minority disputes.

In the longer term, the goal should be a new security system to replace both military alliances—a European security system which will complement and support the United Nations in its task of guaranteeing international peace and security.

Security and cooperation go hand in hand and lasting security cannot be built up without economic and cultural cooperation. The CSCE has a central role to play here too as the only European forum which embraces all European states.

Today, most European cooperation is taking place outside the CSCE—in organizations such as the EC, EFTA, OECD and the Council of Europe and the European Bank for Reconstruction and Development, which was set up last week. The CSCE should not compete with these organizations or try to replace them.

Yet the CSCE needs to be given a firmer structure. Regular meetings of ministers are one aspect of reinforcement. It us also essential that a permanent executive CSCE secretariat is established. It is our view that a decision to set up a secretariat should be taken at the next CSCE Summit Meeting.

Our experience as a host country for the Stockholm Conference encourages us to believe that Stockholm would be a suitable venue for a permanent executive secretariat of the CSCE. We wish to make a substantial contribution here and, in line with our commitment to the CSCE process, Sweden is now proposing Stockholm as the permanent seat for such a secretariat.

A continuous process, moving towards common security and broader, closer cooperation throughout Europe, both within and outside the CSCE framework, will surely facilitate solutions of the problem which have arisen as a result of developments in Central and Eastern Europe.

Solidarity between nations must be one of the driving forces in this process. The transformation taking place in the Soviet Union and the changes in Central and Eastern Europe offer the Soviet Union great opportunities. The Western countries can facilitate changes by assisting the Soviet Union in its reform policies in various ways.

The countries of Central and Eastern Europe are searching for their place in the

Europe of the future. They need solidarity and cooperation with the West if they are to modernize run-down industries and deal with environmental devastation. They need support in an economic reform process which might well lead to dangerous social strains and tensions.

The transition to market economies in Central and Eastern Europe must take place on a socially acceptable basis. Otherwise, the backlash may also threaten democracy. If peace and security in Europe are to be guaranteed, it is essential that inequalities in economic development and living conditions are levelled out.

The vision which has ultimately inspired West European integration has been the unification of the whole of Europe. Today, the realization of this vision has come much closer. This visionary perspective must be constantly kept alive in future integration endeavours within the EC and between the EC and EFTA. President Mitterrand's concept of a European confederation is obviously a case in point.

Sweden's policy towards Europe has always been inspired by a Pan-European vision. This has been true in the Council of Europe, which is the focus for cooperation between all European democracies—and of course in the CSCE. And this also applies today when we are trying to achieve cooperation with the EC as intimate as our policy of neutrality will permit.

The same perspective has also led Sweden and Poland to invite the countries concerned to a Conference on the Baltic environment later this year.

Despite their different security solutions, the Nordic countries have by and large succeeded in maintaining a low degree of tension in their area throughout the post-war period. As countries which are culturally and socially close, we have also built wide-ranging cooperation in a number of spheres. We trust that our experience can also be useful in the context of broader European cooperation. Regional cooperation can and should play a positive role in the Europe of the future.

Tomorrow's Europe must be a Europe which is united in its multiplicity and by ties of varying kinds and strength. But it must also be a Europe based on solidarity. A Europe which has torn down its internal walls must not surround itself with new external barriers.

The security and prosperity of Europe and North America are ultimately dependent on the security and prosperity of other countries and peoples in the world. Conflicts and an arms race outside Europe also expose Europe to risks. And the environmental problems which the world is facing are obviously also a threat to the future of Europe and North America.

At a time when Europe is intensively discussing and planning for new forms for security and cooperation, life is becoming increasingly hard for millions of people in the developing countries. Let me only remind you that the countries of the Third World, weighed down by their burden of debt, are currently paying more interest to the industrialized countries than they receive in development assistance.

There is no doubt a limit to how much underdevelopment global security can tolerate, and to how much poverty democracy can stand.

Democracy and respect for human rights have spread and been reinforced in Europe in a manner which we would not have dared to hope for only a few months ago. This makes it an even more pressing duty to ensure that the best features of the European tradition— belief in universal human rights and solidarity—will guide also our relations with the developing countries.

In the end, this is the only way that a safer world and a safer Europe can be built in the 1990s.

XII. NATO document

London Declaration on a transformed
North Atlantic Alliance

Issued by the Heads of State
and Government participating in the
Meeting of the North Atlantic Council,
London, 5–6 July 1990

1. Europe has entered a new, promising era. Central and Eastern Europe is liberating itself. The Soviet Union has embarked on the long journey toward a free society. The walls that once confined people and ideas are collapsing. Europeans are determining their own destiny. They are choosing freedom. They are choosing economic liberty. They are choosing peace. They are choosing a Europe whole and free. As a consequence, this Alliance must and will adapt.

2. The North Atlantic Alliance has been the most successful defensive alliance in history. As our Alliance enters its fifth decade and looks ahead to a new century, it must continue to provide for the common defence. This Alliance has done much to bring about the new Europe. No-one, however, can be certain of the future. We need to keep standing together, to extend the long peace we have enjoyed these past four decades. Yet our Alliance must be even more an agent of change. It can help build the structures of a more united continent, supporting security and stability with the strength of our shared faith in democracy, the rights of the individual, and the peaceful resolution of disputes. We reaffirm that security and stability do not lie solely in the military dimension, and we intend to enhance the political component of our Alliance as provided for by Article 2 of our Treaty.

3. The unification of Germany means that the division of Europe is also being overcome. A united Germany in the Atlantic Alliance of free democracies and part of the growing political and economic integration of the European Community will be an indispensable factor of stability, which is needed in the heart of Europe. The move within the European Community towards political union, including the development of a European identity in the domain of security, will also contribute to Atlantic solidarity and to the establishment of a just and lasting order of peace throughout the whole of Europe.

4. We recognise that, in the new Europe, the security of every state is inseparably linked to the security of its neighbours. NATO must become an institution where Europeans, Canadians and Americans work together not only for the common defence, but to build new partnerships with all the nations of Europe. The Atlantic Community must reach out to the countries of the East which were our adversaries in the Cold War, and extend to them the hand of friendship.

5. We will remain a defensive alliance and will continue to defend all the territory of all of our members. We have no aggressive intentions and we commit ourselves to the peaceful resolution of all disputes. We will never in any circumstance be the first to use force.

6. The member states of the North Atlantic Alliance propose to the member states of the Warsaw Treaty Organization a joint declaration in which we solemnly state that we are no longer adversaries and reaffirm our intention to refrain from the threat or use of force against the territorial integrity or political independence of any state, or from acting in any other manner inconsistent with the purposes and principles of the United Nations Charter and with the CSCE Final Act. We invite all other CSCE member states to join us in this commitment to non-aggression.

7. In that spirit, and to reflect the changing political role of the Alliance, we today invite President Gorbachev on behalf of the Soviet Union, and representatives of the other Central and Eastern European countries, to come to Brussels and address the North Atlantic Council. We today also invite the governments of the Union of Soviet Socialist Republics, the Czech and Slovak Federal Republic, the Hungarian Republic, the Republic of Poland, the People's Republic of Bulgaria and Romania to come to NATO, not just to visit, but to establish regular diplomatic liaison with

NATO. This will make it possible for us to share with them our thinking and deliberations in this historic period of change.

8. Our Alliance will do its share to overcome the legacy of decades of suspicion. We are ready to intensify military contacts, including those of NATO Military Commanders, with Moscow and other Central and Eastern European capitals.

9. We welcome the invitation to NATO Secretary General Manfred Wörner to visit Moscow and meet with Soviet leaders.

10. Military leaders from throughout Europe gathered earlier this year in Vienna to talk about their forces and doctrine. NATO proposes another such meeting this Autumn to promote common understanding. We intend to establish an entirely different quality of openness in Europe, including an agreement on 'Open Skies'.

11. The significant presence of North American conventional and US nuclear forces in Europe demonstrates the underlying political compact that binds North America's fate to Europe's democracies. But, as Europe changes, we must profoundly alter the way we think about defence.

12. To reduce our military requirements, sound arms control agreements are essential. That is why we put the highest priority on completing this year the first treaty to reduce and limit conventional armed forces in Europe (CFE) along with the completion of a meaningful CSBM package. These talks should remain in continuous session until the work is done. Yet we hope to go further. We propose that, once a CFE Treaty is signed, follow-on talks should begin with the same membership and mandate, with the goal of building on the current agreement with additional measures, including measures to limit manpower in Europe. With this goal in mind, a commitment will be given at the time of signature of the CFE Treaty concerning the manpower levels of a unified Germany.

13. Our objective will be to conclude the negotiations on the follow-on to CFE and CSBMs as soon as possible and looking to the follow-up meeting of the CSCE to be held in Helsinki in 1992. We will seek through new conventional arms control negotiations, within the CSCE framework, further far-reaching measures in the 1990s to limit the offensive capability of conventional armed forces in Europe, so as to prevent any nation from maintaining disproportionate military power on the continent. NATO's High Level Task Force will formulate a detailed position for these follow-on conventional arms control talks. We will make provisions as needed for different regions to redress disparities and to ensure that no one's security is harmed at any stage. Furthermore, we will continue to explore broader arms control and confidence-building opportunities. This is an ambitious agenda, but it matches our goal: enduring peace in Europe.

14. As Soviet troops leave Eastern Europe and a treaty limiting conventional armed forces is implemented, the Alliance's integrated force structure and its strategy will change fundamentally to include the following elements:

– NATO will field smaller and restructured active forces. These forces will be highly mobile and versatile so that Allied leaders will have maximum flexibility in deciding how to respond to a crisis. It will rely increasingly on multinational corps made up of national units.

– NATO will scale back the readiness of its active units, reducing training requirements and the number of exercises.

– NATO will rely more heavily on the ability to build up larger forces if and when they might be needed.

15. To keep the peace, the Alliance must maintain for the foreseeable future an appropriate mix of nuclear and conventional forces, based in Europe, and be kept up to date where necessary. But, as a defensive Alliance, NATO has always stressed that none of its weapons will ever be used except in self-defence and that we seek the lowest and most stable level of nuclear forces needed to secure the prevention of war.

16. The political and military changes in Europe, and the prospects of further changes, now allow the Allies concerned to go further. They will thus modify the size and adapt the tasks of their nuclear deterrent forces. They have concluded that, as a result of the new political and military conditions in Europe, there will be a significantly reduced role for sub-strategic nuclear systems of the shortest range. They have decided specifically that, once negotiations begin on short-range

nuclear forces, the Alliance will propose, in return for reciprocal action by the Soviet Union, the elimination of all its nuclear artillery shells from Europe.

17. New negotiations between the United States and the Soviet Union on the reduction of short-range nuclear forces should begin shortly after a CFE agreement is signed. The Allies concerned will develop an arms control framework for these negotiations which takes into account our requirements for far fewer nuclear weapons, and the diminished need for sub-strategic nuclear systems of the shortest range.

18. Finally, with the total withdrawal of Soviet stationed forces and the implementation of a CFE agreement, the Allies concerned can reduce their reliance on nuclear weapons. These will continue to fulfil an essential role in the overall strategy of the Alliance to prevent war by ensuring that there are no circumstances in which nuclear retaliation in response to military action might be discounted. However, in the transformed Europe, they will be able to adopt a new NATO strategy making nuclear forces truly weapons of last resort.

19. We approve the mandate given in Turnberry to the North Atlantic Council in Permanent Session to oversee the ongoing work on the adaptation of the Alliance to the new circumstances. It should report its conclusions as soon as possible.

20. In the context of these revised plans for defence and arms control, and with the advice of NATO Military Authorities and all member states concerned, NATO will prepare a new Allied military strategy moving away from 'forward defence', where appropriate, towards a reduced forward presence and modifying 'flexible response' to reflect a reduced reliance on nuclear weapons. In that connection, NATO will elaborate new force plans consistent with the revolutionary changes in Europe. NATO will also provide a forum for Allied consultation on the upcoming negotiations on short-range nuclear forces.

21. The Conference on Security and Cooperation in Europe (CSCE) should become more prominent in Europe's future, bringing together the countries of Europe and North America. We support a CSCE Summit later this year in Paris which would include the signature of a CFE agreement and would set new standards for the establishment, and preservation, of free societies. It should endorse, *inter alia*:

– CSCE principles on the right to free and fair elections;
– CSCE commitments to respect and uphold the rule of law;
– CSCE guidelines for enhancing economic cooperation, based on the development of free and competitive market economies; and
– CSCE cooperation on environmental protection.

22. We further propose that the CSCE Summit in Paris decide how the CSCE can be institutionalised to provide a forum for wider political dialogue in a more united Europe. We recommend that CSCE governments establish:

– a programme for regular consultations among member governments at the Heads of State and Government or Ministerial level, at least once each year, with other periodic meetings of officials to prepare for and follow up on these consultations;
– a schedule of CSCE review conferences once every two years to assess progress towards a Europe whole and free;
– a small CSCE secretariat to coordinate these meetings and conferences;
– a CSCE mechanism to monitor elections in all the CSCE countries, on the basis of the Copenhagen Document;
– a CSCE Centre for the Prevention of Conflict that might serve as a forum for exchanges of military information, discussion of unusual military activities, and the conciliation of disputes involving CSCE member states; and
– a CSCE parliamentary body, the Assembly of Europe, to be based on the existing parliamentary assembly of the Council of Europe, in Strasbourg, and include representatives of all CSCE member states.

The sites of these new institutions should reflect the fact that the newly democratic countries of Central and Eastern Europe form part of the political structures of the new Europe.

23. Today, our Alliance begins a major transformation. Working with all the countries of Europe, we are determined to create enduring peace on this continent.

XIII. WTO documents

Declaration of the Consultative Political Committee of the WTO states, Moscow, 7 June 1990

On June 7 the high representatives of the Warsaw Treaty member states held a meeting of the Political Consultative Committee in Moscow. The meeting adopted the following declaration:

I

Modern development in Europe creates conditions for overcoming a bloc security model and the division of the continent. This development is becoming irreversible. It meets the interests of nations wishing to live in mutual harmony, without artificial barriers and ideological hostility. Participants in the meeting favour the formation of a new, all-European security system and the creation of a single Europe of peace and cooperation.

The states represented at the meeting are taking an active part in this dynamic process. This is why they find it necessary to reconsider the character and functions of the Warsaw Treaty. They are sure that only in this case the Warsaw Treaty will be able to reach new topical targets during the transition period, dealing with disarmament and the creation of an all-European security system.

Participants in the meeting are unanimous in their opinion that the ideological enemy image has been overcome in many aspects by mutual efforts of the East and the West, while the East and West notions are again acquiring their purely geographical meaning. They believe that danger could come only from those who would threaten the security of countries in any form, including the threat or use of force, no matter who resorts to it. Confrontation elements contained in documents of the Warsaw Treaty and the North Atlantic Treaty Organisation, that were adopted in the past, are no longer in line with the spirit of the time.

In this new situation the states represented at the meeting will begin to review the character, functions and activities of the Warsaw Treaty, and will start its transformation into a treaty of sovereign states with equal rights, formed on a democratic basis. With this aim

in view they created a provisional commission of government representatives, which will present to the Political Consultative Committee specific proposals on this subject before the end of next October. The proposals will be examined by the Political Consultative Committee before the end of November of this year. Warsaw Treaty Member states want to contribute in this way to the consolidation of peace, security and stability in Europe and to the development of the Helsinki process.

The meeting reiterated the readiness for constructive cooperation with the North Atlantic Alliance, its member states, neutral and non-aligned countries of the continent on a bilateral and multilateral basis in the interests of European stability and disarmament, confidence-building and the affirmation of the defence sufficiency principle.

Participants in the meeting believe that consistent and all-round institutionalisation of the Helsinki process is an important stage of these developments. This is the purpose of proposals submitted recently by some countries-participants in the conference on security and cooperation in Europe. Participants in the meeting expect the first important decisions on this problem to be taken at the forthcoming summit of European countries, the United States and Canada.

Warsaw Treaty member states positively assess some of the steps taken recently by NATO. They expect the new trend of changes in NATO to be accelerated and deepened and to be reflected by corresponding substantial changes in the activities of this alliance.

II

Warsaw Treaty member states went on record in favour of a successful termination of the Vienna talks on conventional armed forces and on confidence- and security-building measures in Europe, so that corresponding agreements could be adopted at a meeting of leaders of the states-participants in the Conference on Security and Cooperation in Europe late in 1990.

So far as external aspects of Germany's reunification are concerned, they expressed their unanimous conviction that it should be carried out in the context of the all-European process and on the basis of its principles, should stimulate and deepen its development, take into consideration lawful security interests of Germany's neighbours and all other states and ensure firm guarantees of the inviolability of European borders.

The states represented at the meeting will actively promote the creation of a European economic and legal space, as well as full implementation of the basic human rights and freedoms.

Participants in the meeting pointed out that the agreements reached at the Soviet–American summit promote a further advance towards disarmament and the improvement of the international situation.

Warsaw Treaty member states express their conviction that all the states-participants in the Helsinki process fully realise their responsibility that the history-making chance to create Europe without blocs and hostility not to be missed.

Proposal of the Czech and Slovak Federal Republic, the German Democratic Republic and the Republic of Poland regarding the institutionalization of the CSCE process, Vienna, 10 July 1990

The participating States of the Conference on Security and Co-operation in Europe,

Proceeding from the fact that the dynamics of present developments in Europe require further improvement in the forms and methods of co-operation among them in all spheres,

Reaffirming the important and positive role the Helsinki process has played and continues to play in the development of European politics,

Agreeing that stabilization and security in Europe require new steps towards the institutionalization of the all-European process, using the experience of the CSCE process and existing European institutions,

Convinced that the process of institutionalization must preserve the existing balance between specific areas of all-European co-operation and should take into account interdependence of political, military, economic, ecological and humanitarian factors,

have agreed as follows:

1. Meetings of Heads of State or Government of the participating States of the CSCE will be held in the capitals of the individual participating States on the basis of rotation at least once every two years. The task of the CSCE summit will be to consider major questions pertaining to implementation of the Helsinki Final Act and other CSCE documents.

2. A Council for Security and Co-operation in Europe, meeting at the level of ministers for foreign affairs as a rule twice a year, will be established.

Meetings of the Council may also take place at the level of ministers other than those for foreign affairs.

The Council may also—at a later stage—meet at ambassador/permanent representative level once a month.

In urgent cases an extraordinary session of the Council may be convened at the request of any participating State.

The Council for Security and Co-operation in Europe will act on the basis of consensus and exercise consultative and co-ordinating functions in all spheres of the CSCE.

Its tasks would include the following:

– To consider current problems of European security, co-operation and human rights and to adopt appropriate measures with a view to increasing the effectiveness of CSCE decisions;

– To consider new proposals regarding European security and co-operation and the development of relations and contacts among participating States;

– To prepare CSCE summits and to implement tasks resulting from them;

– To consider reports from centres and institutions to be established concerning specific problems of European security and co-operation and to co-ordinate their activity;

– To consider possible contacts and co-operation with the United Nations, the Council of Europe and other international organizations.

At a later stage, the Council's activities could gradually replace CSCE follow-up meetings as well as meetings of experts.

The activity of the Council will in no way interfere with the functioning of existing organizations of which participating States are members.

3. In order to provide services for the Council a small permanent secretariat will be established. Its functions will be technical, organizational and administrative. Its headquarters will be in . . .

4. A centre for confidence building, arms control and verification will be established. The Council will determine its tasks and will consider their implementation.

The functions of the centre will include the exchange of information, the notification of movements of military units and military exercises, the registration and co-ordination of inspections and other control activities.

It will also collect and record all information resulting from the implementation of confidence-building measures as well as verification procedures agreed upon in the CSCE process. This information will be available to all CSCE participating States.

The headquarters of the centre will be in . . .

5. In addition, a centre for conflict prevention and settlement will be established.

The main functions of the centre will be to collect information on potential causes of conflict, disputes between States or incidents and to prevent their arising. The centre may propose to the Council measures to eliminate such causes or recommend possible solutions in cases where such conflicts have arisen.

An important task of the centre will be to promote the establishment of a system of peaceful settlement of disputes. They may include consultations, conciliation procedures, mediation, good offices and other measures worked out in the CSCE process.

6. Other bodies may be established to consider specific problems of co-operation in various domains.

7. The frequency of the meeting and conferences agreed upon in the Concluding Document of the Vienna Meeting 1986 should be adhered to.

XIV. Neutral and non-aligned document

Communiqué of the meeting of the ministers for foreign affairs of the neutral and non-aligned countries of the CSCE, Helsinki, 1–2 November 1990

Communiqué

The Ministers for Foreign Affairs of Austria, Cyprus, Finland, Liechtenstein, Malta, San Marino, Sweden, Switzerland and Yugoslavia met in Helsinki on 1–2 November 1990 in order to discuss the CSCE process and the strengthening of its role, assess the preparations for the CSCE Summit in Paris and consider the future cooperation of their countries within the CSCE process.

The Ministers stated the view that the CSCE Summit, to be held in Paris on 19–21 November 1990, will highlight the opening of a new era of relations between the CSCE participating States marked by respect for human rights, development of democracy, market economy and social justice as well as by intensified cooperation in the field of security. They stressed the importance of respect for and putting into practice all the Principles of the Final Act. They recognized that in order to strengthen security and cooperation in Europe any conflict undermining them must be resolved by peaceful means and in conformity with the Final Act Principles.

They discussed the preparations for the Paris Summit under way at the Preparatory Committee in Vienna. They expressed the view that a substantive and future-oriented political document should be adopted at the Summit. They called for further intensification of its preparations and expressed the readiness of their countries to contribute to that end.

The Ministers, recognizing the significance of national minorities in the societies of the CSCE States, expressed support for the convening of a meeting of experts to be held in Switzerland in 1991.

The Ministers reiterated the commitment of their Governments to peaceful settlement of disputes. They stressed the need for a comprehensive method which includes mandatory third-party involvement. Full use should be made of the Meeting of Experts in Valletta in 1991.

They underlined the importance of reaching before the Paris Summit a substantive document at the Negotiations on Confidence- and Security-building Measures (CSBMs). They expressed their satisfaction at the prospect of a major agreement at the Negotiation on Conventional Armed Forces in Europe (CFE) before the Summit. They stressed the importance of the continuation of both negotiations after the Paris Summit. They also considered that a second seminar on military doctrines should be held in Vienna in 1991.

Taking note of the profound changes in the European military environment and recalling the importance they attach to the development of the military security dimension of the CSCE, the Ministers called for the creation of a single CSCE forum for negotiations on military security in Europe. They considered that consultations on a mandate should be opened among all participating States in the spring of 1991 with a view to beginning the new negotiations after the Helsinki CSCE follow-up meeting.

They expressed their firm view that the CSCE participating States should develop political dialogue in order to promote cooperation and security in Europe and that to this end the Paris Summit should take decisions on new structures for the CSCE process. In this context the Ministers considered that it should be decided that regular meetings of participating States should be held at the level of Heads of State or Government every two years, of Foreign Ministers twice a year and of senior officials as appropriate. They voiced their support for establishing a centre for the prevention of conflicts and setting up a CSCE secretariat. They stressed the importance of the creation of a Parliamentary Assembly of the Council of Europe.

They noted the broad exchange of views on the Mediterranean problems and welcomed the results achieved at the Meeting on the Mediterranean in Palma de Mallorca, which also highlighted the close link between security and cooperation in Europe and in the Mediterranean.

The Ministers expressed the view that the Helsinki follow-up meeting, to be opened in March 1992, will have an important role in reviewing and developing further the decisions to be taken at the Paris Summit. They therefore stressed the need for thorough preparations of the Helsinki follow-up meeting.

The Ministers stressed the commitment of their countries to continuing and developing their cooperation within the CSCE process and, in view of the envisaged regular meetings of representatives of CSCE States, expressed their preparedness to meet as frequently as necessary.

The Ministers emphasized the significance they attach to the continuing contribution of the Neutral and Non-aligned countries to the future development of the CSCE process and to the shaping up of a new and democratic Europe in the interest of all.

The Ministers expressed their gratitude to the Government and people of Finland for the excellent organization of the meeting as well as for their warm hospitality.

XV. European Community document

Declaration by the Twelve on CSCE

**77th EPC Ministerial Meeting,
Dublin, 20 February 1990**

At a time of rapid and profound change in Europe, the Twelve emphasise the fundamental role of the CSCE process in fostering co-operation in Europe and advocate its further development and strengthening as a framework of far-reaching reform and stability in the perspective of achieving a just and lasting order of peace in Europe.

In the declaration of the European Council at Strasbourg the Twelve recalled the aims of the Helsinki Final Act to establish new relations between European countries whether in the area of security, economic and technical co-operation, or the human dimension.

On that occasion, the Twelve recalled the importance of the Community as a mooring for a future European equilibrium. In this spirit, they reaffirm their commitment to further community integration towards European union as being of central importance to the future of Europe. The Community and its member states are determined to assume their responsibilities wholeheartedly and play a full part in the CSCE process. They will examine appropriate modalities as far as the Community is concerned in order to achieve that end.

The Meeting of the Heads of State or Government of the CSCE participating states in the course of this year will mark the starting point for a new, more advanced stage of the CSCE process and give it new directions.

The Twelve consider that the meeting should:

– discuss current developments and give the political guidance necessary to strengthen stability in Europe;
– reaffirm the validity of the principle enshrined in the Final Act and of subsequent CSCE commitments, and confirm their determination to respect these and put them into practice, as well as underlining the importance of maintaining balanced progress in all aspects of the CSCE process;
– welcome the outcome of the Vienna Negotiations and affirm the importance of continuing negotiations in the field of arms control and the building of security and confidence in Europe, in the light of political developments, with a view to achieving a lasting framework for security in Europe;
– welcome the results of all intersessional meetings and conferences which will have taken place within the CSCE framework;
– underline the need for full observance of human rights and fundamental freedoms, for economic, financial, technical and environmental co-operation, and for further co-operation in the Mediterranean, as factors of security and stability;
– mandate foreign ministers of the 35 to implement decisions of the Meeting of Heads of State or Government, in particular:
    – to supplement the CSCE commitments by the right to vote at free elections and a better protection of minorities, and to explore the possibility of expanding existing international guarantees for human rights to other participating states;
    – to consider new institutional arrangements within the CSCE process—without however modifying the schedule of meetings already agreed in a number of fields—and focus attention on the specific tasks which the new developments call upon these meetings to perform;
    – to formulate proposals which would define the future role of the CSCE in establishing new relations between the participating states.

They consider that a Preparatory Committee of the 35 CSCE participating states should begin meeting as soon as possible and not later than July 1990 to consider the agenda and organisation of the summit meeting.

The Twelve will begin consultations with the other CSCE participating states to discuss and agree on the date, venue and agenda of the meeting as well as on the organisation of the Preparatory Committee. This will include consultations with other Western countries.

The Twelve consider that the fourth main follow-up meeting of the CSCE which will take place in Helsinki in 1992 could be held at the level of heads of state or government.

XVI. European Council documents

Guidelines on the CSCE, Presidency Conclusions

Special Meeting of the European Council, Dublin, 28 April 1990

ANNEX 1

The changes in Europe that we are witnessing bring with them the opportunity of overcoming the division of our continent and building a new system of relations between the States of Europe, based on the aims and principles of the Helsinki Final Act. The CSCE process, which has already made a significant contribution to change, will serve as a framework to reform and stability on our continent, and should be developed in new directions. The Community and its member States are determined to assume their responsibilities wholeheartedly and to play a full part in the CSCE process; they are considering appropriate arrangements to achieve this end.

There is now wide agreement on the desirability of a Summit Meeting of the CSCE participating States before the end of this year. This would mark the starting point for a more advanced stage of the Helsinki process. The decisions necessary to launch the Summit process should be taken as soon as possible so as to ensure that the preparations essential for its successful outcome are completed in good time. This should include an early decision on the opening date and venue of a Preparatory Committee as well as on the venue of the Summit. For their part, the Twelve propose that the Preparatory Committee could start in July, and the Summit itself could take place in Paris.

The Community and its member States are continuing intensively with their preparations for the Summit. In their Declaration of 20 February, the Twelve have set out the issues which in their view are appropriate for consideration at the Summit. They look in particular towards a balanced development of the CSCE encompassing notably the development of pluralist democracy, the rule of law, human rights, better protection of minorities, human contacts, security, economic cooperation, the environment, further cooperation in the Mediterranean and cooperation in the field of culture.

The CSCE Summit should make it possible to consider new institutional arrangements within the CSCE process, taking also into account proposals made by the Central and Eastern European countries, including the possibility of regular consultative meetings of Foreign Ministers and the establishment of a small administrative Secretariat. It will also provide the opportunity to consider the relationship that should exist between the CSCE process and other relevant institutions, such as the Council of Europe. It should mandate the Foreign Ministers of the 35 accordingly.

Already, the new climate of cooperation that prevails has made possible a practical and forward-looking outcome to the Bonn Conference on Economic Cooperation in Europe. The results obtained there will serve as guidelines for future economic cooperation between the 35. The Community made a major contribution to the success of the Conference. The Bonn Document, which acknowledges the link between political pluralism and market economies, provides a basic orientation for future economic relations and cooperation in Europe.

The Twelve look forward to a similar spirit of cooperation at the Copenhagen Conference on the Human Dimension, and trust it will be possible to achieve major substantial results there also, results which will serve to strengthen the commitment of all the participating States to human rights and enable all Europeans to enjoy to the full their fundamental rights and freedoms.

The Twelve reaffirm the importance of the Mediterranean dimension of the CSCE. Being of the view that the experience of the CSCE process can have positive effects on the Mediterranean basin, they hope that the meeting in Palma de Mallorca will enable progress to be made in this dimension of the CSCE process.

The Twelve are committed to a secure and stable balance of forces in Europe at lower levels. They look to an early successful conclusion to the negotiation on Conventional Armed Forces in Europe, which is taking place in the framework of the CSCE, as well as to the adoption of further Confidence- and

Security-Building Measures. They affirm once again the importance of continuing negotiations in the field of arms control and the building of security and confidence in Europe with a view to achieving a lasting framework for security in Europe.

European Council Presidency Conclusions, Dublin, 25–26 June 1990

Excerpts

(...)

2. Central and Eastern Europe

The European Council welcomed the continuing progress being made in Central and Eastern European countries in establishing pluralist democracy founded on the rule of law, full respect for human rights, and the principles of the market-oriented economy. The European Council reaffirmed the right of individual citizens to participate fully in this process and called on all states to observe this principle without reservation. The European Council welcomed in particular the holding of free elections in Central and Eastern Europe and expressed the hope that these will lead to a fuller realisation of democratic ideals which, of course, entail full respect for the rights of the opposition parties. The European Council expressed its deep satisfaction at the progress already made and in prospect towards overcoming the divisions of Europe and restoring the unity of the continent whose peoples share a common heritage and culture. The European Council recalled the contribution already made by the Community and the Member States to supporting the process of political and economic reform, notably through the G-24, and affirmed its intention to broaden and intensify that approach.

3. CSCE

The European Council reaffirms the important role played by the CSCE in the process of change in Europe. At a time when our continent is actively engaged in surmounting its divisions, the CSCE provides a necessary framework for maintaining stability and promoting cooperation in Europe and for deepening the reforms that are underway.

It attaches great importance to the comprehensive nature of the CSCE process which brings together the peoples and governments of Europe, the United States and Canada.

It welcomes the decision taken by the Member States of the CSCE to convene in Paris a Summit of Heads of State and Government. The European Council proposes the date of 19 November 1990 for this meeting.

For the European Council, this Summit has an exceptional importance. It should be an opportunity to define the crucial role which the CSCE will play in the future architecture of Europe and in establishing a new set of relations between participating States, based on the Helsinki principles, to be further expanded by new commitments and involving a balanced development of the CSCE encompassing notably the development of pluralist democracy, the rule of law, human rights, better protection of minorities, human contacts, security, economic cooperation, the environment, further cooperation in the Mediterranean and cooperation in the field of culture.

The European Council expects that the Summit, among other things, will:

– make a decisive contribution to strengthening stability and cooperation in Europe, and to disarmament;
– take note of the results obtained in talks relating to German unity, in particular its final settlement under international law;
– provide a basic orientation for future economic relations and cooperation in Europe. A closer association between the Community and other States members of the CSCE is an example of such relations and cooperation;
– set out guidelines for a democratic Europe and consolidate the principles of a State based on the rule of law.

The European Council proposes agreement on regular meetings of Heads of State and Government of the CSCE, as well as of Ministers of Foreign Affairs, and the establishment of a small administrative secretariat, as well as the holding of more frequent follow-up meetings. The Summit will also provide the opportunity to consider the relationship between the CSCE process and other relevant institutions, such as the Council of Europe. Furthermore, the Summit could take decisions on new mechanisms in the field of security and cooperation in Europe, including suitable means to avoid conflict and disputes, and the active participation of parliamentary bodies.

The European Community and its Member States intend to assume a leading role in this enterprise and to contribute actively to all discussion within the CSCE process.

Considering the importance of the Paris Summit, the European Council has agreed that the Community and its Member States will strengthen their coordination with a view to defining and expressing a common position on all questions, in the various sectors of the CSCE, in which they have an essential common interest, and taking into account the importance of coordination with the participating states and organisations.

4. Transatlantic relations

The European Council expressed its satisfaction with the developments in the Community's relations with the United States, based on the structure laid down by the European Council in April and characterized by ever closer cooperation. They wish to take this cooperation further. Their commitment to this further cooperation could take the form of a joint transatlantic declaration on relations between the Twelve and the United States and Canada.*

---

* The USA and the European Community and its member states agreed upon a joint transatlantic declaration, to be released simultaneously in Rome, Brussels and Washington, DC, on 23 November 1990. The declaration defined the common goals and principles of US–EC partnership and identified the rules and areas of co-operation: economics, education, science and culture, as well as transnational challenges and the institutional framework for consultation.

XVII. WEU document

Communiqué of the meeting of the WEU Council of Ministers, Brussels, 23 April 1990

1. The Foreign and Defence Ministers of the Western European Union, meeting in Brussels on 23 April 1990, were particularly pleased that the ratification of the Protocol of Accession of Portugal and Spain to the modified Brussels Treaty had been completed.

2. Ministers welcomed the sweeping changes which had taken place in Europe since their meeting in November 1989. The division of Europe is now being overcome. The emergence of new democracies following free elections is opening up new prospects for broader cooperation among Europeans.

They welcomed the return to democratic standards which the elections in the GDR and Hungary represent, and looked forward to those to be held shortly in other countries of Central and Eastern Europe.

The prospect of the forthcoming attainment of German unity, founded on the unequivocal expression of the wishes of the population concerned, is an opportunity for Europe as a whole and an important step forward towards constructing a just and lasting peaceful order.

The united Germany will thus take its place alongside its fellow members of the North Atlantic Alliance and alongside its partners who have chosen to build a European Union.

3. Ministers welcomed the new impetus being given to the CSCE process and the prospect of a conference of Heads of State and/or of Government taking place by the end of 1990.

The CSCE is the framework within which all Europeans, together with the United States and Canada, can establish new relations and develop cooperative structures capable of assuring each one of them that peace and stability will be maintained and their legitimate interests safeguarded.

4. It was with this new prospect in view that Ministers recalled the importance they attach to building a European Union consistent with the Single European Act which they have signed as members of the European Community. They also reaffirmed the importance of the Atlantic Alliance and Western European Union as essential instruments for the security of the member countries and as factors for stability throughout Europe.

The continued presence of the forces of the United States and of Canada stationed in Europe provided a necessary contribution to our common security and overall stability, together with the contribution of WEU countries and their other European partners. Ministers reaffirmed the importance of The Hague Platform and the Comprehensive Concept of arms control and disarmament of the Atlantic Alliance.

5. Ministers stressed the importance they attach to the concluding of a CFE agreement and to the holding of the CSCE summit before the end of the year. They regard such an agreement as an important achievement in the process of improving security and adapting military postures to the far-reaching changes—both military and political—which Europe is witnessing. They considered that the momentum of the negotiation process should be maintained so as to enhance stability, promote cooperative structures and expedite the attainment of a new peace order in Europe. Agreement on new confidence and security-building measures in parallel with a CFE agreement would contribute greatly to that end.

6. European stability continues to be based on the collective and individual commitment of all partners in the Alliance. It is also an essential matter for the Europeans themselves. For the Europeans to enhance their contribution to stability on the European continent and to the protection of their legitimate security interests, a greater degree of cooperation will be fundamental.

Ministers therefore recognized the need to continue working to strengthen the European identity and to promote the process of European integration including the security dimension. This growing identity is destined to be given concrete expression in the form of close, and even new cooperation between the member countries.

In the field of verification of the CFE Treaty and 'Open Skies', Ministers welcomed the specific measures which had been adopted by WEU member countries particularly as regards the opening of national inspection teams to include inspectors from other WEU member countries.

On the subject of the computerized processing of verification data, Ministers welcomed the fact that a WEU group of experts had jointly defined realistic parameters for a system of interconnected data bases, and that this common WEU viewpoint had been taken into account by the Atlantic Alliance.

Ministers also noted the progress which had been made in studying the possibilities for European cooperation in the field of space-based observation systems for the purposes of arms control verification, and also for crisis and environmental monitoring. They called for concrete proposals to be submitted to them at their next meeting, inter alia with a view to examining the possibility of establishing a satellite verification agency.

7. Ministers recognized that European security has an extra-European dimension. As a consequence the European countries follow closely developments in other regions of the world, in particular the Mediterranean and the Middle East.

8. Peace, security and cooperation in Europe depend on an intensification of the dialogue at all levels. With regard to the new tasks for the Organization proposed by the incoming Presidency, Ministers agreed on the opportuneness of establishing contacts for two-way information with the democratically elected governments in Central and Eastern Europe. They instructed the Presidency and the Secretary-General to organize these contacts. Ministers recognized that, by virtue of its activities, the Parliamentary Assembly of WEU has an important role to play in opening up contacts with the countries of Central and Eastern Europe. This has been illustrated by the recent Extraordinary Session of the Assembly held in Luxembourg on 22 and 23 March. Likewise, the WEU Institute for Security Studies, whose establishment was decided upon at the last Council, and which is to begin operation from July this year, also has an active role to play in pooling ideas and in drawing together the new strands of think-

ing being developed in both the East and the West.

9. Ministers congratulated the Belgian Presidency on the particularly active way in which they had conducted the work of WEU. They hoped that, under its impetus and that of the incoming French Presidency, there would be a continued and intensive process of reflexion and concertation among the member countries, particularly with a view to the two major meetings scheduled to take place before the end of the year, namely the CSCE summit and an Atlantic summit both aimed at giving appropriate responses to the changes taking place in Europe.

WEU provides an entirely suitable forum for its members to prepare a common approach to these forthcoming meetings.

XVIII. The Baltic Conference documents

The Baltic Sea Declaration

Adopted by the Heads of Governments and High Political Representatives of the Baltic Sea States, Ronneby, Sweden, 2–3 September 1990*

Heads of Governments and High Political Representatives of the Baltic Sea States, Norway, the Czech and Slovak Federal Republic and the Representative of the Commission of the European Communities

Assembled at Ronneby, Sweden, September 2–3, 1990.

Having exchanged views on increased environmental cooperation in the Baltic Sea area;

Concerned about the continuing threat to the environment of the Baltic Sea; threatening to irreversibly disrupt the ecological balance in the region and seriously curtail the possibilities for sound development in the area;

Welcoming the new climate of understanding and cooperation between the States in the Baltic Sea area, which will make resources available for the protection of the Baltic Sea environment, *inter alia*, through the reduced need for armaments expenditures;

Convinced that strengthening of such cooperation among them will contribute to the implementation of the relevant provisions of the Final Act of the Conference on Security and Cooperation in Europe and the outcome of its follow-up meetings;

Sharing the view of the World Commission on Environment and Development that sustainable development is dependent on future policies in all countries and in all sectors;

Resolved that exploitation of natural resources in the area should be consistent with sustainable development;

Stressing the need for the use and transfer of the best available technology to protect the area and for low-waste and non-waste technologies to be further developed in order to obtain sustainable development;

Aware of the need to take urgent action to protect and preserve for present and future generations the environment of the Baltic Sea area and surrounding land areas, taking into account the particular sensitivity of the marine environment of the area and its importance to adjacent sea areas;

Welcoming the substantial financial support for the protection of the environment of the Baltic Sea area which is already under way or which may be expected from bilateral agreements, the programmes of the EC and the activities of all relevant international financial institutions, in particular

- the World Bank
- the European Investment Bank
- the Nordic Investment Bank

and the new European Bank of Reconstruction and Development, and further welcoming the priority attached to environmental protection in the framework of the programmes of assistance to the process of economic and social reform under way in several countries in the Baltic Sea area;

Welcoming the conclusions adopted by the Conference of Environment Ministers from the European Community and Eastern and Central European countries held in Dublin on 16 June 1990;

Recalling the valuable work of the UN Economic Commission for Europe in the field of environmental protection;

Recalling the 1973 Convention on Fishing and Conservation of the Living Resources in the Baltic Sea and the Belts, the 1974 Convention on the Protection of the Marine Environment of the Baltic Sea area and the 1979 Convention on Long-Range Transboundary Air Pollution;

Recalling the valuable work on environmental protection that has been achieved under the framework provided by the 1974 Convention on the Protection of the Marine Environment of the Baltic Sea area;

Welcoming the decision of the European Communities to establish an Environment Agency and a European Environment Information and Observation Network, which will be open also to the countries of the Baltic area and other plans to start cooperation centres of importance to the Baltic Sea area states in the field of environmental sciences, such as the Baltic Sea Centre in Finland;

Recalling the 9th Meeting of the Helsinki Commission held at ministerial level in

February 1988, and the Declaration on the Protection of the Marine Environment of the Baltic Sea area that was agreed and signed on that occasion;

Reaffirming the principles adopted on May 16th 1990 in the Bergen Ministerial Declaration on Sustainable Development in the ECE Region.

Do hereby declare their firm intention to:

1. Assure the ecological restoration of the Baltic Sea, ensuring the possibility of self-restoration of the marine environment and preservation of its ecological balance;

2. Urgently prepare a joint comprehensive programme for decisive reduction of emissions in order to restore the Baltic Sea to a sound ecological balance. The programme shall be based on concrete national plans provided by the countries concerned;

An ad hoc high level Task Force shall be set up immediately within the Helsinki Commission to coordinate and supplement the analysis for the different parts of the Baltic Sea and to prepare the joint comprehensive programme. The Task Force shall consist of representatives from the Contracting Parties of the Helsinki Convention. The Czech and Slovak Federal Republic, the Kingdom of Norway, the Commission of the European Communities as well as international financial institutions will take part in the work of the Task Force.

The financial institutions participating in the Baltic Sea Conference (European Bank for Reconstruction and Development, European Investment Bank, Nordic Investment Bank, World Bank) are jointly invited as members of the Task Force, to analyze financial and other requirements and to identify and prepare investment projects and accompanying measures for the different parts of the Baltic Sea.

The national plans shall contain relevant decisions, programmes and regulations for the reduction of polluting substances (especially inputs from agriculture, industry, sewage treatment plants and waste) taking into consideration the quantities of major direct and indirect inputs. The national plans shall be submitted to the Task Force by 31 January 1991.

The comprehensive programme should be finalized by the Task Force by the end of 1991 and be subsequently decided upon at ministerial level in the framework of the Helsinki Commission. In the countries concerned, the key elements of the comprehensive programme shall be under implementation by 1993;

3. Undertake and support intensified efforts to reduce as soon as possible the emissions of harmful substances (toxic, persistent and bioaccumulating substances, heavy metals and nutrients) to levels that are in accordance with a restored ecological balance, implementing as a first step the existing commitments by the contracting parties to the Helsinki Convention to reduce such emissions in the order of 50% in the period 1987–1995;

4. Accept the principle of safeguarding the marine ecosystems in the Baltic Sea by substantially reducing the above-mentioned emissions, by the use of the best available technology and other appropriate measures and furthermore to assure sustainable utilization of natural resources and development and use of cleaner technologies, including low-waste and non-waste processes and environmentally non-hazardous products;

5. Promote the reduction of nutrients and other harmful substances entering the Baltic Sea from diffuse sources by the use of the best environmental practice;

6. Require the best available technology for all important industries (e.g. chemical, fertilizer and pulp and paper industries) and promote the installation and improvement of municipal sewage treatment plants, which should include biological treatment and nutrient removal to the level set up within the Helsinki Commission as far as possible and not later than the year 2000;

7. (a) Strengthen the legal and institutional regime, *inter alia* the Helsinki Convention and its Commission, in the field of prevention and control of pollution entering the Baltic Sea, with a view to accelerating the implementation of existing commitments and bringing the Convention with Annexes in line with the development since its adoption in 1974; (b) Promote closer cooperation between the Helsinki and the Gdansk Commissions;

8. Promote further co-operation within the Convention on Long-Range Transboundary Air Pollution with a view to achieving broader implementation of the Helsinki and Sofia protocols and to reaching agreements in appropriate international fora on further

reductions of the emissions of air pollutants from motor vehicles, ships, industries, etc.;

9. Intensify cooperation in the field of environmental sciences, inter alia, in order to strengthen the foundation for designing adequate measures to reduce the most harmful pollution;

10. Promote additionally, through supportive measures, increased transfer of knowledge regarding the environment;

11. Promote further co-operation in the field of transfer of environmentally sound technology, inter alia, through multilateral, bilateral and commercial mechanisms, with the aim to protect the Baltic Sea;

12. Apply the precautionary principle, i.e. to take effective action to avoid potentially damaging impacts of substances that are persistent, toxic and liable to bioaccumulate even where there is lack of full scientific certainty to prove a causal link between emissions and effects. This applies especially when there is reason to assume that certain damage or harmful effects on the marine ecosystems are likely to be caused by such substances;

13. Extend and strengthen the programme of monitoring in order to improve the assessment of the present and future state of the marine environment of the Baltic Sea area and encourage the cooperation between statistical agencies to improve demographic and other statistics relevant to the protection of the Baltic Sea;

14. Develop a comprehensive programme in nature conservation, inter alia, through the establishment of protected areas representing the various Baltic ecosystems and their flora and fauna.

15. Encourage a strengthening of cooperation and facilitation of human contacts in the region to improve the environment of the Baltic Sea, including inter alia participation of local and regional governments, governmental and private institutions, industries and non-governmental organizations in the fields of economy, trade, science, culture, information, etc.;

16. (a) Cooperate within appropriate international fora in improving legal instruments and technical regulations for transport systems aiming at the prevention of adverse environmental impacts on the Baltic Sea area,

inter alia, pollution arising from maritime casualties, and to this end:

– prepare within the Helsinki Commission a joint initiative for strong support of the work within the IMO on a world-wide agreement on new requirements on constructional arrangements for tankers (e.g. double-hull, double-side, double-bottom ships, tank size limitation) to prevent or reduce oil spills resulting from collisions or groundings, and

– support their best efforts to encourage, by economic incentives, e.g. lower fees, the use of tankers with improved construction to minimize the effects of accidents;

(b) Encourage considerably intensified cooperation regarding airborne surveillance between the respective competent authorities;

17. Undertake to integrate environmental considerations into the procedures for planning future development in all economic and social processes;

18. Encourage further commercial and financial cooperation, multilaterally and bilaterally, in order to implement the necessary reduction of emissions, including supportive financial arrangements when appropriate;

19. Recommend that meetings of the Helsinki Commission will continue to be held at the ministerial level at appropriate intervals, in order to examine the implementation of the decisions and recommendations for the protection of the Baltic Sea by the Commission, to follow closely the development of the environmental quality in the Area and agree on further concerted action of effective improvements concerning the Baltic Sea.

---

* The Conference, convened at the initiative of Polish Prime Minister Tadeusz Mazowiecki and Swedish Prime Minister Ingvar Carlsson, assembled at Ronneby, Sweden, the heads of governments and high representatives of Denmark, the FRG, Finland, the GDR, Poland, Sweden, the Soviet Union and representatives of four Soviet republics (Byelorussia, Estonia, Latvia and Russia), as well as Norway and the Czech and Slovak Federal Republic; Lithuania did not accept the invitation as one of the Soviet republics. The Conference adopted two documents: the Baltic Sea Declaration and the Guidelines for the ad hoc High Level Task Force.

Guidelines for the ad hoc High Level Task Force adopted by the Ministers of the Environment participating in the Baltic Sea Conference,
Ronneby, Sweden, 2–3 September 1990

1. In the Baltic Sea Declaration, adopted on 3 September 1990, it was decided to urgently prepare a joint comprehensive programme for decisive reduction of emissions in order to restore the Baltic Sea to a sound ecological balance.

2. It was furthermore decided to set up immediately within the Helsinki Commission an ad hoc High Level Task Force to co-ordinate and supplement the analysis for the different parts of the Baltic Sea and to prepare the joint comprehensive programme.

3. The Task Force shall consist of representatives from the contracting Parties of the Helsinki convention. The Czech and Slovak Federal Republic, the Kingdom of Norway, the Commission of the European Communities as well as international financial institutions will take part in the work of the Task Force.

4. The financial institutions participating in the Baltic Sea Conference (European Bank for Reconstruction and Development, European Investment Bank, Nordic Investment Bank, World Bank) are jointly invited as members of the Task Force to analyze financial and other requirements and to identify and prepare investment projects and accompanying measures for the different parts of the Baltic Sea.

5. As agreed in the Baltic Sea Declaration the national plans shall contain relevant decisions, programmes and regulations for the reduction of polluting substances (especially inputs from agriculture, industry, sewage treatment plants and waste) taking into consideration the quantities of major direct and indirect inputs. The national plans shall be submitted to the Task Force by 31 January 1991.

6. The comprehensive programme by the Task Force should be finalized by the end of 1991 and be subsequently decided upon at ministerial level in the framework of the Helsinki Commission. In the countries concerned the key elements of the comprehensive programme shall be under implementation by 1993.

The long term objective of the programme should be to reach e.g. the following goals:
– the assured recovery of Baltic indigenous species (e.g. seals, blue mussels, bladder wrack);
– ecological restoration of the Baltic Sea, including coastal areas, for fishing and recreational purposes;

7. On the basis of information available through the concrete national plans and the Helsinki Commission and other relevant material, the Task Force shall:
– examine planned and implemented measures to improve the environment of the Baltic Sea Region;
– assess the need for further measures for the restoration of the Baltic Sea to a sound ecological balance bearing in mind investigations of the ecological capacity of the Baltic Sea;
– determine regional priorities for the protection of the Baltic Sea environment.
Additionally, countries adjacent to commonly used river-basins are requested to ensure an ecologically sound river-basin management.

8. In order to mobilize and fully utilize available financial resources, experience and expertise, the Task Force shall promote a most cost-effective implementation of the reduction of pollution.

9. The Executive Secretary of the Helsinki Commission is requested to convene the first meeting of the Task Force before the end of October 1990 and to provide for secretariat resources for the Task Force.

10. The participating countries, the Commission of the European Communities and the financial institutions are asked to nominate their representatives in the Task Force before 20 September 1990.

11. Governments are encouraged to contribute to the work of the Task Force by assisting the secretariat e.g. through financial support and/or providing expertise.

XIX. Documents on unification

Two-plus-Four
Statement made during the Open Skies Conference,
Ottawa, 14 February 1990

The foreign ministers of the Federal Republic of Germany, the German Democratic Republic, France, the United Kingdom, the Soviet Union and the United States had talks in Ottawa. They agreed that the foreign ministers of the Federal Republic of Germany and the German Democratic Republic would meet with the foreign ministers of France, the United Kingdom, the Soviet Union and the United States to discuss external aspects of the establishment of German unity, including the issues of security of the neighbouring states. Preliminary discussions at the official level will begin shortly

---

Goals of German unification
Statements by President George Bush and Chancellor Helmut Kohl,
Washington, DC, 17 May 1990

Excerpts

(...)

President George Bush:

What's clear from all our discussion over the past months, including our extensive talks today, is that the United States and the Federal Republic of Germany share the same approach and have the same goals regarding German unification. We both want a united Germany which enjoys full sovereignty. A united Germany which is a full member of the Western community and of the NATO Alliance, including participation in its integrated military structures. A united Germany which is, as the Federal Republic has been for over 40 years, a model of freedom, tolerance and friendly relations with its neighbors.

During our discussion today, we reviewed the talks in Bonn on May 5 among foreign ministers of the two German states, the United States, Great Britain, France, and the Soviet Union—those are the two-plus-four talks. Chancellor Kohl and I agreed that these talks should terminate all four-power rights and responsibilities at the time of German unification. A united Germany should have full control over all of its territory without any new discriminatory constraints on German sovereignty.

Forty-five years after the end of the war there is no reason that a unified democratic Germany should be in any way singled out for some special status. In keeping with the Helsinki Final Act, Germany should be fully sovereign, free to choose its own alliances and security arrangements. And we agree that U.S. military forces should remain stationed in the united Germany and elsewhere in Europe to continue to promote stability and security.

The chancellor and I also discussed the broad issues of East–West relations. And I expressed my hope for a successful U.S.–Soviet summit at the end of this month, but also reiterated my own concern, which the chancellor shares, about the situation in Lithuania. We reaffirmed our commitment to the opening of a dialogue in good faith between the Soviet leaders and Lithuanian representatives.

We also discussed the forthcoming NATO summit. It will be held in London on July 5 and July 6. And the chancellor and I reviewed my proposal that the summit address the political role that NATO can play in the new Europe; the conventional forces the alliance will need in the time ahead and NATO's goals for conventional arms control; the role of nuclear weapons based in Europe and Western objectives in new nuclear arms control negotiations between the United States and the Soviet Union; and the alliance's common objectives for strengthening the CSCE, Conference on Security and Cooperation in Europe.

At this time of enormous and I would say encouraging change, in Germany and Europe as a whole, we reaffirm the continuing vital role of the North Atlantic Alliance in guaranteeing stability and security. We also want the

CSCE to pursue a more ambitious agenda in helping the rising democracies in Eastern Europe join the community of free nations and have a strong voice in the new Europe.

When I visited Germany last May, I spoke of the Federal Republic and the United States as partners in leadership. The remarkable changes that have occurred in this short year since then have fully confirmed that partnership. And we now look together with hope and confidence to a Germany united in peace and freedom and to a Europe whole and free.

Chancellor, thank you very much for coming, sir.

Chancellor Helmut Kohl:

Allow me to summarize my message in three points. First of all, on behalf of all Germans, I express sincere thanks to the American people, and especially to you, President Bush, for the magnificent support that you have granted from the outset and continue to grant to us Germans during this decade on our path to German unity.

The Americans and Germans stood side by side at the time of the Berlin blockade and the erection of the Berlin Wall. And together, we championed, not least in the difficult days of the Cold War, our vision of freedom, democracy and human rights. Now that this vision is becoming a reality in the whole of Europe, that the Berlin Wall is being torn down and sold as souvenirs, that Germany and its former capital, Berlin, are becoming reunited, there is something that is all the more true. The friendship and partnership with the United States continue to be vital to us Germans. Naturally, this also applies to a united Germany.

A united Germany will remain a member of the North Atlantic Alliance. But in view of the change occurring in Europe, in view of the triumph of human rights, democracy, pluralism and a social market economy in the whole of Europe, the alliance must concentrate more on its traditional political role. As the threat is decreasing appreciably, the alliance must keep the initiative in the field of disarmament and arms control and review its strategy and structure accordingly.

I'm extremely grateful to you, Mr. President, for having presented important and forward-looking proposals. Together, with our allies, we shall chart the course at the NATO summit meeting in London early in July.

Mr. President, allow me to state at this opportunity here, once and again, how important it is going to be for the future of Germany and Europe that the United States take their legitimate place in Germany and in Europe as a whole.

You, Mr. President, and I agreed in our talks that in order to achieve this, the three anchorages must be strengthened. That means NATO as an indispensable transatlantic security link between the European and North American democracies, cooperation between the United States and the European Community. This is going to be of ever-growing importance in view of the completion of the internal market within the European Community by 1992, and also in view of the ever closer political union within the European Community. What is also important is the expansion of the CSCE into a system of assured human rights, guaranteed security and comprehensive cooperation for all 35 member countries.

We continue to strive for a just and lasting peaceful order in Europe in which the division of Europe, also as regards the date, is overcome together with the division of Germany.

Mr. President, for many of us in Germany a dream is coming true now, is becoming reality also for me. German unity and unity of Europe are two sides of the same coin. We have a lot of reasons to be grateful—to be grateful with regard to many who have helped us. But particularly towards our American friends. And you, Mr. President, have a very important role in all this.

Seven points on the unification of Germany*

Statement by Chancellor Helmut Kohl during the Gorbachev–Kohl press conference, Zheleznovodsk, USSR, 16 July 1990

The present press conference concludes two days of talks between President Gorbachev and myself and between our foreign and finance ministers and our delegations. I believe that in terms of the scope and intensity of the talks we have had in Moscow, aboard the plane and here, in the home country of

President Gorbachev, this meeting will highlight a new stage in the history of German–Soviet relations. I consider President Gorbachev's invitation to visit his home place as a special gesture. The special climate of relations between all the participants in the talks has contributed to the further deepening of mutual trust.

Our talks were marked by a high degree of frankness, mutual understanding and personal touch. The conditions created for us have been another plus factor. I mean our cordial meetings with the people of Stavropol and the encounter we had in the field with local peasants during our stopover on the way here. But the most important thing about this meeting is its results. We agree that a major stride has been made on cardinal issues.

This success has become possible because both sides realise that the historic changes taking place in Europe, Germany and the Soviet Union place a special responsibility on us. This is true with respect to the political activities of each of the countries, the development of ties between our two countries and the future of the whole of Europe. President Gorbachev and I agree that we should assume this historic responsibility. And we shall do our best to cope with it. We also understand this task as a special responsibility of our own generation which was a conscious witness of the past war and its consequences and which has now got a very important and, probably, the only chance to build the future of our countries and continents in the conditions of peace, security and freedom.

President Gorbachev and I realise pretty well that German–Soviet relations are acquiring special significance for the future of our peoples and the destiny of Europe. We want to make this clear and we have agreed to conclude, shortly after the unification of Germany, a comprehensive and fundamental bilateral treaty, based on good-neighbourliness, which will regulate our relations for a long period to come. Such a treaty should cover all areas of relations—not only political questions but also mutual security, economics, culture, science and technology, youth exchanges, and so on, and so forth. The aim is to place our relations on a foundation of stability, predictability, trust and interaction in our common future.

Our present talks have enabled us to clarify very important issues which are being discussed under the 'Two-Plus-Four' formula.

According to an agreement which was reached and firmly confirmed at a meeting of six foreign ministers in Berlin last June, the 'Two-Plus-Four' should be completed in due time so that their results could be presented to a meeting of the heads of state and government of the countries participating in the Conference on Security and Cooperation in Europe, scheduled for next November in Paris. With great satisfaction and with President Gorbachev's consent I can state now the following:

First. The unification of Germany will cover the Federal Republic of Germany, the German Democratic Republic and Berlin.

Second. When the unification takes place, the rights and responsibilities of the four powers will be rescinded. Thus, by the moment of its unification a united Germany will have complete and unrestricted sovereignty.

Third. In pursuance of its unrestricted sovereignty a united Germany will be able to freely and independently decide whether it is a part of any bloc and, if so, of which bloc. This accords with the CSCE Final Act. Explaining the position of the government of the Federal Republic, I have stated that a united Germany would like to be a member of the North Atlantic Alliance. I am sure that this also agreed with the opinion of the government of the German Democratic Republic.

Fourth. A united Germany will conclude a bilateral treaty with the Soviet Union on troop pullout from the German Democratic Republic, which is to be completed within three to four years. Simultaneously a provisional treaty will be signed with the Soviet Union, also for three or four years, on the consequences of the introduction of the West German Mark in the GDR.

Fifth. While the Soviet troops remain in the former territory of the German Democratic Republic, the NATO structures will not be extended to this part of Germany. From the very beginning this will not affect the immediate application of Articles 5 and 6 of the NATO Treaty. Bundeswehr troops that are not part of NATO's military organisation, i.e., territorial defence units, can be stationed in the territory of the present German Democratic Republic and Berlin right after the unification of Germany. The troops of the three Western powers should, in our opinion, remain in Berlin after the unification through-out the presence of Soviet troops in the former territory of the German Democratic Republic. The Federal Government will file this request with the three Western powers and will settle the stationing of their troops on the basis of a corresponding treaty with the governments concerned.

Sixth. The Federal Government declares its readiness already at the present Vienna talks to assume a commitment to reduce the armed forces of a united Germany to 370 000 men within three to four years. The reduction is to begin simultaneously with the entering into force of the first Vienna agreement.

Seventh. A united Germany will renounce the manufacture, possession and disposal of atomic, biological and chemical weapons and will remain a member of the nuclear non-proliferation treaty.

Ladies and gentlemen, this joint agreement is a very good position for reaching a timely and successful agreement on the outside aspects of Germany's unification at the 'Two-Plus-Four' talks. As soon as I return home, I will have the necessary contacts with the Government of the German Democratic Republic. I am sure that it will support our appraisal. Simultaneously, we will inform the three Western powers on the results of our present talks. Foreign Minister Genscher will inform the three Western foreign ministers already tomorrow, when he meets with them in Paris.

We and, above all, colleagues Weigel and Sitaryan, have had detailed talks on further possibilities for economic and financial coop-eration on a bilateral and multilateral level. I want to say that President Gorbachev heartily thanked West Germany for its constructive position in the past. We have agreed to con-tinue and specify even more our talks on all our levels.

In conclusion of these talks I would like to heartily thank you, Mr President, for your remarkable hospitality. This hospitality has made a special contribution to our mutual understanding. I will dare to suggest that our personal trust has grown even stronger. I also have ample ground to thank foreign ministers Shevardnadze and Genscher for the wonderful preparations they made for this conference and, in particular, those made within the framework of the 'Two-Plus-Four' talks.

Mr President, I thank you for your hospi-tality. I also want to use this opportunity to invite you, in front of the public of your own country, to Germany. I hope that I will be able to welcome you in my home country of Pfalz.

---

* (Translated from *Pravda*, 18 July 1990.) Federal Chancellor Helmut Kohl reported on the results of the meeting with Mikhail Gorbachev to the Bundestag on 17 July 1990. The full text is pub-lished in *Bulletin des Presse- und Informations-amtes der Bundesregierung*, 18 July 1990.

Two-plus-Four results*
Paris, 17 July 1990

Dumas: Ladies and gentlemen, we are going to report on the work we have done today. There were three rounds, so to speak. In the morning we met, the two-plus-four, the six, the ministers of the Federal Republic of Germany and the Democratic Republic of Germany, the United States, the United Kingdom, France and the USSR. The second period was taken up by a working luncheon which included the minister of Foreign Affairs of Poland. And the third period or round this afternoon with the participation of the Polish minister. And during this third part of this meeting we dealt especially with Polish affairs and questions.

Now ladies and gentlemen, the process of the German reunification puts an end to the sorry period of the Cold War, the division of the German people, and the division of our European Continent. Of course, the reunifica-tion of Germany is something that the German people themselves have to do, and we are happy to note that everything goes all right. But the fact that the partition of Germany was very hard to deal with and the legal situation after the Second World War give rise to, we had to take into account the external circumstances, the effects of such a reunification that was referred to in Stras-bourg at the European Council meeting in December last year, on the initiative of the president of the French Republic. It has been said then that the problem of borders should be solved. That was the reason for which the group of the six has been set up. The six, the two-plus-four, have already met in Bonn and Berlin. These two meetings clarified the issues. And it has been agreed in Berlin, for instance, that our goal should be to reach a consensus and cogency between the reunifica-tion of Germany and its regaining its sovereignty. And it has also been agreed that the group of six should end its work for the summit of the CSCE to be held on the 19th of November in Paris.

I think, we should be happy for the decisions taken since then in several institutions, that is, since our last meeting in Berlin. In particular, I refer to the summit meeting of the countries of the Atlantic Alliance, 5 and 6 July, which put a definitive end to the Cold War and established a new type of relations and security in Europe.[1] That was started in London, and the recent meetings between Mr. Gorbachev and Mr. Genscher in Moscow led to very substantial progress in relations between the Soviet Union and Germany, and a very important step was therefore taken in Moscow.

The ministers of Foreign Affairs, who met today in Paris, took note with great satisfaction of the common statement of Chancellor Kohl and Mr. Gorbachev.[2] After these brief remarks on behalf of my country, I could say that there's no obstacle for a united Germany to be reestablished in its sovereignty before the end of the year. And it's in full conformity with what France asked for and negotiated for quite a long time. It's a very important step in the setting up of a solid and free Europe, entirely freed from past conflicts.

Now, today's meeting. A few words about that. This meeting is to be considered within this general framework and it enabled us to do away with several obstacles and therefore to make another and probably decisive step towards what we call a definitive settlement. We are agreed that Germany herself would decide on the role in the military and political systems that is to be found in the Final Act of Helsinki. The question of Soviet troops in the present territory of the GDR, that will be settled by a bilateral agreement between the USSR and the united Germany. It has been asked from our political directors to start drafting the final settlement I alluded to. But you understood it, I am sure. The main part of our meeting had to do with the problem of borders and especially Oder-Neisse border. The Polish foreign minister participated in that part of our work, and even at the lunch, as provided for when the Ottawa group decided upon it. It think I speak for all my colleagues that we rejoiced in this participation of the Polish minister. And it has been a very fruitful meeting and very positive.

I could say that our meeting enabled us to register a general agreement on the way in which one could settle the problem of the border between Germany and Poland as regards principles and ways and means and the calendar of that settlement.

On the invitation of the Soviet foreign minister, our next meeting, ministerial meeting, will be held on the 12th of September in Moscow. Therefore, this meeting today ends with the satisfaction of all concerned. I am very happy especially that Poland participated in this today and in the general satisfaction we all feel. I am especially happy that this meeting could have taken place in Paris. Now I will give the floor to the Polish foreign minister.

Skubiszewski: Thank you, Mr. Chairman. I would like to express the thankfulness and the joy of the Polish government because my country was represented during this conference and participated in the debate. Especially I am happy that this meeting would have taken place in Paris, in France, and of the results obtained. And I believe that as regards the problem of the border between Germany and Poland, on both sides, that the two German states and Poland are equally satisfied. Raising, that was my main purpose, the question of the confirmation of that border, and decisions have been taken and language has been decided which are entirely satisfactory.

As you know, Poland proposed some time ago that a treaty be concluded between a united Germany and Poland on the basis of a draft we submitted as to where the provisions regarding the border were, the main features and the treaty now will concentrate only on the topic of the border in order to facilitate things, and it is within the realm of legal texts and constitutions, international law and national law of Germany and Poland. But I also think that—and there we concur with our German friends—that one should as soon as possible conclude another treaty in order to settle all questions of good neighborhood between Poland and united Germany. That is something which will take place later.[3]

The border, as I said, has been confirmed. And you know that starting with the Potsdam Agreement in 1945, one always stressed, on both sides, the Polish stand, that we needed a peace settlement in order to determine and delineate the border. After today's decision, it is not anymore necessary because we achieved final results.

In my contribution to the meeting, I referred to other problems also of concern to Poland, in particular the economic question. And I'm in a position to tell you that in this field also we felt that Germany was fully understanding and we had a very favorable proposal from Minister Genscher about a meeting between Germany and Poland this summer in order to discuss the very difficult economic problems rising for Poland as a result of the past situation. And I am prepared to reply to questions you would care to put to me.

Dumas: Mr. Baker has the floor.

Baker: Ladies and gentlemen, about six months ago in Ottawa we started this two-plus-four process. It was a new process designed to fit new times. I think it would be fair to say that our aim was ambitious, but none too ambitious for this new age of European hope and freedom.

Our aim, of course, was to facilitate the peaceful and democratic unification of Germany, as well as the reconciliation of Europe, and today I think we draw much nearer to that target. We are keeping to the pace that's necessary to complete our work and to meet the target, to terminate the residual four-power rights and responsibilities and to accord Germany its full sovereignty at the time of unification in 1990.

Only six weeks ago at the Washington summit, President Bush presented President Gorbachev nine points designed to assure the Soviet Union of our firm intention to address the legitimate political, security and economic interests of the Soviet Union.[4]

Only two weeks ago in London, the NATO nations issued a declaration that translated this intention into instructions, specific commitments to extend a hand to the East, to modify NATO's defensive doctrine and strategies, to expand our commitment to arms control, and to gradually construct new CSCE institutions for the whole of a Europe enjoying freedom and peace.[5]

Only yesterday, the Federal Republic of Germany and the Soviet Union in Stavropol agreed on eight points that will enable us to terminate four-power rights at the time of unification, restoring Germany's full sovereignty and full prerogatives under the Helsinki Final Act, and thereby creating a sound basis for European security and European stability.[6]

Today, of course, we meet with our Polish colleague, Minister Skubiszewski, in recognition of the special interest that all of us have taken in assuring the definitive character of the Polish–German border. We all agree that a unified Germany will consist of the Federal Republic of Germany, the German Democratic Republic, and Berlin. No more, no less. We also agreed, after discussion with and adjustment by our Polish colleague, on a set of principles to guide the final settlement of the border issue. And, of course, we were pleased by the German statement committing to act on the border treaty in the shortest possible time after unification, in line with the commitments already given by the German parliaments. Next, our officials will begin to use the list of external issues they assembled to prepare a draft final settlement document.

In conclusion, the United States is very pleased that we are moving toward a sovereign and united Germany, and we are moving toward a stable security environment for Europe. We are replacing the historical national interests that divided us with a common European and Atlantic interest that unites us. The outcome that has so long eluded us is now within our reach.

By the anniversary of our Ottawa meeting, I expect the United States and the other four powers will welcome the advent of a united, sovereign and democratic Germany, a valuable contributor to the promotion and preservation of a Europe which is whole and a Europe which is free.

Dumas: Thank you. And I shall now give the floor to Mr. Genscher, foreign minister of the Federal Republic of Germany.

Genscher: Ladies and gentlemen, I should like to begin by thanking our host, Mr. Dumas, for the excellent way in which he chaired our meeting today. And I should like to express, too, my particular pleasure at the presence of our Polish colleague, Foreign Minister Skubiszewski, who for many years has worked to strengthen understanding between Poland and Germany. Today, during the sessions in which he participated, we considered the principles which will underline the resolution of the border issue. Of course, we are well aware of the darkest periods of the historical relationship between Germany and Poland.

Today, we have had agreement on these basic principles, not just among those participating in the two-plus-four negotiations, but also with our Polish colleague. And I should like to take this opportunity to express the intention of the government of the Federal Republic of Germany determination to ensure that within the shortest possible time after unification and the return of sovereignty, there will be a border treaty with Poland, which will then be submitted to the Parliament of the united Germany for ratification.

In our discussions today, we also took up the issue of the results of our discussions with the Soviet leadership in recent days in the Soviet Union. These discussions and the results of those discussions have been welcomed by all participants today, and we consider that they represent a success for Europe as a whole, for the new Europe, and that these results have confirmed our expectations that it should be possible to conclude the two-plus-four discussions before the CSCE summit meeting which will take place in Paris in November. We should be able to complete that before the CSCE summit meeting. In this way we should be able to sign the final document this year so that German unification, and return of full sovereignty to Germany, should be possible within this year.

Given this development, which has been accompanied by the successful preparatory work for the CSCE summit meeting and the results of the NATO conference in London, which represented a new relationship between the member countries of the different alliances, of the two alliances, this dynamic process of German unification is clearly exhibiting a positive influence on Europe as a whole. German unification as a contribution to ensuring the unity, the stability of Europe, and to maintaining peace in Europe.

We Germans, of course, are fully aware of the responsibility which this development places upon us, and we welcome the fact that following today's discussions, it is now clear that German unification will be complete by the end of this year. And I should like to thank all of my colleagues who participated in this negotiation, I should like to thank them for their very constructive approach. Thank you.

Dumas: Thank you, Mr. Genscher, and I shall now give the floor to the foreign affairs minister of the Soviet Union.

Shevardnadze:[7] Ladies and gentlemen, I share the general assessments of the meeting that has just taken place, the ministerial meeting that has just taken place, the assessments as outlined by Mr. Dumas and by my other colleagues that preceded me. By the time of the Paris meeting, very important events have taken place that give us reason for confidence that an agreement about the final settlement of the external aspects of German unity will be reached and will be linked up with the process of German unification.

I would like to note the important work that has been done during the two first rounds of the meeting of the six, and also during the ministerial contacts at a bilateral level. It was during those contacts that we reached an understanding about the conditions and the kind of political evolution that would make possible the resolution of issues related to the German settlement.

In particular, let me emphasize the fact that over the past few months there have been contacts among the top leaders of the countries that participated in the two-plus-four mechanism. The meeting between the president of the USSR, Mikhail Gorbachev, and Federal Chancellor Mr. Kohl completed this series of intensive negotiations at the summit level.

So, now, we have before the six the mutual understandings that evolved, that emerged both during the broad political dialogue of the four powers and the two German states, and those that have been made possible as a result of the far-reaching changes taking place within the Warsaw Treaty, NATO, and within the overall European context.

The central problem that we faced at our talks in Ottawa was the determination of the responsibilities and rights of the four powers, and the granting of a full sovereignty to the future united Germany, and the problem of the political, military status of Germany.

For us, from the very outset there was no question—we did not question the fact that the process of the establishment of German unity is taking place on a democratic basis, that we can trust the German people in both parts of Germany, who over the post-war period have proven their commitment to peace and shown their determination to create a kind of society and state that would not threaten anyone and that would be a sound partner for all countries in the West and in the East.

But we, just like others, had to recognize that until very recently, there were certain realities that stood in the way of resolving the issues related to Germany. So, from the very outset, during the work of our mechanism of the six, we established a link between German unification and three other processes, that of reducing military confrontation in Europe and sharing a transition of European countries to defensive doctrines that implement the principle of defense efficiency; that of creating European structures of security and political cooperation; and that of transforming military blocs into political alliances and establishing relationships of partnership between the states that participate in the two alliances.

After the meeting of the political consultative committee of the Warsaw treaty in Moscow and the meetings of our partners in Dublin and London, we have seen a dramatic change, a dramatic headway in all these three areas. We can say without exaggeration that we have in Europe now a qualitatively new political-military situation evolving in Europe today. And that makes it possible to consider the possibility of synchronizing the external and the internal aspects of German unity and of terminating the responsibilities of the Four Powers at the time of unification of the two German states and the granting of the future Germany of full sovereignty. And that means that, as a sovereign state, Germany will decide itself which alliance it is going to belong to. A choice in favor of NATO created difficulties for us, serious problems for us, in a situation when NATO was holding on to its positions of the past. But the forthcoming transformation of this alliance is making it possible for us to take a new look at the role and place of the changing NATO in Europe.

I think that the interests of all European countries are well served by the political statements of the leaders of the FRG and the GDR, that the future Germany will have no weapons of mass destruction, that the size of the Bundeswehr will be limited, will be substantially limited, and also that the military structures of NATO will not extend to the territory of the GDR. Together with the agreement about the stationing of Soviet troops on the territory of Germany during a few years, these constraints will serve as material guarantees of stability in Europe.

We also have a firm understanding that the Soviet Union and a united Germany will conclude a treaty according to which the two sides will not consider themselves as adversaries, will not use force against each other, and will closely cooperate in the political, economic and other areas. We expect that

shortly new European structures of security will emerge, and first of all, a center to prevent and resolve crises. I would like to recall that during the first meeting of the six in Bonn, the Soviet side said that a change in the political-military situation in Europe will make it possible for the USSR to take a different look, to take a new look at the issues of German unity that looked difficult at the time. Currently, we have reason to do so and we can say that we have really taken a constructive and a goodwill approach to the resolution of these issues.

At the current meeting of the ministers, we have decided, as my colleagues have announced here, to arrange our work in practical terms so as to make sure that by the time of the Moscow meeting on the 12th of September we have a draft agreement between the six that the ministers could adopt as a basis and then complete work on it and submit it to the European summit meeting here in Paris.

Today will also go down in history, I'm sure, as a day when the question of the German-Polish border has been definitively settled, settled to the complete satisfaction of our Polish friends. We value the contribution of Minister Skubiszewski to the resolution of this issue, and I would like sincerely to congratulate him and Mr. Genscher, and Mr. Meckel, and the delegation of those three countries on this important occasion.

And finally, I would like to thank my friend, Mr. Roland Dumas, for his effective chairmanship and also for providing a beautiful and elegant setting to our meetings here in Paris.

Dumas: Thank you, I should like to thank you, my dear friend, and I shall now give the floor to the foreign affairs minister of the United Kingdom, Sir Douglas Hurd.

Hurd: Well, Mr. Chairman, you have been a very skillful chairman for us and it will turn out that today we have cracked two nuts: the question of the Polish borders and the shape of the final settlement. But as someone said quite recently—I can't quite remember who— we do have strong teeth. But this couldn't be taken for granted, even a few weeks ago, because several times in this series of talks, doubts have been expressed about the strength of purpose and the prospects for success in completing our task before the end of the year. Those doubts are now retreating. Mr. Shevardnadze talked this morning to us about patient, serene negotiation. Well, that's been practiced here today, it's been practiced at many meetings in the last few months, and because of that, it's coming out right.

When we have met before in the two-plus-four machinery, Mr. Shevardnadze has emphasized that a united Germany would not fit easily into the landscape of a new Europe if everything else remained the same. And he drew particular attention in advance to the importance of the NATO summit in London. And we took serious note of what he then said, and as you have heard today, the London declaration has not disappointed him. As a result of the particular hard work of the governments of the Soviet Union and the Federal Republic of Germany, we are now within sight of reconciling the freedom of a united Germany to choose its own alliance, its own place in Europe, reconciling with the legitimate concerns of the Soviet Union.

Over lunch and this afternoon, we reached agreement on the border question—Polish-German border question. Now, we British have very strong sympathies for historical reasons, for reasons of today also, with the Poles, and I have held several long and fruitful conversations on this problem with Mr. Skubiszewski. It's a great relief, a great satisfaction to us, that agreement has been reached on this. Here are two countries with a very checkered history together, two countries which are not going to be divided, but divided by an agreed international frontier, but united in their commitment to a Europe which is democratic, free, and which sorts out its differences peacefully. That is how it ought to be.

Dumas: Thank you very much. I call on the foreign minister of the German Democratic Republic, Mr. Meckel.

Meckel: I should like to begin, once again by thanking the foreign affairs minister of France for the way in which he chaired the meeting today. And I think that during our discussion, and indeed over the last days and weeks since June 22nd, our meeting in Berlin, we have achieved quite a lot of progress, and I think we have taken a major step forward. We have come much closer to resolving the issues which have brought us together. I would mention in particular the summit meeting in London recently, the meeting in Moscow in recent days. In this respect, in the area of security, much progress has been made, and I think this has taken account of

the way in which the situation in Europe has developed. That's a point I wanted to bring up.

The new relationship between the member countries of NATO and the Warsaw Pact, and the progress which has been made towards an institutionalization of the CSCE process, and just how important this is in security terms is something that was said very clearly: that the concept of security must not be seen in purely military terms, that security is a broader concept. It's not a question of arming against adversaries, but rather working together to attain security and it also has political and economic dimensions.

We consider that what has been said with regard to conventional armed forces, is a very positive starting point. We are very glad indeed that the Federal Republic has taken up our suggestion, namely, that both German states take the initiative to set a ceiling on German forces, go along with this proposal to Vienna, and in the area of conventional forces we are going to propose a Central European solution.

In recent days, the Soviet Union has agreed to German unification and a return of full sovereignty to Germany. The fact that these events have taken place at the same time, we consider a very major step forward. We think, too, that the international treaties which concern these allied rights and responsibilities, we need to study such treaties to see whether they contain restrictions, limitations on sovereignty which correspond to the rights and responsibilities of the allies.

We are particularly pleased that the Soviet Union has stated that it is willing to withdraw Soviet troops from the territory of the German Democratic Republic in the few years, and we think that this is a very positive development. This is the starting point of the treaty proposed between Germany and the Soviet Union, which concerns not just security issues, but all issues concerning our relations, and we consider that this should be based on the renunciation of force on both sides. This is linked to the withdrawal of Soviet nuclear weapons from German territory and the agreement that on the present territory of the GDR, no nuclear weapons should be based there in the future. We think this is a very important undertaking. It is a first important step forward on the road to a situation whereby, on German territory as a whole, no nuclear weapons should be stationed. And we consider that there is quite simply in the new Europe, there will be no need such nuclear weapons on German territory. We consider that security can be maintained without nuclear weapons on German territory.

And I am very pleased that in today's meeting, Mr. Skubiszewski has taken part in the discussion about this issue of German–Polish border, we have made progress. This, in fact, is an issue which we can now consider as having been resolved. We consider that this is in keeping with the responsibility of Germans, who when they consider the past, the checkered history of our relations between our countries, this is something we must be very much aware of.

It's particular significant that shortly after Federal Chancellor Kohl's visit to Moscow, that so shortly after this agreement, that we have been able today to attain agreement. Now, yesterday the agreement concerned German–Soviet relations, today German–Polish relations. This represents a very good prospect for the future. We never again want to see a situation whereby the relationship between Germany and the Soviet Union could represent a danger to Poland.

We are particularly satisfied that Poland has obtained assurances regarding its security today, security, that is, of its border. This is something which has been based on the principle firstly of signing a border treaty with Germany as soon as possible subsequent to the unification of Germany, and then there will be, subsequent to that, negotiations on a general treaty covering relations between both states. We consider that this is a major step forward. We consider that German unification is closely linked to this key question of the definitive nature of the border between Germany and Poland. Today, we have clearly stated that we are prepared, and that before unification, to engage in trilateral discussions with Poland, and covering those issues which are of mutual interest.

Dumas: Thank you very much. Now, you can put your questions to all the ministers. Will you kindly start by telling to whom you're addressing your question, and to tell us what paper you represent.

You have the floor.

Question: I have a question to Minister Skubiszewski. Would you say that what happened today actually foretells the possibility for Poland to become part of united Europe?

Skubiszewski: An important step in the direction you have indicated. There is no question of a united Europe without a united Germany and vice versa. The final regulation of the, or the confirmation of the frontier issue is an important contribution to the stability of the European continent.

As to Poland's return to Europe, I think this can be taken only in the relative terms because Poland was always present in Europe even in the worst times of its postwar history, we have always been part of cultural Europe and part of European civilization. At the present time, we are taking steps to become a member of the Council of Europe in Strasbourg and we also are making preparations for negotiations on the conclusion of an agreement of association with the European Community, to mention just two important steps which are elements of the Polish European policies.

Q: You make reference to economic talks this summer with West Germany. Please give us some details. And everybody's made reference to the border being finally settled, and terms of that settlement. But I haven't heard any of the terms except that the border is where the border is. Can you give us some idea of what the other terms are?

Skubiszewski: As to the economic talks, I can't give you any details regarding our future talks with Federal Germany and possibly also with the German Democratic Republic because this is only the beginning of our thinking about it. In any case, we are involved in talks with the German Democratic Republic on the fate of our various treaties and arrangements of an economic nature which will change—at least, some of them will change—as a result of German unification. And this is an important problem for Poland because the German Democratic Republic has been an important economic partner for Poland.

As to your second question, I cannot speak in detail about the provisions of the instrument that had been discussed today because this is a confidential matter, but I can tell you one thing. Poland was always puzzled by constant references to peace settlement or peace treaty as the final moment of the recognition or confirmation of the frontier. That condition, or requirement, of peace treaty or peace settlement has now disappeared. That's a result of this conference—a stabilizing result.

Q: A question for Mr. Genscher. Herr Genscher, there seem to be many questions here and other places from the Soviets, from Poland about Germany's future, good behavior. What reassurances have you been able to give your dialogue partners here?

Genscher: I would say that the Germany's behavior was not a matter we discussed today. The matter we discussed is that which was pointed out by our German . . . and I would like to just emphasize here to underline what the foreign minister of the Soviet Union said when he spoke about the confidence, the trust which his country has in both German states and the peoples of both German states, and this is a trust which is shared by all participants in this conference.

Q: I have two questions, if I may, to Mr. Genscher. In connection with what Mr. Meckel just said, I would like to know what you think about the positioning of nuclear arms throughout the territory of the GDR. I would like to hear from you how you foresee the future.

My next question is to Mr. Dumas. Are there any elements which perhaps did not go into the general outline of the settlement which are of concern to you in connection with the unification of Germany, be they of economic, political or military nature?

Genscher: During our discussions yesterday with the Soviet leadership, we did attain agreement, and this agreement is one which is shared by the participants of today's conference, according to which it is up to the united Germany to decide as to which, and if it wants to belong to an alliance. And in our discussions with the Soviet leadership, and as our Federal Chancellor said in the press conference in the Soviet Union, he clearly stated that Germany wants to remain a member of the Western alliance for the—into the future. Over a period of three to four years, Soviet troops will continue to be based on the territory of the GDR. This will be based on a treaty which a united and sovereign Germany will sign with the Soviet Union, and at the same time, in the territory of the present GDR forces of the united Germany will be based which will not be under NATO command, which will be responsible for territorial defense.

Following the withdrawal of Soviet troops, German forces—and that includes German forces under NATO command—will be based in the territory of the GDR. These forces will not, however, have nuclear arms at their disposal. This is a clear description of the situa-

tion as it will apply to Germany, in agreement, too, with the Soviet Union, that the Articles 5 and 6 of the NATO treaty will apply as soon as unification takes place. That these provisions, provisions of Articles 5 and 6 of the NATO treaty, will apply also to the territory of the GDR.

Dumas: To answer your last question, as you know, the Ottawa group was set up to deal with the external aspects of German unification. It being understood that internal issues are dealt with preference of the two countries. Among them, there was the question of frontiers between Poland and Germany and to identify the problems which occurred. The working group submitted to us five essential points which we considered also today. The minister of foreign affairs of Poland raised a number of additional problems which will not enter into the final document of the two-plus-four conference but to which he was able to receive replies in the course of the meeting. These replies some of them, find their way into the final settlement. In other cases, they will be in the shape of declarations that we work into this conference, so you need not worry because there will not be any questions which were not dealt with.

Q: For Ministers Genscher, Meckel and Skubiszewski, and the question is, did you refer today to the question of German constitution in the context of the borders? Thank you.

Genscher: The Federal Republic of Germany at an early stage in the framework of the two-plus-four negotiations clearly expressed that those provisions of the constitution of the Federal Republic which concern German unification will be either deleted or modified because the unification of the Federal Republic of Germany and the German Democratic Republic, and Berlin. Once this unification has taken place, German unification will have been completed, and in this way the goal of the constitution—the objective of the constitution will have been attained.

Skubiszewski: It is true that we talked today about the constitutional problems. A constitution is the highest law of the land, and when you provide that the constitution will take account of certain international changes such as the unification of Germany and the confirmation of the border, you thereby imply that you'll have various legal changes which to some extent are subject to international regulations. Other belong to the sovereign decision of the respective countries. I think that part of our debate was very useful.

Meckel: The constitution, of course, is the supreme law of any state. It's a matter for the sovereignty of that country. As has been said, following German unification, it will be necessary to modify the constitution in certain respects. The preamble, in this respect has been mentioned. This specifies that Article 23, this is something which will not in the future be present in the German constitution. Today, we did not actually discuss this matter but there was agreement that the constitutional issues of this kind should not be part of a treaty with another state. There was discussion as to what extent other legal provisions should be mentioned.

We agreed that it is purely self-evident that domestic law must be in line with international law and international obligations, and it is not necessary to specify this in a treaty. And I say this because, and I underline this because I myself have lived in a state for many years which signed many international treaties. However, the domestic law of the GDR quite simply was not adapted to that—was not in line with our international undertakings, and we are particularly sensitive and particularly aware of this issue and to ensure that this is not the case in future in Germany.

Q: This is both for Mr. Shevardnadze and Mr. Genscher. Mr. Meckel referred just now to his hopes for the denuclearization of Germany. To Mr. Shevardnadze, is it still the Soviet Union's goal that the whole of Germany should be denuclearized? And Mr. Genscher, what is your view on this issue?

Shevardnadze: That would be an ideal solution. Yesterday, in Stavropol and also in Moscow we discussed the question of the military-political status of the territory of what is now GDR. And an understanding has been reached that, on that territory, during the presence of the Soviet troops and also after Soviet troops withdraw, there will be no stationing of nuclear weapons. As for the other aspects of that problem, we have a good degree of mutual understanding that after the completion of the Vienna talks—of the first phase of the Vienna talks, we will begin a dialogue about reducing and maybe eventually eliminating tactical nuclear weapons from Europe.

Genscher: Mr. Shevardnadze, I think, has clearly stated that, in the territory of the present-day GDR, following the withdrawal

of the Soviet troops, that, up to that withdrawal, German troops will be stationed, and indeed following that but they will not dispose of nuclear weapons. The remaining issues will be discussed within the alliance and will be discussed at an international level.

Q: Secretary Baker, does the fact that the arrangements between the Soviet Union and the Germans were concluded by them and not by this conference directly, the fact that the United States is no longer in a position to wield the kind of economic clout it once did and the fact that you haven't been asked a question up to this point at this news conference combine to indicate that American influence in Europe is not what it once was, nor will it be.

Baker: I'm glad you're asking your question. You know, I was really beginning to wonder—respond to you by saying that we are extremely happy to see the announcement that came out of the Soviet Union yesterday, because we have worked very long and very hard for exactly this result.

The terms of the agreement that were reached between Chancellor Kohl and President Gorbachev are terms that the United States has supported since as early at least as last December when we called for a unified Germany as a member of the NATO alliance. So, the terms please us very much. And we would draw your attention, if we could, to the nine points that I mentioned in my opening statement and which we have discussed with all of our colleagues here from time to time, particularly with Minister Shevardnadze and President Gorbachev of the Soviet Union. So we're very pleased to see this result. It is a result that we've supported for a long time, and a result that we have worked very hard to achieve.

Genscher: My answer to this, to add to what Mr. Baker has just said, is that Germany has welcomed from the very outset that the United States has supported Germany's march towards unification, and our view of Germany's continued membership of NATO, which will be the result of the free decision on our part, but also the principle of not extending the structure of NATO to the territories of the GDR. This is the result of the joint appraisal of this matter, and we have greatly appreciated the United States' support in this respect. And I still remember what President Gorbachev said yesterday in the final conference with the Federal Chancellor, in which he referred to the importance of the results attained in the London NATO summit, which represented the starting point of a fundamental change in Europe which enabled the Soviet Union to reach agreement with the Federal Republic yesterday. And in this respect, I should just like to emphasize how important a role the president of the United States and the foreign minister - secretary of State of the United States have played in attaining the result at the London NATO summit.

Q: This is to Herr Genscher. In terms of economic aid, what kind of price do you expect to have to pay for the Soviet Union's agreement to German unification? And could you oblige by answering in English please for British television.

Genscher: Yes, but unfortunately, I would prefer to speak in German. I do not think that it is in keeping with the status of our relations with the Soviet Union and the peoples of the Soviet Union, that it is not in keeping to talk about a price paid to buy Soviet agreement. I do not think that's appropriate—a view of that kind is not appropriate. One cannot buy approval; one cannot buy agreement. That is not something we want to do and something that we could not do.

The Federal Republic of Germany and the Soviet Union, however, do agree that a united Germany will be able to contribute to strengthening relations between our two countries and to do so much more effectively than a continuation of the division of Germany. And for this reason, we have agreed that in a treaty which should be signed within 12 months, these prospects for future relations between Germany and the Soviet Union, we will develop these and we will sign an agreement to this effect. We are convinced that our contribution to insuring the success of the economic reform policy in the Soviet Union, this is, we are convinced, not just beneficial to the Soviet Union, but indeed to the development of Europe as a whole. We have a new approach to this matter; and we are convinced that this is something which is clearly going to be to the benefit of all countries of Europe and we believe that all countries are aware of this. Now, when I talk about 'we', I'm not just referring to the Soviet Union and the Federal Republic of Germany, I am also referring to all the states present at this table and, indeed, I believe all those states participating in the CSCE process.

Shevardnadze: Please bear with me. I would like to react—to respond to your question, too. In such terms as the establishment of a state sovereignty of a nation, national unity, and the self-determination of nations, there is no trade and we're not going to trade. And I fully agree with Mr. Genscher on this.

Q: A question for Minister Baker or Minister Skubiszewski. Mr. Baker, you referred to adjustments by the Polish minister on the principles of the border treaty. I wonder if either of you can please elaborate on what the adjustments were?

And secondly, for Minister Shevardnadze, you referred to 'partners', 'our partners in Dublin and London'. Do you regard the NATO countries as partners? And to bring up the question that came up in Bonn, are you preparing to somehow formalize that partnership, if not by an application to NATO, then what comes next?

Baker: Our perhaps joint answer, Minister, by saying that we have adopted five general principles that guide us in addressing the question of borders as it relates to the external aspects of the German unification. And the minister made several suggestions for changes in those principles. I think I'm probably at liberty to certainly mention one of those in which he requested that we have a statement to the effect that the confirmation of the definitive nature of Germany's borders represents an important contribution to the order of peace in Europe, or words generally to that effect. And we picked up on that suggestion and added that to our five principles. There were other suggestions that were made which were followed as well.

Dumas: As chairman of this meeting I'd like to confirm that this amendment was adopted and will figure in the final. Minister Skubiszewski?

Skubiszewski: Mr. President, you spoke up about adaptations. In fact, there were no particular adaptations, but we enlarged on certain issues. We adopted certain clarifications in various ways, as the Secretary of State said, some of them were incorporated into the five principles, others were subject of statements by the interested states. All of this boils down to confirmation of the frontier.

Shevardnadze: When we speak about partnership, I think there should be nothing surprising in that in fact the relations of partnership are something that we are already building with the United States, France, the FRG, Britain, and other countries. And as for the future, well, yes, I am fully confident that we will be real partners because what we are doing is building new relations between countries that belong to the different military-political alliances today.

Many things are changing in the world today. We are entering a period of peace in the development of world civilization. And in that context, we have to build new relations and there is nothing surprising about the fact that we, the adversaries of yesterday, countries that belong to confronting political-military alliances, will become real partners and will cooperate on the basis of the principles of equality and mutual trust.

Q: Could you please be a bit more specific about the changes that you wanted? Did you ask for a change in the preamble to the West German constitution, for example? Did you ask for Article 23 to be taken out of the constitution? Did you ask for a timetable to be put into the two-plus-four agreement to bind the German states to recognize the frontier as quickly as possible?

Skubiszewski: I didn't ask for the changes in the preamble of the constitution nor in Article 23, because I was told some time ago by our German partners that these changes would be brought about. So that was not a subject of discussion today. And so the change of the constitution is a matter to be decided by the country which is responsible for that constitution. We have received satisfactory assurances at—not only we—it was a matter which was first of all discussed in the two-plus-four talks. As to the timetable, there was indeed a problem of various consultations prior to this meeting. Our interest is in the speedy conclusion of the bilateral treaty, the treaty between Poland and united Germany, and we have received the assurance that that treaty would be concluded as soon as possible after the unification of Germany. That corresponds to the Polish position from the outset.

We always envisaged that the signing and ratification of the treaty will take place after unification. But we insisted on the usefulness of talks preparatory to the treaty now, prior to unification, because that might be helpful for what would happen after unification. That I would say is a pragmatic approach.

Dumas: Thank you very much. I would like to thank my six colleagues. Thank you,

ladies and gentlemen for participating in this exchange.

---

* Transcript of the 17 July 1990 press conference by US Secretary of State James Baker, French Foreign Minister Roland Dumas, FRG Foreign Minister Hans-Dietrich Genscher, GDR Foreign Minister Markus Meckel, Polish Foreign Minister Krzysztof Skubiszewski, British Foreign Secretary Douglas Hurd and Soviet Foreign Minister Eduard Shevardnadze following the Two-plus-Four meetings in Paris.

[1] Roland Dumas made a reference to the London Declaration on a transformed North Atlantic Alliance adopted at the NATO Summit (5–6 July 1990); see section XII—NATO document.

[2] For the results of the Gorbachev–Kohl talks as reflected in the statement during the joint press conference see the preceding document.

[3] The draft treaty on the border between Poland and Germany was submitted by the Polish Government to the German side a few days after unification (8 October 1990). The main controversy has been provoked by the German demand to establish a linkage between the negotiation, conclusion and ratification of two treaties: one on frontiers and another on good neighbourliness and co-operation. The negotiation mentioned by Minister Skubiszewski was initiated in Warsaw (30–31 October 1990). The search for a political solution was the subject of the talks between two heads of government, Chancellor Helmut Kohl and Prime Minister Tadeusz Mazowiecki, who met on 8 November 1990 in Frankfurt-on-Oder (Germany) and Slubice (Poland). The Treaty was signed in Warsaw, 14 November 1990, by the respective foreign ministers.

[4] The nine points mentioned by Secretary of State James Baker and presented in June to President Mikhail Gorbachev were reflected in James Baker's statement at the North Atlantic Council; see section I—US documents.

[5] For the text of the London Declaration see section XII—NATO document.

[6] For the agreement reached between the leaders of the Soviet Union and the FRG see the preceding document.

[7] The speech given by Soviet Foreign Minister Eduard Shevardnadze at the 'Two-plus-Four' Paris meeting (16 July 1990) is published in *Vestnik: Soviet Diplomacy Today* (Soviet Ministry for Foreign Affairs), September 1990, pp. 37–38.

The five principles agreed during the
Two-plus-Four talks,
Paris, 18 July 1990

The five principles on the final character of
the borders of Germany, on which the participants of the Paris summit meeting agreed and
which will be included in the concluding
document of the two-plus-four-talks are the
following:

1. The united Germany will comprise the
territory of the Federal Republic of Germany,
the German Democratic Republic and all of
Berlin. Her external borders will definitely be
the borders of the Federal Republic of
Germany as they are on the day when the
final arrangement comes into force. The confirmation of the character of the borders of
Germany is a substantial contribution to the
peace order in Europe.

2. The united Germany and the Republic of
Poland confirm the border existing between
their states in a treaty binding under international law.

3. The united Germany has no territorial
claims against other states and will also not
raise any in the future.

4. The governments of the Federal Republic of Germany and the German Democratic
Republic will guarantee that the constitution
of the unified Germany will not contain any
regulations which are not compatible with
these principles. This applies correspondingly
to the provisions which are set down in the
preamble and in articles 23, para 2, and 146 of
the Basic Law for the Federal Republic of
Germany.

5. The governments of the USSR, the
USA, the United Kingdom and France receive
formally the corresponding obligation and
declaration of the governments of the Federal
Republic of Germany and the German Democratic Republic and emphasize that with their
implementation the definite character of the
borders of Germany will be confirmed.

Translated from the German text published in:
*Dokumentation zu den Zwei-plus-Vier-Verhand-
lungen in Paris*, Pressemitteilung der Botschaft der
BRD, Stockholm, 18 July 1990.

Treaty between the Federal Republic of
Germany and the German Democratic
Republic on the Establishment of the Unity
of Germany,
Berlin, 31 August 1990

Excerpts

The Federal Republic of Germany and the
German Democratic Republic—

Determined to complete in free self-determination the unity of Germany in peace and
freedom as an equal member of the community of nations,

Starting from the wish of the people in the
two parts of Germany to live together in
peace and freedom in an orderly state under
the rule of law, in a democratic and social
federal state,

In grateful respect for those who helped
freedom to appear in a peaceful way, who,
unflustered, kept hold of the task of establishing the unity of Germany,

Aware of the continuity of German history
and bearing in mind the special responsibility
which arises from our past for democratic
development in Germany which is committed
to the respect of human rights and to peace,

Endeavouring to make a contribution by
German unity to the establishment of a European peace order in which borders no longer
separate and in which all European nations
are guaranteed a trustful co-existence,

Aware that the inviolability of borders and
territorial integrity and sovereignty of all
states in Europe within their borders is a
fundamental condition for peace—

Have agreed to conclude a treaty on the
establishment of the unity of Germany with
the following requirements:

Chapter 1
Effect of the Accession

Article 1
Countries (Länder)

(1) With the implementation of the accession
of the German Democratic Republic to the
Federal Republic of Germany in accordance
with Article 23 of the Basic Law, taking
effect on 3 October 1990, the countries
(Länder) of Brandenburg, Mecklenburg-
Vorpommern, Sachsen, Sachsen-Anhalt and
Thüringen become countries (Länder) of the

Federal Republic of Germany. For the creation of and the establishment of borders between these countries (Länder) the regulations of the constitutional law for the creation of countries (Länder) in the German Democratic Republic of 22 July 1990—The Establishment of Länder Law (Ländereinführungsgesetz—GBl. 1 No. 51, p. 955), annex II applies.

(2) The 23 districts of Berlin form the country (das Land) of Berlin.

Article 2
Capital, the Day of German Unity

(1) The capital of Germany is Berlin. The location of the seat of the Parliament and Government will be decided after the establishment of German unity.

(2) As the Day of German Unity, 3 October is by law a public holiday.

(...)

---

* Translated from German. The full text of the Treaty between the Federal Republic of Germany and the German Democratic Republic on the Establishment of the Unity of Germany is published in *Bulletin des Presse- und Informationsamtes der Bundesregierung*, no. 104/S. 877, Bonn, 6 September 1990, pp. 878–1120.

Treaty on the final settlement
with respect to Germany,*
Moscow, 12 September 1990

The Federal Republic of Germany, the German Democratic Republic, the French Republic, the Union of Soviet Socialist Republics, the United Kingdom of Great Britain and Northern Ireland and the United States of America,

Conscious of the fact that their peoples have been living together in peace since 1945;

Mindful of the recent historic changes in Europe which make it possible to overcome the division of the continent;

Having regard to the rights and responsibilities of the Four Powers relating to Berlin and to Germany as a whole, and the corresponding wartime and post-war agreements and decisions of the Four Powers;

Resolved in accordance with their obligations under the Charter of the United Nations to develop friendly relations among nations based on respect for the principle of equal rights and self-determination of peoples, and to take other appropriate measures to strengthen universal peace;

Recalling the principles of the Final Act of the Conference on Security and Cooperation in Europe, signed in Helsinki;

Recognizing that those principles have laid firm foundations for the establishment of a just and lasting peaceful order in Europe;

Determined to take account of everyone's security interests;

Convinced of the need finally to overcome antagonism and to develop cooperation in Europe;

Confirming their readiness to reinforce security, in particular by adopting effective arms control, disarmament and confidence-building measures; their willingness not to regard each other as adversaries but to work for a relationship of trust and cooperation; and accordingly their readiness to consider positively setting up appropriate institutional arrangements within the framework of the Conference on Security and Cooperation in Europe;

Welcoming the fact that the German people, freely exercising their right of self-determination, have expressed their will to bring about the unity of Germany as a state so that they will be able to serve the peace of the world as an equal and sovereign partner in a united Europe;

Convinced that the unification of Germany as a state with definitive borders is a significant contribution to peace and stability in Europe;

Intending to conclude the final settlement with respect to Germany;

Recognizing that thereby, and with the unification of Germany as a democratic and peaceful state, the rights and responsibilities of the Four Powers relating to Berlin and to Germany as a whole lose their function;

Represented by their Ministers for Foreign Affairs who, in accordance with the Ottawa Declaration of 13 February 1990, met in Bonn on 5 May 1990, in Berlin on 22 June 1990, in Paris on 17 July 1990 with the participation of the Minister for Foreign Affairs of the Republic of Poland, and in Moscow on 12 September 1990;

Have agreed as follows:

Article 1

(1) The united Germany shall comprise the territory of the Federal Republic of Germany, the German Democratic Republic and the whole of Berlin. Its external borders shall be the borders of the Federal Republic of Germany and the German Democratic Republic and shall be definitive from the date on which the present Treaty comes into force. The confirmation of the definitive nature of the borders of the united Germany is an essential element of the peaceful order in Europe.

(2) The united Germany and the Republic of Poland shall confirm the existing border between them in a treaty that is binding under international law.

(3) The united Germany has no territorial claims whatsoever against other states and shall not assert any in the future.

(4) The Governments of the Federal Republic of Germany and the German Democratic Republic shall ensure that the constitution of the united Germany does not contain any provision incompatible with these principles. This applies accordingly to the provisions laid down in the preamble, the second sentence of Article 23, and Article 146 of the Basic Law for the Federal Republic of Germany.

(5) The Governments of the French Republic, the Union of Soviet Socialist Republics, the United Kingdom of Great Britain and Northern Ireland and the United States of America take formal note of the corresponding commitments and declarations by the Governments of the Federal Republic of Germany and the German Democratic Republic and declare that their implementation will confirm the definitive nature of the united Germany's borders.

Article 2

The Governments of the Federal Republic of Germany and the German Democratic Republic reaffirm their declarations that only peace will emanate from German soil. According to the constitution of the united Germany, acts tending to and undertaken with the intent to disturb the peaceful relations between nations, especially to prepare for aggressive war, are unconstitutional and a punishable offence. The Governments of the Federal Republic of Germany and the German Democratic Republic declare that the united Germany will never employ any of its weapons except in accordance with its constitution and the Charter of the United Nations.

Article 3

(1) The Governments of the Federal Republic of Germany and the German Democratic Republic reaffirm their renunciation of the manufacture and possession of and control over nuclear, biological and chemical weapons. They declare that the united Germany, too, will abide by these commitments. In particular, rights and obligations arising from the Treaty on the Non-Proliferation of Nuclear Weapons of 1 July 1968 will continue to apply to the united Germany.

(2) The Government of the Federal Republic of Germany, acting in full agreement with the Government of the German Democratic Republic, made the following statement on 30 August 1990 in Vienna at the Negotiations on Conventional Armed Forces in Europe:

'The Government of the Federal Republic of Germany undertakes to reduce the personnel strength of the armed forces of the united Germany to 370, 000 (ground, air and naval forces) within three to four years. This reduction will commence on the entry into force of the first CFE agreement. Within the scope of this overall ceiling no more than 345, 000 will belong to the ground and air forces which, pursuant to the ageed mandate, alone are the subject of the Negotiations on Conventional Armed Forces in Europe. The Federal Government regards its commitment to reduce ground and air forces as a significant German contribution to the reduction of conventional armed forces in Europe. It assumes that in follow-on negotiations the other participants in the negotiations, too, will render their contribution to enhancing security and stability in Europe, including measures to limit personnel strengths'.

The Government of the German Democratic Republic has expressly associated itself with this statement.

(3) The Governments of the French Republic, the Union of Soviet Socialist Republics, the United Kingdom of Great Britain and Northern Ireland and the United States of America take note of these statements by the Governments of the Federal Republic of Germany and the German Democratic Republic.

Article 4

(1) The Governments of the Federal Republic of Germany, the German Democratic Republic and the Union of Soviet Socialist Republics state that the united Germany and the Union of Soviet Socialist Republics will settle by treaty the conditions for and the duration of the presence of Soviet armed forces on the territory of the present German Democratic Republic and of Berlin, as well as the conduct of the withdrawal of these armed forces which will be completed by the end of 1994, in connection with the implementation of the undertaking of the Federal Republic of Germany and the German Democratic Republic referred to in paragraph 2 of Article 3 of the present Treaty.

(2) The Governments of the French Republic, the United Kingdom of Great Britain and Northern Ireland and the United States of America take note of this statement.

Article 5

(1) Until the completion of the withdrawal of the Soviet armed forces from the territory of the present German Democratic Republic and of Berlin in accordance with Article 4 of the present Treaty, only German territorial defence units which are not integrated into the alliance structures to which German armed forces in the rest of German territory are assigned will be stationed in that territory as armed forces of the united Germany. During that period and subject to the provisions of paragraph 2 of this Article, armed forces of other states will not be stationed in that territory or carry out any other military activity there.

(2) For the duration of the presence of Soviet armed forces in the territory of the present German Democratic Republic and of Berlin, armed forces of the French Republic, the United Kingdom of Great Britain and Northern Ireland and the United States of America will, upon German request, remain stationed in Berlin by agreement to this effect between the Government of the united Germany and the Governments of the states concerned. The number of troops and the amount of equipment of all non-German armed forces stationed in Berlin will not be greater than at the time of signature of the present Treaty. New categories of weapons will not be introduced there by non-German armed forces. The Government of the united

Germany will conclude with the Governments of those states which have armed forces stationed in Berlin treaties with conditions which are fair taking account of the relations existing with the states concerned.

(3) Following the completion of the withdrawal of the Soviet armed forces from the territory of the present German Democratic Republic and of Berlin, units of German armed forces assigned to military alliance structures in the same way as those in the rest of German territory may also be stationed in that part of Germany, but without nuclear weapon carriers. This does not apply to conventional weapon systems which may have other capabilities in addition to conventional ones but which in that part of Germany are equipped for a conventional role and designated only for such. Foreign armed forces and nuclear weapons or their carriers will not be stationed in that part of Germany or deployed there.

Article 6

The right of the united Germany to belong to alliances, with all the rights and responsibilities arising therefrom, shall not be affected by the present Treaty.

Article 7

(1) The French Republic, the Union of Soviet Socialist Republics, the United Kingdom of Great Britain and Northern Ireland and the United States of America hereby terminate their responsibilities relating to Berlin and to Germany as a whole. As a result, the corresponding, related quadripartite agreements, decisions and practices are terminated and all related Four Power institutions are dissolved.

(2) The united Germany shall have accordingly full sovereignty over its internal and external affairs.

Article 8

(1) The present Treaty is subject to ratification or acceptance as soon as possible. On the German side it will be ratified by the united Germany. The Treaty will therefore apply to the united Germany.

(2) The instruments of ratification or acceptance shall be deposited with the Government of the united Germany. That Government shall inform the Governments of the other Contracting Parties of the deposit of each instrument of ratification or acceptance.

Article 9

The present Treaty shall enter into force for the united Germany, the French Republic, the Union of Soviet Socialist Republics, the United Kingdom of Great Britain and Northern Ireland and the United States of America on the date of deposit of the last instrument of ratification or acceptance by these states.

Article 10

The original of the present Treaty, of which the English, French, German and Russian texts are equally authentic, shall be deposited with the Government of the Federal Republic of Germany, which shall transmit certified true copies to the Governments of the other Contracting Parties.

AGREED MINUTE:

Any questions with respect to the application of the word 'deployed' as used in the last sentence of paragraph 3 of Article 5 will be decided by the Government of the united Germany in a reasonable and responsible way taking into account the security interests of each Contracting Party as set forth in the preamble.

---

* The Treaty was signed for the FRG by Hans-Dietrich Genscher, Federal Minister for Foreign Affairs; for the GDR by Lothar de Maizière, Prime Minister and Minister for Foreign Affairs; for the French Republic by Roland Dumas, Minister for Foreign Affairs; for the USSR by Eduard Shevardnadze, Minister for Foreign Affairs; for the UK by Douglas Hurd, Secretary of the Foreign Office; and for the USA by James Baker III, Secretary of State. The text in Russian was published in *Isvestia*, 13 September 1990.

The joint letter of the foreign ministers of the Federal Republic of Germany and the German Democratic Republic* (connected with the signing of the Treaty on the final settlement with respect to Germany), Moscow, 12 September 1990

Mr Foreign Minister,
In connection with the signing today of the Treaty on the Final Settlement with Respect to Germany we would like to inform you that the Governments of the Federal Republic of Germany and the German Democratic Republic declared the following in the negotiations:

1. The Joint Declaration of 15 June 1990 by the Governments of the Federal Republic of Germany and the German Democratic Republic on the settlement of outstanding property matters contains inter alia the following observations:

'The expropriations effected on the basis of occupation law or sovereignty (between 1945 and 1949) are irreversible. The Governments of the Soviet Union and the German Democratic Republic do not see any means of revising the measures taken then. The Government of the Federal Republic of Germany takes note of this in the light of the historical development. It is of the opinion that a final decision on any public compensation must be reserved for a future all-German parliament'.

According to Article 41 (1) of the Treaty of 31 August 1990 between the Federal Republic of Germany and the German Democratic Republic Establishing German Unity (Unification Treaty), the aforementioned Joint Declaration forms an integral part of the Treaty. Pursuant to Article 41 (3) of the Unification Treaty, the Federal Republic of Germany will not enact any legislation contradicting the part of the Joint Declaration quoted above.

2. The monuments dedicated to the victims of war and tyranny which have been erected on German soil will be respected and will enjoy the protection of German law. The same applies to the war graves, which will be maintained and looked after.

3. In the united Germany, too, the free democratic basic order will be protected by the Constitution. It provides the basis for ensuring that parties which, by reason of their aims or the behaviour of their adherents, seek to impair or abolish the free democratic basic order as well as associations which are directed against the constitutional order or the concept of international understanding can be prohibited. This also applies to parties and associations with National Socialist aims.

4. On the treaties of the German Democratic Republic, the following has been agreed in Article 12 (1) and (2) of the Treaty of 31 August 1990 between the Federal Republic of Germany and the German Democratic Republic Establishing German Unity:

'The Contracting Parties agree that, as part of the process of establishing German unity, the international treaties concluded by the German Democratic Republic shall be discussed with the contracting parties in terms of the protection of bona fide rights, the interests of the states concerned and the treaty obligations of the Federal Republic of Germany as well as in the light of the principles of a free democratic basic order founded on the rule of law and taking into account the responsibilities of the European Communities in order to regulate or ascertain the continuance, adjustment or termination of such treaties.

The united Germany shall lay down its position on the continuance of international treaties of the German Democratic Republic after consultations with the respective contracting parties and with the European Communities in so far as their responsibilities are affected'.

Accept, Mr Foreign Minister, the assurances of our high consideration.

---

* This note was addressed to the foreign ministers of the Four Powers: France, the UK, the USA and the USSR.

The Four Powers' declaration on the suspension of their rights and responsibilities relating to Berlin and to Germany as a whole,
New York, 1 October 1990

The Governments of the French Republic, the Union of Soviet Socialist Republics, the United Kingdom of Great Britain and Northern Ireland and the United States of America,

Represented by their Ministers for Foreign Affairs meeting at New York on 1 October 1990,

Having regard to the Treaty on the Final Settlement with respect to Germany signed at Moscow on 12 September 1990, which provides for the termination of their rights and responsibilities relating to Berlin and to Germany as a whole,

Declare that the operation of their rights and responsibilities relating to Berlin and to Germany as a whole shall be suspended upon the unification of Germany, pending the entry into force of the Treaty on the Final Settlement with respect to Germany. As a result, the operation of the corresponding, related quadripartite agreements, decisions and practices and all related Four Power institutions shall likewise be suspended upon the unification of Germany.

The Government of the Federal Republic of Germany, represented by its Minister for Foreign Affairs, and the Government of the German Democratic Republic, represented by its Minister for Education and Science, take note of this declaration.

German unification
Letter of Chancellor Helmut Kohl,*
Bonn, 3 October 1990

Dear Prime Minister,

Today, the German nation has become reunited in peace and freedom. Forty-five years after the end of the second world war, which originated from German soil and caused untold suffering in Europe and throughout the world, the painful separation of the Germans has come to an end.

In exercising our right to free self-determination, in harmony with our neighbours and on the basis of the Treaty on the Final Settlement with Respect to Germany, we Germans have today united to form a single state—the Federal Republic of Germany—with complete sovereignty over its internal and external affairs.

On behalf of the German people I would like to thank all those who stood up for our right of self-determination and smoothed our path towards unity. Conscious of the continuity of German history, we particularly appreciate this contribution.

I

Through its regained national unity, our country wants to serve the cause of global peace and advance the unification of Europe. That is the mandate of our time-honoured constitution, the basic law, which will also apply to the united Germany.

At the same time, we stand by our moral and legal obligations resulting from German history.

We know that upon unification, we will also assume greater responsibility within the community of nations as a whole. Our foreign policy will therefore remain geared towards global partnership, close cooperation and a peaceful reconciliation of interests.

In future, German soil will be a source of peace only. We are aware that the inviolability of the borders and respect for the territorial integrity and sovereignty of all states in

Europe is a basic precondition for peace. That is why we have confirmed the final character of the united Germany's borders, including the border with the Republic of Poland. At no time in the future will we make territorial claims on any other country. Now that German unity has been established, we shall discuss with the contracting parties concerned the international treaties of the German Democratic Republic with a view to regulating or confirming their continued application, adjustment or expiry, taking into account protection of confidence, the interests of the states concerned and the contractual obligations of the Federal Republic of Germany, as well as the principles of a free, democratic basic order governed by the rule of law, and respecting the competence of the European Community.

II

The unification of Germany is inextricably linked with that of Europe. We will resolutely continue to strive for European unification with the same determination with which we worked towards German unity.

Important steps are directly before us. Together with our partners in the European Community, we want to complete the single European market by 1992. We are steadily advancing towards economic and monetary union. The united Germany will play an active part in the development of the political union.

The European Community will be open to close cooperation with the other countries in Europe. In particular, we intend to contribute to the development of closer ties between the European Community and the countries of Central, Eastern and South-Eastern Europe which have won their freedom and set out on the path towards political, economic and social reform.

We are convinced that the countries of Europe can best safeguard and strengthen their independence and their citizens' human rights and fundamental freedoms if they work together.

For this reason, an important forum for our cooperation is and remains the Council of Europe.

We are committed to the process of security and cooperation in Europe as a source of hope for the European nations and as a sign-post towards their future unity. We are therefore strongly in favour of this process being intensified and institutionalized.

III

The community of free Western democracies based on shared values and the North Atlantic Treaty Organization have preserved peace and freedom on our continent during difficult decades. That is why the united Germany will continue to be a member of this alliance.

Together with our allies, we also want to develop further this successful alliance in line with the progress made in East–West relations and the changing demands of our time, as well as preserve its role as the basic pillar of new, overarching security structures in Europe.

We advocate a joint declaration by the members of the two alliances in Europe, reaffirming their intention to refrain from the threat or use of force and establishing a new partnership in the development of a just and lasting peaceful order in Europe.

Disarmament and arms control remain key elements of our security policy.

In the context of German unification we have reaffirmed our renunciation of the manufacture and possession of as well as control over nuclear, biological and chemical weapons. The united Germany remains committed to the Non-Proliferation Treaty.

Our willingness to reduce the united Germany's armed forces to 370, 000 is at the same time a contribution to the success of the negotiations on the reduction of conventional forces in Europe. We assume that in the follow-on negotiations the other participating countries, too, will play their part in consolidating security and stability in Europe, not least through measures to restrict force strengths.

On the global level, too, we shall seek disarmament agreements that will enhance stability and security. The principle of gearing the level of forces solely towards self-defence requirements must apply throughout the world.

An agreement on reductions in strategic nuclear weapons between the United States and the Soviet Union, negotiations on reducing American and Soviet short-range nuclear weapons and, not least, a global ban on chemical weapons are still urgently required.

IV

The countries of Africa, Asia and America can continue to count on the solidarity of the united Germany. We will not invest in German unity at their expense.

On the contrary: the end of the conflict in Europe will release intellectual powers and material resources for tackling the central tasks for peace now facing us. For the struggle against poverty and underdevelopment and for the preservation of our natural environment.

Terrorism and drug abuse are challenges to all states throughout the world, which call for joint action. We will shoulder our share of the responsibility.

V

The elimination of the East–West conflict has also opened up new avenues for fully implementing the lofty goals of the United Nations charter. At the same time, the events of the last few weeks have demonstrated to what extent world peace is still endangered by disregard for the principles of the UN charter.

The Federal Republic of Germany wishes to play a part in ensuring that the United Nations fulfills its indispensable role in the process of building a peaceful world and meeting the global challenges we face.

Now that German unity with complete sovereignty has been achieved, the Federal Republic of Germany is prepared to participate in UN measures aiming at preserving and restoring peace through the deployment of its forces, too. We will create the necessary internal conditions for this.

VI

At the beginning of the last decade of this century, we see new opportunities for a world which solves its problems through reconciliation and understanding, and remains committed to the principles of international law. Our country stands shoulder-to-shoulder with all those who are committed to peace, respect for human rights and fundamental freedoms as well as individual well-being.

Now that the burden of division has been lifted from us, we are prepared to redouble our efforts towards shaping a common peaceful future in trustful cooperation with all countries and peoples who share these worthy objectives.

Please accept, dear Prime Minister, the assurances of my highest consideration.

(sgd) Helmut Kohl, Chancellor of the Federal Republic of Germany

---

* Translated from the letter addressed to Tadeusz Mazowiecki, Prime Minister of Poland, and published in *Rzeczpospolita* (daily), 4 October 1990. The same text was addressed to all heads of government with whom the united Germany has diplomatic relations. The original German text was published in *Bulletin des Presse- und Informationsamtes der Bundesregierung*, no. 118, Bonn, 5 October 1990, pp. 1227–1228..

XX. Soviet–German document

**Treaty between the Federal Republic of Germany and the Union of Soviet Socialist Republics on Good-Neighbourliness, Partnership and Cooperation,*
Moscow, 13 September 1990**

The Federal Republic of Germany and the Union of Soviet Socialist Republics,

Conscious of their responsibility for the preservation of peace in Europe and in the world,

Desiring to set the final seal on the past and, through understanding and reconciliation, render a major contribution towards ending the division of Europe,

Convinced of the need to build a new, united Europe on the basis of common values and to create a just and lasting peaceful order in Europe including stable security structures,

Convinced that great importance attaches to human rights and fundamental freedoms as part of the heritage of the whole of Europe and that respect for them is a major prerequisite for progress in developing that peaceful order,

Reaffirming their commitment to the aims and principles enshrined in the United Nations Charter and to the provisions of the Final Act of Helsinki of 1 August 1975 and of subsequent documents adopted by the Conference on Security and Cooperation in Europe,

Resolved to continue the good traditions of their centuries-long history, to make good-neighbourliness, partnership and cooperation the basis of their relations, and to meet the historic challenges that present themselves on the threshold of the third millenium,

Having regard to the foundations established in recent years through the development of cooperation between the Union of Soviet Socialist Republics and the Federal Republic of Germany as well as the German Democratic Republic,

Moved by the desire to further develop and intensify the fruitful and mutually beneficial cooperation between the two States in all fields and to give their mutual relationship a new quality in the interests of their peoples and of peace in Europe,

Taking account of the signing of the Treaty of 12 September 1990 on the Final Settlement with respect to Germany regulating the external aspects of German unity,

Have agreed as follows.

Article 1

The Federal Republic of Germany and the Union of Soviet Socialist Republics will, in developing their relations, be guided by the following principles:

They will respect each other's sovereign equality, territorial integrity and political independence.

They will make the dignity and rights of the individual, concern for the survival of mankind, and preservation of the natural environment the focal point of their policy.

They reaffirm the right of all nations and States to determine their own fate freely and without interference from outside and to proceed with their political, economic, social and cultural development as they see fit.

They uphold the principle that any war, whether nuclear or conventional, must be effectively prevented and peace preserved and developed.

They guarantee the precedence of the universal rules of international law in their domestic and international relations and confirm their resolve to honour their contractual obligations.

They pledge themselves to make use of the creative potential of the individual and modern society with a view to safeguarding peace and enhancing the prosperity of all nations.

Article 2

The Federal Republic of Germany and the Union of Soviet Socialist Republics undertake to respect without qualification the territorial integrity of all States in Europe within their present frontiers.

They declare that they have no territorial claims whatsoever against any State and will not raise any in the future.

They regard and will continue to regard as inviolable the frontiers of all States in Europe as they exist on the day of signature of the present Treaty.

Article 3

The Federal Republic of Germany and the Union of Soviet Socialist Republics reaffirm that they will refrain from any threat or use of force which is directed against the territorial integrity or political independence of the other side or is in any other way incompatible with the aims and principles of the United Nations Charter or with the CSCE Final Act.

They will settle their disputes exclusively by peaceful means and never resort to any of their weapons except for the purpose of individual or collective self-defence. They will never and under no circumstances be the first to employ armed forces against one another or against third States. They call upon all other States to join in this non-aggression commitment.

Should either side become the object of an attack the other side will not afford any military support or other assistance to the aggressor and resort to all measures to settle the conflict in conformity with the principles and procedures of the United Nations and other institutions of collective security.

Article 4

The Federal Republic of Germany and the Union of Soviet Socialist Republics will seek to ensure that armed forces and armaments are substantially reduced by means of binding, effectively verifiable agreements in order to achieve, in conjunction with unilateral measures, a stable balance at a lower level, especially in Europe, which will suffice for defence but not for attack.

The same applies to the multilateral and bilateral enhancement of confidence-building and stabilizing measures.

Article 5

Both sides will support to the best of their ability the process of security and cooperation in Europe on the basis of the Final Act of Helsinki adopted on 1 August 1975 and, with the cooperation of all participating States, develop and intensify that cooperation further still, notably by creating permanent institutions and bodies. The aim of these efforts is the consolidation of peace, stability and security and the coalescence of Europe to form a single area of law, democracy and cooperation in the fields of economy, culture and information.

Article 6

The Federal Republic of Germany and the Union of Soviet Socialist Republics have agreed to hold regular consultations with a view to further developing and intensifying their bilateral relations and coordinating their position on international issues.

Consultations at the highest political level shall be held as necessary but at least once a year.

The Foreign Ministers will meet at least twice a year.

The Defence Ministers will meet at regular intervals.

Other ministers will meet as necessary to discuss matters of mutual interest.

The existing mixed commissions will consider ways and means of intensifying their work. New mixed commissions will be appointed as necessary by mutual agreement.

Article 7

Should a situation arise which in the opinion of either side constitutes a threat to or violation of peace or may lead to dangerous international complications, both sides will immediately make contact with a view to coordinating their positions and agreeing on measures to improve or resolve the situation.

Article 8

The Federal Republic of Germany and the Union of Soviet Socialist Republics have agreed to substantially expand and intensify their bilateral cooperation, especially in the economic, industrial and scientific-technological fields and in the field of environmental protection, with a view to developing their mutual relations on a stable and long-term basis and deepening the trust between the two States and peoples. They will to this end conclude a comprehensive agreement on the development of cooperation in the economic, industrial and scientific-technological fields and, where necessary, separate arrangements on specific matters.

Both sides attach great importance to cooperation in the training of specialists and executive personnel from industry for the development of bilateral relations and are prepared to considerably expand and intensify that cooperation.

Article 9

The Federal Republic of Germany and the Union of Soviet Socialist Republics will further develop and intensify their economic cooperation for their mutual benefit. They will create, as far as their domestic legislation and their obligations under international treaties allow, the most favourable general conditions for entrepreneurial and other economic activity by citizens, enterprises and governmental as well as non-governmental institutions of the other side.

This applies in particular to the treatment of capital investment and investors.

Both sides will encourage the initiatives necessary for economic cooperation by those directly concerned, especially with the aim of fully exploiting the possibilities afforded by the existing treaties and programmes.

Article 10

Both sides will, on the basis of the Agreement of 22 July 1986 concerning Economic and Technological Cooperation, further develop exchanges in this field and implement joint projects. They propose to draw on the achievements of modern science and technology for the sake of the people, their health, and their prosperity. They will promote and support parallel initiatives by researchers and research establishments in this sphere.

Article 11

Convinced that the preservation of the natural sources of life is indispensable for prosperous economic and social development, both sides reaffirm their determination to continue and intensify their cooperation in the field of environmental protection on the basis of the agreement of 25 October 1988.

They propose to solve major problems of environmental protection together, to study harmful effects on the environment, and to develop measures for their prevention. They will participate in the development of coordinated strategies and concepts for a transborder environmental policy within the international, and especially the European, framework.

Article 12

Both sides will seek to extend transport communications (air, rail, sea, inland waterway and road links) between the Federal Republic of Germany and the Union of Soviet Socialist Republics through the use of state-of-the-art technology.

Article 13

Both sides will strive to simplify to a considerable extent, on the basis of reciprocity, the procedure for the issue of visas to citizens of both countries wishing to travel, primarily for business, economic and cultural reasons and for purposes of scientific and technological cooperation.

Article 14

Both sides support comprehensive contacts among people from both countries and the development of cooperation among parties, trade unions, foundations, schools, universities, sports organizations, churches and social institutions, women's associations, environmental protection and other social organizations and associations.

Special attention will be given to the deepening of contacts between the parliaments of the two States.

They welcome cooperation based on partnership between municipalities and regions and between Federal States and Republics of the Union.

An important role falls to the German–Soviet Discussion Forum and cooperation among the media.

Both sides will facilitate the participation of all young people and their organizations in exchanges and other contacts and joint projects.

Article 15

The Federal Republic of Germany and the Union of Soviet Socialist Republics, conscious of the mutual enrichment of the cultures of their peoples over the centuries and of their unmistakable contribution to Europe's common cultural heritage, as well as of the importance of cultural exchange for international understanding, will considerably extend their cultural cooperation.

Both sides will give substance to and fully exploit the agreement on the establishment and work of cultural centres.

Both sides reaffirm their willingness to give all interested persons comprehensive access to the languages and cultures of the other side and will encourage public and private initiatives.

Both sides strongly advocate the creation of wider possibilities for learning the language of the other country in schools, universities and other educational institutions and will for this purpose assist the other side in the training of teachers and make available teaching aids, including the use of television, radio, audio-visual and computer technology. They will support initiatives for the establishment of bilingual schools.

Soviet citizens of German nationality as well as citizens from the Union of Soviet Socialist Republics who have their permanent abode in the Federal Republic of Germany and wish to preserve their language, culture or traditions will be enabled to develop their national, linguistic and cultural identity. Accordingly, both sides will make possible and facilitate promotional measures for the benefit of such persons or their organizations within the framework of their respective laws.

Article 16

The Federal Republic of Germany and the Union of Soviet Socialist Republics will advocate the preservation of cultural treasures of the other side in their territory.

They agree that lost or unlawfully transferred art treasures which are located in their territory will be returned to their owners or their successors.

Article 17

Both sides stress the special importance of humanitarian cooperation in their bilateral relations. They will intensify this cooperation with the assistance of the charitable organizations of both sides.

Article 18

The Government of the Federal Republic of Germany declares that the monuments to Soviet victims of the war and totalitarian rule erected on German soil will be respected and be under the protection of German law.

The same applies to Soviet war graves; they will be preserved and tended.

The Government of the Union of Soviet Socialist Republics will guarantee access to the graves of Germans on Soviet territory, their preservation and upkeep.

The responsible organizations of both sides will intensify their cooperation on these matters.

Article 19

The Federal Republic of Germany and the Union of Soviet Socialist Republics will intensify their mutual assistance in civil and family matters on the basis of the Hague Convention relating to Civil Procedure which they are signatories. Both sides will further develop their mutual assistance in criminal matters, taking into account their legal systems and proceeding in harmony with international law.

The responsible authorities in the Federal Republic of Germany and the Union of Soviet Socialist Republics will cooperate in combating organized crime, terrorism, drug trafficking, illicit interference with civil aviation and maritime shipping, the manufacture or dissemination of counterfeit money, and smuggling, including the illicit transborder movement of works of art. The procedure and conditions for mutual cooperation will be the subject of a separate arrangement.

Article 20

The two Governments will intensify their cooperation within the scope of international organizations, taking into account their mutual interests and each side's cooperation with other countries. They will assist one another in developing cooperation with international, especially European, organizations and institutions of which either side is a member, should the other side express an interest in such cooperation.

Article 21

The present Treaty will not affect the rights and obligations arising from existing bilateral and multilateral agreements which the two sides have concluded with other States. The present Treaty is directed against no one; both sides regard their cooperation as an integral part and dynamic element of the further development of the CSCE process.

Article 22

The present Treaty is subject to ratification; the instruments of ratification will be exchanged as soon as possible in Moscow.

The present Treaty will enter into force on the date of exchange of the instruments of ratification.

The present Treaty will remain in force for twenty years. Thereafter it will be tacitly extended for successive periods of five years

unless either Contracting Party denounces the
Treaty in writing subject to one year's notice
prior to its expiry.

Done at Bonn on 9 November 1990 in
duplicate in the German and Russian languages, both texts being equally authentic.

For the	For the
Federal Republic	Union of Soviet
of Germany	Socialist Republics

---

* The full text of the Treaty was published in
Isvestia (21 September 1990) with the information
that it was approved by the Ministers of Foreign
Affairs, Eduard Shevardnadze and Hans-Dietrich
Genscher, in Moscow, 13 September 1990. The
Treaty was signed by Mikhail Gorbachev and
Helmut Kohl on 9 November 1990 in Bonn.

XXI. CSCE documents

Report on conclusions and recommendations of the Meeting on the Protection of the Environment of the Conference on Security and Co-operation in Europe, *
Sofia, 3 November 1989

In accordance with the mandate of the Concluding Document of the Vienna Meeting of the representatives of the participating States of the Conference on Security and Co-operation in Europe, the Meeting on the Protection of the Environment took place in Sofia, Bulgaria, from 16 October to 3 November 1989.

During the formal opening of the Meeting on the Protection of the Environment, the participants were welcomed by H.E. Mr. Todor Zhivkov, President of the State Council of the People's Republic of Bulgaria. Opening statements were made by representatives of the participating States. The United Nations Economic Commission for Europe (ECE), the United Nations Environment Programme (UNEP) and the International Union for Conservation of Nature and Natural Resources (IUCN) made contributions to the Meeting.

The Meeting reviewed the work already done, or currently under way, in the fields of prevention and control of the transboundary effects of industrial accidents, management of potentially hazardous chemicals, and pollution of transboundary watercourses and international lakes, and examined possibilities for further measures and co-operation, including improved exchange of information.

A general debate in the Plenary included an exchange of views on items 4 and 5 of the agenda and on other relevant provisions of the Vienna Concluding Document.

Subsidiary Working Body I dealt with the legal, administrative and practical aspects of issues such as liability and restoration, systems of alert, assistance upon request, preventive measures, information flows and consultations.

Subsidiary Working Body II dealt with the scientific, technical and technological aspects of issues such as preventive measures, risk assessment, assessment of damage, clean-up, measurement and monitoring.

The participating States are aware of the opportunities, as they became apparent during the Meeting, for increased co-operation in the CSCE process, with regard to the protection of the environment. They reaffirm their will to strengthen their co-operation and intensify efforts aimed at protecting and improving the environment, bearing in mind the need to maintain and restore the ecological balance in air, water and soil. They also recall their commitment in the Vienna Concluding Document to acknowledge the importance of the contribution of persons and organizations dedicated to the protection and improvement of the environment, and to allow them to express their concerns. They reiterate their willingness to promote greater public awareness and understanding of environmental issues.

The participating States reaffirm their respect for the right of individuals, groups and organizations concerned with environmental issues to express freely their views, to associate with others, to peacefully assemble, as well as to obtain, publish and distribute information on these issues, without legal and administrative impediments inconsistent with the CSCE provisions. These individuals, groups and organizations have the right to participate in public debates on environmental issues, as well as to establish and maintain direct and independent contacts at national and international level.

The participating States will also encourage education and instruction on environmental protection, promote the reproduction, circulation and exchange of information and data, as well as of audiovisual and printed material, on environmental issues, and encourage public access to such information, data and material.

The participating States will also stimulate exchange of information and environmental data, and foster scientific and technological co-operation in order to prevent and reduce pollution.

On the basis of the discussions held during the Meeting, the participating States recommend

– that the ECE elaborate an international convention, code of practice or other appropriate legal instruments on the prevention and control of the transboundary effects of industrial accidents;

– the development of international exchange of information and the co-ordination of efforts in order to achieve closer harmonization concerning the management of hazardous chemicals;

– that the ECE elaborate a framework convention on the protection and use of transboundary watercourses and international lakes;

– the implementation of the above recommendations as soon as possible, bearing in mind that the results will be evaluated by the next Follow-up Meeting of the CSCE, to be held in Helsinki in 1992.

These recommendations are developed in parts I, II and III below:

I. Prevention and control of the transboundary effects of industrial accidents

The participating States recognize the importance of developing and applying commonly agreed policies and strategies for appropriate arrangements for the prevention of, and response to, industrial accidents, their consequences and their transboundary impact on man and the environment.

They give special emphasis to the reduction of the risk of accidents, thereby reducing or preventing their adverse transboundary effects; to increasing preparedness for controlling and coping with emergencies in a transboundary context; and to the examination of key elements for clean-up, restoration and liability.

They stress the importance of international co-operation, recognize the value of existing bilateral and multilateral agreements and take into account the work already done or currently under way by various international organizations, in particular the Process for Responding to Technological Accidents (APELL) developed by UNEP and the Code of Conduct on Accidental Pollution of Transboundary Inland Waters of the ECE and the work done by the Organisation for Economic Co-operation and Development (OECD) and by the European Community.

As a common objective they recognize the importance of establishing regional or subregional mechanisms for response, assistance and exchange of information in environmental emergencies. They emphasize the need for effective measures with a view to:

– limiting the frequency and severity of accidents caused by all industrial activities through better measures of prevention;

– preventing adverse effects from accidents through better land-use planning, and

– mitigating the consequences of accidents by developing adequate emergency plans.

In order to achieve these goals the participating States recommend:

– that the ECE elaborate an international convention, code of practice or other appropriate legal instrument which should be based essentially upon the objectives and principles mentioned below, avoiding redundancy and duplication of efforts and building upon work already under way in international organizations, and taking into account work achieved or in progress in other international fora, without prejudice to any existing or future bilateral or multilateral agreements, with due regard to the legislation and practices of participating States, recognizing that such legal instruments should provide for a high level of protection and safety, and develop, *inter alia*, a precise definition of the industrial activities to be covered;

– that the development of all appropriate measures of prevention, preparedness and response shall recognize the combined responsibilities of industry and competent authorities. In meeting them

(i) full responsibility for safe industrial operation and for taking all appropriate measures to prevent accidents rests with the operator of the installation. This means that, *inter alia*, the operator must implement the most appropriate technologies and measures to prevent accidents including on-site emergency planning, ensure appropriate training facilities and managerial structures, to assess risks and provide the public authorities with the necessary information on their assessment;

(ii) the public authorities will, with due regard to national legislation and practices, take some combination of, amongst others, the following measures: setting safety objectives on the basis of a risk evaluation of the installation; applying a licensing system to certain installations; ensuring that, under land-use policies, a safe distance between the installation and the surrounding population is preserved; preparing off-site emergency plans;

– that consultation and exchange of information on the prevention and control of industrial accidents and their transboundary effects be facilitated, *inter alia*, by:

(i) notifying each other of their initial points of contact for industrial accidents covering, as appropriate, regional and local authorities,

(ii) establishing early warning systems and co-ordination on a bilateral and multilateral basis in order to ensure immediate notification, to the competent authorities of the State likely to be affected, of the type and extent of an accident, and of its possible effects on man and the environment;

– that the potentially affected public be given adequate information, *inter alia*, on risks, safety measures, correct behaviour and protection measures and, whenever possible and appropriate, the opportunity to participate, by providing their views and concerns when decisions are being made by public authorities on prevention, preparedness and emergency planning;

– the development of bilateral and multilateral mechanisms for, and conditions of, mutual assistance, co-operation and co-ordination including emergency response for the implementation of measures to control the effects of industrial accidents including *inter alia*, as appropriate, provision for privileges, immunities and facilities for the expeditious performance of assistance functions;

– the enhancement of scientific and technological co-operation, including the exchange of information on best available technologies, for improved environmental protection, industrial safety and emergency response, including criteria for the monitoring and assessment of transboundary damage, and the promotion of research into less dangerous processes in order to limit environmental hazards;

– co-operation for the further development of on-site and off-site training;

– that the 'polluter-pays' principle be applied to physical and juridical persons;

– the consideration of further appropriate ways and means of elaborating principles and guidelines on the nature and scope of liability;

– that disputes be settled peacefully in accordance with procedures to be established in conformity with international law.

II. Management of hazardous chemicals

The participating States agree on the need to facilitate international exchange of information and co-operation on chemicals. They recognize the effects of chemicals on human health and the environment as well as the efforts to facilitate international trade of chemicals. They are also aware of the significance of international agreements and instruments with regard to the transboundary movement of hazardous waste, and to export notification on banned or severely restricted chemicals.

They will build upon the work of international organizations related to hazardous chemicals, in particular the International Programme on Chemical Safety (IPCS), the UNEP International Register of Potentially Toxic Chemicals (IRPTC), the ECE and the Food and Agriculture Organization of the United Nations (FAO), and support the further development of their work. They will take into account the chemicals programmes of the European Community (EC), the Council for Mutual Economic Assistance (CMEA) and the OECD.

In order to strengthen legal and institutional arrangements for the management of chemicals, at least the following elements will be taken into account by the participating States:

– for the prevention of danger to man and the environment, procedures enabling the identification of hazardous properties of chemicals, in particular toxicological and ecotoxicological properties;

– a system for the classification and labelling of chemicals which may involve hazard to man or the environment;

– a notification procedure providing for the mandatory screening of new chemical substances for any hazardous properties;

– systematic investigation of chemicals already on the market, on the basis of priority criteria established with regard to the quantities produced, the suspected hazards, and the utilization of the substances concerned. This investigation would be most productively accomplished through co-operation between the countries involved;

– a comprehensive system for the control of hazardous chemicals, taking into account the risk of exposure, including substitution by non-hazardous or less hazardous chemicals, and, if necessary, limitation or prohibition of their use;

– procedures to facilitate the international exchange of information on chemicals;

– procedures for the proper storage of chemicals to ensure the safety of man and the environment, including questions of location in order to minimize transboundary effects;

– further training in the field of toxicology and ecotoxicology and other relevant disciplines, including an exchange of educational programmes.

International organizations with relevant experience and ongoing programmes will be invited to assist participating countries in implementing the above tasks and to co-ordinate efforts in a step-by-step approach to achieve closer harmonization of legislation and existing practices with regard to chemicals on the basis of the most advanced systems of protection and management. The approach could contain *inter alia* the following elements:

– early and regular exchange of information on relevant national infrastructures, new legislation and regulations, scientific findings, monitoring and assessment procedures, etc.;

– harmonization of methods for chemicals testing and good laboratory practice to facilitate the mutual acceptance of data, and establishment of a minimum set of data for the assessment of chemicals;

– harmonization of classification and labelling systems for hazardous chemicals, especially for the purpose of facilitating the development of international trade and the protection of transit and importing countries;

– criteria for the selection of chemicals for further assessment and management, taking into account *inter alia* the production volume, the suspected hazard and the utilization of chemicals;

– harmonization of notification procedures for new chemical substances, including identification of toxicological and ecotoxicological properties;

– recommendations for the substitution of hazardous chemicals by non-dangerous or less hazardous chemicals.

III. Pollution of transboundary watercourses and international lakes

The participating States agree on the need to define principles for a sustainable use of transboundary watercourses and international lakes as well as to elaborate arrangements to protect them from pollution. For this aim the participating States recommend that the ECE elaborate a framework convention, whereby existing bilateral and multilateral agreements on the protection and use of transboundary watercourses and international lakes, as well as ongoing activities and completed work in other fora, such as the ECE Senior Advisers on Environmental and Water Problems and the United Nations International Law Commission, should be taken into account. Such a framework convention should contain, in particular, the following elements:

Basic principles, such as:

– Pollution of transboundary watercourses and international lakes, contributing also to the pollution of seas, will be prevented or reduced with the aim of sustainable management, conservation of water resources and environmental protection.

– Effective prevention and pollution control measures will be applied at the source wherever possible.

– Regular consultations on issues of mutual interest and implementation of pollution abatement measures will be promoted.

– Warning and alarm systems and contingency plans will be introduced.

– With the aim of prevention, environmental impact assessment and other means of assessment will be developed, adopted and subsequently implemented.

– Water quality will be monitored and assessed and discharges of pollutants will be registered; methods of analysis, monitoring and assessment, including registration of discharges, will be harmonized.

– For transboundary watercourses and international lakes, parties will establish emission limits based, to the extent possible, on the best available technologies specifically applicable to individual sectors or industries or to specific substances; for municipal waste water, at least biological treatment will be introduced; use of no-waste and low-waste technologies will be promoted.

– Parties will apply water quality objectives; the ecosystems approach will be promoted.

– Discharges will be subject to prior licensing by the competent authority; the approved discharges must be monitored and controlled.

– General water management policies covering transboundary waters including ecological and other impacts of water construction works and water regulation will be implemented.

– The 'polluter-pays' principle will be applied to physical and juridical persons.

– Responsibility and liability issues will be examined.

– Disputes will be settled peacefully in accordance with procedures to be established in conformity with international law.

– Scientific and technological information– including best available technologies—will be exchanged where necessary to achieve the goals of the framework convention in accordance with national laws, regulations and practice.

– A reporting system concerning the implementation of the framework convention will be established.

Principles related to commissions and to other forms of co-operation

The States bordering transboundary watercourses and international lakes will conclude, where they do not yet exist, specific agreements on the establishment of bilateral or multilateral commissions or other forms of co-operation where appropriate. Their tasks to be described in the framework convention will be *inter alia*, without prejudice to comparable existing agreements, the following:

– To carry out investigation on the components of the catchment areas of the water bodies concerned and to identify priority uses of waters;

– To carry out joint measuring programmes concerning water quality and quantity;

– To draw up inventories and exchange information on significant discharges;

– To set emission limits for waste water and evaluate the effectiveness of control programmes;

– To set water quality objectives; to introduce the minimum obligation of maintaining at least the existing water quality;

– To develop concerned action programmes for the reduction of pollution loads discharged both from point-sources (municipal; industrial) and from diffuse sources (particularly agriculture);

– To establish alarm and warning procedures;

– To provide for consultations on existing and planned uses of water that are likely to have significant adverse transboundary effects, including water construction works and water regulation;

– To promote co-operation on the exchange of information and on the exchange of best available technologies in accordance with national laws, regulations and practice as well as to encourage co-operation in scientific research programmes.

In cases where a coastal State is directly and significantly affected by pollution from transboundary watercourses, the riparian States can, if they all so agree, invite that coastal State to be involved in the activities of the commission or, where appropriate, in other forms of co-operation.

States are encouraged to enter such specific agreements (e.g. the Danube, the Elbe) parallel to the elaboration of a framework convention.

* * *

The representatives of the participating States express their profound gratitude to the people and Government of Bulgaria for the excellent organization of the Sofia Meeting and the warm hospitality extended to the delegations which participated in the Meeting.

---

* The document based on the proposal submitted by the delegations of Austria, Finland, Sweden, Switzerland and those of Bulgaria, Canada, Cyprus, Czechoslovakia, France in the name of the twelve participating states, members of the European Community, the German Democratic Republic, the Holy See, Hungary, Iceland, Liechtenstein, Malta, Monaco, Norway, Poland, San Marino, Turkey, the Union of Soviet Socialist Republics, the United States of America and Yugoslavia (CSCE/SEM.36/Rev.1) was formally adopted after the new Romanian Government withdrew its reservations at the CSCE Economic Forum in Bonn (19 March–11 April 1990). The relevant statements are contained in *Journal*, no. 2/Rev.1 of the Bonn Conference on Economic Co-operation in Europe.

Document of the Bonn Conference on Economic Co-operation in Europe convened in accordance with the relevant provisions of the Concluding Document of the Vienna Meeting of the Conference on Security and Co-operation in Europe, Bonn, 11 April 1990

The representatives of the participating States of the Conference on Security and Co-operation in Europe (CSCE), Austria, Belgium, Bulgaria, Canada, Cyprus, Czechoslovakia, Denmark, Finland, France, the German

Democratic Republic, the Federal Republic of Germany, Greece, the Holy See, Hungary, Iceland, Ireland, Italy, Liechtenstein, Luxembourg, Malta, Monaco, the Netherlands, Norway, Poland, Portugal, Romania, San Marino, Spain, Sweden, Switzerland, Turkey, the Union of Soviet Socialist Republics, the United Kingdom, the United States of America and Yugoslavia met in Bonn from 19 March to 11 April 1990, in accordance with the provisions relating to the Conference on Economic Co-operation in Europe contained in the Concluding Document of the Vienna Follow-up Meeting of the CSCE. Delegations included members of the business community.

The Conference was opened and closed by the Minister of Economics of the Federal Republic of Germany.

The President, the Chancellor and the Deputy Chancellor and Minister for Foreign Affairs of the Federal Republic of Germany addressed the Conference.

At the opening and concluding plenary meetings statements were made by delegates of the participating States, among them Prime Ministers, Vice Prime Ministers, Ministers, State Secretaries and the Vice-President of the Commission of the European Communities. Contributions were made by the Executive Secretary of the United Nations Economic Commission for Europe (ECE) and the Secretary General of the International Chamber of Commerce (ICC).

The participating States welcome the fact that members of the business community gave the Conference the benefit of their practical experience, thus contributing to its success.

Having in mind the aim of the Conference to provide new impulses for economic relations between participating States, in particular by improving business conditions for commercial exchanges and industrial co-operation and by considering new possibilities for, and ways of, economic co-operation;

Meeting at a time of profound and rapid change,

The participating States,

Confirm their intention to shape a new order of peace, stability and prosperity in Europe based on the comprehensive and balanced concept set out in the Helsinki Final Act and the subsequent documents of the CSCE, and resolve to respect all the principles of the Final Act and to implement all the provisions of the CSCE documents;

Reaffirm the fundamental role of the CSCE in the future of Europe;

Recognize that democratic institutions and economic freedom foster economic and social progress;

Share the common objectives of sustainable economic growth, a rising standard of living, an improved quality of life, expanding employment, efficient use of economic resources and protection of the environment;

Believe that co-operation in the field of economics, science and technology and the environment is an essential element in their overall relations, and that it should become even more prominent in the future;

Resolve to work together to expand their co-operation in that field and to enhance the growth of their economies;

Believe that the success of their co-operation will depend in large measure on prevailing political and economic conditions;

Stress the importance of the political and economic reforms taking place, and of a supportive international economic environment, recognize the particular economic interests and concerns of countries as they achieve a market economy, and acknowledge other difficulties, such as indebtedness, which are to be dealt with in the competent fora;

Consider that the process of economic reform and structural adjustment, with increased reliance on market forces, will enhance economic performance, improve efficiency of the public sector, respond better to the needs and wishes of consumers, improve the conditions for closer co-operation and contribute to a more open world trading system;

Believe that increased integration of all participating countries into the international economic and financial system, in accordance with the internationally recognized rules and involving the acceptance of disciplines as well as benefits, will also facilitate economic co-operation;

Value the important roles of existing multilateral economic institutions and mechanisms;

Consider that increased emphasis on economic co-operation within the CSCE process should take into account the interests of participating States that are developing from an economic point of view and should not detract from development co-operation with, including assistance to, developing countries;

Recognize that the performance of market-based economies relies primarily on the freedom of individual enterprise and the consequent economic growth;

Believe that economic freedom for the individual includes the right freely to own, buy, sell and otherwise utilize property;

Confirm that, while governments provide the overall framework for economic activity, business partners make their own decisions;

Consider that the progressive convergence of economic policies among the participating States opens new long-term perspectives for the strengthening of their economic relations.

Accordingly the participating States,

Recognizing the relationship between political pluralism and market economies, and being committed to the principles concerning:

– Multiparty democracy based on free, periodic and genuine elections;

– The rule of law and equal protection under the law for all, based on respect for human rights and effective, accessible and just legal systems;

– Economic activity that accordingly upholds human dignity and is free from forced labour, discrimination against workers on grounds of race, sex, language, political opinion or religion, or denial of the rights of workers freely to establish or join independent trade unions,

Will endeavour to achieve or maintain the following:

– Fiscal and monetary policies that promote balanced, sustainable economic growth and enhance the ability of markets to function efficiently;

– International and domestic policies aimed at expanding the free flow of trade, capital, investment and repatriation of profits in convertible currencies;

– Free and competitive market economies where prices are based on supply and demand;

– Policies that promote social justice and improve living and working conditions;

– Environmentally sustainable economic growth and development;

– Full recognition and protection of all types of property including private property, and the right of citizens to own and use them, as well as intellectual property rights;

– The right to prompt, just and effective compensation in the event private property is taken for public use;

– Direct contact between customers and suppliers in order to facilitate the exchange of goods and services among companies—whether private or state-owned—and individuals in both domestic and international markets,

Have come to the following conclusions:

A. Development and diversification of economic relations

1. The participating States wish to create favourable conditions for a harmonious development and diversification of their economic relations based on internationally agreed rules and practices. They therefore agree to improve business conditions, facilities and practices for each other's firms in their respective markets, based on freedom of establishment. They agree to permit and encourage direct contacts between businessmen at all levels of commerce and stages of industry and end-users. To that end they will, in accordance with their relevant commitments undertaken in the CSCE process, facilitate the prompt entry, stay and free movement of businessmen in their territory; the participating States will facilitate, on a non-discriminatory basis, the establishment and operation of business offices and firms in their territory, including the renting and purchasing of commercial premises and housing, the acquisition of equipment and transport facilities, access to telecommunications, utilities and social services, the carrying out of audits as well as the unhindered recruitment of local staff required by firms. They encourage direct contacts between representatives of commercial and business organizations and economic institutions. The participating States stress that expeditious processing/treatment of goods and persons at international borders stimulates international trade and they will therefore make their borders more open for that purpose. They also stress the importance of trade facilitation and electronic data interchange for their trade relations.

2. The participating States resolve to publish and make available comprehensive, comparable and timely economic, commercial and demographic information as a basis for economic research, co-operation and efficient conduct of business relations. To that effect they will provide the United Nations Trade Data Bank (COMTRADE) with up-to-date trade figures to at least the three-digit level of the United Nations product classification (SITC–Rev.2). They will also publish

detailed, comparable and up-to-date data on balance of payments and gross national product statistics on at least an annual basis as a step towards their integration in international economic activities. They stress the need for national statistics and accounting systems to conform with international standards.

3. The participating States will, in order to facilitate and promote economic co-operation, undertake comprehensive co-operation between their respective statistical services in the bilateral and multilateral context. The priority areas for such co-operation are the statistics on external trade, capital movements, employment, transport, foreign tourism, environment, energy and other raw materials such as forestry and mineral products and industrial production in addition to other major components of national production and national income accounting. The object of this co-operation is to exchange detailed and complete information on relevant statistical elements available and the techniques and methodology employed, and to correlate statistical data with the aim of achieving comparability of such statistics among participating States. In view of this aim, the participating States welcome a further development of the work of relevant organizations, notably the ECE, regarding statistics.

4. The participating States recognize the particular importance of small and medium-sized enterprises in their economic co-operation. These enterprises will benefit particularly from improvements in the business environment and the strengthening of market forces. Participating States will therefore pay special attention to the creation of a competitive business environment conducive to the development of SMEs. To that end they will endeavour to provide the appropriate economic, legal, banking and fiscal conditions that take account of the specific requirements of SMEs. They will strengthen information channels and networks and encourage dialogue and the exchange of expertise between the interested parties, including authorities, representatives of business and other public and private agencies providing services to business.

5. The participating States are prepared, insofar as the appropriate conditions exist, to provide support for the SME sector by promoting: business co-operation networks, which facilitate the search for business partners; access to information services, including publications and databanks; management and expert training and information on availability of technical know-how and innovations.

6. The participating States confirm the importance they attach to marketing and product promotion as a means of developing trade and industrial and economic co-operation among themselves. They will therefore encourage trade promotion activities including advertising, consulting, factoring and other business services, and the organization of seminars, fairs and exhibitions. They favour the conduct of market research and other marketing activities by both domestic and foreign firms on their respective territories.

7. The participating States recognize the importance, for the economic process, of the development of the human potential. They therefore recognize the value of co-operation in training programmes for managers and specialists in marketing, product promotion and other fields. Insofar as the appropriate conditions exist, such programmes will be held both in host countries and in countries of origin, and under the aegis of vocational training establishments or of companies either in the context of industrial co-operation projects or within ad hoc programmes. They express the view that the operation of relevant bodies, e.g. the European Training Foundation, can contribute to improved co-operation in this field.

B. Industrial co-operation

1. The participating States note that the economic, fiscal, legal and social infrastructure and the political conditions in their countries determine the extent to which the various forms of industrial co-operation including joint ventures and other means of direct foreign investment can be envisaged. Each participating State will assess its possibilities and interests with a view to creating favourable conditions for industrial co-operation. They are aware that such co-operation, based on freedom of establishment and non-discriminatory treatment of different types of ownership including private property, will have a positive influence on managerial and technical know-how, the extent of investments, the quality of production, the exchange and application of technology and marketing opportunities.

2. The participating States recognize the importance of protecting industrial, commercial and intellectual property rights for their co-operation in both trade- and research-related aspects. They will ensure adequate and effective protection and enforcement of industrial, commercial and intellectual property rights, including by fully observing international commitments, and will encourage appropriate arrangements among themselves. They will provide natural and legal persons of other States with guarantees of these rights, including non-discriminatory procedures for their acquisition and access to their courts and appropriate administrative bodies.

3. Among the conditions for the development of industrial co-operation the participating States emphasize the need for market-oriented and stable economic policies, an appropriate and reliable legal and administrative framework, consisting of such elements as: fiscal, competition, bankruptcy, and insolvency legislation; company laws; arbitration procedures (taking due account of the UNCITRAL model law and other relevant arrangements); protection of industrial and intellectual property rights; investment protection in national legislation as well as in the framework of multilateral and bilateral agreements; free transfer of capital and profits in foreign currency; accounting systems; a free flow of economic data and market information; business facilities; and entrepreneurial autonomy.

4. Possible forms of industrial co-operation, such as co-production, specialization, subcontracting, licensing agreements, joint ventures and other forms of investment, will be decided by firms according to the conditions existing and the nature and the objectives of the co-operation.

5. The participating States recognize the importance of comprehensive information on all legal provisions of host countries for foreign investment, joint ventures and other forms of co-operation, including those concerning foreign staff. They encourage host countries to make this information readily and widely available in an up-to-date form.

6. The participating States are prepared, insofar as the appropriate conditions exist, to foster a favourable climate for investment and the different forms of industrial co-operation, on a non-discriminatory basis, notably by concluding further arrangements on avoidance of double taxation and bilateral and mul-

tilateral agreements for investment promotion and protection, with particular reference to the transfer of profits and repatriation of invested capital. In this respect the establishment of measures to support economic development through investment (e.g. industrial parks developed by the host country, tax policies and practical assistance) may be of interest. They encourage a greater exchange of information on industrial co-operation opportunities for interested parties by such means as the holding of business weeks. The participating States agree on the importance of standardization and certification in improving their economic relations; to this end they envisage mutual exchange of information, greater co-operation within existing multilateral organizations and, where appropriate, technical assistance.

C. Co-operation in specific areas

1. The participating States, while acknowledging the role of governments in creating favourable framework conditions, recognize that the initiative of the enterprises directly concerned is of paramount importance in bringing about co-operation in the specific areas covered by this chapter.

2. The participating States consider that they should extend and deepen their co-operation in the field of energy and raw material saving techniques. To that end they favour the marketing of energy conservation and raw material saving technologies and will promote increased energy efficiency. The participating States will also co-operate bilaterally and multilaterally in the field of hydrocarbon technologies, solid fuels and renewable energies and processes for the separation of waste components and their recycling and upgrading. They will also co-operate, e.g. through the International Atomic Energy Agency, in the field of nuclear energy and of the safety of nuclear installations in accordance with their energy policies.

3. The participating States are prepared to exchange information on energy and raw material saving techniques and, insofar as the appropriate conditions exist, to co-operate in the establishment, operation and utilization of European databases in the field of energy. to undertake joint projects to measure energy-combustion-related environmental pollution, to enhance energy efficiency by means of substitution of energy products and to pro-

mote professional training in energy-saving techniques.

4. The participating States note the increasing importance of environmental issues in the context of their economic co-operation. They recognize that it is vital to ensure the environmental sustainability of economic development. They acknowledge the significance of international economic co-operation aimed at securing a more efficient use of energy and raw materials. They will also endeavour to strengthen co-operation in the field of environmentally sound technology.

5. At the Sofia CSCE Meeting on the environment, the participating States agreed on the enhancement of scientific and technological co-operation, including the exchange of information on best available technologies for improved environmental protection, industrial safety and emergency response. The participating States consider that among the areas for co-operation are pollution monitoring, major technological hazard and accident prevention, assessment of chemicals, treatment and disposal of toxic and dangerous waste, as well as prevention and reduction of air and water pollution, especially that of transboundary watercourses and international lakes, and transboundary pollution caused by energy production, conversion and consumption. The participating States recognize the importance of the ECE and UNEP for the promotion of co-operation in the field of the environment.

6. The participating States are prepared, insofar as the appropriate conditions exist, to take the necessary steps in order to stimulate the exchange of know-how, to promote the wider adoption of environmentally sound technologies and to create demonstration projects in the field of environment. Subsequent co-operation in environmental technology should, in principle, be carried out on a commercial basis. Governments should encourage the application of such technology and set adequate emission standards and promote public awareness. The participating States would welcome improved arrangements for gathering and disseminating information on cleaner technologies. They note the important role which information networks for environmental technology transfer could play in promoting the development and application of environmental forecasting techniques and the exchange of information on the

best technology available for preventing damage to the environment, the possibilities of overcoming hazards due to accidents in industrial works and the rational use of natural resources without disturbing the ecological balance. In this context they recognize the valuable contributions of global and regional organizations such as UNEP, ECE and the European Environment Agency.

7. With a view to improving the quality of life the participating States attach priority to techniques designed to promote the health and safety of their populations. They intend to co-operate in assessing the impact of environmental stress on the population by exchanging relevant data on the effects of environmental pollution. They also consider it important to create the conditions enabling the various elements which contribute to an improved quality of life to be developed.

8. The participating States affirm the importance of co-operation in agro-industry and food processing, including natural food production, and welcome increased commercial relations in this field. They will facilitate joint research, training and exchange of know-how as well as the promotion of contacts between potential partners, especially small and medium-sized enterprises.

9. The participating States welcome efforts to promote co-operation among business enterprises producing machinery for the production of consumer goods as a means of responding to the needs of consumers. They stress the importance of increasing co-operation in the consumer goods sector and will encourage greater access to potential consumers of products. In this context, they note that conversion from military to consumer production may give rise to new business opportunities.

10. The participating States recognize that effective town planning can help to redress urban problems causing a substantial deterioration in the quality of life by striking a balance between economic development and environmental protection as well as ensuring the possibility of citizens to freely take part in economic, political, social and cultural life. They will promote closer co-operation, and encourage the exchange of information on town planning, including infrastructure (e.g. transport), housing construction, protection of monuments and restoration of the architectural heritage. They will also encourage the exchange of information on, and new

approaches to, the economic adaptation of structurally weak regions and the alleviation of environmental damage in urban areas.

D. Monetary and financial aspects

1. The participating States consider that the introduction of undistorted internal pricing is essential to economic reform and a necessary step to currency convertibility. They recognize that both are important for economic development and for increased economic co-operation. They agree that progress towards full convertibility and efficient allocation of resources requires a functioning price mechanism which reflects market-determined and undistorted domestic costs, consumer preferences and international prices. The participating States affirm that currency convertibility forges an efficient link between domestic and foreign price systems capable of transmitting adequate price signals for the allocation of resources inside and outside the country, reflecting international competitiveness. Special attention will thus have to be given to the appropriate level of exchange rates in terms of market-determined prices and other convertible currencies. The success of currency convertibility depends largely on the timely and coherent implementation of measures aimed at developing a market economy which should be underpinned by sound fiscal and monetary policies.

2. The participating States are prepared, insofar as the appropriate conditions exist, to co-operate in establishing conditions for an efficient price mechanism and for progress towards convertibility. This could involve fields such as reform of the banking system, introducing a money market, reform of the investment laws, transformation of public enterprises, taxation, structural adjustment policy, organization of a labour and capital market as well as a foreign exchange market and setting up of the legal framework for introducing convertibility. It could also embrace the establishment of statistics which are essential for creating and maintaining stable monetary and financial conditions and for guiding economic policy.

3. The participating States acknowledge that a market-oriented financial system facilitates the expansion of economic co-operation and that financial instruments play an important role in that context. While, in the period of transition to a market economy, public financial support to well-defined projects can serve as a multiplier in the framework of economic reforms, such intervention should not distort the emerging market mechanisms. The participating States agree that capital from private sources will progressively become the principal source of external finance.

4. The participating States look forward to the successful conclusion of negotiations to establish the European Bank for Reconstruction and Development (EBRD). They are prepared, insofar as the appropriate conditions exist, to co-operate through the EBRD and other multilateral financial institutions. Furthermore, they agree to foster a favourable climate for investment, notably by bilateral and multilateral agreements for investment promotion and protection. They also agree to facilitate the provision of technical advice and expert training in improving management skills and setting up market-based financial mechanisms and credit rating systems.

* * *

In view of the profound and rapid changes taking place in Europe, and wishing to maintain the valuable momentum built up at the present Conference, the participating States are of the opinion that further ways to strengthen their co-operation in the field of economics, of science and technology and of the environment should be considered. They suggest that the next follow-up meeting or any other main CSCE meeting at the appropriate level examines the possibilities for expanding and intensifying economic co-operation, including through meetings within the CSCE aimed at periodic review of progress and providing new impulses for economic relations among participating States.

Furthermore, the participating States recognize the increasing importance of the different existing international economic institutions in promoting economic co-operation in their fields of competence. In this respect they see a need for discussion of the specificities and longer-term issues of economic changes and reforms in the participating States and related problems of co-operation among them and to share experiences. To this end, they invite the ECE, in view of its annual session, to develop practical measures in priority areas. They invite the OECD to consider hosting meetings of experts from the CSCE participating States and OECD member States to promote the process of economic reform.

They recommend that the objective of such undertakings is full integration of the reforming countries into the international economic system. They also consider it important that the expertise and experience of the ICC be fully utilized. The participating States suggest co-ordination among the different existing international economic institutions to avoid duplication and to ensure the maximum effectiveness of their work.

As set out in the Concluding Document of the CSCE Vienna Meeting, the Conference on Economic Co-operation in Europe has been attended by representatives of the participating States and of the business community. The informal discussions held in the course of the Conference have led to comments and suggestions by representatives of the business community. A summary of these comments and suggestions is to be found in the Journal of the day.

The representatives of the participating States express their profound gratitude to the Government of the Federal Republic of Germany for the excellent organization of the Conference and the warm hospitality extended to the delegations which participated in the Conference.

Document of the Copenhagen Meeting of the Conference on the Human Dimension of the CSCE,
Copenhagen, 29 June 1990

The representatives of the participating States of the Conference on Security and Co-operation in Europe (CSCE), Austria, Belgium, Bulgaria, Canada, Cyprus, Czechoslovakia, Denmark, Finland, France, the German Democratic Republic, the Federal Republic of Germany, Greece, the Holy See, Hungary, Iceland, Ireland, Italy, Liechtenstein, Luxembourg, Malta, Monaco, the Netherlands, Norway, Poland, Portugal, Romania, San Marino, Spain, Sweden, Switzerland, Turkey, the Union of Soviet Socialist Republics, the United Kingdom, the United States of America and Yugoslavia, met in Copenhagen from 5 to 29 June 1990, in accordance with the provisions relating to the Conference on the Human Dimension of the CSCE contained in the Concluding Document of the Vienna Follow-up Meeting of the CSCE.

The representative of Albania attended the Copenhagen Meeting as observer.

The first Meeting of the Conference was held in Paris from 30 May to 23 June 1989.

The Copenhagen Meeting was opened and closed by the Minister for Foreign Affairs of Denmark.

The formal opening of the Copenhagen Meeting was attended by Her Majesty the Queen of Denmark and His Royal Highness the Prince Consort.

Opening statements were made by Ministers and Deputy Ministers of the participating States.

At a special meeting of the Ministers for Foreign Affairs of the participating States of the CSCE on 5 June 1990, convened on the invitation of the Minister for Foreign Affairs of Denmark, it was agreed to convene a Preparatory Committee in Vienna on 10 July 1990 to prepare a Summit Meeting in Paris of their Heads of State or Government.

The participating States welcome with great satisfaction the fundamental political changes that have occurred in Europe since the first Meeting of the Conference on the Human Dimension of the CSCE in Paris in 1989. They note that the CSCE process has contributed significantly to bringing about these changes and that these developments in turn have greatly advanced the implementation of the provisions of the Final Act and of the other CSCE documents.

They recognize that pluralistic democracy and the rule of law are essential for ensuring respect for all human rights and fundamental freedoms, the development of human contacts and the resolution of other issues of a related humanitarian character. They therefore welcome the commitment expressed by all participating States to the ideals of democracy and political pluralism as well as their common determination to build democratic societies based on free elections and the rule of law.

At the Copenhagen Meeting the participating States held a review of the implementation of their commitments in the field of the human dimension. They considered that the degree of compliance with the commitments contained in the relevant provisions of the CSCE documents had shown a fundamental improvement since the Paris Meeting. They also expressed the view, however, that further steps are required for the full realization of their commitments relating to the human dimension.

The participating States express their conviction that full respect for human rights and fundamental freedoms and the development of societies based on pluralistic democracy and the rule of law are prerequisites for progress in setting up the lasting order of peace, security, justice and co-operation that they seek to establish in Europe. They therefore reaffirm their commitment to implement fully all provisions of the Final Act and of the other CSCE documents relating to the human dimension and undertake to build on the progress they have made.

They recognize that co-operation among themselves, as well as the active involvement of persons, groups, organizations and institutions, will be essential to ensure continuing progress towards their shared objectives.

In order to strengthen respect for, and enjoyment of, human rights and fundamental freedoms, to develop human contacts and to resolve issues of a related humanitarian character, the participating States agree on the following:

I

(1) The participating States express their conviction that the protection and promotion of human rights and fundamental freedoms is one of the basic purposes of government, and reaffirm that the recognition of these rights and freedoms constitutes the foundation of freedom, justice and peace.

(2) They are determined to support and advance those principles of justice which form the basis of the rule of law. They consider that the rule of law does not mean merely a formal legality which assures regularity and consistency in the achievement and enforcement of democratic order, but justice based on the recognition and full acceptance of the supreme value of the human personality and guaranteed by institutions providing a framework for its fullest expression.

(3) They reaffirm that democracy is an inherent element of the rule of law. They recognize the importance of pluralism with regard to political organizations.

(4) They confirm that they will respect each other's right freely to choose and develop, in accordance with international human rights standards, their political, social, economic and cultural systems. In exercising this right, they will ensure that their laws, regulations, practices and policies conform with their obligations under international law and are brought into harmony with the provisions of the Declaration on Principles and other CSCE commitments.

(5) They solemnly declare that among those elements of justice which are essential to the full expression of the inherent dignity and of the equal and inalienable rights of all human beings are the following:

(5.1) – free elections that will be held at reasonable intervals by secret ballot or by equivalent free voting procedure, under conditions which ensure in practice the free expression of the opinion of the electors in the choice of their representatives;

(5.2) – a form of government that is representative in character, in which the executive is accountable to the elected legislature or the electorate;

(5.3) – the duty of the government and public authorities to comply with the constitution and to act in a manner consistent with law;

(5.4) – a clear separation between the State and political parties; in particular, political parties will not be merged with the State;

(5.5) – the activity of the government and the administration as well as that of the judiciary will be exercised in accordance with the system established by law. Respect for that system must be ensured;

(5.6) – military forces and the police will be under the control of, and accountable to, the civil authorities;

(5.7) – human rights and fundamental freedoms will be guaranteed by law and in accordance with their obligations under international law;

(5.8) – legislation, adopted at the end of a public procedure, and regulations will be published, that being the condition for their applicability. Those texts will be accessible to everyone;

(5.9) – all persons are equal before the law and are entitled without any discrimination to the equal protection of the law. In this respect, the law will prohibit any discrimination and guarantee to all persons equal and effective protection against discrimination on any ground;

(5.10) – everyone will have an effective means of redress against administrative decisions, so as to guarantee respect for fundamental rights and ensure legal integrity;

(5.11) – administrative decisions against a person must be fully justifiable and must as a rule indicate the usual remedies available;

(5.12) – the independence of judges and the impartial operation of the public judicial service will be ensured;

(5.13) – the independence of legal practitioners will be recognized and protected, in particular as regards conditions for recruitment and practice;

(5.14) – the rules relating to criminal procedure will contain a clear definition of powers in relation to prosecution and the measures preceding and accompanying prosecution;

(5.15) – any person arrested or detained on a criminal charge will have the right, so that the lawfulness of his arrest or detention can be decided, to be brought promptly before a judge or other officer authorized by law to exercise this function;

(5.16) – in the determination of any criminal charge against him, or of his rights and obligations in a suit at law, everyone will be entitled to a fair and public hearing by a competent, independent and impartial tribunal established by law;

(5.17) – any person prosecuted will have the right to defend himself in person or through prompt legal assistance of his own choosing or, if he does not have sufficient means to pay for legal assistance, to be given it free when the interests of justice so require;

(5.18) – no one will be charged with, tried for or convicted of any criminal offence unless the offence is provided for by a law which defines the elements of the offence with clarity and precision;

(5.19) – everyone will be presumed innocent until proven guilty according to law;

(5.20) – considering the important contribution of international instruments in the field of human rights to the rule of law at a national level, the participating States reaffirm that they will consider acceding to the International Covenant on Civil and Political Rights, the International Covenant on Economic, Social and Cultural Rights and other relevant international instruments, if they have not yet done so;

(5.21) – in order to supplement domestic remedies and better to ensure that the participating States respect the international obligations they have undertaken, the participating States will consider acceding to a regional or global international convention concerning the protection of human rights, such as the European Convention on Human Rights or the Optional Protocol to the International Covenant on Civil and Political Rights, which provide for procedures of individual recourse to international bodies.

(6) The participating States declare that the will of the people, freely and fairly expressed through periodic and genuine elections, is the basis of the authority and legitimacy of all government. The participating States will accordingly respect the right of their citizens to take part in the governing of their country, either directly or through representatives freely chosen by them through fair electoral processes. They recognize their responsibility to defend and protect, in accordance with their laws, their international human rights obligations and their international commitments, the democratic order freely established through the will of the people against the activities of persons, groups or organizations that engage in or refuse to renounce terrorism or violence aimed at the overthrow of that order or of that of another participating State.

(7) To ensure that the will of the people serves as the basis of the authority of government, the participating States will

(7.1) – hold free elections at reasonable intervals, as established by law;

(7.2) – permit all seats in at least one chamber of the national legislature to be freely contested in a popular vote;

(7.3) – guarantee universal and equal suffrage to adult citizens;

(7.4) – ensure that votes are cast by secret ballot or by equivalent free voting procedure, and that they are counted and reported honestly with the official results made public;

(7.5) – respect the right of citizens to seek political or public office, individually or as representatives of political parties or organizations, without discrimination;

(7.6) – respect the right of individuals and groups to establish, in full freedom, their own political parties or other political organizations and provide such political parties and organizations with the necessary legal guarantees to enable them to compete with each other on a basis of equal treatment before the law and by the authorities;

(7.7) – ensure that law and public policy work to permit political campaigning to be conducted in a fair and free atmosphere in which neither administrative action, violence nor intimidation bars the parties and the candidates from freely presenting their views and qualifications, or prevents the voters from learning and discussing them or from casting their vote free of fear of retribution;

(7.8) – provide that no legal or administrative obstacle stands in the way of unimpeded access to the media on a non-discriminatory basis for all political groupings and individuals wishing to participate in the electoral process;

(7.9) – ensure that candidates who obtain the necessary number of votes required by law are duly installed in office and are permitted to remain in office until their term expires or is otherwise brought to an end in a manner that is regulated by law in conformity with democratic parliamentary and constitutional procedures.

(8) The participating States consider that the presence of observers, both foreign and domestic, can enhance the electoral process for States in which elections are taking place. They therefore invite observers from any other CSCE participating States and any appropriate private institutions and organizations who may wish to do so to observe the course of their national election proceedings, to the extent permitted by law. They will also endeavour to facilitate similar access for election proceedings held below the national level. Such observers will undertake not to interfere in the electoral proceedings.

II

(9) The participating States reaffirm that

(9.1) – everyone will have the right to freedom of expression including the right to communication. This right will include freedom to hold opinions and to receive and impart information and ideas without interference by public authority and regardless of frontiers. The exercise of this right may be subject only to such restrictions as are prescribed by law and are consistent with international standards. In particular, no limitation will be imposed on access to, and use of, means of reproducing documents of any kind, while respecting, however, rights relating to intellectual property, including copyright;

(9.2) – everyone will have the right of peaceful assembly and demonstration. Any restrictions which may be placed on the exercise of these rights will be prescribed by law and consistent with international standards;

(9.3) – the right of association will be guaranteed. The right to form and—subject to the general right of a trade union to determine its own membership—freely to join a trade union will be guaranteed. These rights will exclude any prior control. Freedom of association for workers, including the freedom to strike, will be guaranteed, subject to limitations prescribed by law and consistent with international standards;

(9.4) – everyone will have the right to freedom of thought, conscience and religion. This right includes freedom to change one's religion or belief and freedom to manifest one's religion or belief, either alone or in community with others, in public or in private, through worship, teaching, practice and observance. The exercise of these rights may be subject only to such restrictions as are prescribed by law and are consistent with international standards;

(9.5) – they will respect the right of everyone to leave any country, including his own, and to return to his country, consistent with a State's international obligations and CSCE commitments. Restrictions on this right will have the character of very rare exceptions, will be considered necessary only if they respond to a specific public need, pursue a legitimate aim and are proportionate to that aim, and will not be abused or applied in an arbitrary manner;

(9.6) – everyone has the right peacefully to enjoy his property either on his own or in common with others. No one may be deprived of his property except in the public interest and subject to the conditions provided for by law and consistent with international commitments and obligations.

(10) In reaffirming their commitment to ensure effectively the rights of the individual to know and act upon human rights and fundamental freedoms, and to contribute actively, individually or in association with others, to their promotion and protection, the participating States express their commitment to

(10.1) – respect the right of everyone, individually or in association with others, to seek, receive and impart freely views and information on human rights and fundamental freedoms, including the rights to disseminate and publish such views and information;

(10.2) – respect the rights of everyone, individually or in association with others, to study and discuss the observance of human rights and fundamental freedoms and to develop and discuss ideas for improved protection of human rights and better means for ensuring compliance with international human rights standards;

(10.3) – ensure that individuals are permitted to exercise the right to association, including the right to form, join and participate effectively in non-governmental organizations which seek the promotion and protection of human rights and fundamental freedoms, including trade unions and human rights monitoring groups;

(10.4) – allow members of such groups and organizations to have unhindered access to and communication with similar bodies within and outside their countries and with international organizations, to engage in exchanges, contacts and co-operation with such groups and organizations and to solicit, receive and utilize for the purpose of promoting and protecting human rights and fundamental freedoms voluntary financial contributions from national and international sources as provided for by law.

(11) The participating States further affirm that, where violations of human rights and fundamental freedoms are alleged to have occurred, the effective remedies available include

(11.1) – the right of the individual to seek and receive adequate legal assistance;

(11.2) – the right of the individual to seek and receive assistance from others in defending human rights and fundamental freedoms, and to assist others in defending human rights and fundamental freedoms;

(11.3) – the right of individuals or groups acting on their behalf to communicate with international bodies with competence to receive and consider information concerning allegations of human rights abuses.

(12) The participating States, wishing to ensure greater transparency in the implementation of the commitments undertaken in the Vienna Concluding Document under the heading of the human dimension of the CSCE, decide to accept as a confidence-building measure the presence of observers sent by participating States and representatives of non-governmental organizations and other interested persons at proceedings before courts as provided for in national legislation and international law; it is understood that

proceedings may only be held in camera in the circumstances prescribed by law and consistent with obligations under international law and international commitments.

(13) The participating States decide to accord particular attention to the recognition of the rights of the child, his civil rights and his individual freedoms, his economic, social and cultural rights, and his right to special protection against all forms of violence and exploitation. They will consider acceding to the Convention on the Rights of the Child, if they have not yet done so, which was opened for signature by States on 26 January 1990. They will recognize in their domestic legislation the rights of the child as affirmed in the international agreements to which they are Parties.

(14) The participating States agree to encourage the creation, within their countries, of conditions for the training of students and trainees from other participating States, including persons taking vocational and technical courses. They also agree to promote travel by young people from their countries for the purpose of obtaining education in other participating States and to that end to encourage the conclusion, where appropriate, of bilateral and multilateral agreements between their relevant governmental institutions, organizations and educational establishments.

(15) The participating States will act in such a way as to facilitate the transfer of sentenced persons and encourage those participating States which are not Parties to the Convention on the Transfer of Sentenced Persons, signed at Strasbourg on 21 November 1983, to consider acceding to the Convention.

(16) The participating States

(16.1) – reaffirm their commitment to prohibit torture and other cruel, inhuman or degrading treatment or punishment, to take effective legislative, administrative, judicial and other measures to prevent and punish such practices, to protect individuals from any psychiatric or other medical practices that violate human rights and fundamental freedoms and to take effective measures to prevent and punish such practices;

(16.2) – intend, as a matter of urgency, to consider acceding to the Convention against Torture or Other Cruel, Inhuman or Degrading Treatment or Punishment, if they have not yet done so, and recognizing the competences of the Committee against Torture under articles 21 and 22 of the Convention and withdrawing reservations regarding the competence of the Committee under article 20;

(16.3) – stress that no exceptional circumstances whatsoever, whether a state of war or a threat of war, internal political instability or any other public emergency, may be invoked as a justification of torture;

(16.4) – will ensure that education and information regarding the prohibition against torture are fully included in the training of law enforcement personnel, civil or military, medical personnel, public officials and other persons who may be involved in the custody, interrogation or treatment of any individual subjected to any form of arrest, detention or imprisonment;

(16.5) – will keep under systematic review interrogation rules, instructions, methods and practices as well as arrangements for the custody and treatment of persons subjected to any form of arrest, detention or imprisonment in any territory under their jurisdiction, with a view to preventing any cases of torture;

(16.6) – will take up with priority for consideration and for appropriate action, in accordance with the agreed measures and procedures for the effective implementation of the commitments relating to the human dimension of the CSCE, any cases of torture and other inhuman or degrading treatment or punishment made known to them through official channels or coming from any other reliable source of information;

(16.7) – will act upon the understanding that preserving and guaranteeing the life and security of any individual subjected to any form of torture and other inhuman or degrading treatment or punishment will be the sole criterion in determining the urgency and priorities to be accorded in taking appropriate remedial action; and, therefore, the consideration of any cases of torture and other inhuman or degrading treatment or punishment within the framework of any other international body or mechanism may not be invoked as a reason for refraining from considerations and appropriate action in accordance with the agreed measures and procedures for the effective implementation of the commitments relating to the human dimension of the CSCE.

(17) The participating States

(17.1) – recall the commitment undertaken in the Vienna Concluding Document to keep the question of capital punishment under consideration and to co-operate within relevant international organizations;

(17.2) – recall, in this context, the adoption by the General Assembly of the United Nations, on 15 December 1989, of the Second Optional Protocol to the International Covenant on Civil and Political Rights, aiming at the abolition of the death penalty;

(17.3) – note the restrictions and safeguards regarding the use of the death penalty which have been adopted by the international community, in particular article 6 of the International Covenant on Civil and Political Rights;

(17.4) – note the provisions of the Sixth Protocol to the European Convention for the Protection of Human Rights and Fundamental Freedoms, concerning the abolition of the death penalty;

(17.5) – note recent measures taken by a number of participating States towards the abolition of capital punishment;

(17.6) – note the activities of several non-governmental organizations on the question of the death penalty;

(17.7) – will exchange information within the framework of the Conference on the Human Dimension on the question of the abolition of the death penalty and keep that question under consideration;

(17.8) – will make available to the public information regarding the use of the death penalty.

(18) The participating States

(18.1) – note that the United Nations Commission on Human Rights has recognized the right of everyone to have conscientious objections to military service;

(18.2) – note recent measures taken by a number of participating States to permit exemption from compulsory military service on the basis of conscientious objections;

(18.3) – note the activities of several non-governmental organizations on the question of conscientious objections to compulsory military service;

(18.4) – agree to consider introducing, where this has not yet been done, various forms of alternative service, which are compatible with the reasons for conscientious objection, such forms of alternative service being in principle of a non-combatant or civilian nature, in the public interest and of a non-punitive nature;

(18.5) – will make available to the public information on this issue;

(18.6) – will keep under consideration, within the framework of the Conference on the Human Dimension, the relevant questions related to the exemption from compulsory military service, where it exists, of individuals on the basis of conscientious objections to armed service, and will exchange information on these questions.

(19) The participating States affirm that freer movement and contacts among their citizens are important in the context of the protection and promotion of human rights and fundamental freedoms. They will ensure that their policies concerning entry into their territories are fully consistent with the aims set out in the relevant provisions of the Final Act, the Madrid Concluding Document and the Vienna Concluding Document. While reaffirming their determination not to recede from the commitments contained in CSCE documents, they undertake to implement fully and improve present commitments in the field of human contacts, including on a bilateral and multilateral basis. In this context they will

(19.1) – strive to implement the procedures for entry into their territories, including the issuing of visas and passport and customs control, in good faith and without unjustified delay. Where necessary, they will shorten the waiting time for visa decisions, as well as simplify practices and reduce administrative requirements for visa applications;

(19.2) – ensure, in dealing with visa applications, that these are processed as expeditiously as possible in order, inter alia, to take due account of important family, personal or professional considerations, especially in cases of an urgent, humanitarian nature;

(19.3) – endeavour, where necessary, to reduce fees charged in connection with visa applications to the lowest possible level.

(20) The participating States concerned will consult and, where appropriate, co-operate in dealing with problems that might emerge as a result of the increased movement of persons.

(21) The participating States recommend the consideration, at the next CSCE Follow-up Meeting in Helsinki, of the advisability of holding a meeting of experts on consular matters.

(22) The participating States reaffirm that the protection and promotion of the rights of migrant workers have their human dimension. In this context, they

(22.1) – agree that the protection and promotion of the rights of migrant workers are the concern of all participating States and that as such they should be addressed within the CSCE process;

(22.2) – reaffirm their commitment to implement fully in their domestic legislation the rights of migrant workers provided for in international agreements to which they are parties;

(22.3) – consider that, in future international instruments concerning the rights of migrant workers, they should take into account the fact that this issue is of importance for all of them;

(22.4) – express their readiness to examine, at future CSCE meetings, the relevant aspects of the further promotion of the rights of migrant workers and their families.

(23) The participating States reaffirm their conviction expressed in the Vienna Concluding Document that the promotion of economic, social and cultural rights as well as of civil and political rights is of paramount importance for human dignity and for the attainment of the legitimate aspiration of every individual. They also reaffirm their commitment taken in the Document of the Bonn Conference on Economic Co-operation in Europe to the promotion of social justice and the improvement of living and working conditions. In the context of continuing their efforts with a view to achieving progressively the full realization of economic, social and cultural rights by all appropriate means, they will pay special attention to problems in areas of employment, housing, social security, health, education and culture.

(24) The participating States will ensure that the exercise of all the human rights and fundamental freedoms set out above will not be subject to any restrictions except those which are provided by law and are consistent with their obligations under international law, in particular the International Covenant on Civil and Political Rights, and with their international commitments, in particular the Universal Declaration of Human Rights. These restrictions have the character of exceptions. The participating States will ensure that these restrictions are not abused and are not applied in an arbitrary manner, but in such a

way that the effective exercise of these rights is ensured.

Any restriction on rights and freedoms must, in a democratic society, relate to one of the objectives of the applicable law and be strictly proportionate to the aim of that law.

(25) The participating States confirm that any derogations from obligations relating to human rights and fundamental freedoms during a state of public emergency must remain strictly within the limits provided for by international law, in particular the relevant international instruments by which they are bound, especially with respect to rights from which there can be no derogation. They also reaffirm that

(25.1) – measures derogating from such obligations must be taken in strict conformity with the procedural requirements laid down in those instruments;

(25.2) – the imposition of a state of public emergency must be proclaimed officially, publicly, and in accordance with the provisions laid down by law;

(25.3) – measures derogating from obligations will be limited to the extent strictly required by the exigencies of the situation;

(25.4) – such measures will not discriminate solely on the grounds of race, colour, sex, language, religion, social origin or of belonging to a minority.

III

(26) The participating States recognize that vigorous democracy depends on the existence as an integral part of national life of democratic values and practices as well as an extensive range of democratic institutions. They will therefore encourage, facilitate and, where appropriate, support practical co-operative endeavours and the sharing of information, ideas and expertise among themselves and by direct contacts and co-operation between individuals, groups and organizations in areas including the following:

– constitutional law, reform and development,

– electoral legislation, administration and observation,

– establishment and management of courts and legal systems,

– the development of an impartial and effective public service where recruitment and advancement are based on a merit system,

– law enforcement,

– local government and decentralization,

– access to information and protection of privacy,

– developing political parties and their role in pluralistic societies,

– free and independent trade unions,

– co-operative movements,

– developing other forms of free associations and public interest groups,

– journalism, independent media, and intellectual and cultural life,

– the teaching of democratic values, institutions and practices in educational institutions and the fostering of an atmosphere of free enquiry.

Such endeavours may cover the range of co-operation encompassed in the human dimension of the CSCE, including training, exchange of information, books and instructional materials, co-operative programmes and projects, academic and professional exchanges and conferences, scholarships, research grants, provision of expertise and advice, business and scientific contacts and programmes.

(27) The participating States will also facilitate the establishment and strengthening of independent national institutions in the area of human rights and the rule of law, which may also serve as focal points for co-ordination and collaboration between such institutions in the participating States. They propose that co-operation be encouraged between parliamentarians from participating States, including through existing inter-parliamentary associations and, inter alia, through joint commissions, television debates involving parliamentarians, meetings and round-table discussions. They will also encourage existing institutions, such as organizations within the United Nations system and the Council of Europe, to continue and expand the work they have begun in this area.

(28) The participating States recognize the important expertise of the Council of Europe in the field of human rights and fundamental freedoms and agree to consider further ways and means to enable the Council of Europe to make a contribution to the human dimension of the CSCE. They agree that the nature of this contribution could be examined further in a future CSCE forum.

(29) The participating States will consider the idea of convening a meeting or seminar of experts to review and discuss co-operative measures designed to promote and sustain

viable democratic institutions in participating States, including comparative studies of legislation in participating States in the area of human rights and fundamental freedoms, inter alia drawing upon the experience acquired in this area by the Council of Europe and the activities of the Commission 'Democracy through Law'.

IV

(30) The participating States recognize that the questions relating to national minorities can only be satisfactorily resolved in a democratic political framework based on the rule of law, with a functioning independent judiciary. This framework guarantees full respect for human rights and fundamental freedoms, equal rights and status for all citizens, the free expression of all their legitimate interests and aspirations, political pluralism, social tolerance and the implementation of legal rules that place effective restraints on the abuse of governmental power.

They also recognize the important role of non-governmental organizations, including political parties, trade unions, human rights organizations and religious groups, in the promotion of tolerance, cultural diversity and the resolution of questions relating to national minorities.

They further reaffirm that respect for the rights of persons belonging to national minorities as part of universally recognized human rights is an essential factor for peace, justice, stability and democracy in the participating States.

(31) Persons belonging to national minorities have the right to exercise fully and effectively their human rights and fundamental freedoms without any discrimination and in full equality before the law.

The participating States will adopt, where necessary, special measures for the purpose of ensuring to persons belonging to national minorities full equality with the other citizens in the exercise and enjoyment of human rights and fundamental freedoms.

(32) To belong to a national minority is a matter of a person's individual choice and no disadvantage may arise from the exercise of such choice.

Persons belonging to national minorities have the right freely to express, preserve and develop their ethnic, cultural, linguistic or religious identity and to maintain and develop their culture in all its aspects, free of any attempts at assimilation against their will. In particular, they have the right

(32.1) – to use freely their mother tongue in private as well as in public;

(32.2) – to establish and maintain their own educational, cultural and religious institutions, organizations or associations, which can seek voluntary financial and other contributions as well as public assistance, in conformity with national legislation;

(32.3) – to profess and practise their religion, including the acquisition, possession and use of religious materials, and to conduct religious educational activities in their mother tongue;

(32.4) – to establish and maintain unimpeded contacts among themselves within their country as well as contacts across frontiers with citizens of other States with whom they share a common ethnic or national origin, cultural heritage or religious beliefs;

(32.5) – to disseminate, have access to and exchange information in their mother tongue;

(32.6) – to establish and maintain organizations or associations within their country and to participate in international non-governmental organizations.

Persons belonging to national minorities can exercise and enjoy their rights individually as well as in community with other members of their group. No disadvantage may arise for a person belonging to a national minority on account of the exercise or non-exercise of any such rights.

(33) The participating States will protect the ethnic, cultural, linguistic and religious identity of national minorities on their territory and create conditions for the promotion of that identity. They will take the necessary measures to that effect after due consultations, including contacts with organizations or associations of such minorities, in accordance with the decision-making procedures of each State.

Any such measures will be in conformity with the principles of equality and non-discrimination with respect to the other citizens of the participating State concerned.

(34) The participating States will endeavour to ensure that persons belonging to national minorities, notwithstanding the need to learn the official language or languages of the State concerned, have adequate opportunities for instruction of their mother tongue or in their mother tongue, as well as, wherever

possible and necessary, for its use before public authorities, in conformity with applicable national legislation.

In the context of the teaching of history and culture in educational establishments, they will also take account of the history and culture of national minorities.

(35) The participating States will respect the right of persons belonging to national minorities to effective participation in public affairs, including participation in the affairs relating to the protection and promotion of the identity of such minorities.

The participating States note the efforts undertaken to protect and create conditions for the promotion of the ethnic, cultural, linguistic and religious identity of certain national minorities by establishing, as one of the possible means to achieve these aims, appropriate local or autonomous administrations corresponding to the specific historical and territorial circumstances of such minorities and in accordance with the policies of the State concerned.

(36) The participating States recognize the particular importance of increasing constructive co-operation among themselves on questions relating to national minorities. Such co-operation seeks to promote mutual understanding and confidence, friendly and good-neighbourly relations, international peace, security and justice.

Every participating State will promote a climate of mutual respect, understanding, co-operation and solidarity among all persons living on its territory, without distinction as to ethnic or national origin or religion, and will encourage the solution of problems through dialogue based on the principles of the rule of law.

(37) None of these commitments may be interpreted as implying any right to engage in any activity or perform any action in contravention of the purposes and principles of the Charter of the United Nations, other obligations under international law or the provisions of the Final Act, including the principle of territorial integrity of States.

(38) The participating States, in their efforts to protect and promote the rights of persons belonging to national minorities, will fully respect their undertakings under existing human rights conventions and other relevant international instruments and consider adhering to the relevant conventions, if they have

not yet done so, including those providing for a right of complaint by individuals.

(39) The participating States will co-operate closely in the competent international organizations to which they belong, including the United Nations and, as appropriate, the Council of Europe, bearing in mind their ongoing work with respect to questions relating to national minorities.

They will consider convening a meeting of experts for a thorough discussion of the issue of national minorities.

(40) The participating States clearly and unequivocally condemn totalitarianism, racial and ethnic hatred, anti-semitism, xenophobia and discrimination against anyone as well as persecution on religious and ideological grounds. In this context, they also recognize the particular problems of Roma (gypsies).

They declare their firm intention to intensify the efforts to combat these phenomena in all their forms and therefore will

(40.1) – take effective measures, including the adoption, in conformity with their constitutional systems and their international obligations, of such laws as may be necessary, to provide protection against any acts that constitute incitement to violence against persons or groups based on national, racial, ethnic or religious discrimination, hostility or hatred, including anti-semitism;

(40.2) – commit themselves to take appropriate and proportionate measures to protect persons or groups who may be subject to threats or acts of discrimination, hostility or violence as a result of their racial, ethnic, cultural, linguistic or religious identity, and to protect their property;

(40.3) – take effective measures, in conformity with their constitutional systems, at the national, regional and local levels to promote understanding and tolerance, particularly in the fields of education, culture and information;

(40.4) – endeavour to ensure that the objectives of education include special attention to the problem of racial prejudice and hatred and to the development of respect for different civilizations and cultures;

(40.5) – recognize the right of the individual to effective remedies and endeavour to recognize, in conformity with national legislation, the right of interested persons and groups to initiate and support complaints against acts of discrimination, including racist and xenophobic acts;

(40.6) – consider adhering, if they have not yet done so, to the international instruments which address the problem of discrimination and ensure full compliance with the obligations therein, including those relating to the submission of periodic reports;

(40.7) – consider, also, accepting those international mechanisms which allow States and individuals to bring communications relating to discrimination before international bodies.

V

(41) The participating States reaffirm their commitment to the human dimension of the CSCE and emphasize its importance as an integral part of a balanced approach to security and co-operation in Europe. They agree that the Conference on the Human Dimension of the CSCE and the human dimension mechanism described in the section on the human dimension of the CSCE of the Vienna Concluding Document have demonstrated their value as methods of furthering their dialogue and co-operation and assisting in the resolution of relevant specific questions. They express their conviction that these should be continued and developed as part of an expanding CSCE process.

(42) The participating States recognized the need to enhance further the effectiveness of the procedures described in paragraphs 1 to 4 of the section on the human dimension of the CSCE of the Vienna Concluding Document and with this aim decide

(42.1) – to provide in as short a time as possible, but no later than four weeks, a written response to requests for information and to representations made to them in writing by other participating States under paragraph 1;

(42.2) – that the bilateral meetings, as contained in paragraph 2, will take place as soon as possible, as a rule within three weeks of the date of the request;

(42.3) – to refrain, in the course of a bilateral meeting held under paragraph 2, from raising situations and cases not connected with the subject of the meeting, unless both sides have agreed to do so.

(43) The participating States examined practical proposals for new measures aimed at improving the implementation of the commitments relating to the human dimension of the

CSCE. In this regard, they considered proposals related to the sending of observers to examine situations and specific cases, the appointment of rapporteurs to investigate and suggest appropriate solutions, the setting up of a Committee on the Human Dimension of the CSCE, greater involvement of persons, organizations and institutions in the human dimension mechanism and further bilateral and multilateral efforts to promote the resolution of relevant issues.

They decide to continue to discuss thoroughly in subsequent relevant CSCE fora these and other proposals designed to strengthen the human dimension mechanism, and to consider adopting, in the context of the further development of the CSCE process, appropriate new measures. They agree that these measures should contribute to achieving further effective progress, enhance conflict prevention and confidence in the field of the human dimension of the CSCE.

* * *

(44) The representatives of the participating States express their profound gratitude to the people and Government of Denmark for the excellent organization of the Copenhagen Meeting and the warm hospitality extended to the delegations which participated in the Meeting.

(45) In accordance with the provisions relating to the Conference on the Human Dimension of the CSCE contained in the Concluding Document of the Vienna Follow-up Meeting of the CSCE, the third Meeting of the Conference will take place in Moscow from 10 September to 4 October 1991.

ANNEX

Chairman's statement on the access of non-governmental organizations and the media to meetings of the Conference on the Human Dimension

The Chairman notes that the practices of openness and access to the Meetings of the Conference on the Human Dimension, as they were applied at the Vienna Meeting and as contained in Annex XI of the Concluding Document of that Meeting, are of importance to all participating States. In order to follow and build upon those practices at forthcoming CSCE meetings of the Conference on the

Human Dimension, the participating States agree that the following practices of openness and access should be respected:

– free movement by members of interested non-governmental organizations (NGOs) in the Conference premises, except for the areas restricted to delegations and to the services of the Executive Secretariat. Accordingly, badges will be issued to them, at their request, by the Executive Secretariat;

– unimpeded contacts between members of interested NGOs and delegates, as well as with accredited representatives of the media;

– access to official documents of the Conference in all the working languages and also to any document that delegates might wish to communicate to members of interested NGOs;

– the opportunity for members of interested NGOs to transmit to delegates communications relating to the human dimension of the CSCE. Mailboxes for each delegation will be accessible to them for this purpose;

– free access for delegates to all documents emanating from interested NGOs and addressed to the Executive Secretariat for the information of the Conference. Accordingly, the Executive Secretariat will make available to delegates a regularly updated collection of such documents.

They further undertake to guarantee to representatives of the media:

– free movement in the Conference premises, except for the areas restricted to delegations and to the services of the Executive Secretariat. Accordingly, badges will be issued to them by the Executive Secretariat upon presentation of the requisite credentials;

– unimpeded contacts with delegates and with members of interested NGOs;

– access to official documents of the Conference in all the working languages.

The Chairman notes further that this statement will be an Annex to the Document of the Copenhagen Meeting and will be published with it.

Joint Declaration of Twenty-Two States*
Paris, 19 November 1990

The Heads of State or Government of Belgium, Bulgaria, Canada, the Czech and Slovak Federal Republic, Denmark, France, Germany, Greece, Hungary, Iceland, Italy, Luxembourg, the Netherlands, Norway, Poland, Portugal, Romania, Spain, Turkey, the Union of Soviet Socialist Republics, the United Kingdom and the United States of America

– greatly welcoming the historic changes in Europe

– gratified by the growing implementation throughout Europe of a common commitment to pluralist democracy, the rule of law and human rights, which are essential to lasting security on the continent,

– affirming the end of the era of division and confrontation which has lasted for more than four decades, the improvement in relations among their countries and the contribution this makes to the security of all,

– confident that the signature of the Treaty on Conventional Armed Forces in Europe represents a major contribution to the common objective of increased security and stability in Europe, and

– convinced that these developments must form part of a continuing process of cooperation in building the structures of a more united continent,

Issue the following Declaration:

1. The signatories solemnly declare that, in the new era of European relations which is beginning, they are no longer adversaries, will build new partnerships and extend to each other the hand of friendship.

2. They recall their obligations under the Charter of the United Nations and reaffirm all of their commitments under the Helsinki Final Act. They stress that all of the ten Helsinki Principles are of primary significance and that, accordingly, they will be equally and unreservedly applied, each of them being interpreted taking into account the others. In that context, they affirm their obligation and commitment to refrain from the threat or use of force against the territorial integrity or the political independence of any State, from seeking to change existing borders by threat or use of force, and from acting in any other manner inconsistent with the principles and purposes of those documents. None of their weapons will ever be used except in self-defence or otherwise in accordance with the Charter of the United Nations.

3. They recognize that security is indivisible and that the security of each of their

countries is inextricably linked to the security of all States participating in the Conference on Security and Co-operation in Europe.

4. They undertake to maintain only such military capabilities as are necessary to prevent war and provide for effective defence. They will bear in mind the relationship between military capabilities and doctrines.

5. They reaffirm that every State has the right to be or not to be a party to a treaty of alliance.

6. They note with approval the intensification of political and military contacts among them to promote mutual understanding and confidence. They welcome in this context the positive responses made to recent proposals for new regular diplomatic liaison.

7. They declare their determination to contribute actively to conventional, nuclear and chemical arms control and disarmament agreements which enhance security and stability for all. In particular, they call for the early entry into force of the Treaty on Conventional Armed Forces in Europe and commit themselves to continue the process of strengthening peace in Europe through conventional arms control within the framework of the CSCE. They welcome the prospect of new negotiations between the United States and the Soviet Union on the reduction of their short-range nuclear forces.

8. They welcome the contribution that confidence- and security-building measures have made to lessening tensions and fully support the further development of such measures. They reaffirm the importance of the 'Open Skies' initiative and their determination to bring the negotiations to a successful conclusion as soon as possible.

9. They pledge to work together with the other CSCE participating States to strengthen the CSCE process so that it can make an even greater contribution to security and stability in Europe. They recognize in particular the need to enhance political consultations among CSCE participants and to develop other CSCE mechanisms. The are convinced that the Treaty on Conventional Armed Forces in Europe and agreement on a substantial new set of CSBMs, together with new patterns of co-operation in the framework of the CSCE, will lead to increased security and thus to enduring peace and stability in Europe.

10. They believe that the preceding points reflect the deep longing of their peoples for close co-operation and mutual understanding

and declare that they will work steadily for the further development of their relations in accordance with the present Declaration as well as with the principles set forth in the Helsinki Final Act.

The original of this Declaration of which the English, French, German, Italian, Russian and Spanish texts are equally authentic will be transmitted to the Government of France which will retain it in its archives. The Government of France is requested to transmit the text of the Declaration to the Secretary-General of the United Nations, with a view to its circulation to all the members of the organization as an official document of the United Nations, indicating that it is not eligible for registration under Article 102 of the Charter of the United Nations. Each of the signatory States will receive from the Government of France a true copy of this Declaration.

In witness whereof the undersigned High Representatives have subscribed their signatures below.**

---

* The Paris Declaration was issued by the states parties to the Treaty on Conventional Armed Forces in Europe which was signed at the same time. The Parties to the Declaration and Treaty are the NATO and the WTO states. They committed themselves to the objective of ensuring that the numbers of conventional armaments and equipment limited by the Treaty do not exceed 40 000 battle tanks, 60 000 armoured combat vehicles, 40 000 pieces of artillery, 13 600 combat aircraft and 4000 attack helicopters.

The Treaty on Conventional Armed Forces in Europe incorporates the Protocol on Existing Types of Conventional Armaments and Equipment, with an Annex thereto; the Protocol on Procedures Governing the Reclassification of Specific Models or Versions of Combat-Capable Trainer Aircraft Into Unarmed Trainer Aircraft; the Protocol on Procedures Governing the Reduction of Conventional Armaments and Equipment Limited by the Treaty on Conventional Armed Forces in Europe; the Protocol on Procedures Governing the Categorisation of Combat Helicopters and Recategorisation of Multi-Purpose Attack Helicopters; the Protocol on Notification and Exchange of Information, with an Annex on the Format for the Exchange of Information; the Protocol on Inspection; the Protocol on the Joint Consultative Group; and the Protocol on the Provisional Application of Certain Provisions of the Treaty on Conventional Armed Forces in Europe. Each of these documents constitutes an integral part of the Treaty.

As annexes were attached two declarations of 22 states with respect to land-based naval aircraft and with respect to personnel strength, and the declaration by the Government of the Federal Republic of Germany on the personnel strength of the German armed forces. (For the German declaration see section V–FRG documents.)

** The Joint Declaration of Twenty-Two States and the CFE Treaty were signed by the heads of state or government of: Belgium—Prime Minister Wilfried Martens; Canada—Prime Minister Brian Mulroney; the Czech and Slovak Federal Republic—President Vaclav Havel; Denmark—Prime Minister Paul Schluter; France—President François Mitterrand; Germany—Chancellor Helmut Kohl; Greece—Prime Minister Constantine Mitsotakis; Hungary—Prime Minister Jozsef Antall; Iceland—Prime Minister Steingrimur Hermannsson; Italy—Prime Minister Giulio Andreotti; Luxembourg—Prime Minister Jacques Santer; the Netherlands—Prime Minister Ruud Lubbers; Norway—Prime Minister Gro Harlem Brundtland; Poland—Prime Minister Tadeusz Mazowiecki; Portugal—Prime Minister Anibal Cavaco Silva; Romania—President Ion Iliescu; Spain—Prime Minister Felipe González; Turkey—President Turgut Ozal; the USSR—President Mikhail S. Gorbachev; the UK—Prime Minister Margaret Thatcher; and the USA—President George Bush.

Note: The Negotiation on Conventional Armed Forces in Europe (CFE) among 22 states (known before the unification of Germany as the group of 23) began on 6 March 1989. Its mandate, adopted as an integral part of the Vienna CSCE follow-up meeting in 1989, stated: 'These negotiations will be conducted within the framework of the CSCE process.' The Joint Declaration of Twenty-Two States is therefore included here as part of section XXI–CSCE documents, although it is not a document of the 34 CSCE states.

The Charter of Paris for a new Europe*
Paris, 21 November 1990

A NEW ERA OF DEMOCRACY, PEACE AND UNITY

We, the Heads of State or Government of the States participating in the Conference on Security and Co-operation in Europe, have assembled in Paris at a time of profound change and historic expectations. The era of confrontation and division of Europe has ended. We declare that henceforth our relations will be founded on respect and co-operation.

Europe is liberating itself from the legacy of the past. The courage of men and women, the strength of the will of the peoples and the power of the ideas of the Helsinki Final Act have opened a new era of democracy, peace and unity in Europe.

Ours is a time for fulfilling the hopes and expectations our peoples have cherished for decades: steadfast commitment to democracy based on human rights and fundamental freedoms; prosperity through economic liberty and social justice; and equal security for all our countries.

The Ten Principles of the Final Act will guide us towards this ambitious future, just as they have lighted our way towards better relations for the past fifteen years. Full implementation of all CSCE commitments must form the basis for the initiatives we are now taking to enable our nations to live in accordance with their aspirations.

Human rights, democracy and rule of law

We undertake to build, consolidate and strengthen democracy as the only system of government of our nations. In this endeavour, we will abide by the following:

Human rights and fundamental freedoms are the birthright of all human beings, are inalienable and are guaranteed by law. Their protection and promotion is the first responsibility of government. Respect for them is an essential safeguard against an over-mighty State. Their observance and full exercise are the foundation of freedom, justice and peace.

Democratic government is based on the will of the people, expressed regularly through free and fair elections. Democracy has as its foundation respect for the human person and the rule of law. Democracy is the best safeguard of freedom of expression, tolerance of all groups of society, and equality of opportunity for each person.

Democracy, with its representative and pluralist character, entails accountability to the electorate, the obligation of public authorities to comply with the law and justice administered impartially. No one will be above the law.

We affirm that, without discrimination, every individual has the right to:

freedom of thought, conscience and religion or belief,

freedom of expression,

freedom of association and peaceful assembly,

freedom of movement;

no one will be:

subject to arbitrary arrest or detention,

subject to torture or other cruel, inhuman or degrading treatment or punishment;

everyone also has the right:

to know and act upon his rights,

to participate in free and fair elections,

to fair and public trial if charged with an offence,

to own property alone or in association and to exercise individual enterprise,

to enjoy his economic, social and cultural rights.

We affirm that the ethnic, cultural, linguistic and religious identity of national minorities will be protected and that persons belonging to national minorities have the right freely to express, preserve and develop that identity without any discrimination and in full equality before the law.

We will ensure that everyone will enjoy recourse to effective remedies, national or international, against any violation of his rights.

Full respect for these precepts is the bedrock on which we will seek to construct the new Europe.

Our States will co-operate and support each other with the aim of making democratic gains irreversible.

Economic liberty and responsibility

Economic liberty, social justice and environmental responsibility are indispensable for prosperity.

The free will of the individual, exercised in democracy and protected by the rule of law, forms the necessary basis for successful economic and social development. We will promote economic activity which respects and upholds human dignity.

Freedom and political pluralism are necessary elements in our common objective of developing market economies towards sustainable economic growth, prosperity, social justice, expanding employment and efficient use of economic resources. The success of the transition to market economy by countries making efforts to this effect is important and in the interest of us all. It will enable us to share a higher level of prosperity which is our common objective. We will co-operate to this end.

Preservation of the environment is a shared responsibility of all our nations. While supporting national and regional efforts in this field, we must also look to the pressing need for joint action on a wider scale.

Friendly relations among participating states

Now that a new era is dawning in Europe, we are determined to expand and strengthen friendly relations and co-operation among the States of Europe, the United States of America and Canada, and to promote friendship among our peoples.

To uphold and promote democracy, peace and unity in Europe, we solemnly pledge our full commitment to the Ten Principles of the Helsinki Final Act. We affirm the continuing validity of the Ten Principles and our determination to put them into practice. All the Principles apply equally and unreservedly, each of them being interpreted taking into account the others. They form the basis for our relations.

In accordance with our obligations under the Charter of the United Nations and commitments under the Helsinki Final Act, we renew our pledge to refrain from the threat or use of force against the territorial integrity or political independence of any State, or from acting in any other manner inconsistent with the principles or purposes of those documents. We recall that non-compliance with obligations under the Charter of the United Nations constitutes a violation of international law.

We reaffirm our commitment to settle disputes by peaceful means. We decide to develop mechanisms for the prevention and resolution of conflicts among the participating States.

With the ending of the division of Europe, we will strive for a new quality in our security relations while fully respecting each other's freedom of choice in that respect. Security is indivisible and the security of every participating State is inseparably linked to that of all the others. We therefore pledge to co-operate in strengthening confidence and security among us and in promoting arms control and disarmament.

We welcome the Joint Declaration of Twenty-Two States on the improvement of their relations.

Our relations will rest on our common adherence to democratic values and to human rights and fundamental freedoms. We are convinced that in order to strengthen peace and security among our States, the advancement of democracy, and respect for and effective exercise of human rights, are indispensable. We reaffirm the equal rights of peoples and their right to self-determination in conformity with the Charter of the United Nations and with the relevant norms of international law, including those relating to territorial integrity of States.

We are determined to enhance political consultation and to widen co-operation to solve economic, social, environmental, cultural and humanitarian problems. This common resolve and our growing interdependence will help to overcome the mistrust of decades, to increase stability and to build a united Europe.

We want Europe to be a source of peace, open to dialogue and to co-operation with other countries, welcoming exchanges and involved in the search for common responses to the challenges of the future.

Security

Friendly relations among us will benefit from the consolidation of democracy and improved security.

We welcome the signature of the Treaty on Conventional Armed Forces in Europe by twenty-two participating States, which will lead to lower levels of armed forces. We endorse the adoption of a substantial new set of Confidence- and Security-building Measures** which will lead to increased transparency and confidence among all participating States. These are important steps towards enhanced stability and security in Europe.

The unprecedented reduction in armed forces resulting from the Treaty on Conventional Armed Forces in Europe, together with new approaches to security and co-operation within the CSCE process, will lead to a new perception of security in Europe and a new dimension in our relations. In this context we fully recognize the freedom of States to choose their own security arrangements.

Unity

Europe whole and free is calling for a new beginning. We invite our peoples to join in this great endeavour.

We note with great satisfaction the Treaty on the Final Settlement with respect to Germany signed in Moscow on 12 September 1990 and sincerely welcome the fact that the German people have united to become one State in accordance with the principles of the Final Act of the Conference on Security and Co-operation in Europe and in full accord with their neighbours. The establishment of the national unity of Germany is an important contribution to a just and lasting order of peace for a united, democratic Europe aware of its responsibility for stability, peace and co-operation.

The participation of both North American and European States is a fundamental characteristic of the CSCE; it underlies its past achievements and is essential to the future of the CSCE process. An abiding adherence to shared values and our common heritage are the ties which bind us together. With all the rich diversity of our nations, we are united in our commitment to expand our co-operation in all fields. The challenges confronting us can only be met by common action, co-operation and solidarity.

The CSCE and the world

The destiny of our nations is linked to that of all other nations. We support fully the United Nations and the enhancement of its role in promoting international peace, security and justice. We reaffirm our commitment to the principles and purposes of the United Nations as enshrined in the Charter and condemn all violations of these principles. We recognize with satisfaction the growing role of the United Nations in world affairs and its increasing effectiveness, fostered by the improvement in relations among our States.

Aware of the dire need of a great part of the world, we commit ourselves to solidarity with all other countries. Therefore, we issue a call from Paris today to all the nations of the world. We stand ready to join with any and all States in common efforts to protect and advance the community of fundamental human values.

GUIDELINES FOR THE FUTURE

Proceeding from our firm commitment to the full implementation of all CSCE principles and provisions, we now resolve to give a new impetus to a balanced and comprehensive development of our co-operation in order to address the needs and aspirations of our peoples.

Human dimension

We declare our respect for human rights and fundamental freedoms to be irrevocable. We will fully implement and build upon the provisions relating to the human dimension of the CSCE.

Proceeding from the Document of the Copenhagen Meeting of the Conference on the Human Dimension, we will co-operate to strengthen democratic institutions and to promote the application of the rule of law. To that end, we decide to convene a seminar of experts in Oslo from 4 to 15 November 1991.

Determined to foster the rich contribution of national minorities to the life of our societies, we undertake further to improve their situation. We reaffirm our deep conviction that friendly relations among our peoples, as well as peace, justice, stability and democracy, require that the ethnic, cultural, linguistic and religious identity of national minorities be protected and conditions for the promotion of that identity be created. We declare that questions related to national minorities can only be satisfactorily resolved in a democratic political framework. We further acknowledge that the rights of persons belonging to national minorities must be fully respected as part of universal human rights. Being aware of the urgent need for increased co-operation on, as well as better protection of, national minorities, we decide to convene a meeting of experts on national minorities to be held in Geneva from 1 to 19 July 1991.

We express our determination to combat all forms of racial and ethnic hatred, anti-semitism, xenophobia and discrimination against anyone as well as persecution on religious and ideological grounds.

In accordance with our CSCE commitments, we stress that free movement and contacts among our citizens as well as the free flow of information and ideas are crucial for the maintenance and development of free societies and flourishing cultures. We welcome increased tourism and visits among our countries.

The human dimension mechanism has proved its usefulness, and we are consequently determined to expand it to include new procedures involving, *inter alia*, the services of experts or a roster of eminent persons experienced in human rights issues which could be raised under the mechanism. We shall provide, in the context of the mechanism, for individuals to be involved in the protection of their rights. Therefore, we undertake to develop further our commitments in this respect, in particular at the Moscow Meeting of the Conference on the Human Dimension, without prejudice to obligations under existing international instruments to which our States may be parties.

We recognize the important contribution of the Council of Europe to the promotion of human rights and the principles of democracy and the rule of law as well as to the development of cultural co-operation. We welcome moves by several participating States to join the Council of Europe and adhere to its European Convention on Human Rights. We welcome as well the readiness of the Council of Europe to make its experience available to the CSCE.

Security

The changing political and military environment in Europe opens new possibilities for common efforts in the field of military security. We will build on the important achievements attained in the Treaty on Conventional Armed Forces in Europe and in the Negotiations on Confidence- and Security-Building Measures. We undertake to continue the CSBM negotiations under the same mandate, and to seek to conclude them no later than the Follow-up Meeting of the CSCE to be held in Helsinki in 1992. We also welcome the decision of the participating States concerned to continue the CFE negotiation under the same mandate and to seek to conclude it no later than the Helsinki Follow-up Meeting. Following a period for national preparations, we look forward to a more structured co-operation among all participating States on security matters, and to discussions and consultations among the thirty-four participating States aimed at establishing by 1992, from the conclusion of the Helsinki Follow-Up Meeting, new negotiations on disarmament and confidence and security building open to all participating States.

We call for the earliest possible conclusion of the Convention on an effectively verifiable, global and comprehensive ban on chemical weapons, and we intend to be original signatories to it.

We reaffirm the importance of the Open Skies initiative and call for the successful conclusion of the negotiations as soon as possible.

Although the threat of conflict in Europe has diminished, other dangers threaten the stability of our societies. We are determined to co-operate in defending democratic institutions against activities which violate the independence, sovereign equality or territorial integrity of the participating States. These include illegal activities involving outside pressure, coercion and subversion.

We unreservedly condemn, as criminal, all acts, methods and practices of terrorism and express our determination to work for its eradication both bilaterally and through multilateral co-operation. We will also join together in combating illicit trafficking in drugs.

Being aware that an essential complement to the duty of States to refrain from the threat or use of force is the peaceful settlement of disputes, both being essential factors for the maintenance and consolidation of international peace and security, we will not only seek effective ways of preventing, through political means, conflicts which may emerge, but also define, in conformity with international law, appropriate mechanisms for the peaceful resolution of any disputes which may arise. Accordingly, we undertake to seek new forms of co-operation in this area, in particular a range of methods for the peaceful settlement of disputes, including mandatory third-party involvement. We stress that full use should be made in this context of the opportunity of the meeting on the peaceful settlement of disputes which will be convened in Valletta at the beginning of 1991. The Council of Ministers for Foreign Affairs will take into account the Report of the Valletta Meeting.

Economic co-operation

We stress that economic co-operation based on market economy constitutes an essential element of our relations and will be instrumental in the construction of a prosperous and united Europe. Democratic institutions and economic liberty foster economic and social progress, as recognized in the Document of the Bonn Conference on Economic Co-operation, the results of which we strongly support.

We underline that co-operation in the economic field, science and technology is now an important pillar of the CSCE. The participating States should periodically review progress and give new impulses in these fields.

We are convinced that our overall economic co-operation should be expanded, free enterprise encouraged and trade increased and diversified according to GATT rules. We will promote social justice and progress and further the welfare of our peoples. We recognize in this context the importance of effective policies to address the problem of unemployment.

We reaffirm the need to continue to support democratic countries in transition towards the establishment of market economy and the creation of the basis for self-sustained economic and social growth, as already undertaken by the Group of twenty-four countries. We further underline the necessity of their increased integration, involving the acceptance of disciplines as well as benefits, into the international economic and financial system.

We consider that increased emphasis on economic co-operation within the CSCE process should take into account the interests of developing participating States.

We recall the link between respect for and promotion of human rights and fundamental freedoms and scientific progress. Co-operation in the field of science and technology will play an essential role in economic and social development. Therefore, it must evolve towards a greater sharing of appropriate scientific and technological information and knowledge with a view to overcoming the technological gap existing among the participating States. We further encourage the participating States to work together in order to develop human potential and the spirit of free enterprise.

We are determined to give the necessary impetus to co-operation among our States in the fields of energy, transport and tourism for economic and social development. We welcome, in particular, practical steps to create optimal conditions for the economic and rational development of energy resources, with due regard for environmental considerations.

We recognize the important role of the European Community in the political and economic development of Europe. International economic organizations such as the Economic Commission for Europe of the United Nations (ECE/UN), the Bretton Woods Institutions, the Organization for Economic Co-operation and Development (OECD), the European Free Trade Association (EFTA) and the International Chamber of Commerce (ICC) also have a significant task in promoting economic co-operation, which will be further enhanced by the establishment of the European Bank for Reconstruction and Development (EBRD). In order to pursue our objectives, we stress the necessity for effective co-ordination of the activities of these organizations and emphasize the need to find methods for all our States to take part in these activities.

Environment

We recognize the urgent need to tackle the problems of the environment and the importance of individual and co-operative efforts in this area. We pledge to intensify our endeavours to protect and improve our environment in order to restore and maintain a sound ecological balance in air, water and soil. Therefore, we are determined to make full use of the CSCE as a framework for the formulation of common environmental commitments and objectives, and thus to pursue the work reflected in the Report of the Sofia Meeting on the Protection of the Environment.

We emphasize the significant role of a well-informed society in enabling the public and individuals to take initiatives to improve the environment. To this end, we commit ourselves to promote public awareness and education on the environment as well as the public reporting of the environmental impact of policies, projects and programmes.

We attach priority to the introduction of clean and low-waste technology, being aware of the need to support countries which do not yet have their own means for appropriate measures.

We underline that environmental policies should be supported by appropriate legislative measures and administrative structures to ensure their effective implementation.

We stress the need for new measures providing for systematic evaluation of compliance with the existing commitments and, moreover, for the development of more ambitious commitments with regard to notification and exchange of information about the state of the environment and potential environmental hazards. We also welcome the creation of the European Environment Agency (EEA).

We welcome the operational activities, problem-oriented studies and policy reviews in various existing international organizations engaged in the protection of the environment,

such as the United Nations Environment Program (UNEP), the Economic Commission for Europe of the United Nations (ECE/UN) and the Organization for Economic Co-operation and Development (OECD). We emphasize the need for strengthening their co-operation and for their efficient co-ordination.

Culture

We recognize the essential contribution of our common European culture and our shared values in overcoming the division of the continent. Therefore, we underline our attachment to creative freedom and to the protection and promotion of our cultural and spiritual heritage, in all its richness and diversity.

In view of the recent changes in Europe, we stress the increased importance of the Cracow Symposium and we look forward to its consideration of guidelines for intensified co-operation in the field of culture. We invite the Council of Europe to contribute to this Symposium.

In order to promote greater familiarity amongst our peoples, we favour the establishment of cultural centres in cities of other participating States as well as increased co-operation in the audio-visual field and wider exchange in music, theatre, literature and the arts.

We resolve to make special efforts in our national policies to promote better understanding, in particular among young people, through cultural exchanges, co-operation in all fields of education and, more specifically, through teaching and training in the languages of other participating States. We intend to consider first results of this action at the Helsinki Follow-up Meeting in 1992.

Migrant workers

We recognize that the issues of migrant workers and their families legally residing in host countries have economic, cultural and social aspects as well as their human dimension. We reaffirm that the protection and promotion of their rights, as well as the implementation of relevant international obligations, is our common concern.

Mediterranean

We consider that the fundamental political changes that have occurred in Europe have a positive relevance to the Mediterranean region. Thus, we will continue efforts to strengthen security and co-operation in the Mediterranean as an important factor for stability in Europe. We welcome the Report of the Palma de Mallorca Meeting on the Mediterranean, the results of which we all support.

We are concerned with the continuing tensions in the region, and renew our determination to intensify efforts towards finding just, viable and lasting solutions, through peaceful means, to outstanding crucial problems, based on respect for the principles of the Final Act.

We wish to promote favourable conditions for a harmonious development and diversification of relations with the non-participating Mediterranean States. Enhanced co-operation with these States will be pursued with the aim of promoting economic and social development and thereby enhancing stability in the region. To this end, we will strive together with these countries towards a substantial narrowing of the prosperity gap between Europe and its Mediterranean neighbours.

Non-governmental organizations

We recall the major role that non-governmental organizations, religious and other groups and individuals have played in the achievement of the objectives of the CSCE and will further facilitate their activities for the implementation of the CSCE commitments by the participating States. These organizations, groups and individuals must be involved in an appropriate way in the activities and new structures of the CSCE in order to fulfil their important tasks.

NEW STRUCTURES AND INSTITUTIONS OF THE CSCE PROCESS

Our common efforts to consolidate respect for human rights, democracy and the rule of law, to strengthen peace and to promote unity in Europe require a new quality of political dialogue and co-operation and thus development of the structures of the CSCE.

The intensification of our consultations at all levels is of prime importance in shaping our future relations. To this end, we decide on the following:

We, the Heads of State or Government, shall meet next time in Helsinki on the occasion of the CSCE Follow-up Meeting 1992.

Thereafter, we will meet on the occasion of subsequent follow-up meetings.

Our Ministers for Foreign Affairs will meet, as a Council, regularly and at least once a year. These meetings will provide the central forum for political consultations within the CSCE process. The Council will consider issues relevant to the Conference on Security and Co-operation in Europe and take appropriate decisions.

The first meeting of the Council will take place in Berlin.

A Committee of Senior Officials will prepare the meetings of the Council and carry out its decisions. The Committee will review current issues and may take appropriate decisions, including in the form of recommendations to the Council.

Additional meetings of the representatives of the participating States may be agreed upon to discuss questions of urgent concern.

The Council will examine the development of provisions for convening meetings of the Committee of Senior Officials in emergency situations.

Meetings of other Ministers may also be agreed by the participating States.

In order to provide administrative support for these consultations we establish a Secretariat in Prague.

Follow-up meetings of the participating States will be held, as a rule, every two years to allow the participating States to take stock of developments, review the implementation of their commitments and consider further steps in the CSCE process.

We decide to create a Conflict Prevention Centre in Vienna to assist the Council in reducing the risk of conflict.

We decide to establish an Office for Free Elections in Warsaw to facilitate contacts and the exchange of information on elections within participating States.

Recognizing the important role parliamentarians can play in the CSCE process, we call for greater parliamentary involvement in the CSCE, in particular through the creation of a CSCE parliamentary assembly, involving members of parliaments from all participating States. To this end, we urge that contacts be pursued at parliamentary level to discuss the field of activities, working methods and rules of procedure of such a CSCE parliamentary structure, drawing on existing experience and work already undertaken in this field.

We ask our Ministers for Foreign Affairs to review this matter on the occasion of their first meeting as a Council.

* * *

Procedural and organizational modalities relating to certain provisions contained in the Charter of Paris for a New Europe are set out in the Supplementary Document which is adopted together with the Charter of Paris.

We entrust to the Council the further steps which may be required to ensure the implementation of decisions contained in the present document, as well as in the Supplementary Document, and to consider further efforts for the strengthening of security and co-operation in Europe. The Council may adopt any amendment to the Supplementary Document which it may deem appropriate.

* * *

The original of the Charter of Paris for a new Europe, drawn up in English, French, German, Italian, Russian and Spanish, will be transmitted to the Government of the French Republic, which will retain it in its archives. Each of the participating States will receive from the Government of the French Republic a true copy of the Charter of Paris.

The text of the Charter of Paris will be published in each participating State, which will disseminate it and make it known as widely as possible.

The Government of the French Republic is requested to transmit to the Secretary-General of the United Nations the text of the Charter of Paris for a New Europe, which is not eligible for registration under Article 102 of the Charter of the United Nations, with a view to its circulation to all members of the Organization as an official document of the United Nations.

The Government of the French Republic is also requested to transmit the text of the Charter of Paris to all other international organizations mentioned in the text.

Wherefore, we, the undersigned High Representatives of the participating States, mindful of the high political significance we attach to the results of the Summit Meeting, and declaring our determination to act in accordance with the provisions we have adopted, have subscribed our signatures below:

Done at Paris, on 21 November 1990, in the name of (signatures) . . .

* The Charter was signed by the heads of state or government of the 34 CSCE participating states.

** The 34 CSCE states adopted the 1990 Vienna Document on the Negotiations on Confidence- and Security-Building Measures during the Paris Summit Meeting (21 November 1990).

Note: The agenda for the CSCE Summit Meeting (Paris, 19–21 November 1990) was approved by the Foreign Ministers of the 35 CSCE states in New York (2 October 1990). The decision was taken one day before the unification of Germany; since then the number of participating states in the CSCE meetings is 34 (on 3 October 1990 the GDR acceded to the Basic Law of the FRG and ceased to exist as a separate state).

Supplementary document to give effect to certain provisions contained in the Charter of Paris for a New Europe*

Excerpts

Procedures and organizational modalities relating to certain provisions contained in the Charter of Paris for a new Europe, signed in Paris on 21 November 1990, are set out below:

I. INSTITUTIONAL ARRANGEMENTS

A. The Council

1. The Council, consisting of Ministers for Foreign Affairs of the participating States, provides the central forum for regular political consultations within the CSCE process.

2. The Council will:

– consider issues relevant to the Conference on Security and Co-operation in Europe and take appropriate decisions;

– prepare the meetings of Heads of State or Government of the participating States and implement tasks defined and decisions taken by these meetings.

3. The Council will hold meetings regularly and at least once a year.

4. The participating States may agree to hold additional meetings of the Council.

5. The Chair throughout each meeting of the Council will be taken by the representative of the host country.

6. An agenda for the meetings of the Council, including proposals for the venue—on a basis of rotation—and date of the next meeting, will be prepared by the Committee of Senior Officials.

B. The Committee of Senior Officials

1. A Committee of Senior Officials will prepare the work of the Council, carry out its decisions, review current issues and consider future work of the CSCE including its relations with other international fora.

2. In order to prepare the agenda of the meetings of the Council, the Committee will identify the issues for discussion on the basis of suggestions submitted by the participating States. The Committee will finalize a draft agenda shortly before the meeting of the Council.

3. Each participating State will establish a point of contact which will be used to transmit suggestions for the work of the Committee to the Secretariat for collection and circulation and to facilitate communication between the Secretariat and each participating State.

4. Each meeting of the Committee will be chaired by a representative of the State whose Foreign Minister had been Chairman at the preceding Council meeting. Meetings will be convened by the Chairman of the Committee after consultation with the participating States.

Meetings of the Committee will be held at the seat of the Secretariat and will not exceed two days, unless otherwise agreed. Meetings immediately preceding a meeting of the Council will be held at the venue of the Council meeting.

5. Due to practical considerations, the first meeting of the Committee will be held in Vienna from 28 to 29 January 1991. It will be chaired by the representative of Yugoslavia.

C. Emergency mechanism

The Council will discuss the possibility of establishing a mechanism for convening meetings of the Committee of Senior Officials in emergency situations.

D. Follow-up meetings

Follow-up meetings of the participating States will be held as a rule every two years. Their duration will not exceed three months, unless otherwise agreed.

E. The CSCE Secretariat

1. The Secretariat will:
– provide administrative support to the meetings of the Council and of the Committee of Senior Officials;
– maintain an archive of CSCE documentation and circulate documents as requested by the participating States;
– provide information in the public domain regarding the CSCE to individuals, NGOs, international organizations and non-participating States;
– provide support as appropriate to the Executive Secretaries of CSCE summit meetings, follow-up meetings and inter-sessional meetings.

2. The Secretariat will carry out other tasks assigned to it by the Council or the Committee of Senior Officials.

3. In order to carry out the tasks specified above, the Secretariat will consist of the following staff:
– a Director, responsible to the Council through the Committee of Senior Officials;
– three Officers who will be in charge of organization of meetings (including protocol and security), documentation and information, financial and administrative matters. In addition to these functions, the Director may assign other duties within the framework of the tasks of the Secretariat;
– administrative and technical personnel, recruited by the Director.

F. The Conflict Prevention Centre (CPC)

1. The Conflict Prevention Centre (CPC) will assist the Council in reducing the risk of conflict. The Centre's function and structure are described below.

2. During its initial stage of operations the Centre's role will consist in giving support to the implementation of CSBMs such as:
– mechanism for consultation and co-operation as regards unusual military activities;
– annual exchange of military information;
– communications network;
– annual implementation assessment meetings;
– co-operation as regards hazardous incidents of a military nature.

3. The Centre might assume other functions and the above tasks are without prejudice to any additional tasks concerning a procedure for the conciliation of disputes as well as broader tasks relating to dispute settlement,

which may be assigned to it in the future by the Council of the Foreign Ministers.

Consultative Committee

4. The Consultative Committee, composed of representatives from all participating States, will be responsible to the Council. As a rule, these representatives will be the Heads of Delegation to the CSBM negotiations until the Helsinki Follow-up Meeting. The Consultative Committee will:

– hold the meetings of the participating States which may be convened under the mechanism on unusual military activities;
– hold the annual implementation assessment meetings;
– prepare seminars on military doctrine and such other seminars as may be agreed by the participating States;
– supervise the Secretariat of the Centre;
– provide the forum for discussion and clarification, as necessary, of information exchanged under agreed CSBMs;
– have overall responsibility for the communications network within the mandate of the CPC.

5. The Consultative Committee will work according to CSCE procedures. It will determine its own work programme and may decide to hold additional meetings. Meetings of the participating States, convened at the request of one or more participating States according to the procedures concerning unusual military activities, will be organized by the Director of the CPC Secretariat. Until the appointment of the Director this function will be carried out by the Executive Secretary of the CSBM negotiations.

Secretariat

6. The Secretariat will carry out the tasks assigned to it by the Consultative Committee to which it will be responsible. In particular, it will establish and maintain a data bank, for use of all participating States, compiled on the basis of exchanged military information under agreed CSBMs and will publish Yearbooks on that basis.

7. The Secretariat will consist of the following staff:

– a Director;
– two officers in charge of organization of meetings (including protocol and security),

communication, documentation and information, financial and administrative matters;
– administrative and technical personnel recruited by the Director.

* * *

8. The first meeting of the Consultative Committee of the Conflict Prevention Centre will be convened on 3 December 1990 and chaired by Yugoslavia.

G. The Office for Free Elections

1. The function of the Office for Free Elections will be to facilitate contacts and the exchange of information on elections within participating States. The Office will thus foster the implementation of paragraphs 6, 7 and 8 of the Document of the Copenhagen Meeting of the Conference on the Human Dimension of the CSCE (the relevant provisions are contained in Annex I).

2. To this end, the Office will:

– compile information, including information provided by the competent authorities of the participating States, on the dates, procedures and official results of scheduled national elections within participating States, as well as reports of election observations, and provide these on request to governments, parliaments and interested private organizations;
– serve to facilitate contact among governments, parliaments or private organizations wishing to observe elections and competent authorities of the States in which elections are to take place;
– organize and serve as the venue for seminars or other meetings related to election procedures and democratic institutions at the request of the participating States.

3. The Office will take into account the work of and co-operate with other institutions active in this field.

4. The Office will carry out other tasks assigned to it by the Council.

5. The Office's personnel will be composed of:

– a Director, who will be responsible to the Council through the Committee of Senior Officials;
– an Officer;
– administrative and technical personnel, recruited by the Director of the Office.

H. Procedures and modalities concerning CSCE institutions

Staffing arrangements

1. The director of each institution will be of senior rank, seconded by his/her government, and appointed by the Council to a three-year, non-renewable term, on a basis of rotation.

2. In the event that the director can no longer fulfil his functions, the Chairman of the Council will, after consultation with the participating States, appoint a temporary director until the next meeting of the Council.

3. The officers will be seconded by their governments. Their terms of office will normally last two years. An extension of one year may be agreed upon by the director and the participating State seconding the officer.

4. The appointment of officers will be based on a system of rotation which will follow the French alphabetical order. The beginning of the rotation will be determined by lot for each position in the institution. Vacant positions will be offered to the participating States following this order until the position is filled.

5. No participating State will have its nationals occupy more than one seconded position in the CSCE institutions, unless no other participating State is willing to second its national to a vacant position.

6. Each officer will be nominated by the participating State concerned after consultation with the director who will then make the appointment.

7. Administrative and technical personnel will be contracted by the director of the institution. Arrangements will be made, as required, for interpretation and translation services.

8. The director of each institution will determine its working arrangements.

9. Staff will be accredited by the seconding State to the host country where they will enjoy full diplomatic status.

Costs

10. The costs:

– of seconded personnel will be borne by the seconding country;

– of installation of the CSCE institutions will be shared according to CSCE procedures;

– of operation, including cost of official travel of staff once appointed, will be shared according to CSCE procedures;

– of the premises of the institution as well as the necessary security arrangements including those for meetings held at the seat of the institution, will be borne by the host country.

* * *

11. The host countries undertake to enable the institutions to function fully and enter into contractual and financial obligations and to accord them appropriate diplomatic status.

* * *

12. In order to function effectively, CSCE institutional structures created by the Summit will require agreed administrative, financial and personnel arrangements.

13. To this end a panel, chaired by the Executive Secretary of the Preparatory Committee and composed of the Executive Secretaries of the Paris Summit and of the New York Meeting of Foreign Ministers, as well as the representatives of the host countries of the new CSCE institutions, will submit a report and proposals to participating States by the end of December 1990. This report and these proposals will be considered by an *ad hoc* group of experts of the participating States who will meet in Vienna under the responsibility of the Committee of Senior Officials from 14 to 18 January 1991 and make final recommendations on the above. This meeting will be convened and chaired by the representative of the State chairing the Committee of Senior Officials.

14. The Committee of Senior Officials will consider these recommendations and take the necessary decisions at its first meeting.

The first director of each institution will be nominated by the first meeting of the Committee of Senior Officials and confirmed by the Council through a silence procedure within one week. The Executive Secretariat of the CSBM negotiations in Vienna will provide services for the first meeting of the Consultative Committee of the CPC and for the first meeting of the Committee of Senior Officials.

15. The CSCE Secretariat, the Conflict Prevention Centre and the Office for Free Elections are accountable to the Council which is empowered to determine their tasks and methods of operation. Arrangements relating to the procedures, modalities and the locations of these institutions may be reviewed at the Helsinki Follow-up Meeting.

I. Communications

The Council, acting upon recommendation of the Consultative Committee and of the Committee of Senior Officials, as appropriate, may decide that the communication network, established as part of the agreement on additional CSBMs, be used for other CSCE-related purposes.

J. Application of CSCE rules of procedure

The rules of procedure, working methods, the scale of distribution of expenses and other modalities of the CSCE will be applied *mutatis mutandis*, unless otherwise decided.

II. MEETINGS OF EXPERTS

A. Seminar of Experts on Democratic Institutions

The Seminar of Experts on Democratic Institutions will be held in Oslo from Monday, 4 November 1991 to Friday, 15 November 1991. Its purpose is to hold discussions of ways and means of consolidating and strengthening viable democratic institutions in participating States, including comparative studies of legislation on human rights and fundamental freedoms, drawing *inter alia* upon the experience acquired by the Council of Europe and the activities of the Commission 'Democracy through Law'.

The agenda, timetable and other organizational modalities are set out in Annex II.

B. Meeting of Experts on National Minorities

The Meeting of Experts on National Minorities will be held in Geneva from Monday 1 July 1991 to Friday, 19 July 1991. Its purpose is to hold a thorough discussion on the issue of national minorities and of the rights of persons belonging to them, with due attention to the diversity of situations and to the legal, historical, political and economic backgrounds. It will include:

– an exchange of views on practical experience, in particular on national legislation, democratic institutions, international instruments, and other possible forms of co-operation;

– a review of the implementation of the relevant CSCE commitments and consideration of the scope for the improvement of relevant standards;

– a consideration of new measures aimed at improving the implementation of the aforementioned commitments.

The agenda, timetable and other organizational modalities are set out in Annex III.**

(...)

---

* The omitted parts of this supplementary document describe the financial arrangements and cost-effectiveness of the CSCE.

** The agenda, timetable and other organizational modalities of two meetings of experts on Democratic Institutions (Oslo, 4–15 November 1991) and on National Minorities (Geneva, 1–19 July 1991), as well as relevant provisions concerning the function of the Office for Free Elections, were attached to the Supplementary Document in three annexes.

Appendices

Appendix A
Programme of the SIPRI/IPW conference, Potsdam, 8–10 February 1990

A European Peace Order and the Responsibility of the Two German States

8 February 1990

16.00   Professor Max Schmidt, Director of IPW
Welcoming remarks

16.10   Dr Walther Stützle, Director of SIPRI
Opening of the conference

16.30   H. E. Professor Dr Christa Luft
Deputy Prime Minister (Economic Affairs), GDR
The GDR–FRG network of agreements and the future of Europe
Chair: Professor Max Schmidt
Discussion

20.15   Walter Momper
Governing Mayor of Berlin (West)
Berlin and the current European development

9 February 1990

09.30   H. E. Hans-Dietrich Genscher
Federal Minister for Foreign Affairs, FRG
The responsibility of the two German states for a European peace order
Chair: Dr Walther Stützle
Discussion

14.00   The role of the two German states
A Polish view: Professor Wojciech Lamentowicz, Poland
A French view: Professor Dominique Moisï, France
Chair: Dr Adam Daniel Rotfeld, SIPRI
Discussion

16.15   Dr Wolfram Krause,
Head, Committee for Economic Reform, GDR Government
Change and reform in the GDR: the economic challenge

17.00   Professor Kurt Biedenkopf, FRG
             *Change and reform in the GDR: the challenge of integration into
             the European economy*
             Chair: Professor Catherine Kelleher, USA
             Discussion

19.30   Panel with representatives of the political parties/groupings in the
             GDR
             On the eve of the elections in the GDR: European aspects
             Participants: Dr Gregor Gysi, Chairman PDS; Dr Lothar de
             Maizière, Chairman, CDU; Walter Romberg, SPD; Gerhard
             Lindner, LDPD; Bärbel Bohley, New Forum; Günter Bransch,
             Protestant Church; Fred Dumke, NDPD
             Chair: Professor Egon Bahr, SIPRI Governing Board
             Discussion

10 February 1990

09.30   *The future role of the alliances in Europe*
             Introduction by Ferenc Köszeg, Hungary and Professor Catherine
             Kelleher, USA
             Chair: Ambassador Max Jacobson, SIPRI Governing Board
             Discussion

11.45   *The research agenda ahead: lessons for institutes*
             Introduction by Professor Karl Birnbaum, European Peace Univer-
             sity
             Chair: Professor Max Schmidt and Dr Walther Stützle

12.45   Conference summary

Appendix B
List of conference participants

Roland Asmus
The RAND Corporation
USA

Professor Egon Bahr
Member of Parliament,
FRG
Member of the SIPRI Governing Board

Dr Kennette Benedict
Associate Director
Program on Peace and International
 Cooperation
John D. and Catherine T. MacArthur
 Foundation
USA

Dr Christoph Bertram
Diplomatic Correspondent
Die Zeit
FRG

Professor Dr Kurt Biedenkopf
Member of Parliament
FRG

Professor Dr Karl E. Birnbaum
Director of Programme
European University Centre for Peace Studies
Austria

Bärbel Bohley
New Forum
GDR

Günter Bransch
General Superintendent
Protestant Church of the GDR

Frieder Bubl
PDS, International Commission
GDR

David Childs
Institute for German, Austrian and Swiss
 Affairs
University of Nottingham
UK

Dr Fred Dumke, NDPD
GDR

Ambassador Luigi Vittorio Ferraris
Former Head of the Italian Delegation to the
 CSCE and Ambassador in the FRG
Italy

Stephan Finger
Executive Member of the Social Democratic
 Party of Germany
GDR

Dr Anne-Marie Le Gloannec
Centre d'Etudes et de Recherches
 Internationales (CERI)
France

Dr Gregor Gysi
Chairman, PDS
GDR

Dr Peter Hardi
Director
Hungarian Institute for Foreign Relations
Hungary

Günter Hartmann
Deputy Chairman of the NDPD
GDR

Dr Bo Huldt
Director
Swedish Institute of International Affairs

Ambassador Dr Max Jacobson
Finland
Member of the SIPRI Governing Board

Professor Catherine M. Kelleher
Center for International Security Studies
School of Public Affairs
University of Maryland
USA

Dr Wolfram Krause
Chairman, Government's Committee on
 Economic Reforms
GDR

Dr Gert Krell
Director
Foundation for Peace and Conflict Research
FRG

Ferenc Köszeg
Member of the National Praesidium of the
    Alliance of Free Democrats and Editor-in-
    Chief of *Beszélo*
Hungary

Professor Wojciech Lamentowicz
President
Independent Center for International Affairs
Member of the Solidarity Citizens Committee
Poland

Major General Professor Dr Rolf Lehmann
Commandant,
Military Academy 'Friedrich Engels'
GDR

Gerhard Lindner, LDPD
Acting Chairman of the Committee on
    Foreign Relations
GDR

Robert Livingston
American Institute for Contemporary German
    Studies
The Johns Hopkins University
USA

Professor Dr Karlheinz Lohs
Director, Academy of Sciences of the GDR
Member of the SIPRI Governing Board

Dr Michael Ludwig
German Society of Foreign Policy
FRG

Lothar de Maizière
Chairman, CDU
Deputy Head of State Council
GDR

Doc. Ing. Jiri Matousek, Dr. sc.
Senior Research Fellow
Research Centre for Peace and Disarmament
Czecho-Slovakia

Dr Cesare Merlini
President
Institute of International Affairs
Italy

Dr Dominique Moisï
Deputy Director
French Institute of International Relations
France

Professor Roger Morgan
European University Institute
Italy

Professor Dr Hanspeter Neuhold
Director
Austrian Institute of International Policy
Austria

Professor Dr Maciej Perczynski
Director
Polish Institute of International Affairs
Poland

Dr Vladimir V Razmerov
Institute of World Economy and International
    Relations
Academy of Science of the USSR
USSR

Dr Walter Romberg, SPD
GDR

John Roper
Director of Studies
Royal Institute of International Affairs
    (Chatham House)
UK

Dr Adam Daniel Rotfeld
Senior Researcher
SIPRI

Professor Dr Max Schmidt
Director
Institute of International Politics and
    Economics (IPW)
GDR

Wolfgang Schnur
Chairman, Demokratischer Aufbruch
GDR

Dr Friedrich Schorlemmer, SPD
GDR

Dr Manfred Stolpe
Deputy Chairman, Union of Protestant
    Churches
GDR

Professor Dr Michael Stürmer
Director
Foundation for Science and Politics
FRG

Dr Walther Stützle
Director
SIPRI

Karol Szyndzielorz
Foreign Editor
Przeglad Tygodniowy
Poland

Dr László Valki
Head of the Peace Research Section
Hungarian Academy of Sciences
Hungary

Horst Wendt
New Forum
GDR

Observers

Professor Dr Gerhard Basler
Institute of International Politics and
   Economics (IPW)
GDR

Dr Herbert Barth
Ambassador
Ministry of Foreign Affairs
GDR

Dr Klaus Benjowski
Academic Council on Peace Research
GDR

Professor Dr Harald Lange
Institute of International Politics and
   Economics (IPW)
GDR

Name index